Just For Boys™ presents

GUINNESS
SPORTS
1987-88
★ ★ ★ ★
RECORD
BOOK

Editors

David A. Boehm
Editor-in-Chief

Cyd Smith
Assistant Editor

Jim Benagh
Assistant Editor

Peter Matthews
Contributing Editor

 Sterling Publishing Co., Inc.   New York

Weekly Reader Books offers several exciting
card and activity programs. For information,
write to WEEKLY READER BOOKS, P.O. Box 16636,
Columbus, Ohio 43216.

This book is a presentation of **Just For Boys**,™ Weekly Reader Books.
Weekly Reader Books offers book clubs for children from preschool
through high school. For further information write to: **Weekly
Reader Books,** 4343 Equity Drive, Columbus, Ohio 43228.

Published by arrangement with Sterling Publishing Co., Inc.

Just For Boys™ is a trademark of Field Publications.

Weekly Reader is a trademark of Field Publications.

Copyright © 1987 by Guinness Superlatives Ltd.
Published in 1987 by Sterling Publishing Co., Inc.
Two Park Avenue, New York, New York 10016
This book is taken in part from the
  "Guinness Book of World Records" © 1986
Distributed in Canada by Oak Tree Press Ltd.
℅ Canadian Manda Group, P.O. Box 920, Station U
Toronto, Ontario, Canada M8Z 5P9
Manufactured in the United States of America
All rights reserved
Library of Congress Catalog Card No.: 82-642136
Sterling ISBN 0-8069-6452-9 Trade

CONTENTS

Categories

We are *likely* to publish only those records which improve upon previously published records or which are newly significant in having become the subject of widespread and, preferably, worldwide competition. Records in our sense essentially have to be both measureable and comparable to other performances in the same category.

It should be stressed that unique occurrences, interesting peculiarities and the collecting of everyday objects, are not themselves necessarily records. Records which are *qualified* or limited in some way—for example, by age, handicap, day of the week, etc.—cannot be accommodated in a reference work so general as the *Guinness Book of World Records*.

We do not publish records in gratuitously hazardous categories, such as the lowest starting height for a handcuffed, free-fall parachute jump, or the thinnest burning rope suspending a man in a straitjacket from a helicopter. World records claimed on TV specials are not always set according to Guinness rules. Certain innately dangerous but historically significant activities, such as tightrope walking, are included but are best left to professionals. Other categories which have reached the limits of safety, such as sword swallowing and Volkswagen stuffing, have been retired and either are so marked or have been deleted. No further claims will be considered for publication.

We reserve the right to determine in our sole discretion the record to be published and/or deleted and the use of the name of the record holder for purposes of inclusion in the book.

Rules and Procedures

A record attempt should compete *exactly* with the record in the book and the conditions under which it was set. Where there is doubt about the rules, it is recommended that the strictest interpretation be adopted. Contact with the Guinness editorial offices at 33 London Road, Enfield, Middlesex, England or the American editors (212-532-7160) for clarification should be made well in advance of a planned attempt.

If there is a recognized world or national governing body for an activity, that body should be consulted for rules and one of its representatives, whenever possible,

IS IT A RECORD?

should be involved in officiating. For any attempt, expert officiating by impartial witnesses is desirable.

In marathon or endurance events, five-minute rest intervals are permitted, but only AFTER each *completed* hour, except for a few "non-stop" categories in which minimal intervals may be taken only for purposes other than for resting. These rest breaks are optional and may be accumulated (for example, 3 hours of activity earns 15 minutes of rest time, etc.). Violation of the rest-interval rules will disqualify an attempt. The accepted record will be the gross time (that is, the total elapsed time, including rest intervals, from start to finish). However, unused accumulated rest break time cannot be added to the final figure.

In recent years there has been a marked increase in efforts to establish records for sheer endurance in many activities. In the very nature of record-breaking, the duration of such "marathons" will tend to be pushed to greater and greater extremes, and it should be stressed that marathon attempts are not without possible dangers. Those responsible for marathon events would be well counseled to seek medical advice before, and surveillance during, marathons which involve extended periods with little or no sleep.

Documentation and Verification

■ We do *not* normally supply personnel to monitor, invigilate or observe record attempts, but reserve the right to do so. In any case, the burden of proof rests with the claimant. No particular form is required, and no entry fee is payable. Guidelines for documentation are provided below. We cannot accept as accurate any claim that is insufficiently documented.

■ Claimants should obtain independent corroboration in the form of local or national newspaper, radio or TV coverage. Newspaper clippings must be annotated with the name of the newspaper, its place of publication and the date of the issue in which the article appeared. When possible, the name of the reporter and black-and-white and/or color action photographs should also be supplied. Videotapes and audio cassettes should not be sent, but held in reserve in the event further documentation is requested.

■ Claimants should send signed authentication by independent, impartial adult witnesses or representatives of organizations of standing in their community. Where applicable, a signed document showing ratification by a governing body should be supplied (see above). A claim is naturally enhanced by a witness with a high degree of expertise in the area of endeavor.

■ Signed log books should show there has been unremitting surveillance in the case of endurance events. These log books must include, in chronological order, the times of activity and the times and durations of all rest breaks taken. The log books must be legible and readily decipherable. They must include signatures of witnesses with times of entering and leaving (at least two *independent* witnesses must be on hand at all times). Where applicable, score sheets must be kept to demonstrate a satisfactory rate of play.

All submissions become the property of the publishers. The publishers will consider, but not guarantee, the return of material, only if a self-addressed stamped envelope or wrapper is supplied *with sufficient postage.*

Revisions

Notwithstanding the best efforts of the editors, errors in the book, while rare, may occur. In the event of such errors, the sole responsibility of the publishers will be to correct such errors in subsequent editions of the book.

If there are discrepancies between entries in one edition and another, it may be generally assumed that the *later* entry is the product of up-to-date research.

Editorial Offices

Please consult the latest edition of the book before phoning or writing the editorial offices, which are primarily concerned with maintaining and improving the quality of each succeeding edition. **We do not offer advice on choosing a record for anyone to attempt breaking.** Also, we are unable to perform the function of a free general information bureau for quiz competitions and the like. However, we are always happy to hear about new record attempts.

From the American Editors of *Guinness*

The Sports World

Earliest

The origins of sport stem from the time when self-preservation ceased to be the all-consuming human preoccupation. Archery was a hunting skill in Mesolithic times (by *c.* 8000 BC), but did not become an organized sport until later, certainly by about 300 AD, among the Genoese and possibly as early as the 12th century BC, as an archery competition is described in Homer's *Iliad*. The earliest dated evidence for sport is *c.* 2750–2600 BC for wrestling. Ball games by girls, depicted on Middle Kingdom murals at Beni Hasan, Egypt, have been dated to *c.* 2050 BC.

Fastest

The highest speed reached in a non-mechanical sport is in sky-diving, in which a speed of 185 mph is attained in a head-down free-falling position, even in the lower atmosphere. In delayed drops, a speed of 625 mph has been recorded at high rarefied altitudes. The highest projectile speed in any moving ball game is *c.* 188 mph in pelota (jai-alai). This compares with 170 mph (electronically timed) for a golf ball driven off a tee.

Slowest

In amateur wrestling, before the rules were modified toward "brighter wrestling," contestants could be locked in holds for so long that a single bout once lasted for 11 hours 40 min. In the extreme case of the 2-hour-41-min pull in the regimental tug o'war in Jubbulpore, India, Aug 12, 1889, the winning team moved a net distance of 12 ft at an average speed of 0.00084 mph.

Longest

The most protracted sporting contest was an automobile duration test of 222,621 miles (equivalent to 8.93 times around the equator) by Appaurchaux and others in a Ford Taunus at Miranas, France. This was contested over 142 days (July–Nov) in 1963.

The most protracted non-mechanical sporting event is the *Tour de France* cycling race. In 1926 this was over 3,569 miles, lasting 29 days, but is now reduced to 23 days.

HIS OLYMPIC MEDALS RESTORED: Jim Thorpe, the American Indian who was a football star, pole-vaulted to a gold medal in the decathlon of the 1912 Olympics and won a second gold that year, only to have them revoked because he had once received $25 for playing semi-pro baseball, received his medals back postmortem in 1982, seventy years later.

took the silver medal in the high jump, and gold medals in the javelin throw and hurdles in the 1932 Olympics. Turning professional, she first trained as a boxer, and then, switching to golf, eventually won 19 championships, including the US Women's Open and All-American Open. She holds the women's world record also for longest throw of a baseball—296 ft.

Jim Thorpe (US) (1887–1953) excelled at football, baseball, the 10-event decathlon, and the 5-event pentathlon. He won two gold medals in the 1912 Olympics and was declared "the greatest athlete in the world" by King Gustav of Sweden.

Greatest Earnings

The greatest fortune amassed by an individual in sport is an estimated $69 million by the boxer Muhammad Ali Haj (US) to the end of 1981.

The highest-paid woman athlete is tennis player Martina Navratilova (b Prague, Czechoslovakia, Oct 18, 1956) (US) whose career earnings passed $11 million in 1986.

Youngest and Oldest Recordbreakers

The youngest age at which any person has broken a non-mechanical world record is 12 years 298 days for Gertrude Caroline Ederle (b Oct 23, 1906) of the US, who broke the women's 880-yd freestyle swimming world record with 13 min 19.0 sec at Indianapolis, Ind, Aug 17, 1919.

Most Versatile Athletes

Charlotte "Lottie" Dod (1871–1960) won the Wimbledon singles title (1887 to 1893) 5 times, the British Ladies Golf Championship in 1904, an Olympic silver medal for archery in 1908, and represented England at hockey in 1899. She also excelled at skating and tobogganing.

Mildred (Babe) Didrikson Zaharias (US) (1914–56) was an All-American basketball player,

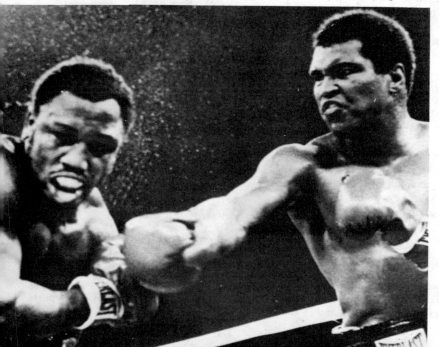

GREATEST EARNER: Muhammad Ali (right) seems to be knocking the stuffing out of Joe Frazier in the "thriller in Manila" when he won $6½ million. Ali's earnings in his 61 fights totaled about $69 million, making him the highest paid in any sport. (AP)

The oldest person to break a world record is Gerhard Weidner (W Germany) (b Mar 15, 1933) who set a 20-mi walk record on May 25, 1974, aged 41 years 71 days.

Youngest and Oldest Champions

The youngest person to have successfully participated in a world title event was a French boy, whose name is not recorded, who coxed the winning Netherlands Olympic pair in rowing at Paris on Aug 26, 1900. He was not more than 10 and may have been as young as 7. The youngest individual Olympic winner was Marjorie Gestring (US) (b Nov 18, 1922), who took the springboard diving title at the age of 13 years 268 days at the Olympic Games in Berlin, Aug 12, 1936. Oscar G. Swahn (see below) was aged 64 years 258 days when he won the gold medal in the 1912 Olympic Running Deer team shooting competition.

Youngest and Oldest Internationals

The youngest age at which any person has won international honors is 8 years in the case of Joy Foster, the Jamaican singles and mixed doubles table tennis champion in 1958. It would appear that the greatest age at which anyone has actively competed for his country is 72 years 280 days in the case of Oscar Gomer Swahn (Sweden) (1847–1927), who won a silver medal for shooting in the Olympic Games at Antwerp on July 26, 1920. He qualified for the 1924 Games, but was unable to participate because of illness.

Largest Field

The largest field for any ball game is that for polo with 12.4 acres, or a maximum length of 300 yd and a width, without side-boards, of 200 yd (with boards the width is 160 yd).

Biggest Sports Contract

In March 1982 the National Football League concluded a deal worth $2.1 billion for 5 years coverage of their games by the 3 major TV networks (ABC, CBS and NBC). This represents $14.2 million for each team in the league.

Largest Crowd

The greatest number of live spectators for any sporting spectacle is the estimated 2,500,000 who annually line the route of the New York Marathon. However, spread over 23 days, it is estimated that more than 10 million see the annual *Tour de France* cycling along the route.

The total attendance at the 1984 Summer Olympic Games was given at 5,797,923 for all sports, including 1,421,627 for soccer and 1,129,465 for track and field.

The largest crowd traveling to any single sporting event is "more than 400,000" for the annual *Grand Prix d'Endurance* motor race on the Sarthe circuit near Le Mans, France. The record stadium crowd was 199,854 paid for the Brazil vs Uruguay soccer match in the Maracaña Municipal Stadium, Rio de Janeiro, Brazil, July 16, 1950.

The largest television audience for a single sporting event (excluding Olympic events) was the esti-

NYC MARATHON DRAWS LARGEST CROWD: About 2,500,000 people annually line the route to watch as many as 19,000 runners race through the 5 boroughs. Here, Alberto Salazar is seen in 1981.

mated 1.5 billion who watched the final game of the 1982 World Cup soccer competition.

Most Participants

The *Bay-to-Breakers* footrace through San Francisco in 1986 (the 75th annual race) was estimated by police to have included 102,000 runners over the 7.6 mi. The 1983 WIBC Championship Tournament attracted 75,480 women bowlers (all of whom paid entry fees) for the 83-day event held Apr 7–July 1 at Showboat Lanes, Las Vegas, Nev.

The most runners in a marathon were the 19,412 in the 1986 NYC Marathon.

In May 1971, the "Ramblin' Raft Race" on the Chattahoochee River at Atlanta, Ga, attracted 37,683 competitors on 8,304 rafts.

Most Athletes

According to a report in 1978, 55 million people are active in sports in the USSR. The country has 3,282 stadiums, 1,435 swimming pools and over 66,000 indoor gymnasia. It is estimated that some 29 percent of the population of E Germany participate in sport regularly.

Worst Disasters

The worst disaster in recent history was when an estimated 604 were killed after some stands at the Hong Kong Jockey Club race course collapsed and caught fire on Feb 26, 1918. During the reign of Antoninus Pius (138–161 AD) the upper wooden tiers in the Circus Maximus, Rome, collapsed during a gladiatorial combat, killing 1,112 spectators.

Heaviest Athlete

The heaviest athlete of all time was the wrestler William J. Cobb of Macon, Ga, who in 1962 was billed as the 802-lb "Happy Humphrey." The heaviest player of a ball game was Bob Pointer, the 487-lb tackle on the 1967 Santa Barbara High School football team.

Longest Reign

The longest reign as a world champion is 33 years (1829–62) by Jacques Edmond Barré (France, 1802–73) at the rarely played game, real (royal) tennis.

Shortest Reign

Olga Rukavishnikova (USSR) (b Mar 13, 1955) held the pentathlon world record for only 0.4 sec at Moscow on July 24, 1980. That is the difference between her second place time of 2 min 04.8 sec in the final 800m event of the Olympic five-event competition, and that of the third-placed Nadezda Tkachenko (USSR), whose overall points came to more than Rukavishnikova's total—5,083 points to 4,937 points.

CZECH ROOM: Strahov Stadium in Prague, Czechoslovakia, is the largest in the world, with space for 240,000 spectators to view mass displays of up to 40,000 gymnasts.

Most Prolific Recordbreaker

Between Jan 24, 1970, and Nov 1, 1977, Vasili Alexeyev (USSR) (b Jan 7, 1942) broke 80 official world records in weight lifting.

Largest Stadiums

The largest stadium is the Strahov Stadium in Praha (Prague), Czechoslovakia. It was completed in 1934 and can easily accommodate 240,000 spectators for mass displays of up to 40,000 Sokol gymnasts.

The largest football (soccer) stadium is the Maracaña Municipal Stadium in Rio de Janeiro, Brazil, which has a normal capacity of 205,000, of whom 155,000 may be seated. A crowd of 199,854 was accommodated for the World Cup final between Brazil and Uruguay on July 16, 1950. A dry moat, 7 ft wide and over 5 ft deep, protects players from spectators and *vice versa*.

The largest covered stadium in the world is the Azteca Stadium, Mexico City, opened in 1968, which has a capacity of 107,000, of whom nearly all are under cover.

The largest retractable roof is being constructed to cover the 60,000-capacity Toronto Blue Jays' new stadium near the CN Tower for completion by Aug 1988. The diameter will be 679 ft.

Largest One-Piece Roof

The transparent acrylic glass "tent" roof over the Munich Olympic Stadium, W Germany, measures 914,940 sq ft in area. It rests on a steel net supported by masts. The roof of longest span is the 680-ft diameter of the Louisiana Superdome in New Orleans. The major axis of the elliptical Texas Stadium, Irving, Tex, completed in 1971 is, however, 784 ft 4 in.

Largest Indoor Arena

The largest indoor stadium is the 13-acre $173-million 273-ft-tall Superdome in New Orleans, La, completed in May 1975. Its maximum seating capacity for conventions is 97,365 or 76,791 for football. Box suites rent for $35,000, excluding the price of admission. A gondola with six 312-in TV screens produces instant replay.

AEROBATICS

World Championships

Held biennially since 1960 (excepting 1974), scoring is based on the system devised by Col José Aresti of Spain. The competitions consist of two compulsory and two free programs. The men's team competition has been won on 5 occasions by the USSR. No individual has won more than one title, the most successful competitor being Igor Egorov (USSR) who won in 1970, was second in 1976, fifth in 1972 and eleventh in 1968. The most successful in the women's competition has been Betty Stewart (US) who has won twice, 1980 and 1982. The US had a clean sweep of all the medals in 1980.

Inverted Flight

The duration record for inverted flight is 4 hours 9 min 5 sec by John "Hal" McClain in a Swick Taylorcraft on Aug 23, 1980 over Houston Raceways, Tex.

Loops

On June 21, 1980, R. Steven Powell performed 2,315⅝ inside loops in a Bellanca Decathlon over Almont, Mich. John McClain achieved 180 outside loops in a Bellanca Super Decathlon on Sept 2, 1978, over Houston, Tex. Ken Ballinger (GB) completed 155 consecutive loops in a Bellanca Citabria on Aug 6, 1983 over Staverton Airport, Cheltenham, Eng.

ARCHERY

Origins

Though the earliest evidence of the existence of bows is seen in the Mesolithic cave paintings in Spain, archery as an organized sport appears to have developed in the 3rd century AD. Competitive archery may, however, date back to the 12th century BC. The world governing body is the *Fédération Internationale de Tir à l'Arc* (FITA), founded in 1931.

OLYMPIC GOLD MEDAL-IST, Darrell Pace (US) (left), had earlier set a target-shooting record of 2,617 out of a possible 2,880 (LA Times). FLIGHT-SHOOTING: April Moon (US) (right), using a handbow, set a women's record (over 1,039 yd) in 1981, and it still stands.

Highest 24-Hour Scores

The record score at target archery over 24 hours by a pair of archers is 51,633 during 48 Portsmouth Rounds (60 arrows at 20 yd with a 2-in-diameter 10 ring) shot by Jimmy Watt and Gordon Danby at the Epsom Showgrounds, Auckland, NZ, Nov 18–19, 1977.

The highest recorded score at field archery is 123,724 by 6 members of the Holland Moss Field Archery Club at Holland Moss Field, Pimbo, Lancashire, Eng, on Apr 28–29, 1983. Bill Chambers set an individual record score of 30,506.

Highest Championship Scores

The highest scores achieved in either a world or Olympic championship for Double FITA rounds are: (Men) 2,617 points (possible 2,880) by Richard McKinney (b Oct 20, 1963) (US) and Darrell Pace (b Oct 23, 1956) (US) and (Women) 2,634 points by Park Jung-ah (S Korea) to win the Asian Games title at Seoul in 1986.

Most Titles

The greatest number of world titles (instituted 1931) ever won by a man is 4 by Hans Deutgen (b Feb 28, 1917) (Sweden), 1947–50. The greatest number won by a woman is 7 by Janina Spychajowa-Kurkowska (b Feb 8, 1901) (Poland), 1931–34, 36, 39 and 47.

Oscar Kessels (Belgium) participated in 21 world championships.

Greatest Pull

Gary Sentman of Roseburg, Ore, drew a longbow weighing a record 176 lb to the maximum draw on the arrow (28¼ in) at Forksville, Pa, Sept 20, 1975.

Olympic Medals

Hubert van Innis (Belgium) (1866–1961) won 6 gold and 3 silver medals in archery events at the 1900 and 1920 Olympic Games.

In 1984, the winners of gold medals were: Darrell Pace (US) with 2,616 points in the men's competition, and Seo Hyang-Soon (S Korea) with 2,568 points in the women's.

Flight Shooting

The longest flight shooting records are achieved in the footbow class. In the unlimited footbow division, Harry Drake (b May 7, 1915) of Lakeside, Calif, holds the record at 1 mile 268 yd, shot at Ivanpah Dry Lake, Calif, Oct 24, 1971, at 3,000-ft altitude. He also holds the regular footbow record with 1,542 yd 34 in, set on Oct 6, 1979. The crossbow record is 1,359 yd 29 in, held by Drake set Oct 14–15, 1967. The female footbow record is 1,113 yd 30 in by Arlyne Rhode (b May 4, 1936) at Wendover, Utah, on Sept 10, 1978. Alan Webster (Eng) set the flight record for the handbow with 1,231 yd 22 in on Oct 2, 1982, and April Moon (US) set a women's record of 1,039 yd 13 in on Sept 13, 1981, both at Ivanpah Dry

ARCHERY WORLD RECORDS

MEN

Event	Name	Record/Maximum	Year
FITA	Darrell Pace (US)	1341/1440	1979
90 m.	Vladimir Esheyev (USSR)	322/360	1980
70 m.	Richard McKinney (US)	342/360	1985
50 m.	Richard McKinney (US)	355/360	1986
30 m.	Takayoshi Matsushita (Japan)	357/360	1986
Team	US (Richard McKinney, Darrell Pace, Jerry Pylypchuk)	3912/4320	1985

WOMEN

Event	Name	Record/Maximum	Year
FITA	Ludmila Arzhannikova (USSR)	1325/1440	1984
70 m.	Natalia Butuzova (USSR)	328/360	1979
60 m.	Ludmila Arzhannikova (USSR)	338/360	1984
60 m.	Kim Jin-ho (S Korea)	338/360	1986
50 m.	Yanzhima Tsyrenzhapova (USSR)	335/360	1985
30 m.	Kim Mi-ja (S Korea)	354/360	1986
Team	S Korea (Kim Mi-ja, Kim Jin-ho, Park Jung-ah)	3935/4320	1986

Lake. The new compound bow records are held by Arlan Reynolds (US) at 1,030 yd 2 ft 11 in, and his wife Sherrie Reynolds at 704 yd 1 ft 9 in, both set at Bonneville Flight Range, Utah, in 1986.

AUTO RACING

Earliest Races

There are various conflicting claims, but the first automobile race was the 201-mile Green Bay-to-Madison, Wis, run in 1878, won by an Osh-kosh steamer.

In 1887, Count Jules Felix Philippe Albert de Dion de Malfiance (1856–1946) won the *La Velocipede* 19.3-mile race in Paris in a De Dion steam quadricy-cle in which he is reputed to have exceeded 37 mph.

The first "real" race was from Paris to Bordeaux and back (732 miles) June 11–13, 1895. The winner was Emile Levassor (1844–97) (France) driving a Panhard-Levassor two-seater with a 1.2-liter Daimler engine developing 3½ hp. His time was 48 hours 47 min (average speed 15.01 mph). The first closed-circuit race was held over 5 laps of a mile dirt track at Narragansett Park, Cranston, RI on Sept 7, 1896. It was won by A. H. Whiting, who drove a Riker electric.

The oldest auto race in the world still being regu-larly run is the R.A.C. Tourist Trophy, first staged on the Isle of Man on Sept 14, 1905. The oldest conti-nental race is the French Grand Prix, first held June 26–27, 1906. The Coppa Florio, in Sicily, has been ir-regularly held since 1900.

Fastest Races

The fastest race in the world is the NASCAR Busch Clash, a 125-mile all-out sprint on the 2½-mile 31-degree banked tri-oval at Daytona International Speedway, Daytona Beach, Fla. In the 1979 event, Elzie Wylie "Buddy" Baker (b Jan 25, 1941) of Charlotte, NC, averaged 194.384 mph in an Oldsmo-bile. Bill Elliott set the world record for a 500 mile race in 1985 when he won at Talladega, Ala at an av-erage speed of 186.288 mph. The NASCAR quali-fying record is 212.229 mph by Bill Elliott in a Ford Thunderbird at Alabama International Motor Speedway, Talladega, Ala on May 1, 1986.

Fastest Drivers

The highest average lap speed attained on any closed circuit is 250.958 mph in a trial by Dr Hans Liebold (b Oct 12, 1926) (Germany) who lapped the 7.85-mile high-speed track at Nardo, Italy, in 1 min 52.67 sec in a Mercedes-Benz C111-IV experimental coupé on May 5, 1979. It was powered by a V8 en-gine with two KKK turbochargers with an output of 500 hp at 6,200 rpm.

The highest average lap speed in an actual race on a closed circuit is 223.401 mph by Rick Mears of Ba-kersfield, Calif, driving a Chevrolet-powered March on the 2-mi Michigan International Speedway, Brooklyn, Mich, July 31, 1986, during the qualifying for the Michigan 500. Mears, in the same car on the same track Nov 17, 1986, was clocked at 233.934 under simulated race conditions and has applied for certification of that time to break his 223.401 record.

The fastest average lap speed on a closed-circuit track by a woman racer is 204.223 by Lyn St. James,

MAN OF LE MANS (left): Jackie Ickx (Belgium) roared to 6 wins in this race, turned in the fastest race lap at almost 149 mph and has been a contender since 1969.

John Winter (W Ger). The race lap record (8.475-mile lap) is 3 min 25.1 sec (average speed 148.61 mph) by Jackie Ickx (Belgium) in a Porsche 962C in 1985. The practice lap record is 3 min 14.8 sec (av. speed 156.62 mph) by Hans Stuck (W Ger) in a Porsche 962C on June 14, 1985.

The most wins by one man is 6 by Jackie Ickx (Belgium), who won in 1969, 75-77 and 81-82.

Most Successful Drivers

Based on the World Drivers' Championships, inaugurated in 1950, the most successful driver is Juan-Manuel Fangio (b Balcarce, Argentina, June 24, 1911), who won five times in 1951, 54-57. He retired in 1958, after having won 24 Grand Prix races (2 shared).

The most successful driver in terms of earnings is Darrell Waltrip (b Feb 5, 1947) of Franklin, Tenn, whose career earnings reached $7,430,635 by the end of 1986, beating total earnings of Richard Lee Petty (b Randleman, NC, July 2, 1937), who has 200 NASCAR Grand National wins, 1958-85. Petty's best season was 1967 with 27 wins. Geoff Bodine won 55 races in 1978. Bill Elliott holds the single year's record of $2,044,468 in NASCAR events in 1985.

The most Grand Prix victories is 27 by Jackie Stewart (b June 11, 1939) of Scotland between Sept 12, 1965 and Aug 5, 1973. Jim Clark (1936-1968) of

(US), in a Mustang Probe on the 2.66-mi Alabama International Motor Speedway in Talladega, Ala, on Nov 26, 1985.

Le Mans

The greatest distance ever covered in the 24-hour *Grand Prix d'Endurance* (first held May 26-27, 1923) on the old Sarthe circuit (8 miles 650 yd) at Le Mans, France, is 3,314.222 miles by Dr Helmut Marko (b Graz, Austria, Apr 27, 1943) and Jonkheer Gijs van Lennep (b Bloemendaal, Netherlands, March 16, 1942) driving a 4,907-cc flat-12 Porsche 917K Group 5 sports car June 12-13, 1971. The record for the current circuit is 3,161,928 miles (average speed 131.747 mph) in a Porsche 956 June 15-16, 1985 by Klaus Ludwig (W Ger), Paulo Barilla (Italy), and

Le Mans 24-Hour Race

The world's most important race for sports cars was first held in 1923. Winners since 1949 when the race was revived after the Second World War:

	Driver	Car	Speed (mph)
1949	Luigi Chinetti/Lord Peter Selsdon	Ferrari	82.27
1950	Louis Rosier/Jean-Louis Rosier	Talbot	89.73
1951	Peter Walker/Peter Whitehead	Jaguar	93.50
1952	Hermann Lang/Fritz Riess	Mercedes	96.67
1953	Anthony Rolt/Duncan Hamilton	Jaguar	105.85
1954	José Froilan Gonzalez/Maurice Trintignant	Ferrari	105.15
1955	Mike Hawthorn/Ivor Bueb	Jaguar	107.07
1956	Ron Flockhart/Ninian Sanderson	Jaguar	104.46
1957	Ron Flockhart/Ivor Bueb	Jaguar	113.85
1958	Phil Hill/Olivier Gendebien	Ferrari	106.20
1959	Roy Salvadori/Carroll Shelby	Aston Martin	112.57
1960	Paul Frère/Olivier Gendebien	Ferrari	109.19
1961	Phil Hill/Olivier Gendebien	Ferrari	115.90
1962	Phil Hill/Olivier Gendebien	Ferrari	115.24
1963	Ludovico Scarfiotti/Lorenzo Bandini	Ferrari	118.10
1964	Jean Guichet/Nino Vaccarella	Ferrari	121.55
1965	Masten Gregory/Jochen Rindt	Ferrari	121.09
1966	Bruce McLaren/Chris Amon	Ford	126.01
1967	Anthony Joseph Foyt/Dan Gurney	Ford	132.49
1968	Pedro Rodriguez/Lucien Bianchi	Ford	115.29
1969	Jackie Ickx/Jackie Oliver	Ford	125.44
1970	Hans Herrmann/Richard Attwood	Porsche	119.29
1971	Helmut Marko/Gijs van Lennep	Porsche	138.142
1972	Graham Hill/Henri Pescarolo	Matra-Simca	121.47
1973	Henri Pescarolo/Gerard Larrousse	Matra-Simca	125.68
1974	Henri Pescarolo/Gerard Larrousse	Matra-Simca	119.27
1975	Jackie Ickx/Derek Bell	Gulf Ford	118.99
1976	Jackie Ickx/Gijs van Lennep	Porsche	123.50
1977	Jackie Ickx/Jurgen Barth/Hurley Haywood	Porsche	120.95
1978	Didier Peroni/Jean-Pierre Jaussaud	Renault Alpine	130.60
1979	Klaus Ludwig/Bill and Don Whittington	Porsche	108.06
1980	Jean-Pierre Jaussaud/Jean Rondeau	Rondeau	119.17
1981	Jackie Ickx/Derek Bell	Porsche	124.87
1982	Jackie Ickx/Derek Bell	Porsche	126.84
1983	Vern Schuppan/Hurley Haywood/Al Holbert	Porsche	130.70
1984	Klaus Ludwig/Henri Pescarolo	Porsche	126.88
1985	Klaus Ludwig/Paulo Barilla/John Winter	Porsche 956	131.74
1986	Hans Stuck/Al Holbert/Derek Bell	Porsche	128.74

Scotland shares the record of Grand Prix victories in one year with 7 in 1963; Alain Prost (France) (b Feb 24, 1955) had 7 in 1984. The most Grand Prix starts is 176 (out of a possible 184) between May 18, 1958, and Jan 26, 1975, by (Norman) Graham Hill (1929–1975). He took part in 90 *consecutive* Grands Prix between Nov 20, 1960 and Oct 5, 1969.

The most Grand Prix points won is 420½ by Niki Lauda (Austria) (b Feb 22, 1949) from 1971 to 1985.

In Indy-car racing, A.J. Foyt, of Houston, Tex, who began racing in 1957, has won 67 races, about 20 more than his nearest competitor through the 1986 season.

Moneywise, on the Indy-car circuit, Bobby Rahal of Dublin, Ohio, became the first driver to earn more than $1 million in one season in 1986, when he earned $1,488,049. The all-time Indy-car money earner is Al Unser, Sr, of Albuquerque, N Mex with $4,816,189 in racing prizes. Unser began his career in 1964 and was still active in 1986.

Youngest and Oldest Grand Prix Winners and Drivers

The youngest Grand Prix winner was Bruce Leslie McLaren (1937–70) of New Zealand, who won the US Grand Prix at Sebring, Fla, on Dec 12, 1959, aged 22 years 104 days. The oldest Grand Prix winner was Tazio Giorgio Nuvolari (1892–1953) of Italy, who won the Albi Grand Prix at Albi, France, on July 14, 1946, aged 53 years 240 days.

The oldest Grand Prix driver was Louis Alexandre Chiron (Monaco, 1899–1979), who finished 6th in the Monaco Grand Prix on May 22, 1955, aged 55

MOST GRAND PRIX VICTORIES: Alain Prost (France), shown in his Formula One car, shares the record of 7 wins in one year (1984) with Jim Clark (Scotland) (1963).

Indianapolis 500

Winners since 1946 (all US except where stated):

	Driver	Car	Speed (mph)
1946	George Robson	Thorne Engineering	114.820
1947	Mauri Rose	Blue Crown Special	116.338
1948	Mauri Rose	Blue Crown Special	119.814
1949	Bill Holland	Blue Crown Special	121.327
1950	Johnny Parsons	Wynn Kurtis Kraft	124.002
1951	Lee Wallard	Belanger	126.224
1952	Troy Ruttman	Agajanian	128.922
1953	Bill Vukovich	Fuel Injection	128.740
1954	Bill Vukovich	Fuel Injection	130.840
1955	Bob Sweikert	John Zink Special	128.209
1956	Pat Flaherty	John Zink Special	128.490
1957	Sam Hanks	Belond Exhaust	135.601
1958	Jimmy Bryan	Belond A. P.	133.791
1959	Rodger Ward	Leader Card Special	135.857
1960	Jim Rathmann	Ken-Paul Special	138.767
1961	A. J. Foyt	Bowes Seal Fast	139.130
1962	Rodger Ward	Leader Card Special	140.293
1963	Parnelli Jones	Agajanian Special	143.137
1964	A. J. Foyt	Sheraton-Thompson Special	147.350
1965	Jim Clark (GB)	Lotus-Ford	150.686
1966	Graham Hill (GB)	American Red Ball	144.317
1967	A. J. Foyt	Sheraton-Thompson Special	151.207
1968	Bobby Unser	Rislone Special	152.882
1969	Mario Andretti	STP Oil Treatment Special	156.867
1970	Al Unser	Johnny Lightning Special	155.749
1971	Al Unser	Johnny Lightning Special	157.735
1972	Mark Donohue	Sunoco McLaren	162.962
1973	Gordon Johncock	STP Double Oil Filter	159.036
1974	Johnny Rutherford	McLaren	158.589
1975	Bobby Unser	Jorgensen Eagle	149.213
1976	Johnny Rutherford	Hygain McLaren	148.725
1977	A. J. Foyt	Gilmore Coyote-Foyt	161.331
1978	Al Unser	Lola-Chapparal Cosworth	161.363
1979	Rick Mears	Penske-Cosworth	158.899
1980	Johnny Rutherford	Chapparal Cosworth	142.862
1981	Bobby Unser	Penske-Cosworth	139.084
1982	Gordon Johncock	Wildcat-Cosworth	162.025
1983	Tom Sneva	March-Cosworth	162.117
1984	Rick Mears	March-Cosworth	163.612
1985	Danny Sullivan	March-Cosworth	152.982
1986	Bobby Rahal	March-Cosworth	170.722

years 292 days. The youngest Grand Prix driver was Michael Christopher Thackwell (b New Zealand, March 30, 1961) who took part in the Canadian Grand Prix in Sept 28, 1980, aged 19 years 182 days.

Oldest and Youngest World Champions

The oldest was Juan-Manuel Fangio, who won his last World Championship Aug 18, 1957, aged 46 years 55 days. The youngest was Emerson Fittipaldi (b São Paulo, Brazil, Dec 12, 1946) who won his first World Championship Sept 10, 1972, aged 25 years 273 days.

Indianapolis 500

The Indianapolis 500-mile race (200 laps) was inaugurated on May 30, 1911. The most successful driver has been Anthony Joseph "A. J." Foyt, Jr (b Houston, Tex, Jan 16, 1935), who won in 1961, 64, 67 and 77.

The record time is 2 hours 55 min 43.48 sec (average speed 170.722 mph) by Bobby Rahal (US) on May 31, 1986, driving a March Cosworth. This was the closest 3-car finish in the 70-year history of the

OLDEST WORLD CHAMPION: Winner of 24 Grand Prix races, Juan-Manuel Fangio (Argentina) won his last race in 1957 when he was more than 46 years old.

race. Bobby Rahal beat Kevin Cogan by 1.4 sec and beat Rick Mears (b 1952, Calif) by 1.8 sec. He did it with a last lap of 209.152 mph, the fastest race lap in Indy history.

Daytona 500

	Driver	Car	Average Speed
1959	Lee Petty	59 Oldsmobile	135.521
1960	Junior Johnson	59 Chevrolet	124.740
1961	Marvin Panch	60 Pontiac	149.601
1962	Fireball Roberts	62 Pontiac	152.529
1963	Tiny Lund	63 Ford	151.566
1964	Richard Petty	64 Plymouth	154.334
1965*	Fred Lorenzen	65 Ford	141.539
1966**	Richard Petty	66 Plymouth	160.627
1967	Mario Andretti	67 Ford	146.926
1968	Cale Yarborough	68 Mercury	143.251
1969	LeeRoy Yarborough	69 Ford	157.950
1970	Pete Hamilton	70 Plymouth	149.601
1971	Richard Petty	71 Plymouth	144.462
1972	A. J. Foyt	71 Mercury	161.550
1973	Richard Petty	73 Dodge	157.205
1974	Richard Petty	74 Dodge	140.894
1975	Benny Parsons	Chevrolet	153.649
1976	David Pearson	Mercury	152.181
1977	Cale Yarborough	Chevrolet	153.218
1978	Bobby Allison	Ford	159.730
1979	Richard Petty	Oldsmobile	143.977
1980	Buddy Baker	Oldsmobile	177.602
1981	Richard Petty	Buick	169.651
1982	Bobby Allison	Buick	153.991
1983	Cale Yarborough	Pontiac	155.979
1984	Cale Yarborough	Chevrolet	150.994
1985	Bill Elliott	Ford	172.265
1986	Geoff Bodine	Chevrolet	148.124

* 332½ miles because of rain
** 495 miles because of rain

MOST NASCAR VICTORIES: Richard Petty has won a total of 200 Grand National races 1958–85, his best season being 1967 with 27 victories.

The qualifying 4-lap record average speed is 216.828 mph, including a one-lap record of 217.581 mph by Rick Mears in a Pennzoil Z-7 with a Cosworth engine on May 10, 1986.

The record prize fund is $4,001,450 for the 1986 race, the 70th. The individual prize record is the $581,062.50 won by Bobby Rahal in 1986.

The first and only woman to qualify for and compete in the Indianapolis 500 is Janet Guthrie (b Mar 7, 1938). She passed her rookie test in May 1976, and earned the right to compete in the qualifying rounds, but was unable to win a place on the starting line when the Vollstedt-Offenhauser she drove was withdrawn from the race after repeated mechanical failures. In the 61st running of the Indianapolis 500, in 1977, Guthrie became the first woman to compete, although her car developed mechanical problems which forced her to retire after 27 laps. In 1978, she completed the race, finishing in ninth place after 190 laps.

Fastest Pit Stop

Bobby Unser (US) took 4 sec to take on fuel on lap 10 of the Indianapolis 500 on May 30, 1976.

Closest Finishes

The closest finish to a World Championship race occurred when Ayrton Senna (Brazil) beat Nigel Mansell (GB) by 0.014 sec in the Spanish Grand Prix at Jerez de la Frontera Apr 13, 1986.

The closest finish in the Indianapolis 500 was in the 1982 race when the winner, Gordon Johncock, crossed the finish line just 0.16 sec before runner-up Rick Mears.

Duration Record

The greatest distance ever covered in one year is 400,000 km (248,548.5 miles) by François Lecot (1879–1949), an innkeeper from Rochetaillée, France, in a 1,900-cc 66-bhp Citroën 11 sedan mainly between Paris and Monte Carlo, from July 22, 1935 to July 26, 1936. He drove on 363 of the 370 days allowed.

Pikes Peak Race

The Pikes Peak Auto Hill Climb, Colorado (instituted 1916) has been won by Bobby Unser 13 times between 1956 and 1974 (10 championship, 2 stock and 1 sports car titles). In the 1979 race Dick Dodge set a record time of 11 min 54.18 sec in a Chevrolet-powered Wells Coyote over the 12.42-mile course, rising from 9,402 to 14,110 ft through 157 curves.

Land Speed Records

The highest speed attained by any wheeled land vehicle is 739.666 mph or Mach 1.0106 (making it the only land vehicle to break the sound barrier) *in a one-way stretch* by the rocket-engined *Budweiser Rocket,* designed by William Frederick, and driven by Stan Barrett at Edwards Air Force Base, California, on Dec 17, 1979. The vehicle, owned by Hal Needham, has a 48,000-hp rocket engine with 6,000 lb of extra thrust from a sidewinder missile. The rear wheels (100-lb solid discs) lifted 10 in off the ground above Mach 0.95, acting as 7,500-rpm gyroscopes.

The official 1-mi land speed record, which is for the average of a two-way run, was set on Oct 4, 1983 when Richard Noble (GB) drove a jet-powered car, *Thrust 2,* at 633.468 mph at Black Rock Desert, Gerlach, Nev. The previous record, 622.287, was set by Gary Gabelich and had stood for 13 years.

The most successful land speed record breaker was Major Malcolm Campbell (1885–1948) (UK). He broke the official record nine times between Sept 25,

HIGHEST AVERAGE SPEED: This Mercedes-Benz C111-IV experimental coupe was recorded on May 5, 1979 at 250.958 mph.

1924, with 146.157 mph in a Sunbeam, and Sept 3, 1935, when he achieved 301.129 mph in the Rolls-Royce-engined *Bluebird*.

Worst Disaster

Drivers have hit spectators with appalling regularity throughout the history of racing, first place doubtless going to Pierre Levegh, who killed 81 spectators as well as himself at Le Mans in 1955.

Earliest Rally

The earliest long rally was promoted by the Parisian daily *Le Matin* in 1907 from Peking to Paris, over about 7,500 miles on June 10. The winner, Prince Scipione Borghese (1872–1927), arrived in Paris on Aug 10, 1907 in his 40-hp Itala accompanied by his chauffeur, Ettore, and Luigi Barzini.

Longest Rallies

The longest rally ever was the *Singapore Airlines* London-Sydney Rally over 19,329 miles, from Covent Garden, London, on Aug 14, 1977, to the Sydney Opera House, won Sept 28, 1977, by Andrew Cowan, Colin Malkin and Michael Broad in a Mercedes 280E.

The longest rally held annually is the Safari Rally (first run 1953 through Kenya, Tanzania and Uganda, now only Kenya), which has been up to 3,874 miles long, as in the 17th Safari held Apr 8–12, 1971. It has been won a record 5 times by Shekhar Mehta (Uganda) in 1973, 79–82.

Monte Carlo

The Monte Carlo Rally (first run 1911) has been won a record 4 times by Sandro Munari (Italy) in 1972, 75–77; and by Walter Röhrl (b Mar 7, 1947) (with co-driver Christian Geistdorfer) in 1980, 1982–84, each time in a different car. Walter Röhrl is also the only man to win two drivers' world championships (inst 1979), 1980 and 1982.

The smallest car to win was an 851-cc Saab driven by Erik Carlsson (b Sweden, March 5, 1929) and Gunnar Häggbom of Sweden, in 1962, and by Carlsson and Gunnar Palm in 1963.

BADMINTON

Origins

A game similar to badminton was played in China in the 2nd millennium BC. The modern game may have evolved *c.* 1870 at Badminton Hall in Avon, England, the seat of the Dukes of Beaufort, or from a game played in India. The first modern rules were codified in Poona, India in 1876. The world's oldest badminton club continuously in existence, founded in 1878, is the Badminton Club of NYC.

International Championships

The International Championship or Thomas Cup (instituted 1948) has been won 8 times by Indonesia, in 1958, 61, 64, 70, 73, 76, 79, and 1984. Indonesians have also won all-England titles 12 times in the last 16 years.

The Ladies International Championship or Uber Cup (instituted 1956) had been won 5 times by Japan (1966, 69, 72, 78 and 81).

Both Cups were won in 1986 by China.

Most Titles

The record for men's singles in the All-England Championship is 8 by Rudy Hartono Kurniawan (b Aug 18, 1948) of Indonesia (1968–74, 76). The most, including doubles, is 21 by G. A. Thomas (Eng), 1903–28. The most, including doubles, by women is 17, a record shared by Muriel Lucas (later Mrs King Adams) (1899–1910) and Mrs G. C. K. Hashman (*née* Judy Devlin) (US) (b Oct 22, 1935), whose wins came from 1954 to 1967, including a record 10 singles titles. Judy Hashman also won 29 US titles.

Marathons

The longest singles match is 78 hours 23 min by Cameron McMullen and Michael Patterson in Wales, Apr 1–4, 1986.

The longest doubles is 77 hours 1 min by Paul Farmer, Andrew Hood, Ben Smith and Loraine Storey in Nottingham, Eng, May 29–June 1, 1984.

Shortest Game

In the 1969 Uber Cup in Tokyo, Japan, Noriko Takagi (later Mrs Nakayama) (Japan) beat Poppy Tumengkol (Indonesia) in 9 min.

Longest Hit

Frank Rugani drove a shuttlecock 79 ft 8½ in in indoor tests at San Jose, Calif, Feb 29, 1964.

24, 1935. President Franklin D. Roosevelt pressed a button at the White House to flick the switch at Crosley Field. Wrigley Field, home of the Chicago Cubs, still remains unlit.

Home Runs

Henry L. (Hank) Aaron (b Feb 5, 1934, Mobile, Ala) broke the major league record set by George H. (Babe) Ruth of 714 home runs in a lifetime when he hit No. 715 on Apr 8, 1974. Between 1954 and 1974

BASEBALL

Earliest Games

The Reverend Thomas Wilson, of Maidstone, Kent, England, wrote disapprovingly, in 1700, of baseball being played on Sundays. The earliest game on record under the Cartwright (Alexander Joy Cartwright, Jr, 1820–92) rules was on June 19, 1846, in Hoboken, NJ, where the "New York Nine" defeated the Knickerbockers 23 to 1 in 4 innings. The earliest all-professional team was the Cincinnati Red Stockings in 1869, who had 56 wins and 1 tie that season.

Night Baseball

The first night game was played on June 2, 1883 (M.E. College vs professionals from Quincy, Ill). The major leagues were slow to adopt this change of program, then considered radical. The Cincinnati Reds were the first big-league team to play under lights when they hosted the Philadelphia Phillies on May

LONG HOMERS: Mickey Mantle can claim 2 "longest" home runs—one was an officially measured 565 ft and the other a trigonometrically measured 643 ft. (NY Yankees)

he hit 733 home runs for the Milwaukee and Atlanta Braves in the National League. In 1975, he switched to the Milwaukee Brewers in the American League and in that year and 1976, when he finally retired, he hit 22 more, bringing his lifetime total to 755, the major league record.

> Mantle's homer in Detroit on Sept 10, 1960, which ascended over the right field roof and is said to have landed in a lumberyard, was measured trigonometrically in 1985 to have traveled 643 ft.

A North American record of almost 800 in a lifetime has been claimed for Josh Gibson (1911–47), mostly for the Homestead Grays of the Negro National League, who was elected in 1972 to the Baseball Hall of Fame in Cooperstown, NY. Gibson is said to have hit 75 round-trippers in one season, in 1931, but no official records were kept.

The most officially recorded home runs hit by a professional player in the US in one season is 72, by Joe Bauman, of the Roswell, NM team, a minor league club, in 1954. The major league record is 61 in 161 games of a 162-game season by Roger Maris (1934–1985) of the NY Yankees, in 1961. George Herman "Babe" Ruth (1895–1948) hit 60 in a 154-game season in 1927.

The longest home run "officially" measured was 618 ft by Roy Edward "Dizzy" Carlyle (1900–56) in a minor league game at Emeryville Ball Park, Calif, July 4, 1929. Babe Ruth hit a 587-ft homer for the Boston Red Sox vs NY Giants in an exhibition game at Tampa, Fla, in 1919. The longest measured home run in a regular-season major league game is 565 ft by Mickey Mantle (b Oct 20, 1931) for the NY Yankees vs Washington Senators on Apr 17, 1953, at Griffith Stadium, Wash DC.

Shortest and Tallest Players

The shortest major league player was surely Eddie Gaedel, a 3-ft-7-in, 65-lb midget, who pinch hit for the St Louis Browns vs the Detroit Tigers on Aug 19, 1951. Wearing number ⅛, the batter with the smallest ever major league strike zone walked on four pitches. Following the game, major league rules were hastily rewritten to prevent the recurrence of such an affair.

The tallest major leaguer was John Alexander Gee (b Dec 7, 1915), a 6-ft-9-in pitcher who spent 6 seasons in the National League: 1939, 41, 43–46.

STRIKEOUT KING: Roger Clemens of the Boston Red Sox fanned 20 Seattle Mariners on Apr 29, 1986, to beat the record of 19 in one game, jointly held by Nolan Ryan, Steve Carlton and Tom Seaver (Boston Red Sox).

LITTLEST MAJOR LEAGUER: Eddie Gaedel, a 26-year-old, 3-ft-7-in pinch hitter for the St Louis Browns, walked on 4 pitches in an Aug 19, 1951 official game against the Detroit Tigers.

MOST CONSECUTIVE INNINGS PLAYED: Cal Ripken, Jr, the Baltimore Oriole shortstop has played all of every inning for 755 games in a unique record of 6,843 innings through 1986. (Jerry Wachter)

Youngest and Oldest Players

The youngest major league player of all time was the Cincinnati pitcher Joe Nuxhall, who started his career in June 1944, aged 15 years 10 months 11 days.

Leroy Satchel Paige (1906?–82) pitched three scoreless innings for the Kansas City Athletics at approximately age 59 in 1965. Baseball's color barrier had kept him out of the major leagues until 1948, when he was a 42-year-old "rookie," and his record of 6 wins and 1 loss helped the Cleveland Indians win the pennant. His birthday is listed as July 7, 1906, but many believe he was born earlier. The Atlanta Braves carried Paige on their roster in 1968 to allow him to qualify for a pension.

Fastest Base Runner

Ernest Evar Swanson (1902–73) took only 13.3 sec to circle the bases at Columbus, Ohio, in 1932, averaging 18.45 mph.

One Day Wonder

John Paciorek of the Houston Colt '45s had a perfect day at bat in his only game in the majors in 1963

with 3 singles, 2 walks, 4 runs scored, and 3 rbi's, for a 1.000 average.

Most Strikeouts

Bobby Bonds in 1970, while playing right field for the San Francisco Giants, fanned 189 times in 157 games.

Fewest Strikeouts

Joe Sewell in 1929, while playing third base for the Cleveland Indians, played in 115 consecutive games, going to bat 437 times without once striking out. In his career stretching 14 years he only struck out 114 times.

Most Strikeouts in an Inning

Seventeen different pitchers hold the record of 4 in an inning. How? The catcher misses on a third strike and the batter gets on base, so the hurler has to fan another batter. The latest pitcher to have 4 K's (strikeouts) in one inning was Mario Soto of the Reds on May 17, 1984 against the Cubs.

Most Foul-Offs

Luke Appling, shortstop for the White Sox in the 1930's, fouled off 14 consecutive pitches from Dizzy Trout of the Tigers. On the 15th pitch, Trout threw his glove instead of the ball.

Hit by Pitch

Ron Hunt, an infielder who played with various National League teams from 1963 to 1974, led the league in getting hit by pitched balls for a record 7 consecutive years. His career total is 243, also a major league record.

Consecutive Innings

Calvin Ripken, Jr, (b Aug 24, 1960) of the Baltimore Orioles set what is believed to be a record for playing every inning of consecutive games, stretching his streak that began June 5, 1982 to 755 games (6,843 innings) through 1986. Ripken played the first six games of the streak at third base, then moved to shortstop. Baseball researchers have found no previous streak longer than 534 games (Buck Freeman, Boston Red Sox, 1901–05).

MAJOR LEAGUE ALL-TIME RECORDS

(including 1986 season)

Individual Batting

Highest percentage, lifetime (5,000 at-bats)
.367 Tyrus R. Cobb, Det AL, 1905–26; Phil AL, 1927–28

Highest percentage, season (500 at-bats)
.438 Hugh Duffy, Bos NL, 1894
Modern Record
.424 Rogers Hornsby, St L NL, 1924

Most games played
3,562 Peter Rose, Cin NL, 1963–78; Phil NL, 1979–83; Mont NL, 1984; Cin NL, 1984–86

Most consecutive games played
2,130 Henry Louis (Lou) Gehrig, NY AL, June 1, 1925 through Apr 30, 1939

Most runs batted in, season
190 Lewis R. (Hack) Wilson, Chi NL, 155 games, 1930

Most runs batted in, game
12 James L. Bottomley, St L NL, Sept 16, 1924

Most runs batted in, lifetime
2,297 Henry L. (Hank) Aaron, Mil NL, 1954–65, Atl NL, 1966–74; Mil AL, 1975–76

Most runs, lifetime
2,244 Tyrus R. Cobb, Det AL, 1905–26; Phil AL, 1927–28

Most base hits, lifetime
4,256 Peter Rose, Cin NL, 1963–78; Phil NL, 1979–83; Mont NL, 1984; Cin NL 1984–86

Most base hits, season
257 George H. Sisler, St L AL, 154 games, 1920

Most hits in succession
12 M. Frank (Pinky) Higgins, Bos AL, June 19–21 (4 games), 1938
Walter Dropo, Det AL, July 14, July 15, 2 games, 1952

Most base hits, consecutive, game
7 Wilbert Robinson, Balt NL, June 10, 1892, 1st game (7-ab), 6-1b, 1-2b
Renaldo Stennett, Pitt NL, Sept 16, 1975 (7-ab), 4-1b, 2-2b, 1-3b
Cesar Gutierrez, Det AL, June 21, 1970, 2nd game (7-ab) 6-1b, 1-2b (12-inning game)

Most times at bat, lifetime
14,053 Peter Rose, Cin NL, 1963–78; Phil NL, 1979–83; Mont NL, 1984; Cin NL, 1984–86

Most consecutive games batted safely, season
56 Joseph P. DiMaggio, NY AL (91 hits—16-2b, 4-3b, 15 hr), May 15 to July 16, 1941

Most total bases, lifetime
6,856 Henry L. (Hank) Aaron, Mil NL, 1954–65; Atl NL, 1966–74; Mil AL, 1975–76

Most total bases, season
457 George H. (Babe) Ruth, NY AL, 152 gs (85 on 1b, 88 on 2b, 48 on 3b, 236 on hr), 1921

Most total bases, game
18 Joseph W. Adcock, Mil NL (1-2b, 4-hr), July 31, 1954

Most one-base hits (singles), season
202 William H. (Wee Willie) Keeler, Balt NL, 128 games, 1898

Most two-base hits, season
67 Earl W. Webb, Bos AL, 151 games, 1931

Most three-base hits, season
36 J. Owen Wilson, Pitts NL, 152 games, 1912

Most home runs, season
61 Roger E. Maris, NY AL (162-game schedule) (30 home, 31 away), 161 gs, 1961
60 George H. (Babe) Ruth, NY AL (154-game schedule) (28 home, 32 away), 151 gs, 1927

Most home runs, lifetime
755 Henry L. Aaron, Mil NL, 1954 (13), 1955 (27), 1956 (26), 1957 (44), 1958 (30), 1959 (39), 1960 (40), 1961 (34), 1962 (45), 1963 (44), 1964 (24), 1965 (32); Atl NL, 1966 (44), 1967 (39), 1968 (29), 1969 (44), 1970 (38), 1971 (47), 1972 (34), 1973 (40), 1974 (20); Mil AL, 1975 (12), 1976 (10)

Most home runs, bases filled, lifetime
23 Henry Louis (Lou) Gehrig, NY AL, 1923–1939

Most home runs with bases filled, season
5 Ernest Banks, Chi NL, May 11, 19, July 17 (1st game), Aug 2, Sept 19, 1955
James E. Gentile, Balt AL, May 9 (2), July 2, 7, Sept 22, 1961

Most home runs, with bases filled, game
2 Anthony M. Lazzeri, NY AL, May 24, 1936
James R. Tabor, Bos AL (2nd game), July 4, 1939
Rudolph York, Bos AL, July 27, 1946
James E. Gentile, Balt AL, May 9, 1961 (consecutive at-bats)
Tony L. Cloninger, Atl NL, July 3, 1966
James T. Northrup Det AL, June 24, 1968 (consecutive at-bats)
Frank Robinson, Balt AL, June 26, 1970 (consecutive at-bats)

Most consecutive games hitting home runs
8 R. Dale Long, Pitt NL, May 19–28, 1956

Most home runs, one doubleheader
5 Stanley F. Musial, St L NL, 1st game (3), 2nd game (2), May 2, 1954
Nathan Colbert, SD NL, 1st game (2), 2nd game (3), Aug 1, 1972

Most bases on balls, game
6 James E. Foxx, Bos AL, June 16, 1938
Andre Thornton, Clev AL, May 2, 1984 (16 inns)

Most bases on balls, season
170 George H. (Babe) Ruth, NY AL, 152 games, 1923

Most hits, pinch-hitter, lifetime
150 Manuel R. Mota, SF NL, 1962; Pitt NL, 1963–1968; Mont NL, 1969; LA NL, 1969–1980

Most consecutive home runs, pinch-hitter
3 Del Unser, Phil NL, June 30, July 5, 10, 1979
Lee Lacy, LA NL, May 2, 6, 17, 1978 (one walk in between)

Most consecutive pinch hits
9 David E. Philley, Phil NL, Sept 9, 11, 12, 13, 19, 20, 27, 28, 1958; Apr 16, 1959

Base Running

Most stolen bases, lifetime
938 Louis C. Brock, Chi NL, 1961–64; St L NL, 1964–79

BASE STEALER SUPREME: Rickey Henderson, while with the Oakland A's in 1982, stole 130 bases in 149 games. **(Steve Babineau photo)**

HIT IN EVERY GAME for 56 games is the record Joe DiMaggio (left) of the Yankees set in 1941, collecting 91 hits in those 2 months. **HOME RUN KING** Hank Aaron (right) did rewrite the record book. The great outfielder hit 755 homers in the major leagues and collected a lifetime record of 2,297 rbi's.

Most stolen bases, season since 1900
130 Rickey Henderson, Oak AL, 149 games, 1982

Most stolen bases, game
7 George F. (Piano Legs) Gore, Chi NL, June 25, 1881
William R. (Sliding Billy) Hamilton, Phil NL, 2nd game, 8 inn, Aug 31, 1894

Modern Record

6 Edward T. Collins, Phil AL, Sept 11 and again Sept 22, 1912

Most times stealing home, lifetime
35 Tyrus R. Cobb, Det AL, 1905–26; Phil AL 1927–28

Fewest times caught stealing, season (50+ attempts)
2 Max Carey, Pitt NL, 1922 (53 atts)

Pitching

Most years
25 James Kaat, Minn AL 1959–73; Chi AL 1973–75; Phil NL 1976–79; NY AL 1979–80; St L NL 1980–83

Most games, lifetime
1,070 J. Hoyt Wilhelm, NY-St L-Atl-Chi-LA (448) NL, 1952–57, 69–72; Clev-Balt-Chi-Cal (622) AL, 1957–69

Most complete games, lifetime
751 Denton T. (Cy) Young, Clev-St L-Bos NL (428); Bos-Clev AL (323), 1890–1911

Most games, season
106 Mike Marshall, LA NL, 1974

Most complete games, season
74 William H. White, Cin NL, 1879

Lowest earned run average, season
0.90 Ferdinand M. Schupp, NY NL, 1916 (140 inn)
1.01 Hubert B. (Dutch) Leonard, Bos AL, 1914 (222 inn)
1.12 Robert Gibson, St L NL, 1968 (305 inn)

Most innings pitched, game
26 Leon J. Cadore, Bklyn NL, May 1, 1920
Joseph Oeschger, Bos NL, May 1, 1920

Most games won, lifetime
511 Denton T. (Cy) Young, Clev NL (239) 1890–98; St L NL (46) 1899–1900; Bos AL (193) 1901–08; Clev AL (29) 1909–11; Bos NL (4) 1911

Most games won, season
60 Charles Radbourn, Providence NL, 1884

Modern Record

41 John D. Chesbro, NY AL, 1904

Most consecutive games won, lifetime
24 Carl O. Hubbell, NY NL, 1936 (16); 1937 (8)

Perfect game—9 innings
1880 John Lee Richmond, Worcester vs Clev NL, June 12   1–0
John M. Ward, Prov vs Buff NL, June 17 AM   5–0
1904 Denton T. (Cy) Young, Bos vs Phil AL, May 5   3–0
1908 Adrian C. Joss, Clev vs Chi AL, Oct 2   1–0
†1917 Ernest G. Shore, Bos vs Wash AL, June 23 (1st g)   4–0
1922 C. C. Robertson, Chi vs Det AL, Apr 30   2–0
*1956 Donald J. Larsen, NY AL vs Bklyn NL, Oct 8   2–0
1964 James P. Bunning, Phil NL vs NY, June 21 (1st g)   6–0
1965 Sanford (Sandy) Koufax, LA NL vs Chi, Sept 9   1–0
1968 James A. (Catfish) Hunter, Oak AL vs Minn, May 8   4–0
1981 Leonard H. Barker II, Cleve AL vs Tor, May 15   3–0
1984 Michael Witt, Cal AL vs Texas, Sept 9, 1984   1–0

†Starting pitcher, "Babe" Ruth, was banished from game by Umpire Brick Owens after an argument. He gave the first batter, Ray Morgan, a base on balls. Shore relieved and while he pitched to second batter, Morgan was caught stealing. Shore then retired next 26 batters to complete the "perfect" game.
*World Series game.

SLUGGERS: Although his home run records have been surpassed, Babe Ruth (left) is unlikely to be forgotten. His .625 batting average in the 1928 World Series is the best ever, as is his career slugging percentage of .690. Roger Maris (right) watches his 60th home run fly into the seats at Yankee Stadium. Maris then hit his record-breaking 61st in the last game of the 1961 season.

Special mention
1959 Harvey Haddix, Jr, Pitt vs Mil NL, May 26, pitched 12 perfect innings, allowed hit in 13th and lost.

Most strikeouts, season
505 Matthew Kilroy, Balt AA, 1886 (Distance 50 ft)
383 L. Nolan Ryan, Cal AL, 1973 (Distance 60 ft 6 in)

Most strikeouts, career
4,277 L. Nolan Ryan, NY NL, Cal AL, Houston NL, 1968–86

Most strikeouts, game (9 inn) since 1900
20 Roger Clemens, Bos AL vs Seat, Apr 29, 1986

Most strikeouts, extra-inning game
21 Thomas E. Cheney, Wash AL vs Balt (16 inns), Sept 12, 1962 (night)

Most no-hit games, lifetime
5 L. Nolan Ryan, Cal AL, 1973 (2)–74–75; Hou NL, 1981

Most consecutive no-hit games
2 John S. Vander Meer, Cin NL, June 11–15, 1938

Most consecutive games won, season
19 Timothy J. Keefe, NY NL, 1888
Richard W. (Rube) Marquard, NY NL, 1912

Most shutout games, season
16 George W. Bradley, St L NL, 1876
Grover C. Alexander, Phil NL, 1916

Most shutout games, lifetime
113 Walter P. Johnson, Wash AL, 21 years, 1907–27

Most consecutive shutout games, season
6 Donald S. Drysdale, LA NL, May 14, 18, 22, 26, 31, June 4, 1968

Most consecutive shutout innings
58 Donald S. Drysdale, LA NL, May 14-June 8, 1968

Most saves, season
46 Dave Righetti, NY AL, 1986

Most saves, lifetime
324 Roland (Rollie) Fingers, Oak AL, 1968–76; SD NL 1977–80; Mil AL 1981–84

Fielding

Best percentage, season, by position

First Base: 1.000
Steven Garvey, SD NL, 1984

Second Base: .9948
Robert Wilfong, Minn AL, 1980

Third Base: .9894
Donald Money, Mil AL, 1974

Shortstop: .9912
Lawrence Bowa, Phil NL, 1979

Outfield: 1.000
Curtis Flood, St L NL, 1966 (based on most chances handled without an error—396)

Catcher: 1.000
Warren (Buddy) Rosar, Phil AL, 1946

Pitcher: 1.000
Randall Jones, SD NL, 1976 (based on most chances handled without an error—112)

Consecutive games, no errors, by position

First Base: 193
Steven Garvey, SD NL, 1983–85

Second Base: 91
Joe Morgan, Cin NL, 1977–78

Third Base: 97
James Davenport, SF NL, 1966–68

Shortstop: 72
Edwin Brinkman, Det AL, 1972

Outfield: 266
Donald Demeter, Phil NL–Det AL, 1962–65

Catcher: 148
Lawrence P. (Yogi) Berra, NY AL, 1957–59

Pitcher: 385
Paul Lindblad, KC-Oak AL, 1966–74

YOUNGEST WINNER of Cy Young award: Dwight Gooden (left) (NY Mets), was only 20 in 1985, when he was unanimously selected. (AP/Wide World Photos). **FASTEST PITCHER:** Nolan Ryan (right) (Houston Astros) had 4,277 strikeouts to the end of the 1986 season. (Angels Photo)

World Series Records

Most series played
14 Lawrence P. (Yogi) Berra, NY, AL, 1947, 49–53, 55–58, 60–63

Highest batting percentage (20 g min.), total series
.391 Louis C. Brock, St L NL, 1964, 67–68 (g-21, ab-87, h-34)

Highest batting percentage, 4 or more games, one series
.625 4-game series, George H. (Babe) Ruth, NY AL, 1928

Most runs, total series
42 Mickey C. Mantle, NY AL, 1951–53, 55–58, 60–64

Most runs, one series
10 Reginald M. Jackson, NY AL, 1977

Most runs batted in, total series
40 Mickey C. Mantle, NY, AL, 1951–53, 55–58, 60–64

Most runs batted in, consecutive times at bat
7 James L. (Dusty) Rhodes, NY NL, first 4 times at bat, 1954

Most base hits, total series
71 Lawrence P. (Yogi) Berra, NY AL, 1947, 49–53, 55–58, 60–63

Most home runs, total series
18 Mickey C. Mantle, NY AL, 1952 (2), 53 (2), 55, 56 (3), 57, 58 (2), 60 (3), 63 (3)

Most home runs, one series
5 Reginald (Reggie) M. Jackson, NY AL, 1977

Most home runs, game
3 George H. (Babe) Ruth, NY AL, Oct 6, 1926; Oct 9, 1928
   Reginald (Reggie) M. Jackson, NY AL, Oct 18, 1977

Pitching in most series
11 Edward C. (Whitey) Ford, NY AL, 1950, 53, 55–58, 60–64

Most victories, total series
10 Edward C. (Whitey) Ford, NY AL, 1950 (1), 55 (2), 56 (1), 57 (1), 60 (2), 61 (2), 62 (1)

Most games won, one series
3 games in 5-game series
   Christy Mathewson, NY NL, 1905
   J. W. Coombs, Phil AL, 1910
   Many others won 3 games in series of more games.

Most victories, no defeats
6 Vernon L. (Lefty) Gomez, NY AL, 1932 (1), 36 (2), 37 (2), 38 (1)

Most shutout games, total series
4 Christy Mathewson, NY NL, 1905 (3), 1913

Most shutout games, one series
3 Christy Mathewson, NY NL, 1905

Most strikeouts, one pitcher, total series
94 Edward C. (Whitey) Ford, NY AL, 1950, 53, 55–58, 60–64

Most strikeouts, one series
23 in 4 games
   Sanford (Sandy) Koufax, LA NL, 1963
18 in 5 games
   Christy Mathewson, NY NL, 1905
20 in 6 games
   C. A. (Chief) Bender, Phil AL, 1911
35 in 7 games
   Robert Gibson, St L NL, 1968
28 in 8 games
   W. H. Dinneen, Bos AL, 1903

Most strikeouts, one pitcher, game
17 Robert Gibson, St L NL, 1968

Most runs batted in, game
6 Robert C. Richardson, NY AL, (4) 1st inn, (2) 4th inn, 1960

Most hits, 7-Game Series
13 Martin Barrett, Bos AL, 1986, Louis Brock, St L NL, 1968
   Robt Richardson, NY AL, 1960

Most Series Won
22 New York AL, 1923, 1927, 1928, 1932, 1936–39, 1941, 1943, 1947, 1949–53, 1956, 1958, 1961, 1962, 1977, 1978

WORLD SERIES HEROES: Reggie Jackson (left) got the name "Mr October" by hitting 5 home runs for the NY Yankees in the 1977 Series and attaining a record slugging average of .755. Stan "The Man" Musial (right) helped the St Louis Cardinals get into 4 series in 5 years, hit 5 home runs in one day, and was selected National League MVP 3 times.

Attendances

The World Series record attendance is 420,784 (6 games with total gate receipts of $2,626,973.44) when the Los Angeles Dodgers beat the Chicago White Sox 4 games to 2, Oct 1–8, 1959.

The single game record is 92,706 for the fifth game (gate receipts $552,774.77) at the Memorial Coliseum (no longer used for baseball), LA, Oct 6, 1959.

The highest seating capacity in a baseball stadium is 74,208 in the Cleveland Municipal Stadium.

The all-time season record for attendance for both leagues has been 46,828,819 in 1984–85.

An estimated 114,000 spectators watched a game between Australia and an American servicemen's team in a "demonstration" during the Dec 1, 1956 Olympics in Melbourne, Australia.

Fastest Pitcher

The fastest recorded pitcher is (Lynn) Nolan Ryan (b Jan 31, 1947) who, on Aug 20, 1974 (then of the California Angels, now of the Houston Astros) at Anaheim Stadium, Calif, was measured to pitch at 100.9 mph.

All Runs Unearned

The Mets scored 16 runs against the Houston Astros on July 27, 1985, winning 16–4, with all the Met runs unearned. Houston made 5 errors in the game.

MOST HITS, MOST AT-BATS, MOST GAMES: Pete Rose, spark plug of the Cincinnati Reds (with the Phillies for 5 years), now manager of the Reds, ended the 1986 season with 4,256 hits (65 more than Cobb) in 3,562 games and 14,053 times at the plate.

In 1893, there was an important rules change that must be considered when looking at batting records. In the early days of the game, pitching was viewed merely as a matter of trying to get the ball over the plate. Any outfielder might be called upon to pitch. But as managers discovered that there was a decisive advantage to having a pitcher who knew how to throw a knuckleball or a spitball, batting averages declined drastically. Thus in 1893 the distance between home plate and the pitcher's rubber was changed from 50 ft to the current 60 ft 6 in. Batting averages soared.

OLDEST IN BASEBALL: Satchel Paige (right) was about 59 (exact age in doubt) when he pitched for the Kansas City Athletics in 1959. He couldn't break into the majors before he was 42 because of the "color barrier." (UPI)

LEGENDARY PITCHER: Denton T. (Cy for "cyclone") Young (below) pitched 751 complete games in his 22-year career including 511 victories (one a perfect game), and averaged 24 wins per season. Now each year the outstanding pitcher in each league is given a Cy Young award.

HERO IN HIS ERA: Christy Mathewson, idol of the Giants, pitched 3 shutouts including 18 strikeouts in the 5-game 1905 World Series. His best pitch was a "fadeaway," a screwball-like pitch that broke away from left-handed batters. →

KNUCKLEBALL PITCHER Hoyt Wilhelm (right) pitched in 1,070 games, 1952–72, and finished 651 games.

Most Strikeouts, Career

Nolan Ryan of the Houston Astros pitched his 4,000th strikeout on July 11, 1985 against the NY Mets, his former team. By the 1986 season's end his total had risen to 4,277. No other pitcher in the history of baseball has achieved such a record. Ryan was the first to eclipse Walter Johnson's (Wash AL) record of 3,508 which he set between 1907 and 1927 and which stood for 55 years until April 27, 1983.

Dwight Gooden (b Nov 16, 1964) of the Mets in the 1984 All-Star Game in San Francisco struck out 6 consecutive AL batters.

Gooden, in 1985, became the youngest pitcher to win the coveted Cy Young Award. He won it by unanimous vote of the 24 sports writers who make the selection.

Managers

Connie Mack (1892–1956) managed in the major leagues for 53 seasons—3 with Pittsburgh (NL), 1894–96, and 50 with the Philadelphia Athletics (AL), the team he owned, 1901–50. He amassed a record 3,776 regular-season victories (952 victories ahead of John McGraw). Eddie Stanky managed the Texas Rangers (AL) for one day (June 23, 1977) before deciding he did not want the job—even though his team beat Minnesota, 10–8. It is believed to be the shortest term for anyone who signed a managerial contract (that is, excluding interim managers).

Charles D. "Casey" Stengel (1890–1975) set records by managing the NY Yankees (AL) in 10 World Series and winning 7 of them, including 5 in a row (1949–53).

Do-Everything Record

Two major league ballplayers, Bert Campaneris (b Mar 12, 1942) and Cesar Tovar (b July 3, 1940), have the distinction of playing each of the nine field positions in a single major league game. Campaneris did it first, on Sept 8, 1965, when his team, the Kansas City Athletics, announced he would. He played one inning at each position, including the full eighth inning as a pitcher and gave up just one run. Tovar duplicated the feat on Sept 22, 1968, when he played for the Minnesota Twins. He pitched a scoreless first inning and retired the first batter, none other than Campaneris. On June 4, 1983, Mike Ashman, a minor league player for the Albany-Colonie A's of the Eastern League, improved upon the Campaneris-Tovar feat by playing 10 positions, including designated hitter, in a game against Nashua.

MOST CONSECUTIVE GAMES: Lou Gehrig played in 2,130 consecutive games, 1925–39, helping the NY Yankees to 6 of their record 22 championships. His 23 grand-slam homers is a career record.

Do-Nothing Record

Toby Harrah of the Texas Rangers (AL) played an entire doubleheader at shortstop on June 26, 1976, without having a chance to make any fielding plays, assists or putouts.

Longest Throw

The longest throw of a 5-5¼-oz (regulation) baseball is 445 ft 10 in by Glen Gorbous (b Canada) Aug 1, 1957. Mildred "Babe" Didrikson (later Mrs George Zaharias) (1914–56) threw a ball 296 ft at Jersey City, NJ, July 25, 1931.

Longest and Shortest Major League Games

The Brooklyn Dodgers and Boston Braves played to a 1–1 tie after 26 innings on May 1, 1920.

The NY Giants needed only 51 min to beat the Philadelphia Phillies, 6–1, in 9 innings on Sept 28, 1919. (A minor league game, Atlanta vs Mobile in the Southern Association on Sept 19, 1910, took only 32 min, it is claimed.)

The Chicago White Sox played the longest ball game in elapsed time—8 hours 6 min—before beating the Milwaukee Brewers, 7–6, in the 25th inning on May 9, 1984 in Chicago. The game was ended with a homer by Harold Baines, making Tom Seaver

"BEST" SHORTSTOP Honus Wagner (left) of the Pittsburgh Pirates in the early 1900's, noted for his base stealing, was elected to the Hall of Fame. Today he is renowned for the baseball card issued in 1910 and called back by the cigarette company because Wagner, a nonsmoker, objected. Wagner never received any money for it, but the card sells for $25,000. (Card supplied by Tom Miceli and B&E Collectibles, Thornwood, NY. Photo by V. J. Holland)

the winning pitcher for pitching the last inning. The game took 2 days, actually. It started on Tuesday night and was still tied at 3–3 when the 1 a.m. curfew caused suspension until Wednesday night.

Fly Ball Stays Up

When the architects planned the Metrodome in Minneapolis they didn't know they had to contend with Dave Kingman, the slugger who has played in the American and National Leagues, who has been known previously for his many home runs and many strikeouts. Now Kingman has entered the *Guinness Book* with a record for a fly ball he hit that went straight up and didn't come down. It happened when he came up to bat for the Oakland Athletics against the Minnesota Twins on the night of May 4, 1984.

The ball penetrated the netting of the fabric ceiling of the dome 180 feet up and rolled around. When it didn't drop down for an infielder to catch it, the umpires didn't know what to call it. It wasn't in the rule book, of course. Was Kingman out, on the supposition that the fly ball would have been caught? They decided that the ball park was at fault and ruled it a "ground rule double." Fair? The A's lost the game anyway, 3–1. P.S. When the groundskeeper got the ball down, it was sent to the Baseball Hall of Fame in Cooperstown, NY.

Ball Drop from a Dirigible

Joe Sprinz, later catcher for the Cleveland Indians, in 1939 was playing for the Seals of the Pacific Coast League, when Lefty O'Doul was his manager. The San Francisco World's Fair was drawing crowds to Treasure Island in the Bay when someone dreamed up the stunt of dropping baseballs from a dirigible from 1,200 ft up for the Seals' players to try to catch. Sprinz was the only one who had dared to try.

"I had to shade my eyes, I saw the ball all the way, but it looked the size of an aspirin tablet," he said later. "The ball hit me in the mouth, my lips were lacerated very badly, 12 cracks in my upper jaw, lost 5 teeth, was knocked out." And he dropped the ball.

Rained-Out Game in Covered Stadium

The first time in baseball history a game in a covered stadium was called because of rain was on June 16, 1976, in Houston. Flooding around the Astrodome prevented anyone getting into the stadium and the game between Houston and Pittsburgh was called.

Running Bases in Reverse

Herman (Germany) Schaefer of the Washington Senators in 1910 stole first base. This was after he had stolen second with a runner on third. Dissatisfied because the catcher had not thrown to second to allow a double steal to begin, he stole first on the next pitch to try again. A new baseball rule (7.08 i) was instituted at once to prevent this happening again.

Longest Game in Baseball History

The longest was a minor league game in 1981 that lasted 33 innings. At the end of 9, the score was tied, 1-1, with the Rochester (NY) Red Wings battling the home team Pawtucket (RI) Red Sox. At the end of 21 it was tied, 2-2, and at the end of 32, the score was still 2-2, when the game was suspended. Two months later, play was resumed and 18 minutes later, Pawtucket scored one run and won. The winning pitcher was the Red Sox' Bob Ojida, whose teammates included Marty Barrett at 2B, Wade Boggs, at 3B, and Rich Gedman catching. The Rochester cleanup batter was Cal Ripken, Jr. The 33rd inning was witnessed by 54 newspaper reporters, got a top-of-page headline in *The New York Times,* and was carried by the national TV networks!

BASKETBALL

Origins

Ollamalitzli was a 16th century Aztec precursor of basketball played in Mexico. If the solid rubber ball was put through a fixed stone ring placed high on one side of the stadium, the player was entitled to the clothing of all the spectators. The captain of the losing team often lost his head (by execution). Another game played much earlier, in the 10th century BC by the Olmecs in Mexico, called *Pok-ta-Pok,* also resembled basketball in its concept of a ring through which a round object was passed.

Modern basketball was devised by the Canadian-born Dr James Naismith (1861–1939) at the Training School of the International YMCA College at Springfield, Mass, in Dec 1891. The first game played under modified rules was on Jan 20, 1892. The first public contest was on March 11, 1892.

The International Amateur Basketball Federation (FIBA) was founded in 1932.

Rule Change

In the 1940's coaches devised a new tactic, "freezing the ball," in order to maintain a leading score. It consisted of dribbling the ball and avoiding shooting it at the basket in order to maintain possession. In a short time this strategy became part of the entire game resulting in slow play and low scores. The lowest ever was when the Fort Wayne Pistons beat the Minneapolis Lakers 19–18, Nov 22, 1950. As attendance dropped as a result of boring play, Danny Biasone, a team owner, conceived of the "24-second rule" which requires a team to make a try at a basket within 24 seconds of gaining possession of the ball or turn possession over to the opposing team. In 1954, the NBA adopted the rule and scores increased dramatically—as did attendance. In international amateur play the 30-second rule is enforced. In college play the rule is 45 seconds.

Most Accurate Shooting

The greatest goal-shooting demonstration was made by a professional, Ted St. Martin, now of Jacksonville, Fla, who, on June 25, 1977, scored 2,036 consecutive free throws.

In a 24-hour period, May 31–June 1, 1975, Fred L. Newman of San Jose, Calif, scored 12,874 baskets out of 13,116 attempts (98.15%). Newman has also made 88 consecutive free throws while blindfolded at the Central YMCA, San Jose, Calif, Feb 5, 1978. On Dec 17, 1986 he made 338 free throws out of 356 attempts in 10 min, for an average accuracy of 94.9%.

In 24 hours, Jeff Liles scored more free throws, 15,138 out of 17,862 taken (but with 84.75% accuracy) at Lakeland Christian School, Lakeland, Fla, Apr 11–12, 1986.

The longest reported string of consecutive free throws made at any level of organized game competition is 126 by Daryl Moreau over 2 seasons (Jan 17, 1978–Jan 9, 1979) of high school play for De La Salle in New Orleans, La. The best reported one-game free throw performance was by Chris McMullin who made all 29 of his foul shots for Dixie College (St. George, Utah) in the NJCAA National Finals on March 16, 1982.

Greatest Attendances

The Harlem Globetrotters played an exhibition to 75,000 in the Olympic Stadium, West Berlin, Germany, in 1951. The largest indoor basketball attendance was 67,596, including 64,682 tickets sold at the box office, for the Indiana Olympic Basketball Tribute at the Hoosier Dome, Indianapolis on July 9, 1984. They saw victories by the US men's and women's Olympic teams over all-star opposition. The record for a women's college game is 22,157 in Iowa City between Univ of Iowa and Ohio State Univ, on Feb 3, 1985. The NBA record is 44,180 on Feb 15, 1986 in Pontiac, Mich, with the Philadelphia 76ers vs Detroit Pistons.

BASKETBALL was only 8 years old when this game in 1900 took place at Barnard College, NYC.

The National Basketball Association's Championship series was established in 1947. Prior to 1949, when it joined with the National Basketball League, the professional circuit was known as the Basketball Association of America.

SERVICE

Most Games, Lifetime
1,328 Kareem Abdul-Jabbar, Mil 1970–75, LA Lakers 1976–86
Most Games, Consecutive, Lifetime
906 Randy Smith, Buf-SD-Cleve-NY 1972–1983
Most Complete Games, Season
79 Wilt Chamberlain, Phil 1962
Most Minutes, Lifetime
51,002 Kareem Abdul-Jabbar, Mil 1970–75, LA Lakers 1976–86
Most Minutes, Season
3,882 Wilt Chamberlain, Phil 1962

SCORING

Most Seasons Leading League
7 Wilt Chamberlain, Phil 1960–62; SF 1963–64; SF-Phil 1965; Phil 1966
Most Points, Lifetime
35,108 Kareem Abdul-Jabbar, Mil 1970–75, LA Lakers 1976–86
Most Points, Season
4,029 Wilt Chamberlain, Phil 1962
Most Points, Game
100 Wilt Chamberlain, Phil vs NY, Mar 2, 1962
Most Points, Half
59 Wilt Chamberlain, Phil vs NY, Mar 2, 1962
Most Points, Quarter
33 George Gervin, SA vs NO, Apr 9, 1978
Most Points, Overtime Period
14 Butch Carter, Ind vs Bos, March 20, 1984
Highest Scoring Average, Lifetime (400+ games)
30.1 Wilt Chamberlain, Phil-SF-LA 1960–73
Highest Scoring Average, Season
50.4 Wilt Chamberlain, Phil 1962

Field Goals Made

Most Field Goals, Lifetime
14,484 Kareem Abdul-Jabbar, Mil 1970–75; LA Lakers 1976–86
Most Field Goals, Season
1,597 Wilt Chamberlain, Phil 1962
Most Field Goals, Game
36 Wilt Chamberlain, Phil vs NY, Mar 2, 1962
Most Field Goals, Half
22 Wilt Chamberlain, Phil vs NY, Mar 2, 1962

NBA Championships

The most National Basketball Association titles have been won by the Boston Celtics with 16 championships from 1957 to 1986. The Celtics also hold the record for consecutive championships with 8 (1959–66).

Most Field Goals, Quarter
13 David Thompson, Den vs Det, Apr 9, 1978
Most 3-Point Field Goals, Game
8 Rick Barry, Hou vs Utah, Feb 9, 1980
John Roche, Den vs Sea, Jan 9, 1982
Most 3-Point Field Goals, Season
92 Darrell Griffith, Utah 1985

Field Goal Percentage

Most Seasons Leading League
9 Wilt Chamberlain, Phil 1961; SF 1963; SF-Phil 1965; Phil 1966–68; LA 1969, 72–73
Highest Percentage, Lifetime
.600 Artis Gilmore, Chi 1977–82; SA 1983–86
Highest Percentage, Season
.727 Wilt Chamberlain, LA 1973

Free Throws Made

Most Free Throws Made, Lifetime
7,694 Oscar Robertson, Cin-Mil 1961–74
Most Free Throws Made, Season
840 Jerry West, LA 1966
Most Free Throws Made, Consecutive, Season
78 Calvin Murphy, Hou Dec 27, 1980–Feb 28, 1981
Most Free Throws Made, Game
28 Wilt Chamberlain, Phil vs NY, Mar 2, 1962
Adrian Dentley, Utah vs Hou, Jan 5, 1984
Most Free Throws Made (No Misses), Game
19 Bob Pettit, St L vs Bos, Nov 22, 1961
Bill Cartwright, NY vs KC, Nov 17, 1981
Most Free Throws Made, Half
19 Oscar Robertson, Cin vs Balt, Dec 27, 1964
Most Free Throws Made, Quarter
14 Rick Barry, SF vs NY, Dec 6, 1966
Pete Maravich, At vs Buff, Nov 28, 1973

Free Throw Percentage

Most Seasons Leading League
7 Bill Sharman, Bos 1953–57, 59, 61
Highest Percentage, Lifetime
.900 Rick Barry, SF-GS-Hou 1966–67, 73–80
Highest Percentage, Season
.958 Calvin Murphy, Hou 1981

REBOUNDS

Most Seasons Leading League
11 Wilt Chamberlain, Phil 1960–62; SF 1963; Phil 1966–68; LA 1969, 71–73
Most Rebounds, Lifetime
23,924 Wilt Chamberlain, Phil-SF-LA 1960–73
Most Rebounds, Season
2,149 Wilt Chamberlain, Phil 1961
Most Rebounds, Game
55 Wilt Chamberlain, Phil vs Bos, Nov 24, 1960
Most Rebounds, Half
32 Bill Russell, Bos vs Phil, Nov 16, 1957
Most Rebounds, Quarter
18 Nate Thurmond, SF vs Balt, Feb 28, 1965
Highest Average (per game), Lifetime
22.9 Wilt Chamberlain, Phil-SF-LA 1960–73
Highest Average (per game), Season
27.2 Wilt Chamberlain, Phil 1961

ASSISTS

Most Seasons Leading League
8 Bob Cousy, Bos 1953–60
Most Assists, Lifetime
9,887 Oscar Robertson, Cin-Mil 1961–74
Most Assists, Season
1,123 Isiah Thomas, Det 1985
Most Assists, Game
29 Kevin Porter, NJ vs Hou, Feb 24, 1978
Most Assists, Half
19 Bob Cousy, Bos vs Minn, Feb 27, 1959
Highest Average (per game), Lifetime
10.68 Earvin (Magic) Johnson, LA Lakers 1979–86
Highest Average (per game), Season
13.86 Isiah Thomas, Detroit 1985

PERSONAL FOULS

Most Personal Fouls, Lifetime
4,193 Elvin Hayes, SD-Hou-Balt/Wash-Hou 1969–84
Most Personal Fouls, Season
386 Darryl Dawkins, NJ 1984
Most Personal Fouls, Game
8 Don Otten, TC vs Sheb, Nov 24, 1949

NBA REGULAR SEASON RECORDS (INCLUDING 1985–86) (*continued*)

STEALS

Most Steals, Season
301 Alvin Robertson, SA, 1986
Highest Steals Average, Season, per game
3.67 Alvin Robertson, SA, 1986
Most Steals, Game
11 Larry Kenon, SA vs KC, Dec 26, 1976

DISQUALIFICATIONS
(Fouling Out of Game)

Most Disqualifications, Lifetime
127 Vern Mikkelsen, Minn, 1950–59
Most Disqualifications, Season
26 Don Meineke, Ft W 1953
Most Games, No Disqualifications, Lifetime
1,045 Wilt Chamberlain, Phil-SF-LA 1960–73 (Entire Career)

NBA PLAYOFF RECORDS
(Through 1986)

Most games played, lifetime
180 Kareem Abdul-Jabbar, Mil-LA Lakers, 15 years
Most points scored, lifetime
4,912 Kareem Abdul-Jabbar, Mil-LA Lakers, 15 years
Most points, game
63 Michael Jordan, Chi vs Bos, Apr 20, 1986 (2 overtimes)
61 Elgin Baylor, LA Lakers vs Bos, Apr 14, 1962
Best scoring average, lifetime
29.1 Jerry West, LA Lakers, 13 years
Most field goals, game
24 Wilt Chamberlain, Phil vs Syr, March 14, 1960
John Havlicek, Bos vs Atl, Apr 1, 1973

Most free throws, lifetime
1,213 Jerry West, LA Lakers, 13 years
Most free throws, game
30 Bob Cousy, Bos vs Syr, March 21, 1953 (4 overtimes)
21 Oscar Robertson, Cin vs Bos, Apr 10, 1963
Most rebounds, lifetime
4,104 Bill Russell, Bos, 13 years
Most rebounds, game
41 Wilt Chamberlain, Phil vs Bos, Apr 5, 1967
Most assists, lifetime
1,278 Earvin (Magic) Johnson, LA Lakers, 7 years
Most assists, game
24 Earvin (Magic) Johnson, LA Lakers vs Phoenix, May 15, 1984

TOP SCORERS: Kareem Abdul-Jabbar, Mil-LA, (left) compiled 35,108 points with 14,484 field goals 1970–86, beating the 31,419 point record of Wilt Chamberlain (below, #13 in Phila uniform) who scored 100 points in one game and never fouled out of his 1,045 games played. Here he is seen jumping over Bill Russell of the Celtics.

BULL'S EYE: Artis Gilmore of the Chicago Bulls leads the NBA with a .600 field goal percentage. The 7-ft-2-in center has raised his percentage by 23 points in 5 years.

Marathon

The longest game is 102 hours by two teams of five from the Sigma Nu fraternity at Indiana Univ of Pennsylvania, Indiana, Penn, April 13–17, 1983.

Tallest Players

The tallest player of all time is reputed to be Suleiman Ali Nashnush (b 1943) who played for the Libyan team in 1962 when he measured 8 ft tall. Aleksandr Sizonenko of the USSR national team is 7 ft 10 in tall. The tallest woman player is Iuliana Semenova (USSR) who played in the 1976 Olympics and is reputed to stand 7 ft 2 in tall and weigh 281 lb.

Olympic Champions

The US won all 7 Olympic titles from the time the sport was introduced to the Games in 1936 until 1972, without losing a single contest. In 1972, in Munich, the US run of 63 consecutive victories was broken when its team lost, 51–50, to the USSR in a much-disputed final game. The US regained the Olympic title in Montreal in 1976, again without losing a game. In 1980 Yugoslavia took the Olympic gold, but the US came back once more in 1984 for a record 9th title.

In women's Olympics, the USSR won in 1976 and 1980, but the US took the gold in 1984.

BUCKET BRIGADE: Bevo Francis (left) scored 113 points in one game for tiny Rio Grande College in 1954. That season, he averaged 46.5 points per game. Starring for Francis Marion College, Pearl Moore (right) topped all collegiate players with 4,061 career points, 16 more than the men's college record, held by Travis Grant of Kentucky State.

Individual Scoring

Marie Boyd (now Eichler) scored 156 points in a girls' high school basketball game for Central HS, Lonaconing, Md, in a 163–3 victory over Ursuline Academy, on Feb 25, 1924. The boys' high school record is 135 points by Danny Heater of Burnsville, W Va, on Jan 26, 1960.

In college play, Clarence (Bevo) Francis of Rio Grande College, Ohio, scored 113 points against Hillsdale on Feb 2, 1954. One year earlier, Francis scored 116 points in a game, but the record was disallowed because the competition was with a two-year school. In women's college basketball, Annette Kennedy of State Univ at Purchase, NY, scored 70 points vs Pratt Institute on Jan 22, 1984, with 34 field goals in 43 attempts.

Wilton Norman (Wilt) Chamberlain (b Aug 21, 1936) holds the professional record with 100 points for the Philadelphia Warriors vs NY Knicks, scored in one game on Mar 2, 1962. During the same season, Wilt set the record for points in a season (4,029).

Kareem Abdul-Jabbar (formerly Lewis Ferdinand Alcindor) (b Apr 16, 1947) has scored a professional career record of 35,108 points from 1970 through the 1986 season for the Milwaukee Bucks and Los Angeles Lakers. Wilt Chamberlain holds the record average of 30.1 points per game for his total of 31,419.

COURT JESTER: Meadowlark Lemon, of the Harlem Globetrotters, whose comic antics have attracted over 80 million fans to the team's games worldwide.

Pearl Moore of Francis Marion College, Florence, SC, scored a record 4,061 points during her college career, 1975–79. The men's college career scoring record is 4,045 points by Travis Grant for Kentucky State, 1969–72.

Mats Wermelin (Sweden), 13, scored all 272 points in a 272–0 win in a regional boys' tournament in Stockholm, Sweden, on Feb 5, 1974.

Longest Field Goal

The longest *measured* field goal in a college game was made from a distance of 89 ft 10 in by Bruce Morris for Marshall Univ vs Appalachian St, Feb 7,

JUMP SHOT FROM UNICYCLE: Manuel Vargas, Jr, of the World Wheelers under the auspices of UNI-BALL® has made more jump shots from a 3-ft-high 24-in-diameter unicycle than anyone in unicycle basketball history. Willie Vargas of the World Wheelers, from a 6-ft-high unicycle, consistently scores 30 points or more per game.

1985. In an AAU game at Pacific Lutheran University on Jan 16, 1970, Steve Myers sank a shot while standing out of bounds at the other end of the court. Though the basket was illegal, the officials gave in to crowd sentiment and allowed the points to count. The distance is claimed to be 92 ft 3½ in from measurements made 10 years later. The longest for a woman is one of 72 ft 6 in by Annette Alverson of Ohio Northern Univ vs Northern Kentucky, Jan 11, 1985.

Team Scoring

The highest game total in the NBA is 370 points in the Detroit Pistons' victory over the Denver Nuggets 186–184 in 1983. The highest in college play is 282, Univ of Nevada—Las Vegas vs Utah State, 1985. Nevada won, 142–140.

World Champions

The USSR has won most titles at both the Men's World Championships (inst. 1950) with three (1967, 1974 and 1982) and Women's (inst. 1953) with six (1959, 1964, 1967, 1971, 1975 and 1983).

Youngest and Oldest

Bill Willoughby (b May 20, 1957) made his NBA debut for the Atlanta Hawks on Oct 23, 1975, when he was 18 years 5 months 3 days old. The oldest NBA player was Bob Cousy (b Aug 9, 1928), who was 41 years 6 months 2 days old when he appeared in the last of seven games he played for the team he was coaching (Cincinnati Royals) during 1969–70.

BIATHLON   See Skiing

BOARDSAILING (Windsurfing)

Windsurfing is a misnomer. If a surfboard with a sail and mast mounted is used as a surfboard the event is called *sailsurfing,* and if a surfboard with a sail and mast mounted is used like a boat this is called *boardsailing* or *sailboarding.*

The idea of adding a sail enabled surfriders to continue practicing their sport even when there were no waves. The sport of boardsailing was included in the Olympic Games for 1984. The sport is governed by the same associations as surfing.

World Championships

The world championships (started in 1973) have been won five times, consecutively, by Stephan van den Berg (Neth) to 1983.

The longest boardsail ever made was by Timothy John Batstone (b Apr 22, 1959) in circumnavigating 1,794 miles around Great Britain May 2–July 10, 1984. He did 70 miles in a single stretch, made 40 sail changes and had zero falls on eight days.

Highest Speed

The record speed for boardsailing is 38.861 knots in a wind of 50 knots by Pascal Maka (France) at Fuerteventura, Canary Islands, on July 21, 1986, in a Gaastra 4 sq m limited edition speed-trial sailboard.

The women's record of 33.77 knots was set by Britt Dunderbeke in the Canary Islands in July 1986 also.

Longest Sail

Starting from Dakar, Senegal, Jan 23, 1986, two French boardsailors, Stéphane Peyron and Alain Pichavant, crossed the Atlantic unescorted on a 31-ft tandem sailboard in 24 days 12 hours 5 min, landing on the West Indies island of Guadeloupe, some 3,000 mi away. They then proceeded to Miami where they were joined by Carolyn Stalins, 18 (a US citizen living in France), and boardsailed to NYC to arrive on July 2 for the Statue of Liberty celebration. The men covered about 5,000 mi in all.

Endurance

Steve Maxted (GB) went 103 hours at Chatham Docks, Kent, Eng, in Aug 1986.

Longest Line

The longest line of boardsails was achieved by 60 windsurfers in tandem at the International Windsurfing Week event in Balk, Holland, on July 2, 1985.

BOBSLEDDING, LUGING AND TOBOGGANING

Origins

The oldest known sled, dated *c.* 6500 BC, was in Heinola, Finland. The first known bobsled race took place at Davos, Switzerland, in 1889.

MOST NORTHERLY BOARDSAILING: John Stephenson (UK), off the coast of Greenland at 76°N, sailed near icebergs within the Arctic Circle.

TRANSATLANTIC BOARDSAIL: Stéphane Peyron, 24 (left) and Alain Pichavant, 25 (both from France), set a record of 3,000 mi in 24½ days on this 31-ft tandem sailboard, traveling from W Africa to Guadeloupe. They later sailed on to NYC for the July 1986 Liberty weekend.

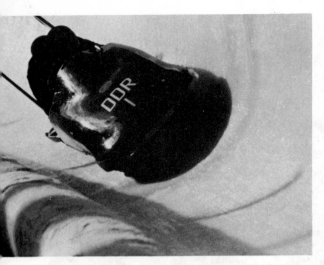

BOB TALE: Meinhard Nehmer and Bernhard Germeshausen, pilots of this East German 2-man bobsled, have each won 3 Olympic golds. Between them, they have also accumulated 4 world titles.

Bobs have two pairs of runners and streamlined cowls. Steering is by means of cables attached to the front runners, which are flexible. The International Federation of Bobsleigh and Tobogganing was formed in 1923, followed by the International Bobsleigh Federation in 1957.

Official international luging (*loojing*) competition, in which the rider adopts a reclining, as opposed to a prone, position, began at Klosters, Switzerland, in 1881. The first European championships were at Reichenberg (now East) Germany, in 1914 and the first world championships at Oslo, Norway, in 1953. The International Luge Federation was formed in 1957. Luging became an Olympic sport in 1964.

Olympic and World Titles

The Olympic 4-man bob title (instituted 1924) has been won 4 times by Switzerland (1924, 36, 56, 72). The US (1932, 36), Switzerland (1948, 80), Italy (1956, 68) W Germany (1952, 72) and E Germany (1976, 84) have won the Olympic 2-man bob event (instituted 1932) twice. The most gold medals won by an individual is 3 by Meinhard Nehmer (b June 13, 1941) (E Germany) and Bernhard Germeshausen (b Aug 21, 1951) (E Germany) in the 1976 two-man, 1976 and 1980 four-man events. The most medals won is 6 (2 gold, 2 silver, 2 bronze) by Eugenio Monti (Italy) (b Jan 23, 1928) from 1956 to 1968. He was a member of 11 world championship crews, 8 two-man and 3 four-man.

In Olympic years, the Olympic champion is also world champion.

The World 4-man bob has been won 15 times by Switzerland (1924, 36, 39, 47, 54–57, 71–73, 75, 82, 83, 86). Italy won the 2-man title 14 times (1954, 56–63, 66, 68–69, 71, 75).

Tobogganing

In tobogganing, the rider lies prone on his (her) belly.

The word "toboggan" comes from the Micmac American Indian word *tobaakan*. The St Moritz Tobogganing Club, Switzerland, founded in 1887 is the oldest toboggan club in the world. It is unique in being the home of the Cresta Run, which dates from 1884, and for the introduction of the one-man racing toboggan skeleton. The course is 3,977 ft long with a drop of 514 ft and the record is 51.31 sec (av. 52.85 mph) by Franco Gansser of Switzerland on Feb 16, 1986. From Junction (2,920 ft), Nico Baracchi (Switz) set a record of 41.58 sec on Feb 21, 1986.

Speeds of 90 mph are sometimes reached.

The greatest number of wins in the Grand National (instituted 1885) is eight by the 1948 Olympic champion Nino Bibbia (Italy) (b Sept 9, 1924) in 1960–64, 66, 68, 73. The greatest number of wins in the Curzon Cup (instituted 1910) is eight by Bibbia in 1950, 57–58, 60, 62–64, 69, who hence won the double in 1960, 62–64.

Luge

Luging was first competed in 1883 in Switzerland, first in world competition in 1955, and first in the Olympics in 1964.

The most successful rider in the world championships is Thomas Köhler (E Ger) (b June 25, 1940), who won the single-seater title in 1962, 64 (Olympic), 66, 67, 73, 76 and shared the two-seater title in 1967 and 68 (Olympic). Köhler and his partner Hans Rinn (E Ger) hold 6 two-seater titles including 2 Olympics (1976 and 1980). Margit Schumann (E Ger) (b Sept 14, 1952) has won the women's championship 5 times—in 1973, 74, 75, 76 (Olympic) and 77.

Paul Hildgartner (Italy) has medaled three times: 1972, Sapporo, Japan, gold, men's doubles (teamed with Walter Plaikner); 1980, Lake Placid, US, silver, men's singles; and 1984, Sarajevo, Yugoslavia, gold, men's singles.

The highest recorded photo-timed speed is 85.38 mph by Asle Strand (Norway) at Tandådalens Linbane, Sälen, Sweden, on May 1, 1982.

BODYBUILDING CHAMPIONS: Arnold Schwarzenegger (Austria, now US) (left) dominated the Mr. Olympia competition in the 1970's. Lee Haney (US) (right) has been the winner for the last 3 years. (Haney photo by Garry Bartlett)

BODYBUILDING

In this new category, information on men's championships has been supplied by the International Federation of Bodybuilders (IFBB), Ben Weider, president, and on women's championships by *Women's Physique World* magazine, Steve Wennerstrom, editor-in-chief.

The Mr. Olympia competition has been dominated by Arnold Schwarzenegger (US) who won 7 titles, 1970–75 and 1980. Lee Haney (US), the current Mr. Olympia, won 3 times, 1984–86. Frank Zane (US) has also won 3 times, 1977–79.

In the Mr. Universe championships, various weight classes are contested. Lee Haney won the heavyweight title in 1982. Multiple winners are Herman Hoffend (W Ger) who won 4 championships, 1983–6 and a 2nd place in 1982, his weight growing from bantamweight to lightweight. Renato Bertagna

(Italy) won 1st place finally in 1979 as a lightweight, after having placed 2nd and 3rd in the short class in 1971, 75, 77 and 78.

In the lightweight division, Heinz Sallmeyer (Austria) won once (1980) and took 2nd place once (1979) while Emmat Sadek (Egypt) took 3rd place 3 times (1984, 85, 86).

In women's contests held by the International Federation of Bodybuilders, the current (1986) Ms. Olympia, Corinna Everson (US) also won that title in 1984, 85 and 86, and the National Women's Championship in 1984. In the IFBB Pro World Championships, Juliette Bergman (Holland) is a first-time winner although she tied for the lightweight World Amateur Championship in 1985 as a lightweight.

In women's contests held by the National Physique Committee, the US Champion in 1986 is Laura Creavalle (Calif) and the National Women's Cham-

FEMALE BODYBUILDING WINNERS: (Left) Corinna Everson, Ms. Olympia 1984–86 and NPC champ 1984; (center) Rachel McLish, Ms. Olympia and US Champion 1980, 82, and Pro World Champion 1982; (right) Carla Dunlap, NPC champ 1981, 82, Ms. Olympia and Pro World Champ 1983. (Photos from "Woman's Physique World" magazine)

pion is Cathey Palyo (Calif), who also won the heavyweight Amateur Championship (IFBB) in 1986. Multiple winners have been Carla Dunlap (US) who won 4 titles (1981, 82, 83), Rachel McLish (US) who also won 4 (1980, 82), Lori Bowen (US) who won 3 (1983, 84) and Corinna Everson 4 titles.

BOWLING

Origins

Bowling can be traced to articles found in the tomb of an Egyptian child of 5200 BC where there were nine pieces of stone to be set up as pins at which a stone "ball" was rolled. The ball first had to roll through an archway made of three pieces of marble. In the Italian Alps about 2,000 years ago, the underhand tossing of stones at an object is believed the beginnings of *bocci,* a game still widely played in Italy and similar to bowling. Martin Luther is credited with the statement that nine was the ideal number of pins. In the British Isles, lawn bowls was preferred to bowling at pins. In the 16th century, bowling at pins was the national sport in Scotland. Early British settlers probably brought lawn bowls to the US and set

up what is known as Bowling Green at the tip of Manhattan Island in NY but perhaps the Dutch under Henry Hudson were the ones to be credited.

In 1841, the Connecticut state legislature prohibited the game and other states followed. Eventually, a tenth pin was added to what had all along been a 9-pin game, to evade the ban.

Organizations

The American Bowling Congress (ABC), established in NY on Sept 9, 1895, was the first body to standardize rules, and the organization now comprises 3,624,575 men who bowl in leagues and tournaments. The Women's International Bowling Congress (WIBC), founded 1916, has a membership of 3,550,566. The Young American Bowling Alliance (YABA) (inst 1982), the successor to the American Junior Bowling Congress and Youth Bowling Assn, has 663,411 youth and collegiate members. The Professional Bowlers Association (PBA), formed in 1958, comprises more than 2,800 of the world's best male bowlers. The Ladies Professional Bowlers Tour has 170 members.

Lanes

In the US there were 8,503 bowling establishments with 157,706 lanes in 1985 and about 68 million bowlers.

The world's largest bowling center (now closed) was the Tokyo World Lanes Center, Japan, with 252 lanes. Currently the largest center is Fukuyana Bowl, Osaka, Japan, which has 144 lanes.

BEST FINISHES: Les Schissler of Denver (bowling here) bowled a 300 game, won 3 ABC crowns in one year in 1966 after winning the singles, All-Events, and being on the winning team in one tournament.

Marathons

Donnie Moore (b 1960), a US Navy petty officer stationed at the Jacksonville, Fla Naval Air Station, bowled 2,028 games in 217 hours, 55 min, July 15–24, 1985, for an average of 9.3 games per hour. He was under medical surveillance, stopping for blood pressure and vital sign checks regularly and on July 22 stopped for 24½ hours for hospital rest and oxygen intake per doctor's orders.

Dorothy Meinecke of Detroit, Mich, bowled 130 games in 16 hours 30 min, non-stop, Jan 24, 1926 for an average of 7.9 games per hour.

World Championships

The Fédération Internationale des Quilleurs world championships were instituted in 1954. The highest pinfall in the individual men's event is 5,963 for 28 games by Ed Luther (US) at Milwaukee, Wis on Aug 28, 1971. In the current schedule of 24 games, the men's record is 5,242 by Mats Karlsson (Sweden) and 4,806 by Bong Coo (Philippines) is the women's record, both set in Nov 1983 at Caracas, Venezuela.

ABC LEAGUE RECORDS

Highest Scores

The highest individual score for three games is 886 by Albert "Allie" Brandt of Lockport, NY, on Oct 25, 1939. Glenn Allison (b 1930) rolled a perfect 900 in a 3-game series in league play on July 1, 1982, at La Habra Bowl, LA, Calif, but the ABC could not recognize the record when an ABC inspector examined the lanes and determined they had been improperly dressed (for other 900 series see *Most Perfect Scores,* below). Highest 3-game team score is 3,858 by Budweisers of St Louis on March 12, 1958.

The highest season average attained in sanctioned competition is 242 by John Ragard of Susquehanna, Pa, for 66 games in 1981–82.

The all-time ABC sanctioned 2-man single-game record is 600 by John Cotta (300) and Steve Lanson (300) on May 1, 1981, at the Manteca, Calif, Bowling Assn Tournament. The 2-man team series record is 1,639 by Tim Foti (794) and Bob Perry (845) in Lodi, NJ on Aug 27, 1986.

Consecutive Strikes

The record for consecutive strikes in sanctioned match play is 33 by John Pezzin (b 1930) at Toledo, Ohio, on March 4, 1976.

Most Perfect Scores

The highest number of sanctioned 300 games is 27 (through 1986) by Elvin Mesger of Sullivan, Mo. The maximum 900 for a three-game series has been recorded five times in unsanctioned competition—by Leon Bentley at Lorain, Ohio, on March 26, 1931; by Joe Sargent at Rochester, NY, in 1934; by Jim Margie in Philadelphia, on Feb 4, 1937; by Bob Brown at Roseville Bowl, Calif, on Apr 12, 1980; and by Glenn Allison (see above) at Whittier, Calif, on July 1, 1982.

FRAME AND FORTUNE: Earl Anthony of Dublin, Calif (left) is the PBA career champion with a lifetime total of 41 titles and earnings of more than $1¼ million. Mark Roth of N Arlington, NJ (right) set a PBA season mark in 1978 when he won 8 titles.

PBA RECORDS

Most Titles

Earl Anthony of Dublin, Calif, has won a lifetime total of 41 PBA titles through Oct 1986. The record number of titles won in one PBA season is 8, by Mark Roth of North Arlington, NJ, in 1978.

Consecutive Titles

Only three bowlers have ever won three consecutive professional tournaments—Dick Weber in 1959, 60, and 61, Johnny Petraglia in 1971, and Mark Roth in 1977.

Perfect Games

A total of 119 perfect (300-pin) games were bowled in PBA tournaments in 1979. Dick Weber rolled 3 perfect games in one tournament (Houston) in 1965, as did Billy Hardwick of Louisville, Ky (in the Japan Gold Cup competition) in 1968, Roy Buckley of Columbus, Ohio (at Chagrin Falls, Ohio) in 1971, John Wilcox (at Detroit), Norm Meyers of St Louis (at Peoria, Ill) in 1979, and Shawn Christensen of Denver (at Denver) in 1984.

Don Johnson of Las Vegas, Nev, bowled at least one perfect game in 11 consecutive seasons (1965–1975). Guppy Troup, of Savannah, Ga, rolled 6 perfect games on the 1979 tour.

Highest Earnings

The greatest lifetime earnings on the Professional Bowlers Association circuit have been won by Earl Anthony who has taken home $1,264,621 through Nov 15, 1986. Mike Aulby holds the season earnings record with $201,200 in 1985.

Highest Score in 24 Hours

A team of 6 called "The Cobras" scored 53,543 in 24 hours at Paderborn (W Ger) Bowling Center, July 24–25, 1986.

Television Bowling

Nelson Burton Jr, St Louis, rolled the best series, 1,050, for four games (278-279-257-236) at Dick Weber Lanes in Florissant, Mo, Feb 11, 1984.

40 □ BOWLING

ABC TOURNAMENT RECORDS

Highest Individual

Highest three-game series in singles is 801 by Mickey Higham of Kansas City, Mo, in 1977. Best three-game total in any ABC event is 833 by Fran Bax of Niagara Falls, NY, in team in 1983. Jim Godman of Lorain, Ohio, holds the record for a nine-game All-Events total with 2,184 (731–749–704) set in Indianapolis, Ind, in 1974. ABC Hall of Famers Fred Bujack of Detroit, Bill Lillard of Houston, and Nelson Burton Jr of St Louis, have won the most championships with 8 each. Bujack shared in 3 team and 4 team All-Events titles between 1949 and 1955, and also won the individual All-Events title in 1955. Lillard bowled on Regular and team All-Events champions in 1955 and 1956, the Classic team champions in 1962 and 1971, and won regular doubles and All-Events titles in 1956. Burton shared in 3 Classic team titles, 2 Classic doubles titles and has won Classic singles twice and Classic All-Events.

Highest Doubles

The ABC national tournament record of 558 was set in 1976 by Les Zikes of Chicago and Tommy Hudson of Akron, Ohio. The record score in a doubles series is 1,453, set in 1952 by John Klares (755) and Steve Nagy (698) of Cleveland.

Perfect Scores

Les Schissler of Denver scored 300 in the Classic team event in 1967, and Ray Williams of Detroit scored 300 in Regular team play in 1974, the first two perfect games bowled in team competition. In all, there have been only forty-six 300 games in the ABC tournament through 1986. There have been 25 perfect games in singles, 16 in doubles, and 5 in team play.

Best Finishes in One Tournament

Les Schissler of Denver won the singles, All-Events, and was on the winning team in 1966 to tie Ed Lubanski of Detroit and Bill Lillard of Houston as the only men to win three ABC crowns in one year. The best four finishes in one ABC tournament were third in singles, second in doubles, third in team and first in All-Events by Bob Strampe, Detroit, in 1967, and first in singles, third in team and doubles and second in All-Events by Paul Kulbaga, Cleveland, in 1960.

Strikes and Spares in a Row

In the greatest finish to win an ABC title, Ed Shay set a record of 12 strikes in a row in 1958, when he scored a perfect game for a total of 733 in singles. Most strikes in a row is 20 by Lou Viet of Milwaukee in 1977.

The most spares in a row is 23, a record set by Lt Hazen Sweet of Battle Creek, Mich, in 1950.

Most Tournament Appearances

Bill Doehrman of Fort Wayne, Ind, competed in 71 consecutive ABC tournaments, beginning in 1908. (No tournaments were held 1943–45.)

Attendance

Largest spectator attendance on one day for an ABC Tournament was 5,257 in Milwaukee in 1952. The total attendance record was set at Las Vegas, Nev, in 1986 with 201,175 in 134 days.

SUPER BOWLER: Jeanne Maiden of Solon, Ohio, has rolled 11 perfect games to set the WIBC career record. She also set a record of 40 consecutive strikes in 1986. (WIBC)

TOP WOMEN BOWLERS: Patty Ann (left) has a record 5-year average of 227.20 and has scored 27 strikes in a row. Rose Walsh (center) became the second woman in history to roll 300 in the 67-year-old WIBC Championship Tournament. Ethel Brunnick (right) participated in a tournament at age 98 in 1986.

Youngest and Oldest Winners

The youngest champion was Ronnie Knapp of New London, Ohio, who was a member of the 1963 Booster team champions when he was 16 years old. The oldest champion was Joe Detloff of Chicago, Ill, who, at the age of 72, was a winner in the 1965 Booster team event. The oldest doubles team in ABC competition totaled 165 years in 1955: Jerry Ameling (83) and Joseph Lehnbeutter (82), both from St Louis. The youngest bowler to score 300 is said to be John Jaszkowski of S Milwaukee, Wis, who performed this feat at age 11, on Mar 13, 1982. The oldest bowler to score 300 is Leo Sites of Wichita, Kans, who performed the feat on Apr 10, 1985 at age 80.

WIBC RECORDS

Highest Scores

Patty Ann of Bloomington, Ill, had a record 227 average in league play in the 1985–86 season, and a record 5-year composite average of 227.20 through 1986. Her record for the highest total in a three-game series was exceeded in 1986 by Jeanne Maiden (see below) who rolled 864.

The highest 5-woman team score for a 3-game series is 3,379 by Freeway Washer of Cleveland in 1960. The highest game score by a 5-woman team is 1,210 by Sheraton Inn, Scranton, Pa in 1982.

Championship Tournaments

The highest score for a 3-game series in the annual WIBC Championship Tournament is 737 by D. D. Jacobson in the 1972 singles competition. The record for one game is 300 by Lori Gensch of Milwaukee in the 1979 doubles event and by Rose Walsh of Pomona, Calif in 1986. The WIBC sanctioned 153,435 leagues in the 1985 season.

Mary Covell of Chicago participated in her 55th WIBC tournament in 1986. The oldest participant was Ethel Brunnick (b Aug 30, 1887) of Santa Monica, Calif, at age 98 in 1986. Mary Ann Keiper of St Louis was only 5 years old when she participated in the 1952 tournament. The youngest champion was Leila Wagner (b July 12, 1960) of Seattle, Wash, who was 18 when she was a member of the championship 5-woman team in 1979.

Dorothy Miller of Chicago has won 10 WIBC Championship Tournament events, the most by an individual. Millie Martorella is the only one to have won 3 WIBC Queen Tournaments, 1967, 1970, and 1971.

The highest lifetime average is 199.14 by Dorothy Fothergill of Lincoln, RI, who has bowled for 10 years but is now inactive.

The largest tournament in 1983 in Las Vegas drew 14,430 teams attracted by a record $1,627,815 in prize money.

Perfect Games

The most 300 games rolled in a career is 11 by Jeanne Maiden of Solon, Ohio. The oldest woman to bowl a perfect game (12 strikes in a row) was Helen Duval of Berkeley, Calif, at age 65 in 1982. Of all the women who rolled a perfect game, the one with the lowest average was Diane Ponza of Santa Cruz, Calif, who had a 112 average in the 1977–78 season.

Consecutive Strikes, Spares and Splits

The record for most consecutive strikes is 40 by Jeanne Maiden (see above). Joan Taylor of Syracuse, NY, made 27 consecutive spares. Shirley Tophigh of Las Vegas, Nev, holds the unenviable record of rolling 14 consecutive splits.

BOXING

Boxing with gloves was depicted on a fresco from the Isle of Thera, Greece, which has been dated to 1520 BC. The earliest prize-ring code of rules was formulated in England, Aug 16, 1743, by the champion pugilist Jack Broughton (1704–89), who reigned from 1729 to 1750. Boxing, which had in 1867 come under the Queensberry Rules, formulated for John Sholto Douglas, 9th Marquess of Queensberry, was not established as a legal sport in Britain until after a ruling of Mr Justice Grantham following the death of Billy Smith (Murray Livingstone) due to a fight on Apr 24, 1901, at Covent Garden, London.

There are two governing bodies, the World Boxing Association (formed as the National Boxing Association in the US in 1920) and the World Boxing Council (formed in 1963). At most weights separate champions are recognized by these two organizations.

Longest Fights

The longest recorded fight with gloves was between Andy Bowen of New Orleans and Jack Burke in New Orleans, Apr 6–7, 1893. The fight lasted 110 rounds (7 hours 19 min from 9:15 p.m. to 4:34 a.m.) but was declared no contest (later changed to a draw) when both men were unable to continue. The longest recorded bare knuckle fight was one of 6 hours 15 min between James Kelly and Jack Smith at Fiery Creek, Dalesford, Australia, Dec 3, 1855. The greatest recorded number of rounds is 276 in 4 hours 30 min, when Jack Jones beat Patsy Tunney in Cheshire, England, in 1825. The longest world title fight was in 1906 when Joe Gans (US) beat Battling Nelson (Den) when Nelson was disqualified in the 42nd round of a scheduled 45-round contest.

BOXING THE WAY IT USED TO BE: No overstuffed gloves, just a taped-off dirt ring. Just $22,500 was the record prize in 1889 for a fight-till-you-drop that went 27 rounds in Port Elizabeth, S Africa, between Jack Cooper and Wolf Bendoff.

TITLE DEEDS: Joe Louis (left) kept the heavyweight title for over 11 years, the longest reign at any weight class. Known as "The Brown Bomber," Louis successfully defended his title a record 25 times. Louis' largest purse, earned in his 8th round KO of Billy Conn in 1946, was $625,916—a far cry from today's high-priced bouts. Ringside seats cost a then-record $100.

Shortest Fights

There is a distinction between the quickest knockout and the shortest fight. A knockout in 10½ sec (including a 10-sec count) occurred on Sept 23, 1946, when Al Couture struck Ralph Walton while the latter was adjusting his mouthpiece in his corner at Lewiston, Me. If the time was accurately taken it is clear that Couture must have been more than halfway across the ring from his own corner at the opening bell.

The shortest fight on record appears to be one in a Golden Gloves tournament in Minneapolis, Minn, Nov 4, 1947, when Mike Collins floored Pat Brownson with his first punch and the contest was stopped, without a count, 4 sec after the bell.

The shortest world title fight was the James J. Jeffries (1875–1953) vs Jack Finnegan heavyweight bout on Apr 6, 1900, won by Jeffries in 55 sec.

The shortest *professional* bout occurred Apr 3, 1936 when Al Carr (Alfred Tramantano) stopped Lew Massey in 7 sec with one punch in New Haven, Conn.

Longest Career

The heavyweight Jem Mace (GB) (1831–1910), known as "the Gypsy," had a career lasting 50 years from 1855 to 1905, when he put on an exhibition bout with Tug Wilson, but his career is not fully documented. Kid Azteca (b Louis Villanueva Parano, 1915, Mexico City) started boxing professionally in 1929 and has a published record that includes at least one bout per year, 1932–61.

Tallest Boxer

The tallest boxer to fight professionally was Gogea Mitu (b 1914) of Rumania in 1935. He was 7 ft 4 in and weighed 327 lb. John Rankin, who won a fight in New Orleans in Nov 1967, also claimed 7 ft 4 in.

WORLD HEAVYWEIGHT CHAMPIONS

Earliest Title Fight

The first world heavyweight title fight, with 3-oz gloves and 3-minute rounds, was between John L. Sullivan (1858–1918) and Dominick McCaffrey on Aug 29, 1885 in Cincinnati, O. It went 6 rounds and Sullivan won.

Longest and Shortest Reigns

The longest reign of any world heavyweight champion is 11 years 252 days by Joe Louis (b Joseph Louis Barrow, 1914–81), from June 22, 1937, when he knocked out James J. Braddock in the 8th round at Chicago until announcing his retirement on March 1, 1949. During his reign Louis made a record 25 defenses of his title. The shortest reign was by Greg Page (US) (b Oct 25, 1958) for 150 days, Dec 1984 to Apr 29, 1985. Ken Norton (US) (b Aug 6, 1945) was recognized by the WBC as champion for 83 days, Mar 18–June 9, 1978.

The longest-lived heavyweight champion was Jack Dempsey, who died May 31, 1983 aged 87 years 341 days.

Oldest and Youngest

The oldest man to win the heavyweight crown was Jersey Joe Walcott (b Arnold Raymond Cream, Jan 31, 1914, at Merchantville, NJ), who knocked out Ezzard Charles on July 18, 1951, in Pittsburgh, when aged 37 years 5 months 18 days. Walcott was the oldest title holder at 38 years 7 months 23 days when he

NEWLY THRONED: Mike Tyson, who knocked out 26 opponents and was unbeaten in 28 bouts, knocked out WBC champion Trevor Berbick in the 2nd round on Nov 22, 1986 in Las Vegas to become at age 20 the youngest ever to wear the heavyweight crown.

THE CHAMP AND HIS MANAGERS: Mike Tyson, wearing his heavyweight champion's gold belt, shows it off, surrounded by his managers, Bill Cayton (left) and Jim Jacobs (right).

lost to Rocky Marciano on Sept 23, 1952. The youngest age at which the world heavyweight title has been won is 20 years 145 days by Mike Tyson (b June 30, 1966), who won the WBC title by beating Trevor Berbick in the 2nd round on Nov 22, 1986, in Las Vegas, Nev.

Undefeated

Rocky Marciano (b Rocco Francis Marchegiano) (1923–69) is the only heavyweight champion to have been undefeated in his entire professional career (1947–1956). His record was 49 wins (43 by KO) and no losses or draws.

Most Recaptures

Muhammad Ali Haj (b Cassius Marcellus Clay, in Louisville, Ky, Jan 17, 1942) is the only man to regain the heavyweight title twice. Ali first won the title on Feb 25, 1964, defeating Sonny Liston. He defeated George Foreman on Oct 30, 1974, having been stripped of his title by the world boxing authorities on Apr 28, 1967. He lost his title to Leon Spinks on Feb 15, 1978, but regained it on Sept 15, 1978 by defeating Spinks in New Orleans.

Heavyweight Champions through the Years

1882 John L. Sullivan (US)
1892 James J. Corbett (US)
1897 Bob Fitzsimmons (GB)
1899 James J. Jeffries (US)
1905 Marvin Hart (US)
1906 Tommy Burns (Can)
1908 Jack Johnson (US)
1915 Jess Willard (US)
1919 Jack Dempsey (US)
1926 Gene Tunney (US)
1930 Max Schmeling (Ger)
1932 Jack Sharkey (US)
1933 Primo Carnera (Ita)
1934 Max Baer (US)
1935 James J. Braddock (US)
1937 Joe Louis (US)
1949 Ezzard Charles (US)
1951 Jersey Joe Walcott (US)
1952 Rocky Marciano (US)
1956 Floyd Patterson (US)
1959 Ingemar Johansson (Swe)
1960 Floyd Patterson (US)
1962 Sonny Liston (US)
1964 Cassius Clay/Muhammad Ali (US)
1965 Ernie Terrell (US)—WBA only till 1967
1968 Joe Frazier (US)—NY State
1968 Jimmy Ellis (US)—WBA
1970 Joe Frazier (US)—undisputed
1973 George Foreman (US)
1974 Muhammad Ali (US)
1978 Leon Spinks (US)
1978 Ken Norton (US)—WBC
1978 Muhammad Ali (US)—WBA
1978 Larry Holmes (US)—WBC, IBF from 1983
1979 John Tate (US)—WBA
1980 Mike Weaver (US)—WBA
1982 Mike Dokes (US)—WBA
1983 Gerry Coetzee (So Afr)—WBA
1984 Tim Witherspoon (US)—WBC
1984 Pinklon Thomas—WBC
1984 Greg Page—WBA
1985 Tony Tubbs (US) WBA
1985 Michael Spinks (US)—WBC, IBF
1986 Trevor Berbick (Canada) WBC
1986 Tim Witherspoon (US) WBA
1986 Mike Tyson (US) WBC

WBC—World Boxing Council, headquartered in Mexico City. President: Jose Sulaiman, who has devoted himself to boxing for 20 years. A substantial portion of WBC's income has been spent furthering the sport, protecting the athletes and improving medical facilities. This is the most highly regarded organization.

WBA—World Boxing Association, headquartered in Panama City, Panama. President: Gilberto Mendoza.

IBF—International Boxing Federation, headquartered in NJ. President: Bob Lee.

These 3 bodies represent national federations of boxing commissions throughout the world, and have a variety of financial and political connections.

Heaviest and Lightest

The heaviest world champion was Primo Carnera (Italy) (1906–67), the "Ambling Alp," who won the title from Jack Sharkey in 6 rounds in NYC, on June 29, 1933. He scaled 267 lb for this fight. He had the longest reach at 85½ in (finger tip to finger tip) and an expanded chest measurement of 53 in.

The lightest was Robert James Fitzsimmons (1863–1917), (b Helston, Cornwall, England) who, at a weight of 167 lb, won the title by knocking out James J. Corbett in 14 rounds at Carson City, Nev, March 17, 1897.

The greatest differential in a world title fight was 86 lb between Carnera (270 lb) and Tommy Loughran (184 lb) of the US, when the former won on points at Miami, Fla, March 1, 1934.

Tallest and Shortest

The tallest world champion was Primo Carnera, who was measured at 6 ft 5.4 in by the Physical Education Director at the Hemingway Gymnasium of Harvard, although he was widely reported and believed in 1933 to be 6 ft 8½ in tall. Jess Willard (1881–1968), who won the title in 1915, was often described as being 6 ft 6¼ in tall, but was in fact 6 ft 5¼ in. The shortest was Tommy Burns (1881–1955) of Canada, world champion from Feb 23, 1906, to Dec 26, 1908, who stood 5 ft 7 in and weighed between 168 and 180 lb.

Knockout Percentage

George Foreman (b Jan 10, 1949) had the highest career knockout percentage of any heavyweight champion. In his 47 professional fights, Foreman KO'd 42 opponents, thus winning 89.36% of his bouts by knockout.

> George Foreman is the only US champion in any weight class to have won, defended, and lost his crown all outside the US. To win his title he defeated Joe Frazier in Kingston, Jamaica, Jan 22, 1973. He defended it against Jose Roman in Tokyo, Japan, Sept 1, 1973, and against Ken Norton in Caracas, Venezuela, Mar 26, 1974. He lost it to Muhammad Ali in Kinshasa, Zaire, Oct 30, 1974. As world champion, this native of Marshall, Tex never fought in his own country.

THE HARDER THEY FALL: (Left) Muhammad Ali is seated on the canvas during his unsuccessful attempt to regain the heavyweight crown from Joe Frazier in New York's Madison Square Garden in 1971. Three years later, Ali knocked out George Foreman in the 8th round (right) in Zaire for the first of his record two recaptures. Foreman KO'd 42 opponents in 47 pro fights. (AP) George Foreman holds a record of his own (see page 46).

WORLD CHAMPIONS (ANY WEIGHT)

Longest Reign

Joe Louis's heavyweight duration record of 11 years 252 days stands for all divisions.

Youngest and Oldest

The youngest at which any world championship has been won is 17 years 176 days by Wilfredo Benitez (b Sept 12, 1958) of Puerto Rico, who won the WBA light-welterweight title, Mar 6, 1976.

The oldest world champion was Archie Moore (b Archibald Lee Wright, Collinsville, Ill, Dec 13, 1913 or 1916), who was recognized as a light-heavyweight champion up to Feb 10, 1962, when his title was removed. He was then between 45 and 48. Bob Fitzsimmons (1863–1917) had the longest career of any official world titleholder with over 31 years from 1883 to 1914. He had his last world title bout on Dec 20, 1905 at the age of 42 years 208 days.

YOUNGEST BOXER to win a world title was Wilfredo Benitez (right), who captured the light-welterweight title when he was only 17½ years old. Benitez is one of only a handful of fighters who have won world titles in 3 different weight classes.

LORD OF THE RING: Rocky Marciano (left) is the only heavyweight champion to go through his entire professional career without a loss. Marciano won all 49 of his bouts, including 43 knockouts.

Most Fights

The greatest recorded number of fights in a career is 1,024 by Bobby Dobbs (US) (1858–1930), who is reported to have fought from 1875 to 1914, a period of 39 years. Abraham Hollandersky, *alias* Abe the Newsboy (US), is reputed to have had 1,309 fights in the 14 years from 1905 to 1918, but many of them were one-round exhibition bouts. Len Wickwar, an English lightweight who fought between 1928–47, had 463 documented fights.

Most Fights Without Loss

Edward Henry (Harry) Greb (US) (1894–1926) was unbeaten in 178 bouts, but these included 117 "no decisions" 1916–23 and 5 were unofficial losses. Of boxers with complete records Packey McFarland (US) (1888–1936) had 97 fights (five draws) in 1905–15 without a defeat. Pedro Carrasco (b Spain, Nov 7, 1943) won 83 consecutive fights from Apr 22, 1964 to Sept 3, 1970, and then drew once and had a further nine wins before his loss to Armando Ramos in a WBC lightweight contest on Feb 18, 1972.

Olympic Gold Medals

In the 1984 Olympics, US boxers won a record total of 9 of the 12 gold medals.

Only two boxers have won three Olympic gold medals: southpaw László Papp (b 1926, Hungary), who took the middleweight (1948) and the light-middleweight titles (1952 and 56), and Cuban heavyweight Teofilo Stevenson (b Mar 23, 1952), who won the gold medal in his division for three successive Games (1972, 76 and 80). The only man to win two titles in one meeting was Oliver L. Kirk (US), who took both the bantam and featherweight titles at St Louis, Mo, in 1904, but he only needed one bout in each class.

The oldest man to win an Olympic gold medal in boxing was Richard K. Gunn (1871–1961) (GB), who won the featherweight title on Oct 27, 1908, in London, aged 38.

Greatest "Tonnage"

The greatest "tonnage" in a world title fight was 488¾ lb when Primo Carnera (259½ lb) fought Paolino Uzcudun (229¼ lb) of Spain, in Rome, Italy, Oct 22, 1933.

The greatest "tonnage" recorded in any fight is 700 lb, when Claude "Humphrey" McBride of Okla at 340 lb knocked out Jimmy Black of Houston at 360 lb in the 3rd round at Oklahoma City, June 1, 1971.

Smallest Champions

The smallest man to win any world title has been Netranoi Vorsingh (b Apr 22, 1959) (Thailand), WBC light-flyweight champion from May to Sept 1978, at 4 ft 11 in tall. Jimmy Wilde (b Merthyr Tydfil, 1892, d 1969, UK), who held the flyweight title from 1916 to 1923, was reputed never to have fought above 108 lb.

Longest Title Fight

The longest world title fight (under Queensberry Rules) was between the lightweights Joe Gans (1874–1910), of the US, and Oscar "Battling" Nelson (1882–1954), the "Durable Dane," at Goldfield, Nev, Sept 3, 1906. It was terminated in the 42nd round when Gans was declared the winner on a foul.

Most Title Bouts

The record number of title bouts in a career is 37, of which 18 ended in "no decision," by 3-time world welterweight champion Jack Britton (US) (1885–1962), from 1915 to 1922.

TALLEST AND HEAVIEST CHAMPION (6 ft 5.4 in, 270 lb at the time) Primo Carnera shows off his strength before winning the heavyweight title in 1933.

Most Titles Simultaneously

The only man to hold world titles at three weights simultaneously was Henry "Homicide Hank" Armstrong (b Dec 12, 1912) of the US, at featherweight, lightweight and welterweight from Aug to Dec 1938.

Most Knockdowns in Title Fights

Vic Toweel (South Africa) knocked down Danny O'Sullivan of London 14 times in 10 rounds in their world bantamweight fight at Johannesburg, Dec 2, 1950, before the latter retired.

Most Recaptures

The only boxer to win a world title five times at one weight is Sugar Ray Robinson (b Walker Smith, Jr, in Detroit, May 3, 1921) who beat Carmen Basilio (US) in the Chicago Stadium on March 25, 1958, to regain the world middleweight title for the fourth time. The other title wins were over Jake LaMotta (US) in Chicago on Feb 14, 1951; Randy Turpin (UK) in NYC on Sept 12, 1951; Carl "Bobo" Olson (US) in Chicago on Dec 9, 1955; and Gene Fullmer (US) in Chicago on May 1, 1957.

Amateur World Championships

Two boxers have won three world championships (instituted 1974): Teofilo Stevenson (Cuba), heavyweight 1974, 1978 and 1986, and Adolfo Horta (b Oct 3, 1957) (Cuba), bantam 1978, feather 1982 and lightweight 1986.

ALL FIGHTS

Highest Earnings in Career

The largest known fortune ever made in a fighting career (or any sports career) is an estimated $69 million (including exhibitions) amassed by Muhammad Ali from Oct 1960 to Dec 1981, in 61 fights comprising 549 rounds.

Largest Purse

The greatest purse for one boxer is $12 million by Sugar Ray Leonard (US) (b May 17, 1956) when he beat Thomas Hearns (US) for the undisputed world welterweight title at Las Vegas, Nev, on Sept 16, 1981. The total purse for both fighters was a record $17.1 million. The purse for the Gerry Cooney vs Larry Holmes heavyweight championship fight, June

BIGGEST PURSE: Sugar Ray Leonard (left) and Thomas Hearns set the world's record for the largest total purse for both fighters of $17.1 million, of which Leonard earned a record share with $12 million (almost three times greater than Joe Louis' lifetime earnings of $3.8 million for 71 fights). (All-Sport)

11, 1982 in Las Vegas, was over $18 million which was split equally.

The largest stake ever fought for in the bare-knuckle era was $22,500 in a 27-round fight when Jack Cooper beat Wolf Bendoff at Port Elizabeth, South Africa, July 26, 1889.

Most Knockouts

The greatest number of knockouts in a career is 145 (129 in professional bouts) by Archie Moore (1936 to 1963). The record for consecutive KO's is 44, set by Lamar Clark of Utah at Las Vegas, Nev,

Jan 11, 1960. He knocked out 6 in one night (5 in the first round) in Bingham Canyon, Utah, on Dec 1, 1958.

Highest and Lowest Attendances

The greatest paid attendance at any boxing fight has been 120,757 (with a ringside price of $27.50) for the Tunney vs Dempsey world heavyweight title fight at the Sesquicentennial Stadium, Philadelphia, Sept 23, 1926. The indoor record is 63,360 for the Spinks vs Ali world heavyweight title fight at the Louisiana Superdome in New Orleans, Sept 15, 1978.

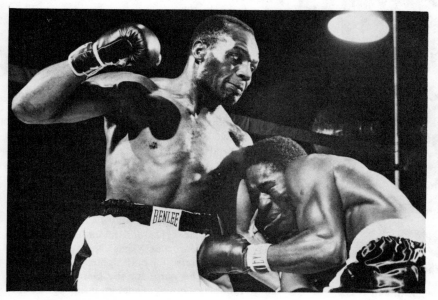

OLDEST HEAVYWEIGHT CHAMP: Jersey Joe Walcott, 37½, in the process of knocking out Ezzard Charles, in a 1951 upset, to win the crown in Pittsburgh. (AP London)

The record for live gate receipts is $7,293,600 for the Larry Holmes vs Gerry Cooney WBC heavyweight title bout in Las Vegas, Nev, on June 11, 1982. The highest non-paying attendance is 135,132 at the Tony Zale vs Billy Pryor fight at Juneau Park, Milwaukee, Wis, Aug 18, 1941.

The smallest attendance at a world heavyweight title fight was 2,434 at the Ali vs Liston fight at Lewiston, Me, May 25, 1965.

Time-Keeping

There is a little known variable in the sport of boxing. While all rule books agree that, under the Queensberry rules, a round lasts 3 min, in fact they often do not. At the Gerrie Coetzee-Michael Dokes heavyweight championship fight (Sept 23, 1984) the rounds were about 3 min, 2 sec. If the correct time had been kept the fighters would have been in their corners when Coetzee knocked out Dokes at 2:58 of round 10. It is not unusual for a timekeeper to be off by as much as a minute. The chairman of the NY State Athletic Commission explained it this way: "With all the excitement, it's sometimes hard to keep exact time."

CANOEING AND KAYAKING

Origins

Modern canoes and kayaks originated with the Indians and Eskimos of North America. French trappers were the first to compete in canoe races (1790).

The acknowledged pioneer of canoeing as a modern sport was John Macgregor (1825–92), a British barrister, in 1865. The Canoe Club was formed on July 26, 1866.

Olympic and World Titles

Gert Fredriksson (b Nov 21, 1919) of Sweden has won the most Olympic gold medals with 6 (1948, 52, 56, 60). The most by a woman is 3 by Ludmila Pinayeva (née Khvedosyuk, b Jan 14, 1936) (USSR) in the 500-m K.1 in 1964 and 1968, and the 500-m K.2 in 1972. The most gold medals at one Games is 3 by Vladimir Parfenovich (b Dec 2, 1958) (USSR) in 1980 and by Ian Ferguson (NZ) (b July 20, 1952) in the 1984 Olympics (one individually at 500 m and 2 on New Zealand boat at 500 m and 1,000 m).

Thirteen titles have been won by Rüdiger Helm (E Ger) (b Oct 6, 1956), 10 world and 3 Olympic between 1976 and 1983. Birgit Fischer (now Schmidt) (E Ger) (b Feb 25, 1962) won all 3 gold medals in the world championships of 1981–3, one in 1979, 2 in 1985, and the kayak singles at the 1980 Olympics for a women's record of 13.

Longest Open Sea Voyage

Beatrice and John Dowd, Ken Beard and Steve Benson (Richard Gillett replaced him mid-journey) paddled 2,170 miles out of a total journey of 2,192 miles from Venezuela to Miami, Fla, via the West Indies from Aug 11, 1977, to Apr 29, 1978, in two Klepper Aerius 20 kayaks.

Eskimo Rolls

The record for 1,000 Eskimo rolls in a kayak is 44 min 7 sec by Steve Flint in Maidstone, Eng, on July 18, 1985. Julian Dean achieved 1,555 continuous rolls at Casterton Swimming Pool, Cumbria, England, taking 1 hour 49 min 45 sec on Dec 6, 1983. A "hand-rolling" record of 100 rolls in 2 min 39.35 sec by Colin Hill at Crystal Palace, London, on Feb 23, 1986.

Highest Speed

The Olympic 1,000-m best performance of 3 min 02.70 sec by the 1980 USSR K4 on July 31, 1980, represents a speed of 12.24 mph. They achieved 13.14 mph over the first quarter of the course.

Downstream Canoeing

The record for canoeing down the Mississippi from Lake Itasca, Minn to the Gulf of Mexico is 23 days 10 hours 20 min by Valerie Fons and Verlen Kruger, Apr 27–May 20, 1984.

Fastest 24 Hours

The solo 24-hour canoe record is 143.32 mi by Dr Chris Greiff (S Africa) in a Jaguar K1 canoe on the Breede River, Robertson to Cape Infanta, Cape Province, S Africa, Aug 11–12, 1985. The women's

CANOEING TOGETHER: Ken Beard and Steve Benson paddle in the Gulf Stream. Along with Beatrice and John Dowd, they completed the longest open sea voyage ever made by canoe.

record is 97.2 mi set by Lydia Formentin on the Swan River, W Australia in 1979.

Longest Journey

The longest journey ever made by canoe is 12,181 miles by father and son Dana and Donald Starkell from Winnipeg, Manitoba, Canada by ocean and river to Belem, Brazil from June 1, 1980 to May 1, 1982. All portages were human powered.

The longest journey without portage or aid of any kind is one of 6,102 miles by Richard H. Grant and Ernest "Moose" Lassy circumnavigating the eastern US from Chicago to New Orleans to Miami to NYC, returning back to Chicago via the Great Lakes, from Sept 22, 1930, to Aug 15, 1931.

DOWNSTREAM CANOEING

River	Miles	Name and Country	Route	Date	Duration
Murray–Darling	1980	Six students of St Albert's College, UNE (Australia)	Gunnedah, NSW to Lake Alexandrina, SA	Dec 1975	—
Mississippi	2552	Valerie Fons and Verlen Kruger (US)	Lake Itasca, Minnesota to Gulf of Mexico	Apr 27– May 20, 1984	23 days 10 hr 20 min
Zaire (Congo)	2600	John and Julie Batchelor (GB)	Mossampanga to Banana	May 8– Sept 12, 1974	128 days
Amazon	3800	Alan Trevor Holman (GB/Aus) (b. 21 Feb 1944)	Quitani, Peru to Cabo Maguavi, Brazil	Aug 9– Dec 3, 1982	116 days
Mississippi–Missouri	3810	Nicholas Francis (GB)	Three Forks, Montana to New Orleans, La.	July 13– Nov 25, 1977	135 days
		Mary Schmidt and Bev Gordon (US)	Three Forks to New Orleans	July 4– Oct 13, 1984	98 days (un-ratified)
Nile	4000	John Goddard (US), Jean Laporte and André Davy (France)	Kagera to the Delta	Nov 1953– July 1954	9 months

Fritz Lindner of Berlin, W Germany, totaled 56,847 mi from 1928 to 1983, for the greatest lifetime distance.

Longest Race

The longest race ever staged was 3,283 mi from Rocky Mountain House, Alberta, to the Expo 67 site at Montreal, Quebec as the Canadian Government Centennial Voyageur Canoe Pageant and Race. Ten canoes represented Canadian provinces and territories. The winner of the race, which took from May 24 to Sept 4, 1967, was the Province of Manitoba canoe *Radisson.*

The longest regularly held canoe race in the US is the Texas Water Safari (instituted 1963) which covers 265 twisting mi from San Marcos to Seadrift, Tex, on the San Marcos and Guadalupe Rivers. Mike Wooley and Howard Gore set the record of 36 hours, 40 min, June 2–3, 1979.

CROQUET

Origins

Some say croquet began in the 12th to 14th century in France when peasants used crude mallets to knock balls through hoops made of bent willow branches. Americans contend that, since one needed a large lawn, or at least a large backyard, peasants could not have invented the game.

It was probably first popular in England as a country-house game in the mid-1600's, when it was called "crokey." Professional groundskeepers were hired and lawns became "greenswards." Oddly enough (according to a recent book by Jack Osborn and Jesse Kornbluth), "one court was made of powdered cockleshell and its wickets were festooned with flowers."

The game has gone through several lapses into obscurity over the years, and in the last century was introduced from England into Australia and the US. The literary group that gathered around Herbert Bayard Swope and Alexander Woollcott in the 1920's (the Algonquin Round Table set which included George S. Kaufman and Dorothy Parker) brought croquet into the limelight. Croquet spread to Hollywood soon after, under the guidance of Darryl Zanuck and Samuel Goldwyn.

Today the U.S. Croquet Association has 250 clubs

as members with 75 of them new in 1985–86. The Palm Beach, Fla, area with 5 championship courts is the largest croquet complex in the western hemisphere.

Marathon

A foursome at Birmingham Univ, Eng, played for 120 hours 25 min, June 14–19, 1986.

USCA National Grand Prix Rankings

These ratings are based on the final standings of all individual competitors entered in major Class "A" 1985 USCA Sanctioned Events, including:

USCA National Singles Championships—NYC
USCA National Doubles Championships—NYC
USCA National Club Team Championships—Palm Beach, Fla.
Five USCA Regional Championships, Invitationals and Club Championships

1. John C. Osborn, NY
2. Jack R. Osborn, NY
3. Ray Bell, Ariz
4. Jim Erwin, NY
5. John Young, Bermuda
6. Donald Degnan, NY
7. Dana Dribben, Fla
8. Debbie Prentis, Fla
9. Archie Burchfield, Ky
10. Nelga Young, Bermuda
11. Barry Fitzpatrick, Calif
12. Michael Watkins, Ga
13. Ren Kraft, Ariz
14. Harold Brown, Ga
15. William Hiltz, NY
    (out of 452 name list)

CROQUET CHAMPION attempts a pass roll: Dana Dribben, a pro at golf, as well as croquet, is shown winning a match in Central Park, NYC. (US Croquet Assn)

USCA National Champions

SINGLES

Year	
1977	J. Archie Peck, Palm Beach
1978	Richard Pearman, Bermuda
1979	J. Archie Peck, Palm Beach
1980	J. Archie Peck, Palm Beach
1981	Richard Pearman, Bermuda
1982	J. Archie Peck, Palm Beach
1983	E. A. (Ted) Prentis IV, Florida & NY
1984	James Bast, Phoenix
1985	Ray Bell, Scottsdale, Ariz
1986	Reid Fleming, Puget Sound, Wash

DOUBLES

Year	
1977	Jack Osborn & J. Archie Peck
1978	E. A. (Ted) Prentis & Arthur Bohner
1979	Jack Osborn & J. Archie Peck
1980	Ted & Ned Prentis
1981	Ted & Ned Prentis
1982	Archie & Mark Burchfield (Kentucky)
1983	Kiley Jones & Richard Illingsworth
1984	James Bast & Ray Bell
1985	Dana Dribben & Ray Bell
1986	Dana Dribben & Ray Bell

CROSS-COUNTRY RUNNING

International Championships

The earliest international cross-country race was run between England and France on a course 9 miles 18 yd long from Ville d'Avray, outside Paris, on March 20, 1898 (England won by 21 points to 69). The inaugural International Cross-Country Championships took place at the Hamilton Park Racecourse, Scotland, on March 28, 1903. Since 1973 the race has been run under the auspices of the International Amateur Athletic Federation.

The greatest margin of victory in the International Cross-Country Championships has been 56 sec, or 390 yd, by Jack T. Holden (England) (b Mar 13, 1907) at Ayr Racecourse, Scotland, March 24, 1934. The narrowest win was that of Jean-Claude Fayolle (France) at Ostend, Belgium, on March 20, 1965, when the timekeepers were unable to separate his time from that of Melvyn Richard Batty (England).

The greatest men's team wins have been those of England, with a minimum of 21 points (the first six runners to finish) on two occasions, 1924 and 1932, at Newcastle, Eng and at the Hippodrome, Brussels, Belgium.

BETTER KNOWN as a marathon and road runner, Grete Waitz (Norway) (right, below) has won 5 victories in the international cross-country championships, 1978–81 and 1983. In the NYC Marathon she won 5 times, in 1978–80, 83 and 86.

ROUGH RUNNING: French runner Alain Mimoun (#1) (below) streaks to one of his four world titles, a record he shares with Jack Holden and Gaston Roelants.

Most Appearances

The runner with the largest number of international championship appearances is Marcel Van de Wattyne of Belgium (b July 7, 1924), who participated in 20 competitions in the years 1946–65. The women's record is 16 by Jean Lockhead of Wales (b Dec 24, 1946), 1967–79, 81, 83–4.

Most Wins

The most victories is 5 in the women's race by Doris Brown-Heritage (US) (b Sept 17, 1942), 1967–71; and by Grete Waitz (*née* Andersen) (Norway) (b Oct 1, 1953), 1978–81, 83.

The greatest number of men's individual victories is 4 by Jack Holden (England) in 1933–35, and 39; by Alain Mimoun-o-Kacha (b Jan 1, 1921) (France) in 1949, 52, 54 and 56; and by Gaston Roelants (b Feb 5, 1937) (Belgium) in 1962, 67, 69 and 72.

Largest Field

The largest recorded field in any cross-country race was 11,763 starters (10,810 finishers) in the 18.6-mi Lidingoloppet near Stockholm, Sweden, Oct 3, 1982.

CURLING

CURLING ACTION: This is the scene at the 1986 contest between Madison (Wis), the US champs, and Sweden for the men's World Curling Championship (US Curling Assn).

Origins

Although a 15th-century bronze figure in the Florence Museum appears to be holding a curling stone, the earliest illustration of the sport was in one of the winter scenes by the Flemish painter Pieter Brueghel, *c.* 1560. The game was introduced into Canada in 1759. Organized administration began in 1838 with the formation of the Grand (later Royal) Caledonian Curling Club, the international legislative body until the foundation of the International Curling Federation in 1966. The first indoor ice rink to introduce curling was in Montreal, Canada in 1807.

Curling stones are made of rare, dense granite, quarried in Wales. Special shoes for curlers are made to grip the ice for walking. A "slider" is worn on one foot to allow a long, smooth follow-through.

Competitions (called "bonspiels") in the US and Canada are organized along state (provincial), regional and national lines, with many local curling clubs and leagues for both men and women participating in the colder parts of America particularly, using skating and hockey arenas occasionally, but mostly ice facilities built specifically for curling.

The US won the first Gordon International Medal series of matches, between Canada and the US, at Montreal in 1884. Demonstrated at the Winter Olympics of 1924, 1932, and 1964, curling is scheduled to be demonstrated once more in the 1988 Winter Games in Calgary, Canada.

Most Titles

The record for the men's World Championship (inst 1959) (now the "International Olympic Committee President's Cup") is 17 wins by Canada (7 Scotch Cups, 9 Silver Brooms, 1 IOC President's Cup). The most Strathcona Cup (inst 1903) wins is 7 by Canada (1903, 09, 12, 23, 38, 57, 65). The US is second. The most women's World Championships (inst 1979) is 3 for Canada (1980, 84, 85).

CURLING MARATHON CHAMPS: Jim Paul and Chris McCrady of Brockville, Canada, curled for 38 hours in 1982.

Largest Rink

The world's largest curling rink is the Big Four Curling Rink, Calgary, Alberta, Canada, opened in 1959 at a cost of Can. $2,250,000. Each of the two floors has 24 sheets of ice, the total accommodating 96 teams and 384 players.

Largest Bonspiels

The largest indoor bonspiel is the Manitoba Bonspiel held in Winnipeg, Canada. There were 848 teams, or rinks, of 4 players in the 1985 tournament, for a total of 3,392 curlers using 171 sheets of curling ice. The largest outdoor bonspiel is the "Grand Match" held on a loch in Scotland when weather is cold enough. It often attracts over 4,000 curlers.

"Perfect" Games

Stu Beagle, of Calgary, Canada, played a perfect game (48 points) against Nova Scotia in the Canadian championships (Brier) at Ft. William (now Thunder Bay), Ontario, on March 8, 1960. Bernice Fekete, of Edmonton, Canada, skipped her rink (team) to two consecutive eight-enders on the same sheet of ice at the Derrick Club, Edmonton, on January 10 and February 6, 1973. Andrew McQuistin, of

Stranraer, Scotland, skipped a Scotland rink to a 1–0 victory over Switzerland, scoring in the tenth end after nine consecutive blank ends, in the Uniroyal World Junior Championships at Kitchener-Waterloo, Ontario, Canada, on March 16, 1980.

Marathon

The longest recorded curling match is one of 67 hours 55 min by the Capital Winter Club of New Brunswick, Canada, Apr 9–12, 1982. The duration record for 2 curlers is 38 hours by Jim Paul and Chris McCrady at the Brockville Country Club, Ont, Canada, Mar 26–28, 1982.

World Championships

The US curler who participated most on world championship teams is Bill Strum of the Superior (Wis) Curling Club, who was on 3 teams (1965, 74, 78) and on 5 USA championship teams (1965, 67, 69, 74, 78). Two others who were on 5 USA championship teams are Bud Somerville of Superior (1965, 68, 69, 74, 78) and Bruce Roberts of Hibbing, Minn (1966, 67, 76, 77, 84).

CYCLING

Earliest Race

The earliest recorded bicycle race was a velocipede race over 2 km (1.24 miles) at the Parc de St Cloud, Paris, on May 31, 1868, won by Dr James Moore (GB) (1847–1935).

The first American bicycle race was held May 24, 1878 in Boston's Beacon Park. Winner C. A. Parker of Harvard University covered the 3-mi course in 12 min, 27 sec.

The time-trial was devised in 1889–90 by F. T. Bidlake to avoid the congestion caused by ordinary mass road racing.

Highest Speed

John Howard (b Aug 16, 1947) of Encinitas, Calif achieved 152.284 mph on July 20, 1985, riding a specially designed 46-lb bike with hydraulic forks and motorcycle wheels, at Bonneville Salt Flats, Utah. A former Olympic cyclist, he rode behind a car modified with a large tail section designed to cut down on air resistance.

Fred Markham recorded an unofficial unpaced 6.832 sec for 200 m (65.484 mph) on a streamlined bicycle on Highway 120, Calif, on May 11, 1986. Riding in the desert valley of Big Sand Flat, Calif (elevation 7,850 ft) Markham and bike designer Gardner Martin claimed an $18,000 prize offered by DuPont Corp to the first person to ride a bicycle 65 mph on level ground, unpaced and without an aiding wind.

The greatest distance ever covered in one hour is 76 miles 604 yd by Leon Vanderstuyft (Belgium) on the Montlhéry Motor Circuit, France, Sept 30, 1928. This was achieved from a standing start paced by a motorcycle ahead. (Cycling rules permit a motorcycle to precede a bicycle in an event of over 10 km.) The 24-hour record behind pace is 860 miles 367 yd by Sir Hubert Ferdinand Opperman (b May 29, 1904) in Melbourne, Australia on May 23, 1932.

One-Hour Distance Records

The greatest distance covered in 60 min unpaced is 31 mi 1,381 yd by Francesco Moser (Italy) at Mexico City on Jan 23, 1984. The International Cycling Union (UCI), which recognizes both sea-level and high-altitude hour records, classifies Moser's Mexico City distance in the high altitude category because it was achieved on a track located at an elevation greater than 600 m (above mean sea level). Moser also holds the sea-level 60 min distance record of 30 mi 1,665.6 yd in Milan, Italy on Oct 3, 1986.

The indoor 60 min distance record is 30 mi 1,742 yd by Viatcheslav Ekimov (USSR), ridden on the Olympic Velodrome in Moscow in Nov 1986.

Jeannie Longo of France holds both the sea-level and high-altitude 60 min unpaced women's records. She cycled 27 mi 147 yds in Oct 1986 in Milan, Italy, for the sea-level mark and 27 miles 1,441 yds, Sept 20, 1986, in Colorado Springs, Colo for the altitude mark.

24-Hour Distance Record

The 24-hour record on the road is 515.8 miles by Teuvo Louhivouri of Finland on Sept 10, 1974.

Indoors, unpaced, the 24-hour record is 516 mi 427 yd by Michael Secrest (b Jan 20, 1953) of Flint, Mich, who cycled this distance at the Montreal (Canada) Olympic Velodrome Mar 13–14, 1985.

Most World Titles

World championships, contested annually, were first staged for amateurs in 1893 and for professionals in 1895. The most wins at a particular event is 10 consecutively by Koichi Nakano (Japan) (b Nov 14, 1955), professional sprint champion 1977–86. The most wins at a men's amateur event is 7 by Daniel Morelon (France) (b July 28, 1944), sprint 1966–7, 69–71, 73, 75; and Leon Meredith (UK) (1882–1930), 100-km motor-paced 1904–5, 1907–9, 11, 13.

The most women's titles is 7 by Beryl Burton (UK) (b May 12, 1937), pursuit 1959–60, 62–63, 66 and road 1960, 67; and by Yvonne Reynders (Belgium) pursuit 1961, 64–65 and road 1959, 61, 63, 66.

SPEEDIEST BIKER: John Howard, riding in the vacuum created behind a large-tail racing car on a specially designed 46-lb bicycle, sped more than 152 mph on Bonneville Salt Flats in July 1985. (Al Gross)

FIRST AMERICAN WINNER of Tour de France: Greg LeMond of Reno, Nev, became the only non-European in 83 years to win the 23-day race in 1986. He was also the only American to win the World Professional Road Championship in Switzerland in 1983. (All-Sport)

Greg LeMond (see below) is the only American ever to win the World Professional Road Championship, taking the title Sept 4, 1983, at Altenrhein, Switzerland.

Tour de France

For the first time in 83 years the Tour de France was won by a non-European, Greg LeMond (b June 26, 1961) of Reno, Nevada. He beat the field in 1986, including his teammate Bernard Hinault (b Nov 14, 1954) (France) who won in 1978, 79, 81, 82 and 85. This race takes about 23 days to stage annually. The longest ever was in 1926 when it lasted for 29 days. It is estimated that as many as 10 million people watch some part of it.

The greatest number of wins in the Tour de France (inaugurated 1903) is 5 by Jacques Anquetil (b Jan 8, 1934) (France), who won in 1957, 1961–64; Eddy Merckx (b June 17, 1945) (Belgium) who won five titles (1969–72, 1974); and Bernard Hinault (see above) who also won 5 times.

The closest race ever was in 1968 when after 2,898.7 mi over 25 days (June 27–July 21) Jan Janssen (Netherlands) (b May 19, 1940) beat Herman van Springel (Belgium) in Paris by 38 sec. The longest course was 3,569 miles on June 20 to July 18, 1926. The length of the course is usually about 3,000 miles, but varies from year to year.

The fastest average speed was 23.51 mph by Bernard Hinault in 1981. The greatest number of participants were 170 starters in 1982 and 1984.

Coast-to-Coast Cycling

The US transcontinental men's unpaced record (West Coast to East Coast) has been cut in half since 1972 (see chart opposite). Pete Penseyres, 43, of Fallbrook, Calif, set the current mark of 8 days 9 hours 47 min in July 1986 during the Race Across AMerica (3,107.3 mi, Huntington Beach, Calif to Atlantic City, NJ). The US transcontinental women's record of 10 days 2 hours 4 min, held by Elaine Mariolle of Berkeley, Calif, was also set during the '86 RAAM.

Lon Haldeman of Harvard, Ill, and his wife Susan Notorangelo-Haldeman set a transcontinental tandem bicycle record of 9 days 20 hours 7 min (Huntington Beach, Calif to Virginia Beach, Va) in April 1986.

Wayne Phillips of Richmond, BC, rode across Canada from Vancouver, BC, to Halifax, Nova Scotia, covering the 3,800 miles in 14 days 22 hours 47 min June 13–28, 1982.

Endurance

Tommy Godwin (1912–75) (GB) in the 365 days of 1939 covered 75,065 miles or an average of 205.65 miles per day. He then completed 100,000 miles in 500 days to May 14, 1940. Jay Aldous and Matt DeWaal cycled 14,290 miles on a round trip from

24-HOUR RECORDHOLDER: Michael Secrest cycled 516+ mi indoors unpaced in March 1985. (Red Roof Inns, Inc, Ohio)

COAST-TO-COAST CYCLING*

US Transcontinental West-East

Date	Name	Mileage	Start–Finish	Days:Hours:Min
Men				
6/29/61	Jerry Hornig		San Francisco to NYC	17: 05: 15
4/22/72	Peter Duker		Santa Monica to NYC	18: 02: 38
3/17/73	Paul Cornish		Santa Monica to NYC	13: 05: 20
8/26/78	John Marino		Santa Monica to NYC	13: 01: 20
6/28/80	John Marino		Santa Monica to NYC	12: 03: 41
7/14/81	Lon Haldeman		Santa Monica to NYC	10: 23: 27
8/14/82	Lon Haldeman	2,986	Santa Monica to NYC	9: 20: 02 Great American Bike Race '82
8/29/84	Pete Penseyres	3,047.4	Huntington Beach to Atlantic City, NJ	9: 13: 13 Race Across America '84
7/31/85	Jonathan Boyer	3,120.2	Huntington Beach to Atlantic City, NJ	9: 02: 06 Race Across America '85
7/14/86	Peter Penseyres	3,107.3	Huntington Beach to Atlantic City, NJ	8: 09: 47 McDonald's Race Across America
Women				
6/15/82	Ann Kovich		Santa Monica to NYC	14: 14: 54
7/13/82	Susan Notorangelo		Santa Monica to NYC	11: 16: 15
8/1/85	Susan Notorangelo-Haldeman	3,120.2	Huntington Beach to Atlantic City, NJ	10: 14: 25 Race Across America '85
7/16/86	Elaine Mariolle	3,107.3	Huntington Beach to Atlantic City, NJ	10: 02: 04 McDonald's Race Across America '86
Trans-Canada				
6/28/82	Wayne Phillips	3,800	Vancouver, B.C. to Halifax, Nova Scotia	14: 22: 47
US Transcontinental East-West				
7/2/81	Lon Haldeman (solo/unpaced)		NY to Santa Monica	12: 18: 49
7/7/81	Len Vreeland (solo/recumbent)		NY to Santa Monica	14: 21: 13
US Double Transcontinental				
10/84	Victor Vincente of America		Santa Monica to NY to Santa Monica	36: 08: 00
7/14/81	Lon Haldeman		NY to Santa Monica to NY	24: 02: 34
US 24-Hour Outdoor Track (San Diego Velodrome)				
4/2/84	Jim Elliott	502.3 mi		
US 24-Hour Indoor Track (Olympic Velodrome, Montreal, Canada)				
3/14/85	Michael Secrest	516 mi, 427 yd		
US 24-Hour Roller Record				
1/21/77	Bruce Hall	792.209 mi		
5/14/83	Richard Gunther	838.7 mi		
US Transcontinental West-East				
9/10/84	Sean O'Keefe 11 years (born 6/6/73), youngest to cross US on a bicycle		Santa Monica to NY	24 days
Death Valley Double Crossing (heat endurance in summer in Calif)				
8/31/86	Jay Levine	220.5 mi	North/South & back	17 hours 51 min 51 sec

*US records from the Ultra Marathon Cycling Association, as of September 1986, courtesy of John Marino.

Place Monument, Salt Lake City, Utah, in 106 days, Apr 2–July 16, 1984.

Nicholas Mark Sanders (b Nov 26, 1957) of Glossop, Eng, circumnavigated the world (13,035 road miles) in 78 days, 3 hours 30 min between July 5 and Sept 21, 1985.

Carlos Vieira cycled for 191 hours "non-stop" at Leiria, Portugal June 8–16, 1983. The distance covered was 1,496.04 mi, and he was moving 98.7% of the time.

Roller Cycling

The greatest distance achieved in 24 hours is 1,560.73 mi by Piet Vitten (Neth) at Midden, Beemster, The Netherlands on Mar 8–9, 1980. Paul Swinnerton (GB) achieved a record 102 mph for 200 meters on rollers on Feb 12, 1982, at Stoke-on-Trent, England.

In a marathon try, Gilbert Bil rode 83 hours 29 min, Dec 1–4, 1985, at Cafe Zuid, The Netherlands.

WATERCYCLE: "The Flying Fish," the fastest non-motorized craft on water, being ridden by Steve Hegg, Olympic cycling medalist.

GOLD MEDALIST: Alexi Grewal (US) (left below) is jubilant as he wins the individual road race in 1984 Olympics.
CYCLO-CROSS (right below): The new activity requires the racers to carry their bikes over a ridge.

Six-Day Races

The greatest number of wins in six-day races is 88 out of 233 events by Patrick Sercu (b June 27, 1944), of Belgium, 1964–83.

Longest One-Day Race

The longest single-day "massed start" road race is the Bordeaux-to-Paris, France, event of 342 to 385 miles. Usually paced over all or part of the route, the highest average speed in 1981 was 29.32 mph by Herman van Springel (Belgium) (b Aug 14, 1943) for 363.1 mi in 13 hours 35 min 18 sec.

The course record in the Spenco 500-mile race, held in Texas in 1984 and 1985, is just over one day. In winning the '85 competition from 302 starters, Thomas Prehn of Boulder, Colo, finished in 24 hours 25 min 36 sec.

Most Olympic Titles

The greatest number of gold medals ever won is 3 by Paul Masson (France) in 1896, Francisco Verri (Italy) in 1906 and Robert Charpentier (France) in 1936. Daniel Morelon (France) won two in 1968 and a third in 1972. He also won a bronze medal in 1964. Marcus Hurley (US) (1884–1950) won 4 events in the "unofficial" cycling competition in the 1904 Games.

Touring

The most participants in a bicycle tour were 27,220 in the 56-mile London-to-Brighton Bike Ride on June 15, 1986.

The longest cycle tour on record is the more than 402,000 miles amassed by Walter Stolle (b Sudetenland, 1926), an itinerant lecturer. From Jan 24, 1959 to Dec 12, 1976, he covered 159 countries, had 5 bicycles stolen and suffered 231 other robberies, along

SIX DAYS ON THE TRACK: Patrick Sercu (Belgium) (leading) won 88 six-day races out of 233 events for a 39% record. The durable cyclist also holds 3 professional speed records for 1 kilometer.

with over 1,000 flat tires. From 1922 to Dec 25, 1973, Tommy Chambers (1903–84) of Glasgow, Scotland, rode a verified total of 799,405 miles.

John Hathaway of Vancouver, Canada, covered 50,600 miles, visiting every continent, from Nov 10, 1974 to Oct 6, 1976.

Veronica and Colin Scargill, of Bedford, England, traveled 18,020 miles around the world, on a tandem, Feb 25, 1974–Aug 27, 1975.

Highest Altitude

Nicholas and Richard Crane cycled their mountain bikes to the summit of Mount Kilimanjaro, Tanzania, 19,340 ft, on Dec 31, 1984.

1984 Olympic Winners

1,000 m Time Trials	
Fredy Schmidthe (W Ger)	1:06.10
1,000 m Sprint	
Mark Gorski (US)	
Individual Points Race	
Roger Ilegems (Belgium)	
4,000 m Individual Pursuit	
Steve Hegg (US)	4:39.35
14,000 m Team Pursuit	
Australia	4:25.99
Individual Road Race	
Alexi Grewal (US)	4 hr 59 min 57 sec
100 km Team Time Trial	
Italy	1 hr 58 min 28 sec
Women's Individual Road Race	
Connie Carpenter-Phinney (US)	2 hr 11 min 14 sec

Unicycle Records

The tallest unicycle ever mastered is one 101 ft 9 in tall ridden by Steve McPeak (with a safety wire or mechanic suspended to an overhead crane) for a distance of 376 ft in Las Vegas in Oct 1980. The freestyle riding of even taller unicycles must inevitably lead to serious injury or fatality.

Hanspeter Beck of Jindabyne, S Australia unicycled 3,876.08 mi in 51 days, 23 hours, 25 min, June 30–Aug 20, 1985, going from W Australia to Melbourne. Brian Davis of Tillicoultry, Scotland rode 901 mi from Land's End to John O'Groats May 16–June 4, 1980 in 19 days 1¾ hours. Floyd Beattie of Athens, O, set a record for 100 mi in 7 hours 18 min 55 sec on Oct 11, 1986. The sprint record from a standing start over 100 meters is 14.89 sec by Floyd

Grandall of Pontiac, Mich, in Tokyo, Japan on Mar 24, 1980.

EQUESTRIAN SPORTS

Origin

Men have ridden horses for 5,000 years. The Athenian general and historian Xenophon wrote a treatise on horsemanship 2,300 years ago, but it was not until the 16th century that schools of horsemanship, or equitation, became established, primarily in Italy and then in France. In Britain the first official competitions were held in 1865 under the auspices of the Royal Dublin Society, while the first jumping contest was at the Agricultural Hall, London in 1869. The dressage event was a direct outcome of the exercises taught in the early Italian and French academies. The Three-Day Event developed from cavalry endurance rides, one of the earliest being from Vienna to Berlin in 1892. There was a jumping event in the Olympic Games of 1900, but a full equestrian program was not instituted until 1912.

Most Olympic Medals

The greatest number of Olympic gold medals is 5 by Hans-Günter Winkler (b July 24, 1926) (W Germany), who won 4 team gold medals as captain in 1956, 60, 64 and 72, and won the individual Grand Prix in 1956. The most team wins in the Prix des Nations is 5 by Germany in 1936, 56, 60, 64, and 1972.

The lowest score obtained by a winner for jumping was no faults, by Frantisek Ventura (Czech) (1895–1969) on "Eliot" in 1928, and by Alwin Schockemöhle (W Ger) (b May 29, 1934) on "Warwick Rex" in 1976. Pierre Jonqueres d'Oriola (France) (b Feb 1, 1920) is the only two-time winner of the individual gold medal, in 1952 and 1964.

In dressage, Henri St Cyr (Swe) has won four golds, including a unique two in the individual competition 1952–56. St Cyr was also a member of the winning Swedish team in 1948, but subsequently they were disqualified because one of them was not a military officer as the rules at that time decreed. Emphasizing the increasingly successful role of women in this sport, the most medals ever won is five by Liselott Linsenhoff (W Ger) between 1956 and 1972.

In the Three-Day Event, Charles Pahud de Mortanges (Hol) won a record four gold medals, including two individual titles, from 1924 to 1932, as well as a team silver.

TWO FOR THE SHOW: Hans-Günter Winkler (West Germany) rode to 5 Olympic gold medals: 4 for team competition and the individual gold in 1956. The show-jumping champion also won 2 world titles.

World Team Championship

Instituted in 1965 as the President's Trophy and renamed the Prince Philip Trophy in 1985, it has been won a record 11 times by Great Britain, 1965, 67, 70, 72–74, 77–79, 83, 85.

Driving

The most wins at the biennial World Driving Championships (inst 1972) is 3, by Great Britain in 1972, 74 and 80; and by Hungary in 1976, 78 and 84.

World Cup

The only World Cup (inst 1969) double winner is Conrad Homfield (US) (b Dec 25, 1951) in 1980 and 1985.

World Titles

The men's world championship in show jumping (instituted 1953) has been won twice by Hans-Günter Winkler of W Germany in 1954 and 1955, and Raimondo d'Inzeo of Italy in 1956 and 1960. The women's title (1965–74) was won twice by Jane "Janou" Tissot (née Lefebvre) (b Saigon, May 14, 1945) of France on "Rocket" in 1970 and 1974. The three-day event was won twice by Bruce Davidson (US) in 1974 and 1978.

Jumping Records

The official *Fédération Equestre Internationale* high jump record is 8 ft 1¼ in by "Huaso," ridden by Capt A. Larraguibel Morales (Chile) at Santiago, Chile, on Feb 5, 1949, but there are several reports of much higher jumps. The most extreme is a 9 ft 6 in clearance by "Ben Bolt" at the 1938 Royal Horse Show in Sydney, Australia.

The greatest height by a woman is 7 ft 8 in by Katrina Towns-Musgrove (Aust) on "Big John" in Cairns in 1978.

The greatest recorded height reached bareback is 7 ft by Michael Whitaker (b Mar 17, 1960) on "Red Flight" in Dublin, Eire, Nov 14, 1982.

The official long jump over water record is 27 ft 6¾ in by "Something" ridden by André Ferreira at Johannesburg, S Africa on April 26, 1975, but there have been many longer jumps recorded. The Australian record is 32 ft 10 in by "Monarch" at Brisbane in 1951, but "Solid Gold" jumped 36 ft 3 in at the Wagga Show, NSW, Australia, in 1936. In the US "Heatherbloom," ridden by Dick Donnelly, is reputed to have cleared 37 ft when high jumping 8 ft 3 in at Richmond, Va. in 1903. The most extreme claim made is for "Jerry M," the 1912 Grand National Steeplechase winner at Aintree, Eng, who is alleged to have jumped 40 ft over water there.

Longest Ride

Thomas L. Gaddie (US) rode 11,217.2 miles from Dallas, Tex, to Fairbanks, Alaska, and back in 295 days, Feb 12–Dec 2, 1980, with seven horses. Henry G. Perry, a stockman from Mollongghip, Victoria, Australia, rode 14,021 mi around Australia in 157 days, May 1–Oct 4, 1985, with 6 horses.

The Bicentennial "Great American Horse Race," begun on May 31, 1976, from Saratoga Springs, NY,

STEEPLECHASE provides thrilling moments. The most extreme claim is for "Jerry M" the 1912 Grand National winner who is alleged to have jumped 40 ft over water.

to Sacramento, Calif (3,500 miles) was won by Virl Norton on "Lord Fauntleroy"—a mule—in 98 days. His actual riding time was 315.47 hours.

First Solo Transcontinental Journey

Nan Jane Aspinwall left San Francisco on horseback on Sept 1, 1910. She arrived in NYC on July 8, 1911, having covered 4,500 miles in 301 days, 108 of which she spent traveling.

Marathon

Ken Nothdurft rode for 112 hours, 30 min at Kingsthorpe, Queensland, Australia, Aug 31–Sept 4, 1985.

FENCING

Origins

Fencing (fighting with single sticks) was practiced as a sport, or as part of a religious ceremony, in Egypt as early as c. 1360 BC.

Swords have been in use as combat weapons since ancient times. The first indication of sword fencing

"HEATHERBLOOM": Flying like a bird, this horse (below) is said to have covered 37 feet in clearing an 8-foot-3-inch jump in 1903. She is here making a demonstration jump of 8 feet 2 inches in 1905.

BALLET WITH SWORDS: Michael Marx (left) bends precariously as he duels with foils to win the 1985 US men's championship. (US Fencing Federation)

as a sport is on a relief in the temple of Medinet Habu, Luxor, Egypt built by Rameses III about 1190 BC.

The modern sport developed directly from the dueling, often to the death, of the Middle Ages. In the early 14th century the Marxbrüder Fencing Guild was flourishing in Frankfurt, Germany. In Britain, Edward I had specifically banned fencing tournaments in the City of London in 1285. Henry VIII, some 250 years later, founded the Corporation of Masters of Defence which was probably the first governing body of any sport in Britain. The mask was introduced by a Frenchman, La Boessière in about 1780.

There are three swords used today. With the foil, first used in France as a practice weapon for the short court sword in the 17th century, only the trunk of the body is acceptable as a target. The épée, established in the mid-19th century, is rather heavier and more rigid than the foil and has the whole body as a valid target. The saber, introduced by the Italians in the late-19th century, has cutting edges on the front and back of the blade, and can only score on the whole

body from the waist upwards. In foil and épée, hits are scored with the point of the weapon, but with the saber, scoring is allowed using all of the front edge and part of the back edge of the blade.

US Championships

Peter Westbrook (b Apr 1952) of the NY Fencers Club won the saber title in the Div. I National Championships for the 10th time, tying Norman Armitage's record in number of titles and setting a record in number of consecutive titles, 8, for any event in the Fencing Championships. Michael Marx of Salle Auriol in Portland, Ore (b July 1958) won the 1986 Div. I Foil Championships for the 5th time, the first one to do so since Joseph Levis won his 6th title in 1954. Lee Shelley of Hackensack, NJ (b May 1956), representing Salle Santelli of NJ, won his 3rd épée title, closing on Paul Pesthy's 5 titles in men's épée. Caitlin Bilodeaux of Boston, Mass (b Mar 1965) representing the NY Fencers Club won the women's foil title for the first time, having captured junior titles in recent years. In women's épée, a recent addition to the women's events, Vincent Bradford, of Austin, Tex (b Mar 1955), came from a 2-year retirement to capture the title for the 3rd time in its 4-year existence.

Most Olympic Titles

Fencing was included in the first modern Olympics in 1896.

The greatest number of individual Olympic gold medals won is 3 by Ramón Fonst (Cuba) (1883–1959) in 1900 and 1904 (2) and Nedo Nadi (Italy) (1894–1952) in 1912 and 1920 (2). Nadi also won 3 team gold medals in 1920 making a then unprecedented total of 5 gold medals at one Olympic meet.

Edoardo Mangiarotti (Italy) (b Apr 7, 1919) holds the record of 13 Olympic medals (6 gold, 5 silver, 2 bronze), won in the foil and épée competitions from 1936 to 1960.

The most gold medals won by a woman is four (one individual, three team) by Elena Novikova- Belova (USSR) (b July 28, 1947) from 1968 to 1976, and the record for all medals is 7 (2 gold, 3 silver, 2 bronze), by Ildikó Sagi-Retjö (formerly Ujlaki-Retjö) (Hungary) (b May 11, 1937) from 1960 to 1976.

The 1984 Olympics gold medalists were: Mauro Numa (Italy) in the foil, Philippe Boisse (France) in the épée, Jean-Francois Lamour (France) in the saber, Jujie Luan (China) in the women's foil. In the team events, Italy won the foil and saber, and W Germany took the épée and women's foil.

World Championships

Other than at the Olympic Games, genuine world championships were not introduced until 1937, although the European titles, inaugurated in 1921 for men, were styled "world championships."

The greatest number of individual world titles won is 5 by Aleksandr Romankov (USSR) (b Nov 7, 1953) at foil, 1974, 77, 79, 82–3, but note that Christian d'Oriola (France) won 4 world titles (1947, 49, 53–54) and also won 2 individual Olympic titles. Four women foilists have won 3 world titles: Helene Mayer (Germany) (1910–53) 1929, 31, 37; Ellen Müller-Preiss (Austria), Ilona Schacherer-Elek (Hungary) (b May 17, 1907) 1934–5, 51; and Cornelia Hanisch (W Ger) (b June 12, 1952) 1979, 81, 85. Of these only Ilona Schacherer-Elek also won 2 individual Olympic titles (1936 and 48).

Amateur Fencing Association

The most titles won at one weapon is 10 at women's foil by Gillian Sheen (now Donaldson), 1949, 51–58, 60.

FOILED: Christian d'Oriola (left) merited his opponent's complete attention. The French foilist won 4 world titles and 2 Olympic golds. He was also a member of 2 gold-medal-winning French foil teams.

FIELD HOCKEY

Origins

A representation of two players with curved snagging sticks apparently in an orthodox "bully" position was found in Tomb No. 17 at Beni Hasan, Egypt, and has been dated to *c.* 2050 B.C. There is a reference to the game in Lincolnshire, England, in 1277. The Fédération Internationale de Hockey was formed on Jan 7, 1924.

The first international match was the Wales *vs.* Ireland match on Jan 26, 1895. Ireland won 3–0.

Highest International Score

The highest score in international field hockey was when India defeated the US 24–1 at Los Angeles, in the 1932 Olympic Games. The Indians were Olympic Champions from the re-inception of Olympic hockey in 1928 until 1960, when Pakistan beat them 1–0 at Rome. They had their eighth win in 1980. Of the 9 Indians who have won 3 Olympic gold medals, two have also won a silver medal—Leslie Walter Claudius in 1948, 1952, 1956 and 1960 (silver), and Udham Singh (b Aug 4, 1928) in 1952, 1956, 1964 and 1960 (silver).

The highest score in a women's international match occurred when England defeated France 23–0 at Merton, Surrey, on Feb 3, 1923. A women's tournament was added to the Olympic Games in 1980, and the winners have been Zimbabwe in 1980, and The Netherlands in 1984.

Most Goals Scored

The greatest number of goals scored in international hockey is 150 by Paul Litjens (Neth) (b Nov 9, 1947) in 112 games.

Greatest Goalkeeping

Richard James Allen (b June 4, 1902) (India) did not concede a goal during the 1928 Olympic Tournament and only a total of 3 in the following two Olympics of 1932 and 1936. In these three Games India scored a total of 102 goals.

Marathon

Two teams of 11 from Beech Springs Venture Unit, Baldock, Eng, played for 44 hours 11 min July 19–21, 1986.

SCRAMBLE! Field hockey in the US has lagged behind Europe in popularity of the game, but women collegians participate in contests regularly under the NCAA. (NCAA News)

Longest Game

The longest international game on record was one of 145 min (into the sixth period of extra time), when Netherlands beat Spain 1–0 in the Olympic tournament at Mexico City on Oct 25, 1968.

Highest Attendance

There were 65,165 at the women's hockey match between Eng and the US at Wembley, London, on Mar 11, 1978.

A.I.A.W.

1975	West Chester State, Pa
1976	West Chester State
1977	West Chester State
1978	West Chester State
1979	California State-Long Beach
1980	Penn State

NCAA Division I

1981	Univ of Connecticut
1982–4	Old Dominion Univ
1985	Univ of Connecticut

FISHING

Origins

From time immemorial men have fished the seas and rivers of the world for food, but fishing for pleasure and leisure seems to have been practiced in Egypt, according to wall paintings, from the 5th Dynasty, 2470–2320 BC. On tomb inscriptions, Amenemhat, a prince of Beni Hasan, is described as "overseer of the swamps of enjoyment," a reference interpreted as fishing grounds.

Freshwater Casting

The longest freshwater cast ratified under ICF (International Casting Federation) rules is 574 ft 2 in by Walter Kummerow (W Germany), for the Bait Distance Double-Handed 30-g event held at Lenzerheide, Switzerland, in the 1968 Championships.

The longest Fly Distance Double-Handed cast is 257 ft 2 in by Sverne Scheen (Norway) also set at Lenzerheide in Sept 1968.

Longest Fight

The longest recorded fight between a fisherman and a fish is 32 hours 5 min by Donal Heatley (NZ) (b 1938) with a black marlin (estimated length 20 ft and weight 1,500 lb) off Mayor Island off Tauranga, New Zealand, Jan 21–22, 1968. It towed the 12-ton launch 50 miles before breaking the line.

World Championships

The *Confédération Internationale de la Pêche Sportive* championships were inaugurated as European championships in 1953. They were recognized as World Championships in 1957. France won 12 times between 1956 and 1981 and Robert Tesse (France) took the individual title uniquely three times, 1959–60, 65. The record weight (team) is 76 lb 8 oz in 3 hours by W Germany in the Neckar at Mannheim, W Germany on Sept 21, 1980. The individual record is 37 lb 7 oz by Wolf-Rüdiger Kremkus (W Germany) at Mannheim on Sept 20, 1980. The most fish caught is 652 by Jacques Isenbaert (Belgium) at Dunajvaros, Yugoslavia on Aug 27, 1967.

Most Fish Caught in a Season

In 77 days of fishing from Apr 1 to Oct 31, 1984, David Romeo of East Meadow, NY, caught on rod

CAUGHT 3,001 BASS in one season: The champ, David Romeo of East Meadow, NY, holds up a 5 lb-5 oz, 21 ⅝-in-long catch he made in 1986. (Photo by Bruce Cooper)

and reel 3,001 largemouth bass in the fresh waters of NY State and Florida, the most ever caught in a season. Mr. Romeo, who doesn't like eating fish but enjoys catching them, threw back all but 24 of them for this and legal reasons. His log books helped the environment conservation people to make "informed bass management decisions."

Bass, Anyone?

If you're a bass-fisher, you should check into Indiana State University at Terre Haute, where 10,000 enrollees from ten states take courses sponsored by the school's Bass Fishing Institute.

Spear-Fishing

The largest fish ever taken underwater was an 804-lb giant black grouper by Don Pinder of the Miami Triton Club, Fla, in 1955.

FISHING WORLD RECORDS

Selected Sea and Freshwater fish records taken by tackle as ratified by the International Game Fish Association to Sept 1986.

Species	Weight in lb	oz	Name of Angler	Location	Date
Amberjack	155	10	Joseph Dawson	Challenger Bank, Bermuda	June 24, 1981
Barracuda††	83	0	K. J. W. Hackett §§	Lagos, Nigeria	Jan 13, 1952
Bass (Giant Sea)	563	8	James D. McAdam, Jr	Anacapa Island, Calif	Aug 20, 1968
Bass (Striped)	78	8	Albert R. McReynolds	Atlantic City, NJ	Sept 21, 1982
Bluefish	31	12	James M. Hussey	Hatteras, NC	Jan 30, 1972
Carp†	57	13	David Nikolow	Potomac, Wash, DC	June 19, 1983
Cod	98	12	Alphonse J. Bielevich	Isle of Shoals, NH	June 8, 1969
Mackerel, Spanish	12	0	John F. Colligan	Ft Pierce, Fla	Nov 17, 1984
Marlin (Black)	1,560	0	Alfred C. Glassell, Jr	Cabo Blanco, Peru	Aug 4, 1953
Marlin (Atlantic Blue)	1,282	0	Larry Martin	St Thomas, US VI	Aug 6, 1977
Marlin (Pacific Blue)	1,376	0	Jay Wm. deBeaubien	Kaaiwi Point, Kona, Hawaii	May 31, 1982
Marlin (Striped)	494	0	Bill Boniface	Tutukaka, NZ	Jan 16, 1986
Marlin (White)	181	14	Evandro Luiz Coser	Vitoria, Brazil	Dec 8, 1979
Pike (Northern)	46	2	Peter Dubuc	Sacandaga Reservoir, NY	Sept 15, 1940
Sailfish (Atlantic)	128	1	Harm Steyn	Luanda, Angola	Mar 27, 1974
Sailfish (Pacific)	221	0	C. W. Stewart	Santa Cruz I, Ecuador	Feb 12, 1947
Salmon (Chinook)§	97	4	Les Anderson	Kenai River, Alaska	May 17, 1985
Salmon, Sockeye	12	8	Mike Boswell	Situk River, Yakutat, Alaska	June 23, 1983
Shark (Blue)	437	0	Peter Hyde	Catherine Bay, NSW, Aust	Oct 2, 1976
Shark (Hammerhead)	991	0	Allen Ogle	Sarasota, Fla	May 30, 1982
Shark (Mako)**	1,080	0	James L. Melanson	Montauk, NY	Aug 26, 1979
Shark (White or Man-eating)	2,664	0***	Alfred Dean	Ceduna, S Aust	Apr 21, 1959
Shark (Porbeagle)	465	0	Jorge Potier	Cornwall, England	July 23, 1976
Shark (Thresher)‡	802	0	Dianne North	Tutukaka, NZ	Feb 8, 1981
Shark (Tiger)	1,780	0	Walter Maxwell	Cherry Grove, SC	June 14, 1964
Sturgeon‡‡	468	0	Joey Pallotta, III	Benicia, Calif	July 9, 1983
Swordfish	1,182	0	L. E. Marron	Iquique, Chile	May 7, 1953
Tarpon	283	0	M. Salazar	Lake Maracaibo, Venez	Mar 19, 1956
Trout (Brook)	14	8	Dr. W. J. Cook	Nipigon R, Ont, Can	July 1916
Trout (Lake)¶	65	0	Larry Daunis	Great Bear Lake, NWT, Can	Aug 8, 1970
Tuna (Allison or Yellowfin)	388	12	Curt Wiesenhutter	San Benedicto Is, Mex	Apr 1, 1977
Tuna (Atlantic Big-eyed)	375	8	Cecil Browne	Ocean City, Md	Aug 26, 1977
Tuna (Pacific Big-eyed)	435	0	Dr Russel V. A. Lee	Cabo Blanco, Peru	Apr 17, 1957
Tuna (Bluefin)	1,496	0	Ken Fraser	Aulds Cove, Nova Scotia	Oct 26, 1979
Wahoo	149	0	John Pirovano	Cat Cay, Bahamas	June 15, 1962
Weakfish	19	2	Dennis R. Rooney	Jones Beach, NY	Oct 11, 1984

†† A barracuda weighing 103 lb 4 oz was caught on an untested line by Chester Benet at West End, Bahamas, on Aug 11, 1932. Another weighing 48 lb 6 oz was caught barehanded by Thomas B. Pace at Panama City Beach, Fla, on Apr 19, 1974. §§ Hackett was only 11 years 137 days old at the time. † A carp weighing 83 lb 8 oz was taken (not by rod) near Pretoria, South Africa. A 60-lb specimen was taken by bow and arrow by Ben A. Topham in Wythe Co, Va, on July 5, 1970. § A salmon weighing 126 lb 8 oz was taken (not by rod) near Petersburg, Alaska. ** A 1,295-lb specimen was taken by two anglers off Natal, South Africa, on March 17, 1939, and a 1,500-lb specimen harpooned inside Durban Harbour, South Africa, in 1933. ‡ W. W. Dowding caught a 922-lb thresher shark in 1937 on an untested line. ‡‡ An 834-lb sturgeon was landed (not by a rod) by Garry Oling at Albion, BC, Canada, from the Fraser River on Aug 11, 1981. ¶ A 102-lb trout was taken from Lake Athabasca, northern Saskatchewan, Canada, on Aug 8, 1961. *** Unofficial 3,450 lb specimen caught on overweight line, Aug 1986 off Montauk, NY.

Smallest Catch

The smallest fish ever to win a competition was a smelt weighing 1/16 of an oz, caught by Peter Christian at Buckenham Ferry, Norfolk, England, on Jan 9, 1977. This beat 107 other competitors who failed to catch anything.

Largest Catches

Yet to be ratified is the largest fish ever caught by rod and line: A great white shark, 18 ft 9 in long, weighing 3,450 lb was landed off Montauk Marine Basin, LI, NY in August 1986 by Donnie Braddick and Frank Mundus. The shark fought for two hours, but this could not be accepted as a record because the men used a 150-lb test nylon line, heavier than the 130-lb IGFA limit.

The largest fish ever caught on a rod is an officially ratified man-eating great white shark (*Carcharodon carcharias*) weighing 2,664 lb, and measuring 16 ft 10 in long, caught by Alf Dean at Denial Bay, near Ceduna, South Australia, on Apr 21, 1959. In June 1978 a great white shark measuring 29 ft 6 in in length and weighing over 10,000 lb was harpooned and landed by fishermen in the harbor of San Miguel, Azores.

A white pointer shark weighing 3,388 lb was caught on a rod by Clive Green off Albany, W Australia, on Apr 26, 1976, but this will remain unratified as whale meat was used as bait.

The largest marine animal ever killed by *hand* harpoon was a blue whale 97 ft in length by Archer Davidson in Twofold Bay, NSW, Australia, in 1910. Its tail flukes measured 20 ft across and its jaw bone 23 ft 4 in.

The biggest single freshwater catch ever ratified

REEL WINNERS: 1,282-lb Atlantic blue marlin (left) caught by Larry Martin in the Virgin Isles in 1977. (Center) MOST VALUABLE FISH: A prize of $250,000, the most money ever paid for a fish, awaited Al McReynolds of Atlantic City, NJ, when he caught this 78-lb-8-oz striped bass off a jetty after a 2-hour fight in Sept 1982. (Right) Ken Fraser with his 1,496-lb bluefin tuna landed after a 45-min fight off Nova Scotia, Canada, for an all-tackle record.

was on the Snake River, Idaho, in 1956 when Willard Cravens caught a white sturgeon weighing 360 lb. However, that may not be the last word as two years previously, in the same river, Glenn Howard claims to have caught one which weighed 394 lb.

The heaviest game fish caught on rod and line is a 468-lb sturgeon by Joey Pallotta on July 9, 1983 off Benicia, Calif. An 834-lb freshwater sturgeon was *landed* by Garry Oling from the Fraser River, Albion, Brit Columbia, on Aug 11, 1981.

Most Valuable Fish

It was a modern version of an old fairy tale. When Al McReynolds went fishing one stormy night, the fish he caught brought fame and fortune. In this case, the magic was supplied by ABU-Garcia, a leading

manufacturer of fishing tackle, through a contest that offered a $250,000 reward for landing an all-tackle world record fish in one of four categories.

McReynolds, 36, and his friend Pat Erdman were fishing from a jetty in their hometown, Atlantic City, NJ, on the night of Sept 21, 1982, when McReynolds hooked and, after a 2-hour fight, landed a 78-lb-8-oz striped bass—a world record for rod and reel. As one ordeal had ended, another began. McReynolds had to wait for the IGFA and ABU-Garcia to determine that the record was legitimate—a process that took nearly 5 months. Testing even included having the fish x-rayed to determine no stones or weights had been added to make the fish heavier.

It all ended happily on Feb 11, 1983, at the Explorers Club in NYC when McReynolds received a check for $250,000—the most money ever paid for a fish.

A claim has been made that two fishermen won $500,000 each in a fishing contest in Puget Sound, Wash in 1983. The objective was to catch one of 8 tagged fish. The two reportedly succeeded and split the $1 million prize.

FOOTBALL

Origins

The origin of modern football stems from the "Boston Game" as played at Harvard. Harvard declined to participate in the inaugural meeting of the Intercollegiate Football Association in NYC in Oct 1873, on the grounds that the proposed rules were based on the non-handling "Association" code of English football. Instead, Harvard accepted a proposal from McGill University of Montreal, which played the more closely akin English Rugby Football. The first football match under the Harvard Rules was thus played against McGill at Cambridge, Mass, in May 1874. Most sports historians point to a contest between Rutgers and Princeton at New Brunswick, NJ, on Nov 6, 1869, as the first football game, but many American soccer historians regard this contest as the first intercollegiate *soccer* game. (Rutgers won the game, 6 goals to 4, and there were 25 players to a side.) In Nov 1876, a new Intercollegiate Football Association, with a pioneer membership of 5 colleges, was inaugurated at Springfield, Mass, to reconcile the conflicting versions of the sport. It was not until 1880 that the game, because of the organizational genius of Walter Camp of Yale, began to take its modern form. Among other things,

he reduced the number of players on a side to 11, which it is today (and defined their positions), and also replaced the scrum with the line of scrimmage.

Professional football dates from the Latrobe, Pa vs Jeannette, Pa match at Latrobe, in Aug 1895. The National Football League was founded in Canton, Ohio, in 1920, although it did not adopt its present name until 1922. The year 1969 was the final year in which professional football was divided into separate National and American Leagues, for record purposes.

Most Prolific Recordbreaker

After he finished his 4-year career at Portland State U in 1980, Neil Lomax held 90 NCAA football records and was tied for two other records, mostly on the basis of his passing feats. No other football player, past or present, has been remotely close to holding that many records—in any college sport.

College Series Records

The oldest collegiate series still contested is that between Yale and Princeton dating from 1873, or 3 years before the passing of the Springfield rules, with 109 games played through the 1986 season. The most regularly contested series is between Lafayette and Lehigh, who have met 122 times, 1884 to 1986.

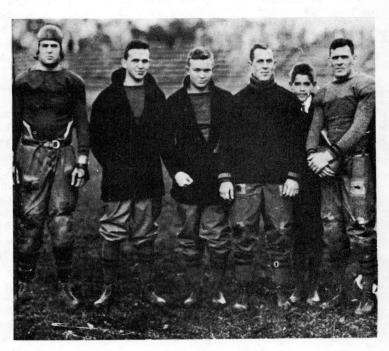

FAMOUS FOOTBALLER: The man who played for Army and went on to become President is the third from the left in this photo—Dwight D. Eisenhower.

SUPER-BOWL RECORD: When the Chicago Bears beat the New Eng Patriots 46–10 in Jan 1986, it was the biggest margin of victory ever in the annual classic. This is how play looked at ground level. (All Sport)

Yale University became the only college to win more than 700 games when it finished the 1979 season with a total of 701 victories in 107 seasons. Yale has 736 wins in 114 seasons to the end of 1986.

All-America Brothers

Twice have three brothers made All-America at the same school. The first trio were the Wistert brothers at Mich, all of whom were tackles. Francis was honored in 1933, Albert in 1942, Alvin in 1948–49. At Oklahoma, defensive lineman Lucious Selmon was an All-America in 1973 and he was followed by his brothers Leroy, a defensive tackle, and Dewey, an offensive guard, in 1975.

Jim Thorpe vs Dwight D. Eisenhower

The two met in 1912 when Thorpe was playing for the Carlisle School for Indians (Pa) and Eisenhower was playing for Army (West Point, NY). Eisenhower and another back were instructed to follow Thorpe wherever he went. In the third quarter of the game they both hit Thorpe so hard that the pair of them were dazed and were taken out of the game by their coach. Thorpe played to the end.

Ban Football!

Although remembered as one of the most athletic of presidents, Theodore Roosevelt threatened to ban college football in 1905. Eighteen players had died of injuries that year and 73 were seriously hurt. One of Roosevelt's sons, a freshman at Harvard, came home from the first day of practice with a black eye. At the President's urging, the flying wedge was outlawed as a move, and a neutral zone between opposing lines was instituted. Roosevelt's demands to outlaw rough play led to the Rules Committee legalizing the forward pass in 1906.

First Televised Football Game

Fordham U, NYC, was the host to Waynesburg, a Pa school, in the first football game ever televised—in 1939. Fordham won, 34–7.

ALL-TIME NATIONAL FOOTBALL LEAGUE RECORDS
(Through 1986 Season)

SERVICE

Most Seasons, Active Player
26 George Blanda, Chi Bears, 1949–58; Balt, 1950; AFL: Hou, 1960–66; Oak, 1967–75

Most Games Played, Lifetime
340 George Blanda, Chi Bears, 1949–58; Balt, 1950; AFL: Hou, 1960–66; Oak, 1967–75

Most Consecutive Games Played, Lifetime
282 Jim Marshall, Cleve, 1960; Minn, 1961–79

Most Seasons, Head Coach
40 George Halas, Chi Bears, 1920–29, 33–42, 46–55, 58–67

SCORING

Most Seasons Leading League
5 Don Hutson, GB, 1940–44
Gino Cappelletti, Bos, 1961, 63–66 (AFL)

Most Points, Lifetime
2,002 George Blanda, Chi Bears, 1949–58; Balt, 1950; AFL: Hou, 1960–66; Oak, 1967–75 (9-td, 943-pat, 335-fg)

Most Points, Season
176 Paul Hornung, GB, 1960 (15-td, 41-pat, 15-fg)

Most Points, Rookie Season
132 Gale Sayers, Chi Bears, 1965 (22-td)

Most Points, Game
40 Ernie Nevers, Chi Cards vs Chi Bears, Nov 28, 1929 (6-td, 4-pat)

Most Consecutive Games, Scoring
151 Fred Cox, Minn 1963-73

Touchdowns

Most Seasons Leading League
8 Don Hutson, GB, 1935–38, 41–44

Most Touchdowns, Lifetime
126 Jim Brown, Cleve, 1957–65 (106-r, 20-p)

Most Touchdowns, Season
24 John Riggins, Wash (24-r), 1983

Most Touchdowns, Rookie Season
22 Gale Sayers, Chi Bears, 1965 (14-r,6-p, 1-prb, 1-krb)

Most Touchdowns, Game
6 Ernie Nevers, Chi Cards vs Chi Bears, Nov 28, 1929 (6-r)
William (Dub) Jones, Cleve vs Chi Bears, Nov 25, 1951 (4-r, 2-p)
Gale Sayers, Chi Bears vs SF, Dec 12, 1965 (4-r, 1-p, 1-prb)

Most Consecutive Games Scoring Touchdowns
18 Lenny Moore, Balt, 1963–65

Points After Touchdown

Most Seasons Leading League
8 George Blanda, Chi Bears, 1956; AFL: Hou, 1961–62; Oak, 1967–69, 72, 74

Most Points After Touchdown, Lifetime
959 George Blanda, Chi Bears, 1949–58; Balt, 1950; AFL: Hou, 1960–66; Oak, 1967–69, 72, 74

Most Points After Touchdown, Season
66 Uwe von Schamann, Miami 1984

Most Points After Touchdown, Game
9 Marlin (Pat) Harder, Chi Cards vs NY, Oct 17, 1948
Bob Waterfield, LA vs Balt, Oct 22, 1950
Charlie Gogolak, Wash vs NY Giants, Nov 27, 1966

Most Consecutive Points After Touchdown
234 Tommy Davis, SF, 1959–65

Most Points After Touchdown (no misses), Game
9 Marlin (Pat) Harder, Chi Cards vs NY Giants, Oct 17, 1948
Bob Waterfield, LA Rams vs Balt, Oct 22, 1950

Field Goals

Most Seasons Leading League
5 Lou Groza, Cleve, 1950, 52–54, 57

Most Field Goals, Lifetime
373 Jan Stenerud KC 1967–69; Gr Bay 1980–83, Minn 1984–85

Most Field Goals, Season
35 Ali Haji-Sheikh, NY Giants, 1983

Most Field Goals, Game
7 Jim Bakken, St L vs Pitt, Sept 24, 1967

Most Consecutive Games, Field Goals
31 Fred Cox, Minn, 1968–70

Highest Field Goal Percentage, Season
95.24 Mark Mosely, Wash, 1982 (20–21)

Most Consecutive Field Goals
23 Mark Mosely. Wash, 1981–82

Longest Field Goal
63 yd Tom Dempsey, NO vs Det, Nov 8, 1970

RUSHING

Most Seasons Leading League
8 Jim Brown, Cleve, 1957–61, 63–65

Most Yards Gained, Lifetime
16,193 Walter Payton, Chi Bears, 1975–86

Most Yards Gained, Season
2,105 Eric Dickerson, LA Rams, 1984

Most Yards Gained, Game
275 Walter Payton, Chi Bears vs Minn, Nov 20, 1977

Longest Run from Scrimmage
99 Tony Dorsett, Dall vs Minn, Jan 3, 1983 (td)

Highest Average Gain, Lifetime (799 att)
5.2 Jim Brown, Cleve, 1957–65 (2,359–12,312)

HEADED FOR THE SUPER BOWL: Owner George Halas (standing center, in raincoat and baseball hat) coached the Chicago Bears for 40 seasons, piling up a record 325 victories. Here he watches Gale Sayers in 1965 take off around end. The Bears did not win their first Super Bowl until Jan 1986, long after Halas had passed away.

Most Yards Gained Passing, Season
  5,084 Dan Marino, Miami, 1984

Most Touchdown Passes, Lifetime
  342 Fran Tarkenton, Minn
      1961–66, 72–78; NY Giants
      1967–71

Most Touchdown Passes, Season
  48 Dan Marino, Miami, 1984

Most Touchdown Passes, Game
  7 Sid Luckman, Chi Bears v
      NY Giants, Nov 14, 1943
      Adrian Burk, Phil vs Wash
      Oct 17, 1954
      George Blanda, Hou vs NY
      Titans, Nov 19, 1961 (AFL)
      Y. A. Tittle, NY vs Wash, Oct
      28, 1962
      Joe Kapp, Minn vs Balt, Sep
      28, 1969

Most Touchdown Passes, Consecutive
Games
  47 John Unitas, Balt, 1956–60

Passing Efficiency, Lifetime (1,500 att)
  63.2 Joe Montana, SF 1979–86;
      (1,818–2,878)

Passing Efficiency, Season (100 att)
  70.55 Ken Anderson, Cin, 1982
      (309–218)

Passing Efficiency, Game (20 att)
  90.9 Ken Anderson, Cin vs Pitt,
      Nov 10, 1974 (22–20)

RUSHING RECORDHOLDER: Walter Payton of the 1986 Super-Bowl Champion Chicago Bears set a record in 1984 for 58 games with 100 yds or more gained. In 1977 he broke the record for yds gained in one game (275). He rushed 16,193 yds in his career through 1986. (UPI—Bettmann Archive)

Highest Average Gain, Game (10 att)
  17.1 Marion Motley, Cleve vs Pitt,
      Oct 29, 1950 (11–188)
Most Touchdowns Rushing, Lifetime
  106 Jim Brown, Cleve, 1957–65
      Walter Payton, Chi Bears
      1975–86
Most Touchdowns Rushing, Season
  24 John Riggins, Wash, 1983
Most Touchdowns Rushing, Game
  6 Ernie Nevers, Chi Cards vs
      Chi Bears, Nov 28, 1929

PASSING

Most Seasons Leading League
  6 Sammy Baugh, Wash, 1937,
      40, 43, 45, 47, 49
Most Passes Attempted, Lifetime
  6,467 Fran Tarkenton, Minn,
      1961–66, 72–78; NY
      Giants, 1967–71
Most Passes Attempted, Season
  623 Dan Marino, Miami, 1986
Most Passes Attempted, Game
  68 George Blanda, Hou vs Buff,
      Nov 1, 1964 (AFL) (37 com-
      pletions)
Most Passes Completed, Lifetime
  3,686 Fran Tarkenton, Minn,
      1961–66, 72–78; NY Giants,
      1967–71

Most Passes Completed, Season
  378 Dan Marino, Miami, 1986
Most Passes Completed, Game
  42 Richard Todd, NY Jets vs SF,
      Sept 21, 1980 (59 attempts)
Most Consecutive Passes Completed
  20 Ken Anderson, Cin vs Hou,
      Jan 2, 1983
Longest Pass Completion (all tds)
  99 Frank Filchock (to Farkas),
      Wash vs Pitt, Oct 15, 1939
      George Izo (to Mitchell), Wash
      vs Cleve, Sept 15, 1963
      Karl Sweetan (to Studstill),
      Det vs Balt, Oct 16, 1966
      C. A. Jurgensen (to Allen),
      Wash vs Chi Bears, Sept 15,
      1968
      Jim Plunkett (to Branch) LA
      Raiders vs Wash Oct 2, 1983
      Ron Jaworski (to Quick) Phil
      vs Atl, Nov 10, 1985
Most Yards Gained Passing, Lifetime
  47,003 Fran Tarkenton, Minn,
      1961–66, 72–78; NY Giants,
      1967–71
Most Yards Gained Passing, Game
  554 Norm Van Brocklin, LA vs
      NY Yanks, Sept 28, 1951
      (41–27)

Passes Had Intercepted

Most Passes Intercepted, Game
  8 Jim Hardy, Chi Cards vs Phil,
      Sept 24, 1950 (39 attempts)
Most Consecutive Passes Attempted,
None Intercepted
  294 Bryan (Bart) Starr, GB,
      1964–65
Fewest Passes Intercepted, Season
(Qualifiers)
  1 Joe Ferguson, Buff, 1976 (151
      attempts)
Lowest Percentage Passes Intercepted,
Lifetime (1,500 att)
  2.64 Joe Montana, SF 1979–86
      (2,878–76)
Lowest Percentage Passes Intercepted,
Season (Qualifiers)
  0.66 Joe Ferguson, Buff, 1976
      (151–1)

PASS RECEPTIONS

Most Seasons Leading League
  8 Don Hutson, GB, 1936–37, 39,
      41–45
Most Pass Receptions, Lifetime
  750 Charley Joiner, Hou 1969–72,
      Cinc 1972–75, SD 1976–86
Most Pass Receptions, Season
  106 Art Monk, Wash, 1984
Most Pass Receptions, Game
  18 Tom Fears, LA Rams vs GB,
      Dec 3, 1950 (189 yd)

Longest Pass Reception (all tds)
99 Andy Farkas (Filchock), Wash vs Pitt, Oct 15, 1939
Bobby Mitchell (Izo), Wash vs Cleve, Sept 15, 1963
Pat Studstill (Sweetan), Det vs Balt, Oct 16, 1966
Gerry Allen (Jurgensen), Wash vs Chi Bears, Sept 15, 1968
Cliff Branch (Plunkett), LA Raiders vs Wash, Oct 2, 1983
Mike Quick (Jaworski), Phil vs Atl, Nov 10, 1985

Most Consecutive Games, Pass Receptions
139 Steve Largent, Seattle, 1976–86

Most Pass Receptions by a Running Back, Game
17 Clark Gaines, NY Jets vs SF, Sept 21, 1980

Most Yards Gained Pass Receptions, Game
309 Stephone Paige, KC vs SD, Dec 22, 1985

Touchdowns Receiving

Most Touchdown Passes, Lifetime
99 Don Hutson, GB, 1935–45

Most Touchdown Passes, Season
18 Mark Clayton, Miami, 1984

Most Touchdown Passes, Game
5 Bob Shaw, Chi Cards vs Balt, Oct 2, 1950
Kellen Winslow, SD vs Oak, Nov 22, 1981

Most Consecutive Games, Touchdown Passes
11 Elroy (Crazy Legs) Hirsch, LA Rams, 1950–51
Gilbert (Buddy) Dial, Pitt, 1959–60

PASS INTERCEPTIONS

Most Interceptions by, Lifetime
81 Paul Krause, Wash (28), 1964–67; Minn (53), 1968–79

Most Interceptions by, Season
14 Richard (Night Train) Lane, LA Rams, 1952

Most Interceptions by, Game
4 By 17 players, twice by Jerry Norton St L vs Wash, Nov 20, 1960; St L vs Pitt, Nov 26, 1961

Most Touchdowns Interception Returns, Lifetime
9 Ken Houston, Hou 1967–79; Wash 1973–80

PUNTING

Most Seasons Leading League
4 Sammy Baugh, Wash, 1940–43
Jerrel Wilson, AFL: KC, 1965, 68; NFL: KC, 1972–73

Most Punts, Season
114 Bob Parsons, Chi, 1981

Most Punts, Lifetime
1,083 John James, Atl 1972–81, Det 1982, Hou 1982–84

Longest Punt
98 yd Steve O'Neal, NY Jets vs Den, Sept 21, 1969 (AFL)

Most Punts, Game
14 Dick Nesbitt, Chi Cards vs Chi Bears, Nov 30, 1933
Keith Molesworth, Chi Bears vs GB, Dec 10, 1933
Sammy Baugh, Wash vs Phil, Nov 5, 1939
John Kinscherf, NY Giants vs Det, Nov 7, 1943
George Taliaferro, NY Yanks vs LA Rams, Sept 28, 1951

Average Yardage Punting

Highest Punting Average, Lifetime (300 punts)
45.1 yd Sammy Baugh, Wash, 1937–52 (338)

Highest Punting Average, Season (20 punts)
51.4 yd Sammy Baugh, Wash, 1940 (35)

Highest Punting Average, Game (4 punts)
61.8 yd Bob Cifers, Det vs Chi Bears, Nov 24, 1946

KICKOFF RETURNS
Yardage Returning Kickoffs

Most Yards Gained, Lifetime
6,922 Ron Smith, Chi Bears, 1965, 70–72; Atl, 1966–67; LA 1968–69; SD, 1973; Oak, 1974

Most Yards Gained, Season
1,345 George (Buster) Rhymes, Minn 1985

Most Yards Gained, Game
294 Wally Triplett, Det vs LA, Oct 29, 1950 (4)

Longest Kickoff Return for Touchdown
106 Al Carmichael, GB vs Chi Bears, Oct 7, 1956
Noland Smith, KC vs Den, Dec 17, 1967 (AFL)
Roy Green, St L vs Dall, Oct 21, 1979

Highest Average, Lifetime (75 returns)
30.6 Gale Sayers, Chi Bears, 1965–71

Ave. Yardage Kickoff Returns

Highest Average, Season (15 returns)
41.1 Travis Williams, GB, 1967 (18)

Highest Average, Game (3 returns)
73.5 Wally Triplett, Det vs LA Rams, Oct 29, 1950 (4–294)

Touchdowns Returning Kickoffs

Most Touchdowns, Lifetime
6 Ollie Matson, Chi Cards, 1952 (2), 54, 56, 58 (2)
Gale Sayers, Chi Bears, 1965, 66 (2), 67 (3)
Travis Williams, GB, 1967 (4), 69, 71

Most Touchdowns, Season
4 Travis Williams, GB, 1967
Cecil Turner, Chi Bears, 1970

Most Touchdowns, Game
2 Thomas (Tim) Brown, Phil vs Dall, Nov 6, 1966
Travis Williams, GB vs Cleve, Nov 12, 1967

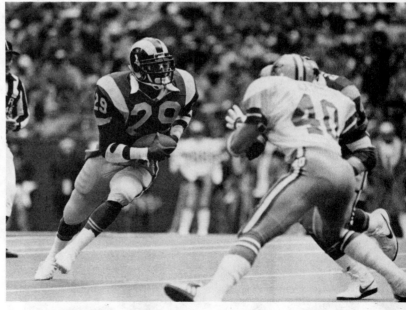

RUSHING RECORD of 2,105 yds in one season was set by Eric Dickerson (LA Rams) in his peak year 1984, eclipsing O.J. Simpson's record of 2,003 which had held for 11 years. (UPI—Bettmann Archive)

PUNT RETURNS
Yardage Returning Punts

Most Yards Gained, Lifetime
3,123 Billy Johnson, Hou 1974–80, Atl 1982–86

Most Yards Gained, Season
692 Fulton Walker, LA Raiders 1985

Most Yards Gained, Game
207 Le Roy Irvin, LA Rams vs Atl, Oct 11, 1981

Longest Punt Return (all tds)
98 Gil LeFebvre, Cin vs Brk, Dec 3, 1933
Charlie West, Minn vs Wash, Nov 3, 1968
Dennis Morgan, Dall vs St L, Oct 13, 1974

Highest Average, Lifetime (75 or more returns)
12.78 George McAfee, Chi Bears, 1940–41, 1945–50

Highest Average, Season (Qualifiers)
23.0 Herb Rich, Balt, 1950

Highest Average, Game (3 returns)
47.7 Chuck Latourette, St L vs NO, Sept 29, 1968

Touchdowns Returning Punts

Most Touchdowns, Lifetime
8 Jack Christiansen, Det, 1951–58
Rick Upchurch, Den, 1975–83

Most Touchdowns, Season
4 Jack Christiansen, Det, 1951
Rick Upchurch, Den, 1976

Most Touchdowns, Game
2 Jack Christiansen, Det vs LA Rams, Oct 14, 1951; vs GB, Nov 22, 1951
Dick Christy, NY Titans vs Den, Sept 24, 1961
Rick Upchurch, Den vs Cleve, Sept 26, 1976
LeRoy Irvin, LA Rams vs Atl, Oct 11, 1981

FUMBLES

Most Fumbles, Lifetime
105 Roman Gabriel, LA Rams, 1962–72; Phil, 1973–77

Most Fumbles, Season
17 Dan Pastorini, Hou, 1973
Warren Moon, Hou 1984

Most Fumbles, Game
7 Len Dawson, KC vs SD, Nov 15, 1964 (AFL)

Longest Fumble Return
104 Jack Tatum, Oak vs GB, Sept 24, 1972

Most Opponents' Fumbles Recovered, Lifetime
29 Jim Marshall, Cleve, 1960; Minn, 1961–79

Most Opponents' Fumbles Recovered, Season
9 Don Hultz, Minn, 1963

Most Opponents' Fumbles Recovered, Game
3 by 9 players 1949–86

LONGEST FIELD GOAL: Tom Dempsey (New Orleans Saints) kicked a record 63-yard field goal on the last play of an NFL game to beat the Detroit Lions 19–17 on Nov 8, 1970. Dempsey, who was born with only half a right foot and only part of his right arm, wore a special shoe for placekicking. He reportedly once kicked a 57-yarder without a shoe in a semipro game.

SUPER BOWL RECORDS
(Through 1987 Game)

Most points, lifetime
24 Franco Harris, Pitt, 4 games (4 td)

Most points, game
18 Roger Craig, SF vs Miami, Jan 20, 1985 (3 td)

Most field goals, lifetime
5 Ray Wersching, SF, 2 games

Most field goals, game
4 Don Chandler, GB vs. Oak, Jan 14, 1968
Ray Wersching, SF vs Cin, Jan 24, 1982

Longest field goal
48 Jan Stenerud, KC vs Minn, Jan 11, 1970
Rick Karlis, Den vs NY Giants Jan 25, 1987

Most yards rushing, lifetime
354 Franco Harris, Pitt, 4 games

Most yards rushing, game
191 Marcus Allen, LA Raiders vs Wash, Jan 22, 1984

Most yards passing, lifetime
932 Terry Bradshaw, Pitt, 4 games

Most yards, passing, game
331 Joe Montana, SF vs Miami, Jan 20, 1985

Most passes completed, lifetime
61 Roger Staubach, Dallas, 4 games

Most passes completed, game
29 Dan Marino, Miami vs SF, Jan 20, 1985

Most touchdown passes, lifetime
9 Terry Bradshaw, Pitt, 4 games

Most touchdown passes, game
4 Terry Bradshaw, Pitt vs Dallas, Jan 21, 1979

Longest completed pass
80 Jim Plunkett to Kenny King, Oak Raiders vs Phil, Jan 25, 1981

Best passing pct, game
.880 Phil Simms, NY Giants vs Den (22 of 25), Jan 25, 1987

Most yards receiving, lifetime
364 Lynn Swann, Pitt, 4 games

Most yards receiving, game
161 Lynn Swann, Pitt vs Dallas, Jan 18, 1976

Most receptions, lifetime
16 Lynn Swann, Pitt, 4 games

Most receptions, game
11 Dan Rose, Cin vs SF, Jan 24, 1982

Most interceptions, game
3 Rod Martin, Oak Raiders vs Phil, Jan 25, 1981

Longest punt
62 Rich Camarillo, NE Patriots vs Chi Bears, Jan 26, 1986

Longest punt return
34 Darrell Green, Wash vs LA Raiders, Jan 22, 1984

Longest kickoff return
98 Fulton Walker, Miami vs Wash, Jan 30, 1983

and AFL champions. The Pittsburgh Steelers have the most Super Bowl victories with 4 (1975–76, 79–80). The 1972 Miami Dolphins had the best record for one season, including playoffs and Super Bowl (played Jan 1973), with 17 wins and no losses or ties.

Shortest Touchdown Pass

When the Dallas Cowboys had only 2 inches to go for a touchdown against the Washington Redskins on Oct 9, 1960, quarterback Eddie LeBaron did the unexpected. Knowing that everyone was looking to a powerful thrust at the line by the heaviest plunging back on his team, LeBaron took the ball from center and instead of handing it off to his fullback, slipped into the pocket and unleashed a short pass over the left side to his left end Bielski to set a world record for the shortest distance gained by a pass for a touchdown—2 inches.

STRONG ARM: Fran Tarkenton set lifetime NFL records by attempting 6,467 passes and completing 3,686 of them during his 18-year career with the NY Giants and Minn Vikings. Tarkenton, who holds career passing records for touchdowns (342) and yards gained (47,003), was elected to the Hall of Fame in 1986.

Longest Streaks

The longest collegiate winning streak is 47 straight by Oklahoma. The longest unbeaten streak is 63 games (59 won, 4 tied) by Washington from 1907 to 1917. Macalaster University of St Paul, Minn, ended a record 50-game losing streak when, with 11 sec remaining in the game, a 23-yd field goal beat Mount Senario, 17–14, on Sept 6, 1980. It was Macalaster's first victory since Oct 11, 1974.

NFL Champions

The Green Bay Packers have won a record 11 NFL titles from 1929 through 1967. The Packers also won the first two Super Bowls (instituted Jan 1967), when the games were a competition between NFL

SUPER PASSING: Phil Simms (NY Giants), most valuable player in the 1987 Super Bowl set 2 major records, completing 10 passes in a row and finishing with 22 out of 25 attempts for a record .880 percentage.

MODERN MAJOR-COLLEGE INDIVIDUAL RECORDS
(Through 1986 Season)

Points

Most in a Game	43	Jim Brown (Syracuse)	1956
Most in a Season	174	Lydell Mitchell (Penn State)	1971
	174	Mike Rozier (Nebraska)	1983
Most in a Career	368	Luis Zendejas (Ariz State)	1981–84

Touchdowns

Most in a Game	7	Arnold Boykin (Mississippi)	1951
Most in a Season	29	Lydell Mitchell (Penn State)	1971
	29	Mike Rozier (Nebraska)	1983
Most in a Career	59	Glenn Davis (Army)	1943–46
	59	Tony Dorsett (Pittsburgh)	1973–76

Field Goals

Most in a Game	7	Mike Prindle (W Mich)	1984
		Dale Klein (Nebraska)	1985
Most in a Season	29	John Lee (UCLA)	1984
Most in a Career	80	Jeff Jaeger (Washington)	1983–86
Most Consecutively (Career)	30	Chuck Nelson (Washington)	1981–82

Other Season Records

Yards Gained Rushing	2,342 yd	Marcus Allen (So Cal)	1981
Highest Average Gain per Rush (min. 150 attempts)	9.35 yd	Greg Pruitt (Oklahoma)	1971
Most Passes Attempted	511	Robbie Bosco (Brigham Young)	1985
Most Passes Completed	338	Robbie Bosco (Brigham Young)	1985
Most Touchdown Passes	47	Jim McMahon (Brigham Young)	1980
Most Yards Gained Passing	4,571 yd	Jim McMahon (Brigham Young)	1980
Most Passes Caught	134	Howard Twilley (Tulsa)	1965
Most Yards Gained on Catches	1,779 yd	Howard Twilley (Tulsa)	1965
Most Touchdown Passes Caught	18	Tom Reynolds (San Diego St)	1969
Most Passes Intercepted by	14	Al Worley (Washington)	1968
Highest Punting Average (min. 30 punts)	49.8 yd	Reggie Roby (Iowa)	1981

Highest Score

The most points ever scored (by one team and both teams) in a college football game was 222 by Georgia Tech, Atlanta, Ga, against Cumberland University of Lebanon, Tenn on Oct 7, 1916. Tech also set records for the most points scored in one quarter (63), most touchdowns (32) and points after touchdown (30) in a game, and the largest victory margin (Cumberland did not score).

College Record Passer

Doug Flutie of Boston College became the first major college player to pass for more than 10,000 yards in a career. His next-to-last game of the 1984 season on Nov 23 saw him complete 34 of 46 passes for 472 yards and 3 touchdowns with no interceptions in a victory over the University of Miami, 47–45. The winning touchdown pass of 64 yards came in the last seconds of play in the Orange Bowl before 30,235 spectators and millions on a national TV hookup. The receiver of the final pass and many others of Flutie's passes was Gerald Phelan, his roommate.

Super Bowl Winners

1967 Green Bay Packers (NFL)
1968 Green Bay Packers (NFL)
1969 New York Jets (AFL)
1970 Kansas City Chiefs (AFL)
1971 Baltimore Colts (AFC)
1972 Dallas Cowboys (NFC)
1973 Miami Dolphins (AFC)
1974 Miami Dolphins (AFC)
1975 Pittsburgh Steelers (AFC)
1976 Pittsburgh Steelers (AFC)
1977 Oakland Raiders (AFC)
1978 Dallas Cowboys (NFC)
1979 Pittsburgh Steelers (AFC)
1980 Pittsburgh Steelers (AFC)
1981 Oakland Raiders (AFC)
1982 San Francisco 49ers (NFC)
1983 Washington Redskins (NFC)
1984 Los Angeles Raiders (AFC)
1985 San Francisco 49ers (NFC)
1986 Chicago Bears (NFC)
1987 New York Giants (NFC)

The highest victory margin was in 1986 when the

PUTTING THE FOOT IN FOOTBALL: Steve O'Neal (#20) of the NY Jets follows through on his punt from the end zone in Denver's Mile High Stadium. The line of scrimmage (from which punts are measured) had been the 1-yd line. The ball, which sailed well over the receiver's head, bounced and rolled to the Denver 1-yd line—a 98-yd punt! (Pro-Football Hall of Fame)

Bears beat the New England Patriots by 36 points, 46-10. This was also the most points scored by a winning team.

A record $550,000 per 30 sec was charged by NBC for advertising on the telecast.

Coaching Records

The longest-serving head coach was Amos Alonzo Stagg (1862–1965), who served Springfield in 1890–91, Chicago from 1892 to 1932 and College of the Pacific from 1933 to 1946, making a total of 57 years. He later served as an assistant coach to his son.

The record for most victories by a coach of a professional team is 325, by George Halas (1895–1983), who coached the Chicago Bears, 1920–29, 33–42, 46–55, 58–67.

In 1948, Bennie Oosterbaan, an assistant coach at Mich, his alma mater, was elevated to head coach. He won all 9 games and the national championship, becoming the first and only man to do that as a first-year head coach.

In 1986, Eddie Robinson of Grambling State University (Louisiana) won his 336th game, all at Grambling, in his 44 years there, to become the winningest coach in college football history. The previous record of 323 had been set by Paul "Bear" Bryant in 1982. Bryant had coached at Maryland (1945), Kentucky (1946–53), Texas A&M (1954–57) and Alabama (1958–82).

Worst Attendance

The worst attendance for a college football game was recorded on Nov 12, 1955 at Pullman, Washington. The game was between Wash State and San Jose State. It was played in spite of high winds and a temperature of 0°F. Total paid attendance: 1.

GAMES AND PASTIMES

BACKGAMMON

Forerunners of the game have been traced back to a dice and a board game found in excavations at Ur, dated to 3000 BC. Later the Romans played a game remarkably similar to the modern one. The name "Backgammon" is variously ascribed to Welsh ("little battle"), or Saxon ("back game"). Modern variations include the American Acey Deucey.

At present there are no world championships held, but a points rating system may soon be introduced internationally, thereby enabling players to be ranked.

Marathon

Dick Newcomb and Greg Peterson of Rockford, Ill, played backgammon for 151 hours 11 min, June 30–July 6, 1978.

BLACKJACK

Marathon

Earl Arnall, a dealer at the King 8 Casino in Las Vegas, Nev, spent 190 hours at the blackjack table, June 22–30, 1977. Ardeth Hardy set the women's mark of 169 hours 47 min of continuous dealing during the same period. Both took 5-min rest breaks after each hour.

BRIDGE (CONTRACT)

Bridge (corruption of Biritch) is thought to be either of Levantine origin, similar games having been played there in the early 1870's, or to have come from the East—probably India.

Auction bridge (highest bidder names trump) was invented *c.* 1902. The contract principle, present in several games (notably the French game *Plafond, c.* 1917), was introduced to bridge by Harold S. Vanderbilt (US) on Nov 1, 1925, during a Caribbean voyage aboard the SS *Finland*. The new version became a worldwide craze after the US vs GB challenge match between Rumanian-born Ely Culbertson (1891–1955) and Lt-Col Walter Thomas More Buller (1887–1938) at Almack's Club, London, Sept 1930. The US won the 200-hand match by 4,845 points.

On June 14, 1986, for the first time, a tournament was simultaneously held worldwide sponsored by the Epsom Computer Corp with about 50,000 pairs participating.

Most World Titles

The World Championship (Bermuda Bowl) has been won most often by Italy's Blue Team (*Squadra Azzura*), 1957–9, 61–3, 65–7, 69, 73–5. Italy also won the Olympiad in 1964, 68 and 72. Giorgio Belladonna (b 1923) was on all these winning teams.

Most Durable Player

Oswald Jacoby (b Dec 8, 1902, Dallas, Tex, d 1984) was a world-rank competitor for 52 years after winning his first world title in 1931. In Oct 1967, he became the first player to amass 10,000 master points. He retired in July 1983 but came back in Nov 1983 to be part of a team that won the North America team championship. (He also won the World Backgammon title.)

The bridge player with the longest unbroken record of competition in an ACBL annual is Jay T. Feigus (b 1892) of Middleton, NJ, who in 1985 played in his 56th consecutive Goldman Trophy contest. He twice finished in second place.

Most Master Points

In the latest ranking list based on Master Points awarded by the World Bridge Federation, the leading male player in the world was Giorgio Belladonna, a member of Italy's Blue Team, with 1,821¼ points, followed by four more Italians. The world's leading woman player is Dorothy Hayden Truscott (US) with 331¼ points.

As for master points awarded by the American Contract Bridge League, the leader was Barry Crane of Los Angeles (b 1927 Detroit, d July 5, 1985) who won a total of 35,137.6 points just before he died. Only 4 other players have even reached 25,000. The leader now is Paul Soloway with 26,119.41 points.

Youngest Life Masters

Dougie Hsieh (NYC) was 11 years 306 days when he reached the rank of Life Master in the ACBL, and youngest ever to win a regional championship.

Adair Gellman of Bethesda, Md, became the youngest-ever female life master at age 14 years 6 months 4 days on Oct 24, 1983, breaking a record that had stood for 6 years. Then on Nov 5, 1983, just 12 days later, she was toppled from her peak by a still younger lady, Patricia Thomas of Las Cruces, NM,

who was 14 years and 28 days. According to bridge columnist Alan Truscott of *The NY Times,* Miss Thomas joined the ACBL when barely 10 and became a senior master at the age of 11.

Most Players

Most competitors in play simultaneously: 4,444 at 1,111 tables during the 1979 Summer North American Championships at Las Vegas, Nev. Largest bridge tournament on record: 1979 Summer North American Championships with 18,517½ in ten days at the Las Vegas Hilton hotel.

Marathon

The longest recorded session was 186 hours 38 min by Jonathan Noad, Jeremy Cohen, Robert Pinder and Andrew Bale at Ariel Hotel, Hayes, Eng, Sept 20–28, 1986.

CHECKERS

Checkers, also known as draughts, has origins earlier than chess. It was played in Egypt in the second millennium BC. The earliest book on the game was by Antonio Torquemada of Valencia, Spain in 1547. There have been four US vs GB international matches (crossboard) in 1905, 27, 73, and 83, three won by the US and one by GB.

Walter Hellman (1916–75) (US) won a record 6 world championships, 1948–67. Melvin Pomeroy (US) was internationally undefeated from 1914 until

his death in 1933. Marion Tinsley (Tallahassee, Fla) has been the world champion since 1975.

Most Opponents

Nathan Cohen of Portland, Maine, played 172 opponents, 5 to 10 at a time, in 4 hours on July 26, 1981, and won every game, in an exhibition at a picnic.

Con McCarrick (Ireland) was reported as having played a record 154 games simultaneously, winning 136, drawing 17, and losing one, in 4½ hours at Dundalk, County Louth, Ireland, Mar 14, 1982.

Newell W. Banks (b Detroit, Mich, Oct 10, 1887) played 140 games simultaneously, winning 133 and drawing 7, in Chicago in 1933. His playing time was 145 min, so averaging about one move per sec. In 1947 he played blindfolded for 4 hours per day for 45 consecutive days, winning 1,331 games, drawing 54 and losing only 2, while playing six games at a time.

Longest and Shortest Games

In competition the prescribed rate of play is not less than 30 moves per hour with the average game lasting about 90 min. In 1958 a match between Dr Marion Tinsley (US) and Derek Oldbury (GB) lasted 7 hours 30 min. The shortest possible game is one of 20 moves, composed by Alan Malcolm Beckerson (GB) in 1977.

The longest session is 138 hours, 28 min by Greg Davis and Mark Schumacher at Denny's Restaurant, Nunawading, Australia, Aug 26–Sept 1, 1985.

CHESS

The game originated in ancient India under the name Chaturanga (literally "four-corps")— an army game. The name chess is derived from the Persian word *shah*. The earliest reference is from the Middle Persian Karnamak (*c.* 590–628), though there are grounds for believing its origins are from the 2nd century, owing to the discovery, announced in Dec 1972, of two ivory chessmen in the Uzbek Soviet Republic, datable to that century. The *Fédération Internationale des Echecs* was established in 1924. There were an estimated 7 million registered players in the USSR in 1973.

The game of chess has led to the publication of at least 20,000 books, more than for any other game.

Most Opponents

Vlastimil Hort (b Jan 12, 1944) (Czechoslovakia), in Seltjarnes, Iceland, Apr 23–24, 1977, played 550 opponents, including a record 201 simultaneously. He only lost ten games.

Dimitrije Bjelica (Yugoslavia) played 301 opponents simultaneously (258 wins, 36 draws, 7 losses) in 9 hours on Sept 18, 1982, at Sarajevo, Yugoslavia. Bjelica's weight dropped by 4½ lb as he walked a total of 12.4 miles.

WORLD CHESS CHAMPIONS: During his tenure (1975–85) Anatoliy Karpov (left) averaged 45.2 consecutive games annually, gaining the title as most active champion. When Gary Kasparov (right) first defeated Karpov on Nov 9, 1985, he was 22 years 210 days old, making him the youngest world champion ever. Both are Russian.

Erik G. J. Knoppert (Neth) (b Sept 20, 1959) played 500 games of 10-min chess against opponents averaging 2,002 on the Elo scale in 67 hours 58 min, Sept 13–16, 1985. He scored 413 points (1 for win, ½ for draw), a success rate of 82.6%.

The record for most consecutive games played is 663 by Vlastimil Hort over 32½ hours at Porz, W Germany on Oct 5–6, 1984. He played 60–100 opponents at a time, scoring over 80% and averaging 30 moves per game.

George Koltanowski (Belgium, later of US) tackled 56 opponents "blindfold" and won 50, drew 6, lost 0 in 9¾ hours at the Fairmont Hotel, San Francisco, on Dec 13, 1960.

Longest Games

The master game with the most moves on record was when Yedael Stepak (b Aug 21, 1940) (Israel) beat Yaakov Mashian (b Dec 17, 1943) (Iran, later Israel) in 193 moves in Tel Aviv, Israel, March 23–Apr 16, 1980. The total playing time was 24½ hours.

The slowest reported move (before modern rules) in an official event is reputed to have been played by Louis Paulsen (1833–91) (Germany) against Paul Charles Morphy (1837–84) (US) on Oct 29, 1857. The game ended in a draw on move 56 after 15 hours of play, of which Paulsen used most of the allotted time. Grandmaster Friedrich Sämisch (1896–1975) (Germany) ran out of the allotted time (2½ hours for 45 moves) after only 12 moves, in Prague, Czechoslovakia, in 1938.

World Champions

World champions have been generally recognized since 1886. The longest undisputed tenure was 26 years 337 days by Dr Emanuel Lasker (1868–1941) of Germany, from 1894 to 1921. Robert J. (Bobby) Fischer (b Chicago, March 9, 1943) is reckoned on the officially adopted Elo system to be the greatest Grandmaster of all time at 2,785. Anatoliy Karpov (USSR) (b May 23, 1951) was world champion 1975–85, with a rating lower than that of Gary Kasparov (USSR) (b Apr 13, 1963), rated 2,715, to whom he lost his title in Nov 1985. In a prior match in early 1985, the two set a record for draws in a championship match, 40. Kasparov at 2,740 is currently the highest-ranked player.

The women's world championship was held by Vera Menchik-Stevenson (1906–44) (USSR, later GB) from 1927 till her death, and was successfully defended a record 7 times. Nona Gaprindashvili (USSR) (b May 3, 1941) held the title from 1962 to 1978, and defended successfully 4 times. The high-

WOMEN'S CHESS CHAMPION: Nona Gaprindashvili (USSR) held the world title for 16 years, during which she defended it successfully 4 times. (AP)

est-rated woman player is Zsusza Polgar (Hungary) at 2,455.

The youngest world champion is Gary Kasparov who, at 22 years 210 days on Nov 9, 1985, beat Anatoliy Karpov (see above). Maya Chiburdanidze (b Jan 17, 1961) of Tbilisi (USSR) won the women's title in 1978 in a women-only match at the age of 17. The oldest was Wilhelm Steinitz (1836–1900) (Czech) who was 58 years 10 days old when he lost his title to Lasker on May 26, 1894.

José Raúl Capablanca (1888–1942) (Cuba) lost

LARGEST CLAY CHESS SET: The King and Queen are 49 in tall, but the Knight at 53 in is taller. The set was created from tile and built by John Nartker of Cincinnati, O.

only 34 games in his adult career, 1909–39, for the fewest games lost by a world champion. He was unbeaten from Feb 10, 1916, to Mar 21, 1924, and was world champion from 1921 to 1927.

Marathon

The longest recorded session is one of 200 hours by Roger Long and Graham Croft in Bristol, Eng, May 11–19, 1984.

CRIBBAGE

The invention of the game (once called Cribbidge) is credited to the English dramatist Sir John Suckling (1609–42). It is estimated that some ten million people play in the US alone.

Rare Hands

William E. Johnson of Waltham, Mass, had 4 maximum 29-point hands, 1974–81. Also, Mrs Mary Matheson of Springhill, Nova Scotia, had 4 between 1974 and 1985. Paul Nault of Athol, Mass, had two such hands within eight games in a tournament on March 19, 1977. Derek Hearne dealt two hands of six clubs with the turn-up card the remaining club on Feb 8, 1976, in Blackpool, Lancashire, England. Bill Rogers of Burnaby, BC, Canada scored 29 in the crib in 1975.

Marathon

Geoff Lee, Ken Whyatt, Ray Charles and Paul Branson played for 120 hours at the RAOB Club, Mapperley, England, Mar 16–21, 1982.

DARTS

The game of darts was originated by archers using heavily weighted 10-in throwing arrows for self-defense in close quarters fighting. The "dartes" were used in Ireland in the 16th century and darts was played on the *Mayflower* by the Plymouth pilgrims in 1620. The modern game dates from at least 1896 when Brian Gamlin of Bury, Lancashire, England, is credited with inventing the present numbering system on the board. The first recorded score of 180 (three triple 20's) was by John Reader at the Highbury Tavern in Sussex, England, in 1902. Today there are an estimated 6 million darts players in the British Isles.

Marathon

Raymond Azzorpardi and Alan Alden played for 134 hours 54 min at the Bank of Valletta Sports and Social Club, Marsa, Malta, Dec 11–17, 1985.

Most Titles

Eric Bristow (b Apr 25, 1957) (GB) has the most wins in the World Masters Championships (instituted 1974) with 5, in 1977, 79, 81, 83 and 84. He has also won the World Professional Championship (instituted 1978) 5 times, 1980–1 and 1984–86. In 1983 he completed a unique treble when he also won the World Cup Singles twice, 1983 and 1985. Six men have won the annual *News of the World* individual championship twice, most recently Eric Bristow in 1983 and 1984 and Bobby George in 1978 and 1986. John Lowe (b July 21, 1945) (GB) is the only man to have won each of the four major world titles: World Masters (1976 and 80), World Professional (1979), World Cup Singles (1981), and *News of the World* (1981).

Fastest 301 Match

The fastest time taken for a match of three games of 301, finishing on doubles, is 1 min 47 sec by Keith Deller on BBC-TV's *Record Breakers* program on Oct 22, 1985.

Fastest "Round the Board"

The record time for going round the board clockwise in "doubles" at arm's length is 9.2 sec by Dennis Gower at the Millers Arms, Hastings, England on Oct 12, 1975 and 14.5 sec in numerical order by Jim Pike (1903–60) at the Craven Club, Newmarket, England in March 1944. The record for this feat at the 9-ft throwing distance, retrieving own darts, is 2 min 13 sec by Bill Duddy (b Sept 29, 1932) at The Plough, Harringey, London, England on Oct 29, 1972.

Lowest Possible Scores

Scores of 201 in four darts, 301 in six darts, 401 in seven darts and 501 in nine darts, have been achieved on numerous occasions. The lowest number of darts thrown for a score of 1,001 is 19 by Cliff Inglis (b 1935) (160, 180, 140, 180, 121, 180, 40) at the Bromfield Men's Club, Devon, England on Nov 11, 1975.

MAJOR DARTS TITLE WINNER: John Lowe (GB) is the only man to have won all 4 major world titles: Masters, Pro, Cup Singles and "News of the World" tournaments. (Syndication Intl.)

Linda Batten (b Nov 26, 1954) set a women's 3,001 record of 117 darts at Enfield, Eng, Apr 2, 1986.

A score of 3,001 in 75 darts was thrown by Mike Gregory (GB) (b Dec 16, 1956) at the Stones Cross Hotel, Norton, Eng in Sept 1985.

MARBLES

Origins

Marbles may have been a children's game in ancient Egypt. It was introduced into Britain by the Romans in the 1st century AD and became a competitive sport under the British Marbles Board of Control in 1926.

Most Championships

The British Championship (established 1926) has been won most often by the Toucan Terribles with 20 consecutive titles (1956–75). Three founder members, Len Smith, Jack and Charlie Dempsey, played in every title win. They were finally beaten in 1976 by the Pernod Rams, captained by Len Smith's son, Paul. Len Smith (b Oct 13, 1917) has won the indi-

vidual title 15 times (1957–64, 1966, 1968–73) but lost in 1974 to his son Alan.

Speed Record

The record for clearing the ring (between 5¾ and 6¼ ft in diameter) of 49 marbles is 2 min 57 sec by the Toucan Terribles at Worthing, West Sussex, Eng, in 1971.

MONOPOLY®

The patentee of Monopoly, the world's most popular proprietary board game of which Parker Brothers has sold in excess of 80 million copies, was Charles Darrow (1889–1967). He invented the patented version of the game in 1933, while an unemployed heating engineer, using the street names of Atlantic City, NJ, where he spent his vacations.

Marathon

The longest game by four players ratified by Parker Brothers is 660 hours by Caara Fritz, Randy Smith, Phil Bennett, and Terry Sweatt in Atlanta, Ga July 12–Aug 8, 1981.

POKER

In the 1983 World Series of Poker held in Las Vegas, Nev, Tom McEvoy, a former Mich accountant, topped 107 other contestants, and with a $100 buy-in won the $540,000 top prize.

Joe Marquis dealt for 109 hours in a 7-card stud game at the Nevada Club in Laughlin, Nev, July 5–9, 1985, for the longest poker game on record.

LONGEST POKER GAME DEALER: Joe Marquis, Jr., of Del Webb's Nevada Club, Laughlin, Nev, dealt for 109 hours nonstop in July 1985 for an endurance record.

POOL AND BILLIARDS

Pool

Pool or championship pocket billiards with numbered balls began to become standardized *c.* 1890. The greatest exponents were Ralph Greenleaf (US) (1899–1950), who won the "world" professional title 19 times (1919–1937), and "Willie" Mosconi (US) (b June 27, 1913), who dominated the game from 1941 to 1957.

Michael Eufemia holds the record for the greatest continuous run in a straight pool match, pocketing 625 balls without a miss on Feb 2, 1960 before a large crowd at Logan's Billiard Academy, Brooklyn, NY.

The greatest number of balls to be pocketed in 24 hours is 15,780 by Vic Elliott at the Royal George, Lincoln, Eng, Apr 2–3, 1985.

The record time for pocketing all 15 balls in a speed competition is 40.06 sec by Ross McInnes (b Jan 19, 1955) at Clacton, Essex, Eng on Sept 11, 1983.

The longest game is 300 hours 16 min by Barry Wicks and Derek Shaw; also by Paul Haslam and Vincent Moore; all at the New Inn, Galgate, Lancaster, Eng, May 21–June 2, 1984. A claim of 384 hours 3 min in Eng in Aug 1984 has not been verified because of discrepancies in rest break times.

3-Cushion Billiards

This pocketless variation dates back to 1878. The world governing body, *Union Mondiale de Billiard*, was formed in 1928. The most successful exponent, 1906–52, was William F. Hoppe (1887–1959), who won 51 billiards championships in all forms between 1906 and 1952. The most UMB titles have been won by Raymond Ceulemans (Belgium) (b July 12, 1935) with 19 (1963–66, 1968–73, 1975–81, 83, 85).

ROULETTE

Longest Run

The longest run in an ungaffed (*i.e.* true) wheel reliably recorded is six successive coups (in No. 10) at El San Juan Hotel, Puerto Rico, July 9, 1959. The odds with a double zero were 3,010,936,383 to 1 or 1 in 38^6. The longest "marathon" on record is one of 31 days from Apr 10 to May 11, 1970, at The Casino de Macao, to test the validity or invalidity of certain contentions in 20,000 spins.

POOL ON TV: The new game of "7-Ball Pool" is attracting audiences, not only in America, but also in Italy and Australia. Willie Mosconi (right) came out of retirement to meet the challenge of Minnesota Fats (left) at 7-Ball, the game invented by William D. Cayton (center).

SCRABBLE® CROSSWORD GAME

The crossword game was invented by Alfred M. Butts in 1931 and was developed, refined and trademarked as Scrabble Crossword Game by James Brunot in 1948. He sold the North American rights to Selchow & Righter Company, NY, the European rights to J. W. Spear & Sons, London, and the Australian rights to Murfett Regency Pty Ltd, Melbourne.

The longest continuous run of Scrabble Crossword Games is 153 hours by Peter Finan and Neil Smith at St Anselm's College, Merseyside, Eng, Aug 18–24, 1984. Ken Cardozo (GB) played for 155 hours 48 min against various opponents Dec 5–11, 1984, at "Perfect Pizza," Fulham, Eng.

TABLE SOCCER

A marathon record of 62 hours 7 min was set by Paul Chambers and Timothy Peters in Hull, Eng, Oct 27–29, 1986.

Twin Galaxies crowned 3 "Players of the Year" for 1985 in a contest on Dynamo Soccer Tables in Salt Lake City, U, June 28–30. Best goalie: Mike Bowers of Denver, Colo, who registered 77% on blocking and 69% on clearing. Best forward: Tony Bacon of Seattle, Wash, who registered 62% on passing and 43% on scoring. Fastest shot: John Morgan of Salt Lake City, who achieved a speed of 28.22 mph measured by electronic equipment.

THROWING

In boomerang throwing, two new records were set in 1986. The longest distance for throw-and-return was 396.98 ft (121 m) achieved by Christian Jabet (France) on Apr 5, 1986 near Lyon, France. Dr. Larry Ruhf (US) set a record of 2 min 31 sec for keeping a boomerang aloft in a throw-and-catch contest in Catskill, NY, sponsored by the US Boomerang Assoc and Palenville Interarts, Inc.

The greatest distance any inert object heavier than air has been thrown is 1,298 ft (433 yd) in the case of the Skyro flying ring by Tom McRann (b Jan 17, 1950) of Menlo Park, Calif on May 21, 1986 at Great America Park, Santa Clara, Calif.

In Frisbee (flying disc) throwing. Don Cain of East Brunswick, NJ set the record for maximum time aloft by keeping a flying disc in the air for 16.72 sec in Phila, Pa, on May 26, 1984. For women, the time-aloft record is 11.47 sec, set in Sonoma, Calif, by Denise Garfield on Oct 5, 1980.

The greatest distance achieved for throwing a flying disc, running, and catching it is 272.6 ft by Steve Bentley on Apr 8, 1982, at Sacramento, Calif. The women's record is 196.9 ft by Judy Horowitz of NYC on June 29, 1985 at LaMirada, Calif.

FLYING DISC RECORD: Don Cain of East Brunswick, NJ, shows how he sent off the disc that stayed aloft a record 16.72 sec on May 26, 1984. (Photo by Michael Chianese)

FASTEST DISC THROW: Alan Bonopane holds the record for tossing a Frisbee—74 mph—and for throwing discs for 250 mi in 24 hours with his partner Dan Roddick. (Donnell A. Tate Photography)

The world record for outdoor distance is 550.8 ft by Frank Aquilera of LaPuente, Calif at Las Vegas, Nev, Feb 4, 1984. The indoor distance record is held by Van Miller of Tempe, Ariz, with a 399-ft toss at Flagstaff, Ariz, on Sept 18, 1982.

Liz Reeves holds the women's outdoor distance record (401.5 ft, set in Surrey, England, June 14, 1980), while the women's indoor distance record belongs to Suzanne Fields, of Boston, who threw 229.6 ft in Cedar Falls, Iowa, Apr 26, 1981.

The 24-hour group distance record is 428.02 miles set in Vernon, Conn, by the South Windsor Ultimate Frisbee disc Team, July 8–9, 1977. Dan Roddick and Alan Bonopane of Pasadena, Calif, hold the outdoor world record for 24-hour pair distance with 250.02 miles, Dec 30–31, 1979. Jamie Knerr and Keith Biery set the indoor 24-hour pair distance mark with 298.37 miles, Aug 14–15, 1982, at Allentown, Pa.

The Prince George's Community College Flying High Club set the group marathon mark with 1,198 hours, June 1–July 22, 1983. The two-person marathon record is held by Jamie Knerr and Keith Biery, who played 110 hours 40 min in Allentown, Pa, Aug 23–27, 1981.

Alan Bonopane threw a professional model Frisbee disc at a speed of 74 mph and his teammate Tim Selinske made a clean catch of the throw on Aug 25, 1980 in San Marino, Calif.

TWISTER

Twister is played on a mat of 24 colored dots. Players place their hands and feet on the dots and move them to other dots according to the results of an arrow spun on a board. As hands and feet become twisted, players fall and are eliminated. The last one to remain on all fours is the winner.

Mass Twister games are played with contestants starting with three players per mat and consolidating as some are eliminated. The record for the greatest number of participants in one game was set on Apr 19, 1986 by 4,034 students at the State Univ of NY at Albany. The winner was Jennifer Ratcliff of Wellesley, Mass.

GLIDING

Humans have sought to emulate the birds from early times, and the first successful "glider pilot" may well have been the mythical Daedalus, of Athens, who made wings for himself and his son Icarus to escape captivity. Icarus soared too near the sun and melted the wax with which the wings were fastened, but according to legend his father flew from Crete to

Sicily. Evidence has been found by Isadore William Deiches that gliders were used in ancient Egypt, c. 2500–1500 BC. In Italy, about 1500 AD Leonardo da Vinci defined the difference between gliding and powered flight in some drawings, and at the same period Danti of Perugia, an Italian mathematician, is said to have actually flown.

Emanuel Swedenborg (1688–1772) of Sweden made sketches of gliders c. 1714. The earliest man-carrying glider was designed by Sir George Cayley (1773–1857) and carried his coachman (possibly John Appleby) about 500 yd across a valley in Brompton Dale, Yorkshire, England, in the summer

HANG GLIDER taking off down a runway.

SELECTED SOARING WORLD RECORDS (SINGLE-SEATERS)

DISTANCE
> 907.7 miles   Hans-Werner Grosse (W Germany) in an ASW-12 on Apr 25, 1972, from Lübeck to Biarritz.

DECLARED GOAL FLIGHT
> 779.4 miles   Bruce Drake, David Speight, S. H. "Dick" Georgeson (all NZ) all in Nimbus 2s, from Te Anau to Te Araroa, Jan 14, 1978.

ABSOLUTE ALTITUDE
> 46,267 ft   Paul F. Bikle, Jr (US) in a Schweizer SGS 1-23E over Mojave, Calif (released at 3,963 feet) on Feb 25, 1961 (also record altitude gain—42,303 ft).

> (women)   41,460 ft   Sabrina Jackintell (US) in an Astir CS Feb 14, 1979.

GOAL AND RETURN
> 1,023.4 miles   Tom Knauff (US) in a Nimbus 3 from Williamsport, Pa, to Knoxville, Tenn on April 25, 1983.

SPEED OVER TRIANGULAR COURSE

100 km	121.36 mph	Ingo Renner (Australia) in a Nimbus 3 on Dec 14, 1982.
300 km	98.59 mph	Hans-Werner Grosse (W Germany) in an ASW-17 over Australia on Dec 24, 1980.
500 km	99.20 mph	Hans-Werner Grosse (W Germany) in an ASW-22 on Dec 20, 1983.
750 km	89.25 mph	Hans-Werner Grosse (W Germany) in an ASW-17 over Australia, on Jan 6, 1982.
1,000 km	90.32 mph	Hans-Werner Grosse (W Germany) in an ASW-17 over Australia, on Jan 3, 1979.
1,250 km	82.79 mph	Hans-Werner Grosse (W Germany) in an ASW-17 over Australia, on Dec 9, 1980.

of 1853. Gliders now attain speeds claimed at over 200 mph.

Most World Titles

The most world individual championships (instituted 1948) won is 3 by Helmut Reichmann (b 1942) (W Germany) in 1970, 74 and 78; and Douglas George Lee (b Nov 7, 1945) (GB) in 1976, 78 and 81.

The women's single-seater world record for absolute altitude is 41,449 ft by Sabrina Jackintell (US) in an Astir GS on Feb 14, 1979.

HANG GLIDING

In the 11th century, the monk Eilmer is reported to have flown from the 60-ft-tall tower of Malmesbury Abbey, Wiltshire, England. The earliest modern pioneer was Otto Lilienthal (1848–96) of Germany who made about 2,500 flights in gliders of his own construction between 1891 and 1896. Professor Francis Rogallo of NASA developed a flexible "wing" in the 1950's from his research into space capsule re-entries.

The official FAI record for the farthest distance covered is 186.80 mi by John Pendry (GB) in an Airwave Magic 3, Horseshoe Meadows, Owens Valley, Calif, to Summit Mt, Monitor Range, Nev in July 1983.

The official FAI height gain record in a flexible-wing glider is 14,250 ft by Larry Tudor (US) at Horseshoe Meadows, Calif, Aug 4, 1985. The height gain record for a flex-wing micro-light glider is 16,168 ft by Bob Calvert (GB).

For distance to declared goal Klaus Kohmstedt (W Ger) glided 140.5 mi to a record over Owens Valley, Calif on July 13, 1983. He also holds the out-and-return distance to a goal record of 107.25 mi over Owens Valley set on June 15, 1983.

The women record holders are Judy Leden (GB) for 145.34 mi distance in a straight line; Lori Judy (US) for 77.38 mi for out-and-return; Jean Little (US) for 27.99 mi for distance to declared goal over Cerro Gordo, Calif on June 15, 1983; and Page Pfieffer (US) for 10,800 ft gain of height over Owens on July 12, 1980.

John Bird piloted a hang glider from the greatest height (39,000 ft from the ground) when he was released from a hot-air balloon. He landed in Edmonton, Canada, on Aug 29, 1982, touching down 50 mi from his point of departure.

James W. Will, 37, of Honolulu stayed aloft for 34 hours over Makapuu and Waimanolo, Oahu, Hawaii, for an unofficial endurance record.

GOLF

Origins

It has been suggested that golf originated with Scottish shepherds using their crooks to knock pebbles into rabbit holes. This may be apocryphal, but somewhat firmer evidence exists. A stained glass window in Gloucester Cathedral, dating from 1350, portrays a golfer-like figure, but the earliest mention of golf occurs in a prohibiting law passed by the

GOLFING FIRSTS: The young Mary, Queen of Scots, playing golf at St Andrews in 1563, following in the footsteps of her grandfather, James IV, who was the first golfer in history that we know by name. She was accused of playing golf only a few days after her husband's death.

Scottish Parliament in March 1457, under which "golff be utterly cryit doune and not usit."

The Romans had a cognate game called *paganica,* which may have been carried to Britain before 400 AD. The Chinese National Golf Association claims the game is of Chinese origin ("*Ch'ui Wan*—the ball-hitting game") from the 3rd or 2nd century BC. There were official ordinances prohibiting a ball game with clubs in Belgium and Holland from 1360. Gutta-percha balls succeeded feather balls in 1848, and were in turn succeeded in 1902 by rubber-cored balls, invented in 1899 by Coburn Haskell (US). Steel shafts were authorized in the US in 1925.

Golf was first played on the moon in Feb 1971 by Capt Alan Shepard (US), commander of the Apollo XIV spacecraft.

Oldest Clubs

The oldest club of which there is written evidence is the Gentleman Golfers (now the Honourable Company of Edinburgh Golfers) formed in March 1744—10 years prior to the institution of the Royal and Ancient Club of St Andrews, Fife, Scotland.

However, the Royal Burgess Golfing Society of Edinburgh claim to have been founded in 1735. The oldest existing club in North America is the Royal Montreal Club (Nov 1873) and the oldest in the US is St Andrews, Westchester County, NY (1888). An older claim is by the Foxbury Country Club, Clarion County, Pa (1887).

Longest Course

The world's longest course is the par-77, 8,325-yd International GC, Bolton, Mass, from the "Tiger" tees, remodeled in 1969 by Robert Trent Jones.

Highest and Lowest Courses

The highest golf course in the world is the Tuctu Golf Club in Morococha, Peru, which is 14,335 ft above sea level at its lowest point. Golf has, however, been played in Tibet at an altitude of over 16,000 ft.

The lowest golf course in the world was that of the now defunct Sodom and Gomorrah Golfing Society at Kallia (Qulya), on the northern shores of the Dead Sea, 1,250 ft below sea level. Currently the lowest is the par-70 Furnace Creek Golf Course, Death Valley, Calif, at a disputed average of 178–272 ft below sea level.

Biggest Bunkers

The world's biggest trap is Hell's Half Acre which stretches 200 yd across the fairway at the 585-yd 7th hole of the Pine Valley course, Clementon, NJ. Highest bunker is the 19-ft deep 115-yd-long trap along the 16th hole at the new PGA West course in Palm Springs, Calif.

Longest Hole

The longest hole in the world is the 7th hole (par 7) of 909 yd at the Sano Course, Satsuki GC, Japan.

Largest Green

Probably the largest green in the world is that of the par-6, 695-yd 5th hole at International GC, Bolton, Mass, with an area greater than 28,000 sq ft.

Lowest Scores for 9 and 18 Holes

Three professional players are recorded to have played a long course (over 6,000 yd) for a score of 57:

Bill Burke at the Normandie Golf Club, St Louis (6,389 yds, par 71) on May 20, 1970; Tom Ward at the Searcy (Ark) Country Club (6,098 yds, par 70) in 1981; Augie Navarro at the Sim Park Golf Course (Wichita, Kans) in 1982.

Alfred Edward Smith (1903–85), the English professional at Woolacombe, achieved an 18-hole score of 55 (15 under bogey 70) on his home course on Jan 1, 1936.

Nine holes in 25 (4, 3, 3, 2, 3, 3, 1, 4, 2) was recorded by A. J. "Bill" Burke in his round of 57 (32 + 25) (see above), and by teenager Douglas Beecher at the Pitman (NJ) Country Club (3,150 yd, par 35) in 1976. The tournament record is 27 by Mike Souchak (US) (b May 1927) for the second nine (par 35) first round of the 1955 Texas Open; Andy North (US) (b Mar 9, 1950) second nine (par 34), first round, 1975 BC Open at En-Joie GC, Endicott, NY; and Jose Maria Canizares (Spain) (b Feb 18, 1947), first nine, third round, in the 1978 Swiss Open on the 6,811-yd Crans-Sur course, and by Robert Lee (GB) (b Oct 12, 1961) first nine, first round, in the Monte Carlo Open on the 6,249 yd Mont Agel course on June 28, 1985.

The US PGA tournament record for 18 holes is 59 (30 + 29) by Al Geiberger (b Sept 1, 1937) in the sec-

RECORDS IN THE 20's: Walter Hagen (US) blasting from a bunker at the 17th green at Holylake in the 1923 British Open. He did not win that year but he did win that event 4 times, the US Open twice and the PGA 5 times. (Radio Times—Hulton)

SURPRISE WINNERS: Playing as an amateur, Bobby Jones (left) won his first of 4 US Opens in 1923 when he was 21 years old. Bernhard Langer of W Germany surprisingly won the US Masters in 1985, one of only 6 times in its 51-year history that a non-American has won this tournament.

ON COURSE: "SLAMMIN' " Sam Snead (left) carded a 59 for 18 holes and 122 for 36 in the 1959 Greenbrier Open. Snead has been credited with 134 tournament victories since 1934. Mickey Wright (below) celebrates her record-tying 4th US Women's Open title. Her 62 is the all-time women's best for a full-size 18-hole course.

MOST WINS IN MAJOR TOURNAMENTS

US Open	Willie Anderson (1880–1910)	4	1901–03–04–05
	Robert Tyre Jones, Jr (1902–71)	4	1923–26–29–30
	W. Ben Hogan (b Aug 13, 1912)	4	1948–50–51–53
	Jack William Nicklaus (b Jan 21, 1940)	4	1962–67–72–80
US Amateur	R. T. Jones, Jr	5	1924–25–27–28–30
British Open	Harry Vardon (1870–1937)	6	1896–98–99, 1903–11–14
British Amateur	John Ball (1861–1940)	8	1888–90–92–94–99, 1907–10–12
PGA Championship (US)	Walter C. Hagen (1892–1969)	5	1921–24–25–26–27
	Jack W. Nicklaus	5	1963–71–73–75–80
Masters Championship (US)	Jack W. Nicklaus	6	1963–65–66–72–75–86
US Women's Open	Elizabeth (Betsy) Earle-Rawls (b May 4, 1928)	4	1951–53–57–60
	"Mickey" Wright (b Feb 14, 1935)	4	1958–59–61–64
US Women's Amateur	Mrs Glenna Vare (*née* Collett) (b June 20, 1903)	6	1922–25–28–29–30–35

ond round of the Danny Thomas Classic, on the 72-par, 7,249-yd Colonial CC course, Memphis, Tenn, June 10, 1977.

In non-PGA tournaments, Samuel Jackson Snead (b May 27, 1912) had 59 in the Greenbrier Open (now called the Sam Snead Festival), at White Sulphur Springs, W Va, on May 16, 1959; Gary Player (South Africa) (b Nov 1, 1935) carded 59 in the second round of the Brazilian Open in Rio de Janeiro on Nov 29, 1974; and David Jagger (GB) also had 59 in a Pro-Am tournament prior to the 1973 Nigerian Open at Ikoyi Golf Club, Lagos.

Women's Lowest Scores

The lowest recorded score on an 18-hole course (over 6,000 yd) for a woman is 62 (30 + 32) by Mary (Mickey) Kathryn Wright (b Feb 14, 1935), of Dallas, on the Hogan Park Course (6,286 yd) at Midland, Tex, in Nov 1964.

Wanda Morgan (b March 22, 1910) recorded a score of 60 (31 + 29) on the Westgate and Birchington Golf Club course, Kent, England, over 18 holes (5,002 yd) on July 11, 1929.

HIGHEST EARNINGS: Besides winning 20 major tournaments (71 in all) for a record, Jack Nicklaus (right) has earned more than $4,800,000 in prize money. Nicklaus is the only golfer who has won all 5 major titles twice. (E. D. Lacey) Arnold Palmer (below) prepares to putt as his many followers, known as Arnie's Army, look on. Palmer won the Masters 4 times and played on 6 winning teams in World Cup play. He was the first golfer to reach $1 million in career earnings.

MOST TOURNAMENT VICTORIES: Byron Nelson (left) in 1945 won 18 tournaments (plus one unofficial), including 11 in a row. He might have won more, but the Masters and the British and US Opens were not contested during the war years. Kathy Whitworth (center) has won 88 LPGA contests in 23 touring years through 1985. BIGGEST PRIZE WINNER: Johnny Miller (right) captured the $500,000 prize offered by Sun City, a course in an enclave in S Africa in 1982, after a playoff against Severiano Ballesteros of Spain (opposite).

The LPGA record for 9 holes is held by Pat Bradley who scored 28 in Denver, Colo, Aug 24, 1984.

Lowest Scores for 36 Holes

The record for 36 holes is 122 (59 + 63) by Sam Snead in the 1959 Greenbrier Open (now called the Sam Snead Festival) (non-PGA) (see above), May 16–17, 1959. Horton Smith (see below) scored 121 (63 + 58) on a short course on Dec 21, 1928.

Floyd Satterlee Rood used the entire United States as a course, when he played from the Pacific surf to the Atlantic surf from Sept 14, 1963 to Oct 3, 1964 in 114,737 strokes. He lost 3,511 balls on the 3,397.7 mi-trail.

Lowest Scores for 72 Holes

The lowest recorded score on a first-class course is 255 (29 under par) by Leonard Peter Tupling (b Apr 6, 1950) (GB) in the Nigerian Open at Ikoyi Golf Club, Lagos, in Feb 1981, made up of 63, 66, 62 and 64 (average 63.75 per round). Horton Smith (1908–63), twice US Masters Champion, scored 245 (63, 58, 61 and 63) for 72 holes on the 4,700-yd course (par 64) at Catalina Country Club, Calif, to win the Catalina Open, Dec 21–23, 1928.

The lowest 72 holes in a US professional event is 257 (60, 68, 64 and 65) by Mike Souchak in the 1955 Texas Open at San Antonio.

The lowest 72 holes in an Open championship in Europe is 262 by Percy Alliss (1897–1975) of Britain, with 67, 66, 66 and 63 in the Italian Open Championship at San Remo in 1932, and by Lu Liang Huan (b Dec 10, 1935) (Taiwan) in the 1971 French Open at Biarritz. Kelvin D. G. Nagle (b Dec 21, 1920) of Australia shot 261 in the Hong Kong Open in 1961.

Lowest Score with One Club

Playing only with a 6-iron, Thad Daber of Durham, NC, won the 1985 World One Club Championship with a record score of 73 on the 6,037-yd Lochmere Golf Club course in Cary, NC on Nov 10, 1985, against 142 other contenders. He beat the previous record set in 1982 by Terry Beardsley, a pro at Franklin, Wis by 3 strokes.

Longest Drive

In long-driving contests 330 yd is rarely surpassed at sea level.

In officially regulated long-driving contests over level ground the greatest distance recorded is 392 yd by Tommie Campbell (b July 24, 1927) (Foxrock

LEADING PROS: Severiano Ballesteros (Spain) (left) began winning major tournaments in 1979 when he was victorious in the British Open. Then he won the Masters in 1980 and 1983, and the British Open again in 1984. Here he is preparing to enter the water to retrieve an errant shot. (Phil Sheldon) Nancy Lopez (center) in 1985 set a season record by winning $416,472, only to be beaten in 1986 by Pat Bradley (right) who earned $489,749 in tournament play. Bradley shot a record 28 for 9 holes in 1984. (Lopez photo by All-Sport; Bradley photo LPGA by SPORTSELL)

Golf Club), a member of the Irish PGA, made at Dun Laoghaire, Co Dublin, in July 1964.

The USPGA record is 341 yd by Jack William Nicklaus (b Columbus, Ohio, Jan 21, 1940), then weighing 206 lb, in July 1963.

In an official PGA long-driving contest at 5,200-ft altitude in Denver, Colo, at the John F. Kennedy Golf Course, on a clear day with a slight wind against him, Jack L. Hamm of Denver drove a ball 406 yd on July 12, 1986. The contest required the drive to land on a 40-ft wide fairway.

Liam Higgins (Ireland) drove a Spalding Top Flite ball 634.1 yd on an airport runway at Baldonnel Military Airport, Dublin, Ireland, Sept 25, 1984.

The longest on an ordinary course is 515 yd by Michael Hoke Austin (b Feb 17, 1910) of Los Angeles, in the US National Seniors Open Championship at Las Vegas, Nev, Sept 25, 1974. Aided by an

LONGEST DRIVE: Ireland's Tommie Campbell (right) holds the world record with the distance of 392 yards in Dublin in 1964.

estimated 35-mph tailwind, the 6-ft-2-in 210-lb golfer drove the ball on the fly to within a yard of the green on the par-4, 450-yd 5th hole of the Winterwood Course. The ball rolled 65 yd past the flagstick.

Arthur Lynskey claimed a drive of 200 yd out and 2 miles down off Pikes Peak, Colo, (14,110 ft) June 28, 1968.

A drive of 2,640 yd (1½ miles) across ice was achieved by an Australian meteorologist named Nils Lied at Mawson Base, Antarctica, in 1962. On the moon, the energy expended on a mundane 300-yd drive would achieve, craters permitting, a distance of a mile.

Longest Hitter

The golfer regarded as the longest consistent hitter the game has ever known is the 6-ft-5-in-tall, 230-lb George Bayer (US) (b Sept 17, 1925), the 1957 Canadian Open Champion. His longest measured drive was one of 420 yd at the fourth in the Las Vegas Invitational in 1953. It was measured as a precaution against litigation since the ball struck a spectator. Bayer also drove a ball pin high on a 426-yd hole in Tucson, Ariz. Radar measurements show that an 87-mph impact velocity for a golf ball falls to 46 mph in 3.0 sec.

Biggest Winning Margin

The greatest margin of victory in a major tournament is 21 strokes by Jerry Pate (b Sept 15, 1953) (US) in the Colombian Open with 262 on Dec 10–13, 1981.

Cecilia Leitch won the Canadian Ladies Open Championship in 1921 by the highest margin for a major title, 17 up and 15 to play.

Most Tournament Wins

The record for winning tournaments in a single season is 18 (plus one unofficial), including a record 11 consecutively, by Byron Nelson (b Feb 4, 1912) (US), March 8–Aug 4, 1945.

Sam Snead has won 84 official USPGA tour events to Dec 1979, and has been credited with a total 134 tournament victories since 1934.

Kathy Whitworth (b Sept 27, 1939) (US) topped this with her 88th LPGA victory through 1985, her 23rd year on the tour. Mickey Wright (US) won a record 13 tournaments in one year, 1963.

Jack Nicklaus (US) is the only golfer who has won all five major titles (British Open, US Open, Masters, PGA and US Amateur) twice, while setting a record

LONGEST PUTT: Cary Middlecoff holed an 86-foot putt on the 13th green at the Augusta National, Georgia, in 1955. The record putt helped him to win the Masters.

total of 20 major tournament victories (1959–86). His remarkable record in the US Open is 4 firsts, 8 seconds and 2 thirds. Nicklaus has accumulated 71 PGA tournament wins in all.

In 1930 Bobby Jones achieved a unique "Grand Slam" of the US and British Open and British and US Amateur titles.

Longest Putt

The longest recorded holed putt in a major tournament was one of 86 ft on the vast 13th green at the Augusta National, Ga, by Cary Middlecoff (b Jan 1921) in the 1955 Masters Tournament.

Bobby Jones was reputed to have holed a putt in excess of 100 ft on the 5th green in the first round of the 1927 British Open at St Andrews, Scotland.

Bob Cook (US) sank a putt measured at 140 ft 2¾ in on the 18th at St Andrew's, Scotland, in the International Fourball Pro-Am Tournament on Oct. 1, 1976.

Highest Earnings

The greatest amount ever won in official US PGA golf prizes is $4,857,494 by Jack Nicklaus through May 1986.

The record for a year in US PGA events is $653,296 by Greg Norman (Aust) in 1986. His worldwide earnings were over $1 million.

The highest LPGA career earnings by a woman is $2,283,946 by Pat Bradley (b Mar 24, 1951) through 1986, a year in which she set a season record of $489,749, beating Nancy Lopez' 1985 winnings of $416,472.

US Open

This championship was inaugurated in 1895. The lowest 72-hole aggregate is 272 (63, 71, 70, 68) by Jack Nicklaus on the Lower Course (7,015 yd) at Baltusrol Golf Club, Springfield, NJ, June 12–15, 1980. The lowest score for 18 holes is 63 by Johnny Miller (b Apr 29, 1947) of Calif on the 6,921-yd, par-71 Oakmont, Pa, course on June 17, 1973, and Jack Nicklaus and Tom Weiskopf (b Nov 9, 1942), both on June 12, 1980.

The winners:

		Score
1895	Horace Rawlins	173
1896	James Foulis	152
1897	Joe Lloyd	162
1898	Fred Herd	328
1899	Willie Smith	315
1900	Harry Vardon (GB)	313
1901	Willie Anderson	331
1902	Laurie Auchterlonie	307
1903	Willie Anderson	307
1904	Willie Anderson	303
1905	Willie Anderson	314
1906	Alex Smith	295
1907	Alex Ross	302
1908	Fred McLeod	322
1909	George Sargent	290
1910	Alex Smith	298
1911	John McDermott	307
1912	John McDermott	294
1913	Francis Ouimet	304
1914	Walter Hagen	290
1915	Jerome Travers	297
1916	Charles Evans, Jr	286
1919	Walter Hagen	301
1920	Edward Ray (GB)	295
1921	Jim Barnes	289
1922	Gene Sarazen	288
1923	Robert T. Jones, Jr	296
1924	Cyril Walker	297
1925	Willie Macfarlane	291
1926	Robert T. Jones, Jr	293
1927	Tommy Armour	301
1928	Johnny Farrell	294
1929	Robert T. Jones, Jr	294
1930	Robert T. Jones, Jr	287
1931	Billy Burke	292
1932	Gene Sarazen	286
1933	John Goodman	287
1934	Olin Dutra	293
1935	Sam Parks, Jr	299
1936	Tony Manero	282
1937	Ralph Guldahl	281
1938	Ralph Guldahl	284
1939	Byron Nelson	284
1940	Lawson Little	287
1941	Craig Wood	284
1946	Lloyd Mangrum	284
1947	Lew Worsham	282
1948	Ben Hogan	276

1949	Cary Middlecoff	286
1950	Ben Hogan	287
1951	Ben Hogan	287
1952	Julius Boros	281
1953	Ben Hogan	283
1954	Ed Furgol	284
1955	Jack Fleck	287
1956	Cary Middlecoff	281
1957	Dick Mayer	282
1958	Tommy Bolt	283
1959	Billy Casper	282
1960	Arnold Palmer	280
1961	Gene Littler	281
1962	Jack Nicklaus	283
1963	Julius Boros	293
1964	Ken Venturi	278
1965	Gary Player (S Afr)	282
1966	Billy Casper	278
1967	Jack Nicklaus	275
1968	Lee Trevino	275
1969	Orville Moody	281
1970	Tony Jacklin (GB)	281
1971	Lee Trevino	280
1972	Jack Nicklaus	290
1973	Johnny Miller	279
1974	Hale Irwin	287
1975	Lou Graham	287
1976	Jerry Pate	277
1977	Hubert Green	278
1978	Andy North	285
1979	Hale Irwin	284
1980	Jack Nicklaus	272
1981	David Graham (Aust)	273
1982	Tom Watson	282
1983	Larry Nelson	280
1984	Fuzzy Zoeller	276
1985	Andy North	279
1986	Ray Floyd	279

The longest delayed result in any national open championship occurred in the 1931 US Open at Toledo, Ohio. George von Elm (1901–61) and Bill Burke (1902–72) tied at 292, then tied the first replay at 149. Burke won the second replay by a single stroke after 72 extra holes.

Youngest and Oldest Champions

The youngest winner of the British Open was Tom Morris, Jr (1851–75) at Prestwick, Ayrshire, Scotland, in 1868, aged 17 years 249 days. The oldest British Open champion was "Old Tom" Morris (1821–1908) who was aged 46 years 99 days when he won in 1867. In modern times, the oldest was 1967 champion Roberto de Vicenzo (Argentina), when aged 44 years 93 days.

The oldest US Amateur Champion was Jack Westland (b Dec 14, 1904) at Seattle, Wash, on Aug 23, 1952, aged 47 years 253 days. The oldest US Open Champion was Raymond Floyd at 43 years 284 days on June 15, 1986. Isabella "Belle" Robertson (b Apr 11, 1936) won the 1986 Scottish Women's Championship aged 50 years 43 days.

US Masters

The lowest score in the US Masters (instituted at the 6,980-yd Augusta National Golf Course, Ga, in 1934) was 271 by Jack Nicklaus in 1965 and Raymond Floyd (b Sept 4, 1942) in 1976. Jack Nicklaus has won most often—6 times. The lowest round is 63 by Nick Price (b Jan 28, 1957) (Zimbabwe) in 1986. The oldest champion was Jack Nicklaus at 46 years 114 days in 1986, and the youngest was Severiano Ballesteros (Spain) aged 23 years 4 days in 1980.

The winners:

	Score
1934 Horton Smith	284
1935 Gene Sarazen	282
1936 Horton Smith	285
1937 Byron Nelson	283
1938 Henry Picard	285
1939 Ralph Gudahl	279
1940 Jimmy Demaret	280
1941 Craig Wood	280
1942 Byron Nelson	280
1946 Herman Keiser	282
1947 Jimmy Demaret	281
1948 Claude Harmon	279
1949 Sam Snead	282
1950 Jimmy Demaret	283
1951 Ben Hogan	280
1952 Sam Snead	286
1953 Ben Hogan	274
1954 Sam Snead	289
1955 Cary Middlecoff	279
1956 Jack Burke	289
1957 Doug Ford	283
1958 Arnold Palmer	284
1959 Art Wall	284
1960 Arnold Palmer	282
1961 Gary Player (S Afr)	280
1962 Arnold Palmer	280
1963 Jack Nicklaus	286
1964 Arnold Palmer	276
1965 Jack Nicklaus	271
1966 Jack Nicklaus	288
1967 Gay Brewer	280
1968 Bob Goalby	277
1969 George Archer	281
1970 Billy Casper	279
1971 Charles Coody	279
1972 Jack Nicklaus	286
1973 Tommy Aaron	283
1974 Gary Player (S Afr)	278
1975 Jack Nicklaus	276
1976 Ray Floyd	271
1977 Tom Watson	276
1978 Gary Player (S Afr)	277
1979 Fuzzy Zoeller	280
1980 Severiano Ballesteros (Spain)	275
1981 Tom Watson	280
1982 Craig Stadler	284
1983 Severiano Ballesteros (Spain)	280
1984 Ben Crenshaw	277
1985 Bernhard Langer (W Ger)	282
1986 Jack Nicklaus	279

British Open

The Open Championship was inaugurated in 1860 at Prestwick, Strathclyde, Scotland. The lowest score for 9 holes is 28 by Denis Durnian (b June 30, 1950) at Royal Birdale, Southport, Eng, in the second round on July 15, 1983.

The lowest scoring round in the Open itself is 63 by Mark Hayes (US, b July 12, 1949) at Turnberry, Strathclyde, Scotland, in the second round on July 7, 1977, and by Isao Aoki (Japan) (b Aug 31, 1942) in the third round at Muirfield, July 19, 1980. Greg Norman (Aust) equaled the record of 63 at Turnberry, July 18, 1986. Henry Cotton (GB) at Royal St George's, Sandwich, Kent, England, completed the first 36 holes in 132 (67 + 65) on June 27, 1934.

The lowest 72-hole aggregate is 268 (68, 70, 65, 65) by Tom Watson (US) (b Sept 4, 1949) at Turnberry, Scotland, ending on July 9, 1977.

The winners:

	Score
1860 Willie Park, Sr	174
1861 Tom Morris, Sr	163
1862 Tom Morris, Sr	163
1863 Willie Park, Sr	168
1864 Tom Morris, Sr	167
1865 Andrew Strath	162
1866 Willie Park, Sr	167
1867 Tom Morris, Sr	170
1868 Tom Morris, Jr	170
1869 Tom Morris, Jr	154
1870 Tom Morris, Jr	149
1871 Not held	
1872 Tom Morris, Jr	166
1873 Tom Kidd	179
1874 Mungo Park	159
1875 Willie Park, Sr	166
1876 Robert Martin	176
1877 Jamie Anderson	160
1878 Jamie Anderson	157
1879 Jamie Anderson	170
1880 Robert Ferguson	162
1881 Robert Ferguson	170
1882 Robert Ferguson	171
1883 Willie Fernie	159
1884 Jack Simpson	160
1885 Bob Martin	171
1886 David Brown	157
1887 Willie Park, Jr	161
1888 Jack Burns	171
1889 Willie Park, Jr	155
1890 John Ball	164
1891 Hugh Kirkaldy	169
1892 Harold Hilton	305
1893 William Auchterlonie	322
1894 John Taylor	326
1895 John Taylor	322
1896 Harry Vardon	316
1897 Harry Hilton	314
1898 Harry Vardon	307
1899 Harry Vardon	310
1900 John Taylor	309
1901 James Braid	309
1902 Alexander Herd	307
1903 Harry Vardon	300
1904 Jack White	296

1905 James Braid	318
1906 James Braid	300
1907 Arnaud Massy (France)	312
1908 James Braid	291
1909 John Taylor	295
1910 James Braid	299
1911 Harry Vardon	303
1912 Edward (Ted) Ray	295
1913 John Taylor	304
1914 Harry Vardon	306
1920 George Duncan	303
1921 Jock Hutchinson (US)	296
1922 Walter Hagen (US)	300
1923 Arthur Havers	295
1924 Walter Hagen (US)	301
1925 James Barnes (US)	300
1926 Robert T. Jones, Jr (US)	291
1927 Robert T. Jones, Jr (US)	285
1928 Walter Hagen (US)	292
1929 Walter Hagen (US)	292
1930 Robert T. Jones, Jr (US)	291
1931 Tommy Armour (US)	296
1932 Gene Sarazen (US)	283
1933 Denny Shute (US)	292
1934 Henry Cotton	283
1935 Alfred Perry	283
1936 Alfred Padgham	287
1937 Henry Cotton	283
1938 Reg Whitcombe	295
1939 Richard Burton	290
1946 Sam Snead (US)	290
1947 Fred Daly	293
1948 Henry Cotton	284
1949 Bobby Locke (S Afr)	283
1950 Bobby Locke (S Afr)	279
1951 Max Faulkner	285
1952 Bobby Locke (S Afr)	287
1953 Ben Hogan (US)	282
1954 Peter Thomson (Aus)	283
1955 Peter Thomson (Aus)	281
1956 Peter Thomson (Aus)	286
1957 Bobby Locke (S Afr)	279
1958 Peter Thomson (Aus)	278
1959 Gary Player (S Afr)	284
1960 Kel Nagle (Aus)	278
1961 Arnold Palmer (US)	284
1962 Arnold Palmer (US)	276
1963 Bob Charles (NZ)	277
1964 Tony Lema (US)	279
1965 Peter Thomson (Aus)	285
1966 Jack Nicklaus (US)	282
1967 Robert de Vicenzo (Arg)	278
1968 Gary Player (S Afr)	299
1969 Tony Jacklin	280
1970 Jack Nicklaus (US)	283
1971 Lee Trevino (US)	278
1972 Lee Trevino (US)	278
1973 Tom Weiskopf (US)	276
1974 Gary Player (S Afr)	282
1975 Tom Watson (US)	279
1976 Johnny Miller (US)	279
1977 Tom Watson (US)	268
1978 Jack Nicklaus (US)	281
1979 Severiano Ballesteros (Spain)	283
1980 Tom Watson (US)	271
1981 Bill Rogers (US)	276
1982 Tom Watson (US)	284
1983 Tom Watson (US)	275
1984 Severiano Ballesteros (Spain)	276
1985 Sandy Lyle (UK)	282
1986 Greg Norman (Australia)	280

18 HOLES IN 28 MINUTES: Gary Wright played a regulation course of 6,039 yd in Queensland, Australia, in record time, waiting for the ball to stop rolling each time. His score? Don't ask.

US PGA Championship

The Professional Golfers' Association championship was first held in 1916 as a match play tournament but since 1958 it has been contested over 72 holes of stroke play. It has been won a record five times by Walter Hagen between 1921 and 1927, and Jack Nicklaus between 1963 and 1980. The oldest champion was Julius Boros at 48 years 18 days in 1968 and the youngest was Gene Sarazen aged 20 years 5 months 20 days in 1922. Since 1958 the greatest margin of victory has been the seven-stroke lead by Nicklaus in 1980. The lowest aggregate was 271 by Bobby Nichols at Columbus, Ohio in 1964, and the lowest round was 63 by Bruce Crampton in 1975 and Ray Floyd in 1982. The lowest score for 36 holes has been 131 by Hal Sutton (65, 66) in 1983. The 54-hole mark is 202 (69, 66, 67) by Raymond Floyd in 1969.

The winners:

1916 James Barnes	1937 Denny Shute
1919 James Barnes	1938 Paul Runyan
1920 Jock Hutchison	1939 Henry Picard
1921 Walter Hagen	1940 Byron Nelson
1922 Gene Sarazen	1941 Vic Ghezzi
1923 Gene Sarazen	1942 Sam Snead
1924 Walter Hagen	1943 Not held
1925 Walter Hagen	1944 Bob Hamilton
1926 Walter Hagen	1945 Byron Nelson
1927 Walter Hagen	1946 Ben Hogan
1928 Leo Diegel	1947 Jim Ferrier
1929 Leo Diegel	1948 Ben Hogan
1930 Tommy Armour	1949 Sam Snead
1931 Tom Creavy	1950 Chandler Harper
1932 Olin Dutra	1951 Sam Snead
1933 Gene Sarazen	1952 Jim Turnesa
1934 Paul Runyan	1953 Walter Burkemo
1935 Johnny Revolta	1954 Chick Harbert
1936 Denny Shute	1955 Doug Ford
	1956 Jack Burke

	Score
1957 Lionel Hebert	
1958 Dow Finsterwald	276
1959 Bob Rosburg	277
1960 Jay Hebert	281

1961 Jerry Barber	277
1962 Gary Player (S Afr)	278
1963 Jack Nicklaus	279
1964 Bob Nichols	271
1965 Dave Marr	280
1966 Al Geiberger	280
1967 Don January	281
1968 Julius Boros	281
1969 Ray Floyd	276
1970 Dave Stockton	279
1971 Jack Nicklaus	281
1972 Gary Player (S Afr)	281
1973 Jack Nicklaus	277
1974 Lee Trevino	276
1975 Jack Nicklaus	276
1976 Dave Stockton	281
1977 Lanny Wadkins	282
1978 John Mahaffey	276
1979 David Graham (Aus)	272
1980 Jack Nicklaus	274
1981 Larry Nelson	273
1982 Ray Floyd	272
1983 Hal Sutton	274
1984 Lee Trevino	273
1985 Hubert Green	278
1986 Bob Tway	276

US Amateur

Initially held in the same week and at the same venue as the first US Open in 1895. Bobby Jones won a record five times between 1924 and 1930, having first qualified for the tournament in 1916, aged 14 yr 5½ months, the youngest ever to do so. The oldest player to win the title was Jack Westland, aged 47 years 8 months 9 days in 1952, while the youngest was Robert Gardner at 19 years 5 months in 1909. (Three years later, in 1912, Gardner broke the world pole vault record becoming the first to clear 13 ft.)

The winners:

1895 Charles Macdonald	1900 Walter Travis
1896 H. J. Whigham	1901 Walter Travis
1897 H. J. Whigham	1902 Louis James
1898 Findlay Douglas	1903 Walter Travis
1899 H. M. Harriman	1904 Chandler Egan

1905 Chandler Egan	1949 Charles Coe
1906 Eben Byers	1950 Sam Urzetta
1907 Jerome Travers	1951 Billy Maxwell
1908 Jerome Travers	1952 Jack Westland
1909 Robert Gardner	1953 Gene Littler
1910 William Fownes, Jr	1954 Arnold Palmer
1911 Harold Hilton (GB)	1955 Harvie Ward
1912 Jerome Travers	1956 Harvie Ward
1913 Jerome Travers	1957 Hillman Robbins
1914 Francis Ouimet	1958 Charles Coe
1915 Robert Gardner	1959 Jack Nicklaus
1916 Charles Evans, Jr	1960 Deane Beman
1919 Davidson Herron	1961 Jack Nicklaus
1920 Charles Evans, Jr	1962 Labron Harris
1921 Jesse Gullford	1963 Deane Beman
1922 Jesse Sweetser	1964 Bill Campbell
1923 Max Marston	1965 Bob Murphy
1924 Robert T. Jones, Jr	1966 Gary Cowan (Can)
1925 Robert T. Jones, Jr	1967 Bob Dickson
1926 George Von Elm	1968 Bruce Fleisher
1927 Robert T. Jones, Jr	1969 Steve Melnyk
1928 Robert T. Jones, Jr	1970 Lanny Wadkins
1929 Harrison Johnston	1971 Gary Cowan (Can)
1930 Robert T. Jones, Jr	1972 Marvin Giles
1931 Francis Ouimet	1973 Craig Stadler
1932 Ross Somerville (Can)	1974 Jerry Pate
1933 George Dunlap, Jr	1975 Fred Ridley
1934 Lawson Little	1976 Bill Sander
1935 Lawson Little	1977 John Fought
1936 John Fisher	1978 John Cook
1937 John Goodman	1979 Mark O'Meara
1938 William Turnesa	1980 Hal Sutton
1939 Marvin Ward	1981 Nathaniel Crosby
1940 Richard Chapman	1982 Jay Sigel
1941 Marvin Ward	1983 Jay Sigel
1946 Stanley Bishop	1984 Scott Vertplank
1947 Robert Riegel	1985 Sam Randolph
1948 William Turnesa	1986 Stewart Alexander

Most Rounds in a Day

The greatest number of holes played on foot in 24 hours is 504 holes (28 rounds) by Bill Ridge (US) on June 26, 1986, at the Bob-O-Link Country Club.

Using golf carts for transport, Mark Rich Matthews played 724 holes at the 6,048-yd Rockwood Municipal Golf Course in Fort Worth, Tex, June 27–28, 1986. Terry Zachary played 391 holes in 12 hours on the 6,706-yd course at Connaught Golf Club, Alberta, Canada on June 16, 1986. Dr. R. C. "Dick" Hardison, aged 61, played 236 holes under USGA rules in 12 hours at Sea Mountain GC, Punaluu, Hawaii July 31, 1984, maintaining an average score of 76 per round, with an average time per hole of 3.05 min. His best round was a 68, achieved in 49 min 58 sec, including a second nine of 30 in 24 min 28 sec. He used seven fore caddies and 26 electric golf carts, which he drove himself.

The most holes played on foot in a week (168 hours) is 1,128 by Steve Hylton at the Mason Rudolph Golf Club (6,060 yd), Clarksville, Tenn, Aug 25–31, 1980.

US Women's Open

This tournament was first held in 1946, and currently is played over 72 holes of stroke play. Betsy Rawls won a record four times between 1951 and 1960, and this was equalled by Mickey Wright between 1958 and 1964. The oldest champion was Fay Crocker (Uru) at 40 years 11 months in 1955, while the youngest was Catherine Lacoste (France) at 22 years 5 days in 1967, when she became the only amateur player to win the title. The greatest margin of victory was by Babe Didrikson Zaharias who beat Betty Hicks by 12 strokes in 1954. The lowest aggregate score has been 280 (70, 70, 68, 72) by Amy Alcott in 1980, and the lowest round was 65 by Sally Little in 1978. The record for 36 holes is 139 by Carol Mann and Donna Caponi in 1970, the latter going on to a 54-hole score of 210.

The winners:

	Score
1946 Patty Berg beat Betty Jameson 5 and 4	
1947 Betty Jameson	295
1948 Mildred Zaharias	300
1949 Louise Suggs	291
1950 Mildred Zaharias	291
1951 Betsy Rawls	293
1952 Louise Suggs	284
1953 Betsy Rawls	302
1954 Mildred Zaharias	291
1955 Fay Crocker (Uru)	299
1956 Kathy Cornelius	302
1957 Betsy Rawls	299
1958 Mickey Wright	290
1959 Mickey Wright	287
1960 Betsy Rawls	292
1961 Mickey Wright	293
1962 Murle Lindstrom	301
1963 Mary Mills	289
1964 Mickey Wright	290
1965 Carol Mann	290
1966 Sandra Spuzich	297
1967 Catherine Lacoste (France)	294
1968 Sue Berning	289
1969 Donna Caponi	294
1970 Donna Caponi	287
1971 JoAnne Carner	288
1972 Sue Maxwell Berning	290
1973 Sue Maxwell Berning	290
1974 Sandra Haynie	295
1975 Sandra Palmer	295
1976 JoAnne Carner	292
1977 Hollis Stacy	298
1978 Hollis Stacy	289
1979 Jerilyn Britz	284
1980 Amy Alcott	280
1981 Pat Bradley	279
1982 Janet Alex	283
1983 Jan Stephenson	290
1984 Hollis Stacy	290
1985 Kathy Baker	280
1986 Jane Geddes	287

Biggest Prize Putt

Jack Nicklaus' total earnings went up by $240,000 when he sank an 8-foot putt on the 18th green of the

DRIVING ACROSS THE RIVER THAMES: Tony Jacklin (GB), winner of the 1969 British Open and 1970 US Open, drives from the roof of the Savoy Hotel, London, 125 ft above street level. His longest drive was about 353 yds but it fell short of the opposite bank. (Daily Express)

Desert Highlands course in Scottsdale, Ariz, on Nov 25, 1984 in a "Skins" match against Arnold Palmer, Gary Player and Tom Watson. All three of his opponents missed their birdie putts from further distances and Nicklaus won the accumulated prize money.

Most Shots One Hole

The highest number of strokes taken at a single hole in a major tournament was achieved in the inaugural Open Championship at Prestwick, Scotland, in 1860, when an unnamed player took 21. In the 1938 US Open, Ray Ainsley achieved instant fame when he took 19 strokes at the par-4 16th hole. Most of them were in an attempt to hit the ball out of a fast-moving brook. Hans Merrell of Mogadore, Ohio, took 19 strokes on the par-3, 222-yd 16th during the Bing Crosby tournament at Cypress Point Club, Del Monte, Calif, on Jan 17, 1959. At Biarritz, France in 1888 it was reported that Chevalier von Cittern took 316 for 18 holes, thus averaging 17.55 strokes per hole.

The story to top them all concerns a lady player in the qualifying round of a tournament in Shawnee-on-Delaware, Pa in the early part of the century. Her card showed she took 166 strokes for the short 130-yd 16th hole. Her tee shot landed and floated in a nearby river, and, with her meticulous husband, she set out in a boat and eventually beached the ball 1½ mi downstream. From there she had to play through a forest until finally she holed the ball. A. J. Lewis, playing at Peacehaven, Sussex, Eng, in 1890 had 156 putts on one green without holing the ball.

Fastest Rounds

With such variations in lengths of courses, speed records, even for rounds under par, are of little comparative value. Rick Baker completed 18 holes (6,142 yd) in 25 min 48.47 sec at Surfer's Paradise, Queensland, Australia, Sept 4, 1982, but this test permitted striking the ball while it was still moving. The record for a still ball is 28 min 5 sec by Gary Wright (b Nov 27, 1946) at Tewantin-Noosa Golf Club, Queensland, Australia (18 holes, 6,039 yd), on Dec 9, 1980.

Seventy-seven players completed the 18-hole 6,502 yd Kern City course, Calif, in 10 min 30 sec on Aug 24, 1984 using only one ball. They scored 80!

Richest Prize

The greatest first-place prize money was $500,000 (total purse $1.1 million) won by Johnny Miller (US) (b Apr 29, 1947) in 1982, and by Raymond Floyd (b Sept 4, 1942) in 1983 at Sun City, Bophuthatswana, S Africa. After 72-hole scores of 277, Miller beat Severiano Ballesteros (Spain) (who won $160,000 for second place) and Floyd beat Craig Stadler in play-offs.

US Women's Amateur Championship

Instituted in Nov 1895, and currently 36 final holes of match play after 36 qualifying holes of stroke play. Glenna Collett Vare won a record 6 titles between 1922 and 1935. The oldest champion was Dorothy Campbell-Hurd (GB) aged 41 years 4 months when winning her third title in 1924, and the youngest was

Laura Baugh at 16 years 2 months 21 days in 1971. Margaret Curtis beat her sister, Harriot, in the 1907 final—they later presented the Curtis Cup for competition between the US and GB.

Ryder Cup

The biennial Ryder Cup (instituted 1927) professional match between the US and GB (Europe since 1979) has been won by the US 21½–4½. In 1985, GB-Europe won 16½ to US 11½ in Eng. William Earl "Billy" Casper (b San Diego, Calif, June 24, 1931) has the record of winning most matches, with 20 won out of 37 (1961–75). Neil Cales (GB) played in a record 40 matches (1961–77).

World Cup (formerly Canada Cup)

The World Cup (instituted 1953), contested over 72 holes of stroke play by teams of two with scores aggregated, has been won most often by the US with 16 victories between 1955 and 1983. In 1985, the winning team was Canada with a score of 559 for Dan Halldorson and Dave Barr, combined. The only men on six winning teams have been Arnold Palmer (b Sept 10, 1929) (1960, 62–64, 66–67) and Jack Nicklaus (1963–64, 66–67, 71, 73). The only man to take the individual title three times is Jack Nicklaus (US) in 1963–64, 1971. The lowest aggregate score for 144 holes is 545 by Australia, Bruce Devlin (b Oct 10, 1937) and David Graham (b May 23, 1946) at San Isidro, Buenos Aires, Argentina, Nov 12–15, 1970, and the lowest score by an individual winner was 269 by Roberto de Vicenzo (b Buenos Aires, Argentina, Apr 14, 1923) on the same occasion.

Walker Cup

The US versus Great Britain–Ireland series instituted in 1921 (for the Walker Cup since 1922), now biennial, has been won by the US 27½–2½ to date. In 1985, the US won 13-11 in NJ. Joe Carr (GB–I) played in 10 contests (1947–67).

Longest Span

Jacqueline Ann Mercer (*née* Smith) (b Apr 5, 1929) won her first South African title at Humewood GC, Port Elizabeth, in 1948, and her fourth title at Port Elizabeth GC on May 4, 1979, 31 years later.

HOLES-IN-ONE

Golf Digest was notified in 1984 of 39,828 holes-in-one, and in 1985 of 43,386, so averaging 119 per day.

Longest

The longest straight hole shot in one is the 10th hole (447 yd) at Miracle Hills GC, Omaha, Neb. Robert Mitera achieved a hole-in-one there on Oct 7, 1965. Mitera, aged 21 and 5 ft 6 in tall, weighed 165

LARGEST DRIVING RANGE: This 3-tier structure in Tokyo, Japan, accommodates 300 golfers at a time.

OLDEST TO SHOOT A HOLE-IN-ONE: Otto Bucher (Switz) (left), who holed-in-one at the age of 99 years 244 days, pictured with Seve Ballesteros (Spain), whose brother runs the club where the feat was achieved in 1985.

Most Aces

The most aces in one year is 30 by Scott Palmer June 5, 1983–May 31, 1984, all on holes between 130 and 350 yd in length at Balboa Park, San Diego, Calif. He also made 4 aces in 4 consecutive rounds, Oct 9–12, 1983.

The greatest number of holes-in-one reported in a career is 87 by Harry Lee Bonner 1967 to 1986, most at his home 9-hole course of Las Gallinas, San Rafael, Calif.

Douglas Porteous, 28, aced 4 holes over 39 consecutive holes—the 3rd and 6th on Sept 26, and the 5th on Sept 28 at Ruchill GC, Glasgow, Scotland, and the 6th at the Clydebank and District GC Course on Sept 30, 1974. Robert Taylor holed the 188-yd 16th hole at Hunstanton, Norfolk, England, on three successive days—May 31, June 1 and 2, 1974. On May 12, 1984, Joe Lucius of Tiffin, Ohio, aced for the 13th time the par-3, 141-yd 15th hole at the Mohawk Golf Club. Lucius has 10 aces for the 10th hole on the same course, and 31 aces in all.

lb. A two-handicap player, he normally drove 245 yd. A 50-mph gust carried his shot over a 290-yd drop-off. The group in front testified to the remaining distance.

The longest dogleg achieved in one is the 480-yd 5th hole at Hope CC, Ark, by Larry Bruce on Nov 15, 1962.

The women's record is 393 yd by Marie Robie of Wollaston, Mass, on the first hole of the Furnace Brook GC, Sept 4, 1949.

Consecutive

There is no recorded instance of a golfer performing three consecutive holes-in-one, but there are at least 16 cases of "aces" being achieved in two consecutive holes, of which the greatest was Norman L. Manley's unique "double albatross" on two par-4 holes (330-yd 7th and 290-yd 8th) on the Del Valle CC course, Saugus, Calif, on Sept 2, 1964.

The first woman ever to card consecutive aces is Sue Prell, on the 13th and 14th holes at Chatswood GC, Sydney, Australia, on May 29, 1977.

The closest recorded instances of a golfer getting 3 consecutive holes-in-one were by the Rev Harold Snider (b July 4, 1900) who aced the 8th, 13th and 14th holes of the par-3 Ironwood course in Phoenix, Ariz, on June 9, 1976, and the late Dr Joseph Boydstone on the 3rd, 4th and 9th at Bakersfield GC, Calif on Oct 10, 1962.

Youngest and Oldest

The youngest golfer recorded to have shot a hole-in-one was Coby Orr (aged 5) of Littleton, Colo, on the 103-yd fifth hole at the Riverside GC, San Antonio, Tex, in 1975. *Golf Digest* credits Tommy Moore (6 yrs 1 month 7 days) of Hagerstown, Md with being the youngest for an ace he shot on a 145-yd hole in 1969.

The oldest golfer to have performed the feat is Otto Bucher (Switz) (b May 12, 1885) aged 99 years 244 days on Jan 13, 1985 when he aced the 130-yd 12th hole at La Manga GC, Spain.

The oldest woman to score an ace is Erna Ross, aged 95 years 257 days, who holed-in-one on the 112-yd 17th hole of the Everglades Club, Palm Beach, Fla, on May 25, 1986.

The oldest player to score his age is C. Arthur Thompson (1869–1975) of Victoria, BC, Canada, who scored 103 on the Uplands course of 6,215 yd when age 103 in 1973.

Largest Tournament

The Volkswagen Grand Prix Open Amateur Championship in the UK attracted a record 321,778 (206,820 men and 114,958 women) competitors in 1984.

GYMNASTICS

Earliest References

Tumbling and similar exercises were performed *c.* 2600 BC as religious rituals in China, but it was the Greeks who coined the word gymnastics. A primitive form was practiced in the ancient Olympic Games, but it was not until Johann Friedrich Simon began to teach at Basedow's Gymnasium in Dessau, Germany, in 1776 that the foundations of the modern sport were laid. The first national federation was formed in Germany in 1860 and the International Gymnastics Federation was founded in Liège, Belgium in 1881. The sport was included at the first modern Olympic Games at Athens in 1896.

Current events for men are: floor exercises, horse vault, rings, pommel horse, parallel bars and horizontal bar, while for women they are: floor exercises, horse vault, asymmetrical bars, and balance beam.

World Championships

In Olympic years, the Olympic title is the World Championship title.

The greatest number of individual titles won by a man in the World Championships including Olympics is 10 by Boris Shakhlin (USSR) between 1954 and 1964. He was also on three winning teams. The women's record is 12 individual wins and 5 team titles by Larissa Semyonovna Latynina (b Dec 27, 1934, retired 1966) of the USSR, between 1956 and 1964. She has the most medals, 33, of which 18 are Olympic medals. Japan has won the men's team title a record 5 times (1962, 66, 70, 74, 78) and the USSR the women's team title on 9 occasions (1954, 58, 62, 70, 74, 78, 81, 83 and 85).

Olympic Medalists

Japan has won 5 men's team titles (1960, 64, 68, 72, 76) and the USSR has won the women's title 8 times (1952–80).

The only men to win 6 individual gold medals are Boris Shakhlin (b Jan 21, 1932) (USSR), with one in 1956, 4 (2 shared) in 1960 and one in 1964; and Nikolai Andrianov (b Oct 14, 1952) (USSR) with one in 1972, 4 in 1976 and one in 1980.

The most successful woman has been Vera Caslavska-Odlozil (b May 3, 1942) (Czechoslovakia), with 7 individual gold medals, 3 in 1964 and 4 (one shared) in 1968. Larissa Latynina of the USSR won 6 individual and 3 team gold medals for a total of 9. She also won 5 silver and 4 bronze for an all-time record total of 18 Olympic medals.

Ecaterina Szabo (Romania) won 4 gold medals and a silver—the most in the 1984 Games at any sport.

The most medals for a male gymnast is 15 by Ni-

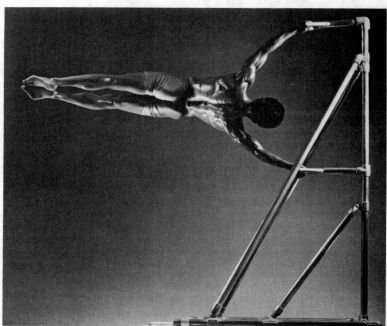

FLAG PUSHOUTS: David Luna of Santa Monica, Calif, defied gravity in stretching his body out like a flag for a record 20 times in succession at the San Diego Sports Medicine Center in Aug 1982. (Cynthia Moore)

UPSIDE-DOWNERS: Mary Lou Retton (US) (left) won the gold medal in the 1984 Olympics as the best all-around gymnast. Aleksandr Ditiatin (USSR) (above) is the only person to win a medal in all 8 categories in one Games (1980, Moscow).

kolai Andrianov (USSR), 7 gold, 5 silver and 3 bronze, 1972–80. Aleksandr Ditiatin (USSR) (b Aug 7, 1957) is the only man to win a medal in all eight categories in the same Games, with 3 gold, 4 silver and 1 bronze at Moscow in 1980.

Nadia Comaneci (b Nov 12, 1961) (Romania) was the first gymnast to be awarded a perfect score of 10.00 in the Olympic Games, in the 1976 Montreal Olympics. She ended the competition with a total of 7 such marks (4 on the uneven parallel bars, 3 on the balance beam). Since then Nelli Kim (USSR) in the same Games, and a number of others have received marks of 10.00.

In the 1984 Olympics a record 16 perfect marks of 10.00 were awarded.

Largest Gymnasium

The world's largest gymnasium is Yale University's 9-story Payne Whitney Gymnasium at New Haven, Conn, completed in 1932 and valued at $18 million.

American Cup Titles

Olympic gold medalist Mary Lou Retton (b 1968) of Fairmont, W Va won her first American Cup in 1983 in NYC and has not relinquished the title since that competition. She is the only female gymnast to hold the title for three straight years. US gymnast Kurt Thomas won the title three years in a row from 1978 to 1980.

Chinning the Bar

The greatest number of continuous chin-ups (from a dead hang position) is 170 by Lee Chin Yong (b Aug 15, 1925) at Backyon Gymnasium, Seoul, Korea on May 10, 1983. Robert Chisnall (b Dec 9, 1952) performed 22 one-arm (his right) chin-ups, from a ring, 18 two-finger chins and 12 one-finger chins, from a nylon strap on Dec 3, 1982 at Queen's Univ, Kingston, Ont, Canada.

Olympic Games

The 1984 gold medalists:

Men

Individual All-Round

Koji Gushiken (Jap) 118,700 pts

Floor Exercises

Li Ning (China) 19,925 pts

Pommel Horse

tie Li Ning (China) 19,950 pts
tie P. Vidmar (US) 19,950 pts

Rings

tie Koji Gushiken (Jap) 19,850 pts
tie Li Ning (China) 19,850 pts

Horse Vault

Lou Yun (China) 19,950 pts

Parallel Bars

Bart Conner (US) 19,950 pts

Horizontal Bar

Shinji Morisue (Jap) 20,000 pts

Women

Individual All-Round

Mary Lou Retton (US) 79,175 pts

Floor Exercises

Ecaterina Szabo (Romania) 19,975 pts

Horse Vault

Ecaterina Szabo (Romania) 19,875 pts

Balance Beam

tie Simona Pauca (Romania) 19,800 pts
tie Ecaterina Szabo (Romania) 19,800 pts

Uneven Parallel (Asymmetrical) Bars

tie Ma Yauhong (China) 19,950 pts
tie J. McNamara (US) 19,950 pts

Rhythmic Individual All-Around

Lori Fung (Can) 5,795 pts

ON THE BEAM: Larissa Latynina earned 18 Olympic medals—the record for either sex in any sport. Nine were gold. Latynina also won 10 individual and 5 team titles in the World Championships.

MOST SUCCESSFUL WOMAN GYMNAST (below) in the Olympics has been Vera Caslavska-Odlozil (Czech) with 7 individual golds. (Tony Duffy-All Sport)

Youngest International Competitors

Pasakevi "Voula" Kouna (b Dec 6, 1971) was aged 9 years 299 days at the start of the Balkan Games at Serres, Greece on Oct 1–4, 1981, when she represented Greece. Olga Bicherova (b Oct 26, 1966) won the women's world title at 15 years 33 days in Nov 1981. The youngest men's champion was Dmitri Relozerchev (USSR) at 16 years 315 days at Budapest, Hungary in 1983.

A PERFECT "10": Nadia Comaneci (Romania) (left and right above) was 14 years old when she made Olympic history as the first gymnast ever to be awarded a perfect score. Her unprecedented feat came during the 1976 Olympics in Montreal. She went on to earn 6 more 10's for a remarkable total of 7 flawless routines (4 on uneven parallel bars and 3 on the balance beam).

STYLE in Gymnastics: Nelli Kim (USSR) (left) shows why she won 1976 and 1980 Olympic golds. (Right) Erica Schiller (USSR) demonstrates Rhythmic Gymnastics, first included in Olympic Games of 1984.

Modern Rhythmic Gymnastics

This recent addition to the female side of the sport incorporates exercises with different hand-held apparatus, including ribbons, balls, ropes, hoops and Indian clubs. The most overall titles won in world championships is 3 by Maria Gigova (Bulgaria) in 1969, 71, and 73 (shared), while the most individual apparatus titles is 9 by Gigova and Galina Shugurova (USSR). The latter has also won a record total of 14 medals. This category of the sport was included in the Olympic Games for the first time in 1984.

World Cup Titles

In the first World Cup competition, in London in 1975, Ludmilla Tourischeva (now Mrs. Valeriy Borzov) (b Oct 7, 1952) (USSR) won all 5 gold medals.

Largest Gymnastic Display

The greatest number of gymnasts to give a display at the same time are the 30,000–40,000 from the Sokol movement who perform annually in the Strahov Stadium in Prague, Czechoslovakia before some 240,000 spectators.

Sit-Ups

Tim Kides of West NY, NJ, a 21-year-old sophomore at Glassboro (NJ) State College, set a record of 72,746 sit-ups with his legs straight, with no weights or anyone holding his legs, in 64 hours Nov 13–15, 1985, beating the former record of 45,005 set in July 1985.

Louis Scripa, Jr, did 43,418 sit-ups within 24 hours in Sacramento, Calif, on Oct 6–7, 1984. As for leg raises, Scripa did 21,598 in 6 hours in Fairfield, Calif on Dec 8, 1983.

Rope Climbing

The US Amateur Athletic Union (AAU) records are tantamount to world records: 20 ft (hands alone), 2.8 sec, by Don Perry, at Champaign, Ill, on Apr 3, 1954; 25 ft (hands alone), 4.7 sec, by Garvin S. Smith at Los Angeles, on Apr 19, 1947.

Moving Human Tower

The NSA Roller Gymnastics Team built a tower of 120 gymnasts 5 stories high, and it moved to music 30 ft in 20 sec on July 3, 1986 at Madison Sq Garden,

GYMNASTIC GOLDS: The only men to win 6 gold medals in the Olympics are these two Russians, Boris Shakhlin (left) and Nikolai Andrianov.

MOVING TOWER: A record 5-story pyramid on roller skates was achieved by the NSA Roller Gymnastics Team on July 3, 1986 in Madison Sq Garden, NYC. NYC, before 18,000 spectators. It was part of the NSA (Nichiren Shoshu Soka Gakkai) of America 2nd Youth Music Festival.

Sargent Jump

Devised by, and named after, an eminent American professor of physical education in the 1920s, this exercise measures the differential between the height reached by a person's fingertips with feet flat on the ground, and that reached by jumping. The record is 48 in by Darrell Griffith (US) of the University of Louisville in 1976. Olympic Pentathlon champion Mary E. Peters (GB) reportedly jumped 30 in in Calif in 1972.

ROPE-JUMP CHAMP: Katsumi Suzuki (Japan), amazes spectators when he performs a quadruple turn in which he jumps about 4 ft in the air and turns the rope 4 times under his feet and around his body before landing back on the floor. He performed this feat 51 times in a row for a world record in 1975. He has also beaten all competitors in making consecutive treble turns (381) and double turns (10,133)—all without a stop or a miss. (Photo by Dean Moon)

Parallel Bar Dips

Roger Perez (b July 11, 1962) of Sacramento, Calif, performed a record 718 parallel bar dips in an hour on Dec 14, 1983. Jack LaLanne (b 1914) is reported to have done 1,000 in Oakland, Calif, in 1945.

Push-Ups

Jack Atherton did 29,601 push-ups in 24 hours, July 11–12, 1986, at HMP Featherstone, Eng.

Colin Hewick (GB) did 3,856 one-arm push-ups in 5 hours at Bodyworld Health Club, Hull, Eng, on June 13, 1986.

Chung Kwun Ying (Hong Kong) did 2,750 handstand push-ups at Government City Hall, Hong Kong, on May 18, 1986. John Deckert (GB) did 4,500 fingertip push-ups at the Congleton Leisure Centre, Cheshire, Eng, June 28, 1986 in 5 hours. Harry Lee Welch completed 100 one-finger push-ups in Durham, NC, Mar 31, 1985. Adam Parsons, a retired Lt Col in the USAF, achieved a documented 1,293,850 push-ups in the year 1985 in Akron, O.

Somersaults

Ashrita Furman (US) performed 7,400 forward rolls over 12 miles 390 yards from Boston to Lexington, Mass, in Apr 1986.

Corporal Wayne Wright (GB) of the Royal Engineers, made a successful dive-and-tucked somersault over 37 men at Old Park Barracks, Dover, Kent, England on July 30, 1980.

Shigeru Iwasaki (b 1960) backwards somersaulted over 50 m (54.68 yd) in 10.8 sec in Tokyo, March 30, 1980.

HANDSTAND PUSH-UP CHAMPION: 8-year-old Chung Kwun Ying pushed-up 2,750 times consecutively like this in Hong Kong, May 18, 1986. (AP)

ROPE JUMPING

The longest recorded rope-jumping marathon was one of 13 hours 12 min 11 sec by George Hood at Nuuanu YMCA, Honolulu, Hawaii, on Oct 18, 1986. John Baber skip-ran the 10-mi People Classic road race at Williamstown, Mass, in 78 min 40 sec on Apr 27, 1986.

Other rope-jumping records made without a break:

Most turns in 1 minute	418	Tyrone Krohn	Middletown (NY) HS	July 10, 1984
Most turns in 10 seconds	128	Albert Rayner	Birmingham, Eng	Nov 19, 1982
Most turns in 1 hour	8,320	Tyrone Krohn	WABC-TV, NY	Dec 20, 1985
Most doubles (with cross)	1,664	Sean Birch	Kerry, Ireland	Apr 27, 1984
Double turns	10,133	Katsumi Suzuki (Japan)	Saitama	Sept 29, 1979
Treble turns	381	Katsumi Suzuki (Japan)	Saitama	May 29, 1975
Quadruple turns	51	Katsumi Suzuki (Japan)	Saitama	May 29, 1975
Quintuple turns	6	Hideyuki Tateda (Japan)	Aomori	June 19, 1982
Duration	1,264 miles	Tom Morris (Aust)	Brisbane-Cairns	1963
Most on a single rope	160	(50 m rope) Shimizu Iida	Shizuoka-ken, Japan	Dec 10, 1982
(minimum 12 turns obligatory)		Junior High School		
Most turns on single rope				
(team of 90)	97	Erimomisaki School	Hokkaido, Japan	May 28, 1983
On a tightrope (consecutive)	58	Bryan Andrew (né Dewhurst)	TROS TV, Holland	Aug 6, 1981

Jumping Jacks

The greatest number of side-straddle hops is 45,027 in 12 hours 23 min by Ashrita Furman (see previous page) on Dec 4, 1986, at Civic Park, San Francisco.

HANDBALL

U.S. Handball Association National Champions

PROFESSIONAL SINGLES
1951	Walter Plekan
1952	Vic Hershkowitz
1953	Bob Brady
1954	Vic Hershkowitz
1955–57	Jim Jacobs
1958–59	John Sloan
1960	Jim Jacobs
1961	John Sloan
1962–63	Oscar Obert
1964–65	Jim Jacobs
1966–67	Paul Haber
1968	Simon (Stuffy) Singer
1969–71	Paul Haber
1972	Fred Lewis
1973	Terry Mack
1974–76	Fred Lewis
1977	Naty Alvarado
1978	Fred Lewis
1979–80	Naty Alvarado
1981	Fred Lewis
1982–85	Naty Alvarado

FOUR-WALL DOUBLES
1951–52	Frank Coyle and Bill Baier
1953	Sam Haber and Harry Dreyfus
1954–56	Sam Haber and Ken Schneider
1957–59	Phil Collins and John Sloan
1960	Jim Jacobs and Dick Weisman
1961	John Sloan and Vic Hershkowitz
1962–63	Jim Jacobs and Marty Decatur
1964	John Sloan and Phil Elbert
1965	Jim Jacobs and Marty Decatur
1966	Pete Tyson and Bob Lindsay
1967–68	Jim Jacobs and Marty Decatur
1969	Lou Kramberg and Lou Russo
1970	Carl Obert and Rudy Obert
1971	Ray Neveau and Simie Fein
1972	Kent Fusselman and Al Drews
1973–74	Ray Neveau and Simie Fein
1975	Steve Lott and Marty Decatur
1976	Dan O'Connor and Gary Rohrer
1977	Matt Kelley and Skip McDowell
1978–79	Marty Decatur and Simon (Stuffy) Singer
1980	Skip McDowell and Harry Robertson
1981	Jack Roberts and Tom Kopatich
1982–85	Vern Roberts and Naty Alvarado

Origin

Handball is a game of ancient Celtic origin. In the early 19th century only a front wall was used, but later side and back walls were added. The court is now standardized 60 feet by 30 feet in Ireland,

OFF THE WALL: Jim Jacobs has been the most successful player in the USHA National Four-Wall Championships with 6 singles and 6 doubles titles.

Ghana and Australia, and 40 feet by 20 feet in Canada, Mexico and the US. The game is played with both a hard and soft ball in Ireland, and a soft ball only, elsewhere.

The earliest international contest was in New York City in 1887, between the champions of the US and Ireland.

Handball was introduced into the Olympic Games at Berlin in 1936 as an 11-a-side outdoor game with Germany winning, but when re-introduced in 1972 it was an indoor game with seven-a-side, the standard size of team since 1952.

Most Titles

The most successful player in the U.S.H.A. National Four-Wall Championships has been James Jacobs (US), who won a record 6 singles titles (1955–56–57–60–64–65) and shared in 6 doubles titles (1960–62–63–65–67–68). Martin Decatur has won 8 doubles titles (1962–63–65–67–68–75–78–79),

5 of these with Jacobs as his partner. Fred Lewis has also won 6 singles titles (1972–74–75–76–78–81).

One-wall handball is played almost exclusively in NYC at almost 2,000 one-wall courts, in playgrounds and schools. Among the most successful players have been Steve Sandler, Oscar Obert and Vic Hershkowitz. The current singles champion is Eddie Golden.

Olympics and World Championships

Three Olympic titles have been won both by the USSR (men 1976, women 1976 and 1980) and by Yugoslavia (men 1972 and 1984, women 1984). World championships were inaugurated in New York in October, 1964, with competitors from Australia, Canada, Ireland, Mexico and the US. The US is the only nation to have won twice, with victories in 1964 and 1967 (shared). The Super Cup, contested by men's Olympic and World Champions, was first held in 1979. W Germany and the USSR have each won once.

Marathon

Two teams of 11 from Castlebridge Handball Club, Ireland, played for 45 hours 50 min, Sept 26–28, 1986.

HARNESS RACING

Origins

Trotting races were held in Valkenburg, Netherlands, in 1554. In England the trotting gait (the simultaneous use of the diagonally opposite legs) was known in the 16th century. The sulky first appeared in harness racing in 1829. Pacers thrust out their fore and hind legs simultaneously on one side.

Greatest Winnings

The greatest amount won by a trotting horse is $3,041,262 by "Ideal du Gazeau" (France) to July 23, 1983. The record for a pacing horse is $3,225,563 by "Nihilator" to his retirement on Nov 29, 1985.

The greatest award won by any harness horse is the $3,225,653 won by the pacer "Nihilator," who was victorious in 35 of 38 races, 1984–85. He also holds the single season winnings record with $1,864,286 in 1985.

The largest purse ever was $2,161,000 for the Woodrow Wilson 2-year-olds race at Meadowlands, NJ, on Aug 16, 1984, of which a record $1,080,500 went to the winner "Nihilator" driven by Billy O'Donnell (b May 4, 1948).

Highest Prices

The highest price ever paid for a pacer is for "Nihilator," who was syndicated for $19.2 million in 1984, topping the record of $10 million set by his father, "Niatross," in 1979.

MOST VALUABLE PACER: "Nihilator," who was syndicated for a record $19.2 million, won a record $3,225,653 in 1984–85, victorious in 35 of 38 races.

HARNESS RACING RECORDS AGAINST TIME

TROTTING

Time Trial (mile track)	1:54.0	"Arndon" (driver, Delvin Miller) (US), at Lexington, Ky	Oct 6, 1982
Race Record (mile)	1:53.4	"Cornstalk" (driver, Howard Beissinger) (US) at Springfield, Ill	Aug 15, 1984

PACING

Time Trial (mile track)	1:49.1	"Niatross" (driver, Clint Galbraith) (US) at Lexington, Ky	Oct 1, 1980
Race Record (mile)	1:49.3	"Nihilator" (driver, Bill O'Donnell) (Can), at East Rutherford, NJ	Aug 3, 1985

The highest price paid for a trotter is $5.25 million for "Mystic Park" by Lana Lobell Farms from Allen, Gerald and Irving Wechter of NY and Robert Lester of Florida, announced on July 13, 1982.

Most Successful Driver

The most successful sulky driver in North America has been Herve Filion (Canada) (b Quebec, Feb 1, 1940) who reached a record of 9,755 wins and $51,227,880 in purse money by Nov 1, 1986. A fellow Canadian, Michel Lachance, broke Filion's 1974 season record of 637 victories by winning 708 races in 1986 (to Dec 1). Filion won the North American championship for the 13th time in 1982. The greatest earnings in a year is $10,207,372 by Billy O'Donnell, who won 419 races in 1985.

HOCKEY

Origins

There is pictorial evidence of a hockey-like game (Kalv) being played on ice in The Netherlands in the early 16th century. The game probably was first played in North America on Dec 25, 1855, at Kingston, Ontario, Canada, but Halifax also lays claim to priority.

The International Ice Hockey Federation was founded in 1908. The National Hockey League was inaugurated in 1917. The World Hockey Association was formed in 1971 and disbanded in 1979 when 4 of its teams joined the NHL.

World Championships and Olympic Games

World Championships were first held for amateurs in 1920 in conjunction with the Olympic Games, which were also considered as World Champion-

ships up to 1968. From 1977 World Championships have been open to professionals. The USSR has won 20 world titles between 1954 and 1986, including the Olympic titles of 1956, 64 and 68. They have won 3 further Olympic titles in 1972, 76 and 84. Canada won 19 titles between 1920 and 1961, including 6 Olympic titles (1920, 24, 32, 48 and 52). The longest Olympic career is that of Richard Torriani (b Oct 1, 1911) (Switzerland) from 1928 to 1948. The most gold medals won by any player is 3; this was achieved by 4 USSR players in the 1964, 68 and 72 Games—Vitaliy Davidov, Aleksandr Ragulin, Anatoliy Firssov and Viktor Kuzkin. Goalie Vladimir Tretiak (USSR) won 3 golds (1972, 1976 and 1984) as well as a silver in 1980.

Longest Season

The only man ever to play 82 games in a 78-game season is Ross Lonsberry. He began the 1971–72 season with the Los Angeles Kings where he played 50 games. Then, in January, he was traded to the Philadelphia Flyers (who had played only 46 games at the time) where he finished out the season (32 more games).

Brad Marsh (b Mar 31, 1958) played 83 games (17 with Calgary and 66 with Philadelphia) during an 80-game season in 1981–82.

Longest Career

Gordie Howe (b March 31, 1928, Floral, Saskatchewan, Canada) skated 25 years for the Detroit Red Wings from 1946–47 through the 1970–71 season, playing in a total of 1,687 NHL regular-season games.

After leaving the Red Wings, he ended a 2-year retirement to skate with his two sons as teammates and played for 6 more seasons with the Houston Aeros and the New England Whalers of the World Hockey Association, participating in 497 games.

With the incorporation of the (now Hartford)

GOAL ORIENTED: Wayne Gretzky showed he was no flash-in-the-pan when, in 1982, he began breaking assist and most-points records and also set a goal-scoring record by netting 92 goals, including a record 10 hat tricks. In 1984, he scored 10 hat tricks again (total of 37 to the end of the 1986 season) and in 1986, a point record of 215 and an assist record of 163 in a season. (Edmonton Oilers)

Whalers into the NHL for the 1979–80 season, Gordie Howe skated in all 80 regular season games (for a record total of 1,767) in his record 26th year in that league. The remarkable 52-year-old grandfather was again selected as an NHL all-star, more times than any other player. Including Howe's 157 NHL playoff appearances, he skated in 2,421 "major league" games in all.

Longest Game

The longest game was 2 hours 56 min 30 sec (playing time) when the Detroit Red Wings eventually beat the Montreal Maroons 1-0 in the 17th minute of the sixth period of overtime at the Forum, Montreal, at 2:25 a.m. on March 25, 1936, 5 hours 51 min after the opening faceoff. Norm Smith, goaltender for the Red Wings, turned aside 92 shots in registering the NHL's longest single shutout.

Longest Streaks

In the 1981–82 season, the NY Islanders won 15 consecutive games, Jan 21–Feb 20, 1982. The longest a team has ever gone without a defeat is 35 games, set by the Philadelphia Flyers with 25 wins and 10 ties from Oct 14, 1979, to Jan 6, 1980.

Fastest Player

The highest speed measured for any player is 29.7 mph (without the puck) for Bobby Hull (then of the Chicago Black Hawks) (b Jan 3, 1939). The highest puck speed is also attributed to Hull, whose left-handed slap shot has been measured at 118.3 mph. Also known as the "Golden Jet," Hull is the only player besides Gordie Howe to score over 1,000 goals in NHL and WHA play.

ROCKET MAN: Maurice "Rocket" Richard beats the Boston goaltender to score one of his record 82 Stanley Cup goals, this one in the 1953 finals. Of those 82 goals, 18 were game winners with 6 coming in overtime. Maurice Richard's brother, Henri "Pocket Rocket" Richard, played in and won 11 finals as part of his record 180 playoff-game appearances. (David Biers)

(Through 1985–86 Season; the number of a year refers to the season that commenced in the year before.)

REGULAR SEASON

Service

Most Seasons
  26 Gordie Howe, Det, 1947–71; Hart, 1980
Most Games, Lifetime
  1,767 Gordie Howe, Det, 1947–71; Hart, 1980
Consecutive Games Played
  914 Gary Unger, Tor-Det-St L-Atl, Feb 24, 1968–Dec 21, 1979

Scoring

Most Points, Lifetime
  1,850 Gordie Howe, Det, 1947–71; Hart, 1980
Most Points, Season
  215 Wayne Gretzky, Edm, 1986
Most Points, Game
  10 Darryl Sittler, Tor vs Bos, Feb 7, 1976
Most Points, Period
  6 Bryan Trottier, NY Isl vs NY Ran, Dec 23, 1978
Consecutive Games Scoring Points
  51 Wayne Gretzky, Edm, Oct 5, 1983–Jan 27, 1984
Most Goals, Lifetime
  801 Gordie Howe, Det, 1947–71; Hart, 1980
Most Goals, Season
  92 Wayne Gretzky, Edm, 1982
Most Goals, Game
  7 Joe Malone, Que Bulldogs vs Tor St Pat, Jan 31, 1920
Most Goals, One Period
  4 Harvey Jackson, Tor vs St L, Nov 20, 1934
     Max Bentley, Chi vs NY Ran, Jan 28, 1943
     Clint Smith, Chi vs Mont, Mar 4, 1945
     Red Berenson, St L vs Phil, Nov 7, 1968
     Wayne Gretzky, Edm vs St L, Feb 18, 1981
     Grant Mulvey, Chi vs St L, Feb 3, 1982
     Bryan Trottier, NY Isl vs Phil, Feb 13, 1982

Most Hat Tricks (3 or more goals in a game), Lifetime
  37 Wayne Gretzky, Edm, 1980–86
     Mike Bossy, NY Isl 1978–86
Most Hat Tricks, Season
  10 Wayne Gretzky, Edm, 1982, 1984
Consecutive Games Scoring Goals
  16 Harry Broadbent, Ottawa, 1921–22
Most Assists, Lifetime
  1,049 Gordie Howe, Det, 1947–71; Hart, 1980
Most Assists, Season
  163 Wayne Gretzky, Edm, 1986
Most Assists, Game
  7 Billy Taylor, Det vs Chi, Mar 16, 1947
     Wayne Gretzky, Edm vs Wash, Feb 15, 1982; vs Chi Dec 11, 1985
Most Assists, Period
  5 Dale Hawerchuk, Win vs LA, Mar 6, 1984

Goaltending

Games Played, Lifetime
  971 Terry Sawchuk, Det-Bos-Tor-LA-NY Ran, 1950–70
Shutouts, Lifetime
  103 Terry Sawchuk, Det-Bos-Tor-LA-NY Ran, 1950–70
Shutouts, Season
  22 George Hainsworth, Mont, 1929
Consecutive Scoreless Streak
  461 min 29 sec Alex Connell, Ottawa, 1927–28
Consecutive Games Without Defeat
  32 Gerry Cheevers, Bos, Nov 14, 1971–Mar 27, 1972
Most Saves, One Game
  70 Roy Worters, Pitt Pirates vs NY Americans, Dec 24, 1925

Penalties

Most Minutes Penalized, Lifetime
  3,515 David (Tiger) Williams, Tor-Van-Det-LA, 1975–86

Most Minutes Penalized, Season
  472 Dave Schultz, Phil, 1975
Most Minutes Penalized, Game
  67 Randy Holt, LA vs Phil, Mar 11, 1979

STANLEY CUP

Most Games, Lifetime
  180 Henri Richard, Mont, 1956–69, 1971–75
Most Points, Lifetime
  176 Jean Beliveau, Mont, 1954–69, 1971
Most Points, Season
  47 Wayne Gretzky, Edm, 1985
Most Points, Game
  7 Wayne Gretzky, Edm, vs Calg, Apr 17, 1983
     Wayne Gretzky, Edm vs Win, Apr 25, 1985
Most Goals, Lifetime
  83 Mike Bossy, NY Isl, 1978–86
Most Goals, Season
  19 Reggie Leach, Phil, 1976
Most Goals, Game
  5 Maurice Richard, Mont vs Tor, Mar 23, 1944
     Darryl Sittler, Tor vs Phil, Apr 22, 1976
     Reggie Leach, Phil vs Bos, May 6, 1976
Most Assists, Lifetime
  111 Wayne Gretzky, Edm, 1980–86
Most Assists, Season
  30 Wayne Gretzky, Edm, 1985
Most Assists, Game
  6 Mikko Leinonen, NY Ran vs Phil, Apr 8, 1982
Most Shutouts by Goalie, Lifetime
  14 Jacques Plante, Mont, 1953–63; St L, 1969–70
Most Victories by Goalie, Lifetime
  88 Billy Smith, NY Isl, 1975–85

Stanley Cup

This cup, presented by the Governor-General Lord Stanley (original cost $48.67), became emblematic of world professional team supremacy 33 years after the first contest at Montreal in 1893. It has been won most often by the Montreal Canadiens, with 23 wins in 1916, 24, 30–31, 44, 46, 53, 56–60 (a record 5 straight), 65–66, 68–69, 71, 73, 76–79, 86. Henri Richard played in his eleventh finals in 1973.

Winners from 1970 are:

1970 Boston Bruins
1971 Montreal Canadiens
1972 Boston Bruins
1973 Montreal Canadiens
1974 Philadelphia Flyers
1975 Philadelphia Flyers
1976 Montreal Canadiens
1977 Montreal Canadiens
1978 Montreal Canadiens

1979 Montreal Canadiens
1980 New York Islanders
1981 New York Islanders
1982 New York Islanders
1983 New York Islanders
1984 Edmonton Oilers
1985 Edmonton Oilers
1986 Montreal Canadiens

Goaltender's Goal

The only goaltender to score a goal in an NHL game is Billy Smith (NY Islanders), against the Colorado Rockies in Denver, Nov 28, 1979. After the Rockies had removed their goaltender in favor of an extra skater during a delayed penalty, a Colorado defenseman's errant centering pass sent the puck skidding nearly the full length of the ice and into his own untended goal. Goalie Smith was the last Islander to touch the puck and was credited with the goal even though he did not take the actual "shot."

Penalties

The most any team has been penalized in one season is the 2,621 min assessed against the Philadelphia Flyers in 1980–81. The most penalty-filled game was a contest between Boston and Minnesota in Boston on Feb 26, 1981, with a total of 84 penalties (42 by each team) for 406 min (211 min by Minnesota).

FASTEST SKATER: Bobby Hull was timed at 29.7 mph. His slap shot went screaming at goaltenders at 118.3 mph. Hull was the only player besides Gordie Howe to score 1,000 NHL and WHA goals.

GOALIE SCORES GOAL: Billy Smith (above) became the only goaltender to be credited with scoring an NHL goal. He was the last Islander to touch the puck (in making a save) before the Colorado Rockies accidentally put the puck in their own net.

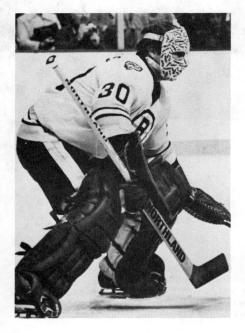

THE PUCK STOPS HERE: Gerry Cheevers (left) who drew stitch marks on his mask whenever it protected him from injury, went 32 straight games, without a loss for the Bruins in 1971-72. As the Bruins' coach in 1982-83, he found himself rooting for his goalie, Pete Peeters, to break the record, but Peeters' streak ended at 31 consecutive undefeated games. (Boston Bruins)

MOST HAT TRICKS: Mike Bossy, right wing of the NY Islanders, has tied Wayne Gretzky with 37 hat tricks. He also has the most goals (83) in Stanley Cup play.

FASTEST GOAL: Bryan Trottier of the NY Islanders scored a goal 5 sec after the opening whistle on Mar 22, 1984.

Fastest Scoring

Toronto scored 8 goals against the NY Americans in 4 min 52 sec on March 19, 1938.

The fastest goal ever scored from the opening whistle came at 5 sec of the first period. This occurred twice, most recently by Bryan Trottier of the NY Islanders vs Boston Bruins on Mar 22, 1984. The previous time was by Doug Smail of the Winnipeg Jets against St Louis on Dec 20, 1981. Claude Provost of the Canadiens scored a goal against Boston after 4 sec of the opening of the second period on Nov 9, 1957.

The Boston Bruins set an NHL record with three goals in a span of 20 sec against the Vancouver Canucks on Feb 25, 1971. Left winger John Bucyk began the record-breaking feat with a goal at the 4 min 50 sec mark of the third period. Center Ed Westfall scored 12 sec later at 5 min 2 sec, while defenseman Ted Green rounded out the surge with a goal at the 5 min 10 sec mark.

The fastest scoring record is held by Bill Mosienko

LONGEST CAREER: Gordie Howe played in the NHL for 26 seasons and collected career records for most games (1,767), goals (801), assists (1,049), and points (1,850), was selected as an all-star a record 21 times, and also collected 500 stitches in his face.

MOST 3-GOAL GAMES: Phil Esposito, in his 18-year NHL career (with Chi-NY-Bos) scored 3 goals or more in 32 games. (Al Ruelle)

(Chicago) who scored 3 goals in 21 sec against the NY Rangers on March 23, 1952. In a playoff game Pat LaFontaine of the NY Islanders scored 2 goals in 22 sec vs Edmonton Oilers, May 19, 1984.

Gus Bodnar (Toronto Maple Leafs) scored a goal against the NY Rangers at 15 sec of the first period of *his first NHL game* on Oct 30, 1943. Later in his career, while with Chicago, Bodnar again entered the record book when he assisted on all 3 of Bill Mosienko's quick goals.

Several fast scoring feats have been reported from non-NHL competition: Kim D. Miles scored in 3 sec for Univ of Guelph vs Univ of W Ontario on Feb 11, 1975; Steve D'Innocenzo scored 3 goals in 12 sec for Holliston vs Westwood in a high school game in Mass on Jan 9, 1982; Clifford "Fido" Purpur, 38, scored 4 goals in 25 sec for the Grand Forks AMerks vs Winnipeg All Stars in Grand Forks, ND, on Jan 29, 1950. In team play, the Skara Ishockeyclubb, Sweden, scored 3 goals in 11 sec against Orebro IK at Skara on Oct 18, 1981; the Vernon Cougars scored 5 goals in 56 sec against Salmon Arm Aces at Vernon, BC, Canada, on Aug 6, 1982; the Kamloops Knights of Columbus scored 7 goals in 2 min 22 sec vs Prince George Vikings on Jan 25, 1980.

Team Scoring

The greatest number of goals recorded in a World Championship match has been 47-0 when Canada beat Denmark on Feb 12, 1949.

The Edmonton Oilers set an NHL record of 446 goals in the 1983–84 season.

The NHL record for both teams is 21 goals, scored when the Montreal Canadiens beat the Toronto St Patricks at Montreal 14-7 on Jan 10, 1920. The most goals ever scored by one team in a single game was set by the Canadiens, when they defeated the Quebec Bulldogs on March 3, 1920 by a score of 16-3.

The most goals in a period is 9 by the Buffalo Sabres in the second period of their 14–4 victory over Toronto on March 19, 1981.

The Detroit Red Wings scored 15 consecutive goals without an answering tally when they defeated the NY Rangers 15-0 on Jan 23, 1944.

HORSE RACING

Origins

There is evidence that men were riding horses, as distinct from riding in chariots pulled by horses, in Assyria and Egypt *c* 1400 BC. However, early organized racing appears to have been confined to chariots, for which the Roman method used riders with a foot on each of two horses. The first racing on horseback was by the Greeks in the 33rd Olympic Games in 648 BC. The earliest recorded race in Britain was at Netherby, Cumbria in 210 AD between Arabian horses brought to Britain by the Roman Emperor, Lucius Septimius Severus. The first recognizable regular race meeting was that held at Smithfield, London at the weekly horse fairs on Fridays in 1174. The first known prize money was a purse of gold presented by Richard I (the Lion-heart) in 1195 for a race between knights over a distance of 3 mi.

Organized horse racing began in New York State at least as early as March 1668. The original Charleston (Va) Jockey Club, organized in 1734, was the world's first.

Racing colors (silks) became compulsory in 1889.

All thoroughbred horses in the world today are descended from at least one of three great stallions, which were imported into Britain in the 17th and 18th centuries. The "Darley Arabian" was brought from Aleppo, Syria by the British Consul Richard

GREATEST MONEY-WINNING HORSE AND JOCKEY: "John Henry" (#1A, in foreground), with Bill Shoemaker up, is first to the wire for the $600,000 first prize in the 1½-mile 1981 Arlington Million. The first horse ever to pass $6 million in purses, "John Henry" was purchased as a yearling for only $1,100 and changed hands seven times before Sam Rubin bought him for $25,000 in 1978. He retired in July 1985.

MOST SUCCESSFUL JOCKEY: Bill (Willie) Shoemaker, winner of the 1986 Kentucky Derby, is only 94 lb and 4 ft 11 in tall, and has made over $110 million for the owners of the 38,853 mounts he has ridden. (Gerry Cranham)

Darley of Yorkshire *c* 1704; the "Byerley Turk" was brought to England from Turkey *c* 1685 and used by Captain Byerley as a charger in Ireland; and the Godolphin Barb—the latter word derived from the Barbary Coast of North Africa—was originally brought from France by Edward Coke in about 1735 and then acquired by the Earl of Godolphin.

Largest Prizes

The richest races ever held are the Breeders' Cup 7-race meetings, run most recently at Santa Anita Park, Calif, on Nov 1, 1986, which paid $10 million total in prize money. This included a total purse of $3 million to the top winners of the 1¼-mi Breeders' Cup Classic.

Victories

The horse with the best win-loss record was "Kincsem," a Hungarian mare foaled in 1874, who was unbeaten in 54 races (1876–79), including the English Goodwood Cup of 1878.

The longest winning sequence is 56 races, in Puerto Rico 1953–5, by "Camarero," foaled in 1951. He had 73 wins in 77 starts altogether. The most wins in a career is 137 from 159 starts by "Galgo Jr" (foaled 1928) in Puerto Rico between 1930 and 1936; in 1931 he won a record 30 races in one year. The only horse to win the same race in 7 successive years was "Doctor Syntax" (foaled 1811) in the Preston Gold Cup, 1815–21.

Dead Heats

There is no recorded case in turf history of a quintuple dead heat. The nearest approach was in the Astley Stakes at Lewes, England, on Aug 6, 1880, when "Mazurka," "Wandering Nun" and "Scobell" triple dead-heated for first place, just ahead of "Cumberland" and "Thora," who dead-heated for fourth place. Each of the five jockeys thought he had won. The only three known examples of a quadruple dead heat were between "Honest Harry," "Miss Decoy," "Young Daffodil" and "Peteria" at Bogside, England, on June 7, 1808; between "Defaulter," "The Squire of Malton," "Reindeer" and "Pulcherrima" in the Omnibus Stakes at The Hoo, England, on Apr 26, 1851; and between "Overreach," "Lady Go-Lightly," "Gamester" and "The Unexpected" at Newmarket, England, on Oct 22, 1855.

Since the introduction of the photo-finish, the highest number of horses in a dead heat has been three, on several occasions.

Greatest Winnings

The most won in a single race is $2.6 million by "Spend a Buck" on May 27, 1985 at Garden State Park in Cherry Hill, NJ. This included a $2 million bonus for also winning the Kentucky Derby and 2 preparatory races at Garden State Park.

The greatest amount ever won by a horse is $6,597,947 by the gelding "John Henry" (foaled 1975) from 1977 to July 1985, when he was retired.

HORSES' SPEED RECORDS

Distance	Time mph	Name	Course	Date
¼ mile	20.8s. 43.26	*Big Racket* (Mex)	Mexico City, Mex	Feb 5, 1945
½ mile	44.4s. 40.54	*Sonido* (Ven)	‡Caracas, Ven	June 28, 1970
	44.4s. 40.54	*Western Romance* (Can)	Calgary, Can	Apr 19, 1980
	44.4s. 40.54	*Northern Spike* (Can)	Winnipeg, Can	Apr 23, 1982
⅝ mile	53.6s. 41.98†	*Indigenous* (GB)	‡*Epsom, Eng	June 2, 1960
	53.89s. 41.75††	*Raffingora* (GB)	‡*Epsom, Eng	June 5, 1970
	55.2s. 40.76	*Chinook Pass* (US)	Seattle, Wash	Sept 17, 1982
¾ mile	1m. 06.2s. 40.78	*Broken Tendril* (GB)	*Brighton, Eng	Aug 6, 1929
	1m. 07.2s. 40.18	*Grey Papa* (US)	Longacres, Wash	Sept 4, 1972
	1m. 07.2s. 40.18	*Petro D. Jay* (US)	Phoenix, Ariz	May 9, 1982
Mile	1m. 31.8s. 39.21	*Soueida* (GB)	*Brighton, Eng	Sept 19, 1963
	1m. 31.8s. 39.21	*Loose Cover* (GB)	*Brighton, Eng	June 9, 1966
		Traditional Miss (GB)	Chepstow, Wales	June 27, 1981
		Traditional Miss (GB)	Chepstow, Wales	Aug, 31 1981
1¼ miles	1m. 57.4s. 38.33	*Double Discount* (US)	Arcadia, Calif	Oct 9, 1977
1½ miles	2m. 23.0s. 37.76	*Fiddle Isle* (US)	Arcadia, Calif	Mar 21, 1970
		John Henry (US)	Arcadia, Calif	Mar 16, 1980
2 miles	3m. 16.75s.	*Il Tempo* (NZ)	Trentham, Wellington, NZ	Jan 17, 1970
2½ miles	4m. 14.6s. 35.35	*Miss Grillo* (US)	Pimlico, Md	Nov 12, 1948
3 miles	5m. 15.0s. 34.29	*Farragut* (Mex)	Aguascalientes, Mex	Mar 9, 1941

* Course downhill for ¼ of a mile.
† Hand-timed.   †† Electrically timed.   ‡ Straight courses.

"All Along" (foaled 1979) won $3,018,420 in France and the US 1981–84 to become the leading money winner among mares.

Topmost Tipster

The only recorded instance of a racing correspondent forecasting ten out of ten winners on a race card was at Delaware Park, Wilmington, Del, on July 28, 1974, by Charles Lamb of the *Baltimore News American*.

Greatest Pay-Out

Three bettors shared the Sweep Six pool at Exhibition Park, Vancouver, BC, on July 10, 1982, each winning $579,129 (US) for a $2 (Canadian) ticket in what is believed to be the biggest single payoff in racing history.

Most Valuable Horses

The most expensive horse ever is the 1983 Irish Derby winner "Shareef Dancer." Reportedly 40 shares in the horse were sold at $1 million each in 1983 by his owner, Sheikh Mohammed Bin Rashid al Maktoum.

The highest price for a yearling is $13.1 million for "Seattle Dancer" on July 23, 1985, in Keeneland, Ky, by Robert Sangster and partners.

Triple Crown

Eleven horses have won all three races in one season which constitute the American Triple Crown (Kentucky Derby, Preakness Stakes and the Belmont Stakes). This feat was first achieved by "Sir Barton" in 1919, and most recently by "Seattle Slew" in 1977 and "Affirmed" in 1978.

The only Triple Crown winner to sire another winner was "Gallant Fox," the 1930 winner, who sired "Omaha," who won in 1935. The only jockey to ride two Triple Crown winners is Eddie Arcaro (b Feb 19, 1916), on "Whirlaway" (1941) and "Citation" (1948).

Owners

The most lifetime wins by an owner is 4,775 by Marion Van Berg in N America in the 35 years up to his death in 1971.

The most winners by an owner in one year is 494 by Dan R. Lasater (US) in 1974. The greatest amount won in a year is $3,070,225 by John Franks in 1984.

Kentucky Derby Winners

1¼ miles at Churchill Downs, Louisville, Kentucky; first held in 1875.

Year *Winner,* Jockey

1875 *Aristides,* O. Lewis
1876 *Vagrant,* R. Swim
1877 *Baden Baden,* W. Walker
1878 *Day Star,* J. Carter
1879 *Lord Murphy,* C. Schauer
1880 *Fonso,* G. Lewis
1881 *Hindoo,* J. McLaughlin
1882 *Apollo,* B. Hurd
1883 *Leonatus,* W. Donohue
1884 *Buchanan,* I. Murphy
1885 *Joe Cotton,* E. Henderson
1886 *Ben Ali,* P. Duffy
1887 *Montrose,* I. Lewis
1888 *Macbeth II,* G. Covington
1889 *Spokane,* T. Kiley
1890 *Riley,* I. Murphy
1891 *Kingman,* I. Murphy
1892 *Azra,* A. Clayton
1893 *Lookout,* E. Kunze
1894 *Chant,* F. Goodale
1895 *Halma,* J. Perkins
1896 *Ben Brush,* W. Simms
1899 *Manuel,* F. Taral
1900 *Lieutenant Gibson,* J. Boland
1901 *His Eminence,* J. Winkfield
1902 *Alan-a-Dale,* J. Winkfield
1903 *Judge Himes,* H. Booker
1904 *Elwood,* F. Prior
1905 *Agile,* J. Martin
1906 *Sir Huon,* R. Troxler
1907 *Pink Star,* A. Minder
1908 *Stone Street,* A. Pickens
1909 *Wintergreen,* V. Powers
1910 *Donau,* F. Herbert
1911 *Meridian,* G. Archibald
1912 *Worth,* C. H. Shilling
1913 *Donerail,* R. Goose
1914 *Old Rosebud,* J. McCabe
1915 *Regret,* J. Nutter
1916 *George Smith,* J. Loftus
1917 *Omar Khayyam,* C. Borel
1918 *Exterminator,* W. Knapp
1919 *Sir Barton,* J. Loftus
1920 *Paul Jones,* T. Rice
1921 *Behave Yourself,* C. Thompson
1922 *Morvich,* A. Johnson
1923 *Zev,* E. Sande
1924 *Black Gold,* J. D. Mahoney
1925 *Flying Ebony,* E. Sande
1926 *Bubbling Over,* A. Johnson
1927 *Whiskery,* L. McAtee
1928 *Reigh Count,* C. Lang
1929 *Clyde Van Dusen,* L. McAtee
1930 *Gallant Fox,* E. Sande
1931 *Twenty Grand,* C. Kurtsinger
1932 *Burgoo King,* E. James
1933 *Brokers Tip,* D. Meade
1934 *Cavalcade,* M. Garner
1935 *Omaha,* W. Saunders
1936 *Bold Venture,* I. Hanford
1937 *War Admiral,* C. Kurtsinger
1938 *Lawrin,* E. Arcaro
1939 *Johnstown,* J. Stout
1940 *Gallahadion,* C. Bierman
1941 *Whirlaway,* E. Arcaro
1942 *Shut Out,* W. D. Wright
1943 *Count Fleet,* J. Longden

RECORDHOLDING MARE: In 1983, the 4-year-old "All Along" earned a record $2,138,963 in the US and France, and retired after 1984 with a lifetime total of $3,018,420.

1944 *Pensive*, C. McCreary
1945 *Hoop, Jr.*, E. Arcaro
1946 *Assault*, W. Mehrtens
1947 *Jet Pilot*, E. Guerin
1948 *Citation*, E. Arcaro
1949 *Ponder*, S. Brooks
1950 *Middleground*, W. Boland
1951 *Count Turf*, C. McCreary
1952 *Hill Gail*, E. Arcaro
1953 *Dark Star*, H. Moreno
1954 *Determine*, R. York
1955 *Swaps*, W. Shoemaker
1956 *Needles*, D. Erb
1957 *Iron Liege*, W. Hartack
1958 *Tim Tam*, I. Valenzuela
1959 *Tomy Lee*, W. Shoemaker
1960 *Venetian Way*, W. Hartack
1961 *Carry Back*, J. Sellers
1962 *Decidedly*, W. Hartack
1963 *Chateaugay*, B. Baeza
1964 *Northern Dancer*, W. Hartack
1965 *Lucky Debonair*, W. Shoemaker
1966 *Kauai King*, D. Brumfield
1967 *Proud Clarion*, R. Ussery
1968 *Forward Pass**, I. Valenzuela

1969 *Majestic Prince*, W. Hartack
1970 *Dust Commander*, M. Manganello
1971 *Canonero II*, G. Avila
1972 *Riva Ridge*, R. Turcotte
1973 *Secretariat*, R. Turcotte
1974 *Cannonade*, A. Cordero
1975 *Foolish Pleasure*, J. Vasquez
1976 *Bold Forbes*, A. Cordero
1977 *Seattle Slew*, J. Cruguet
1978 *Affirmed*, S. Cauthen
1979 *Spectacular Bid*, R. Franklin
1980 *Genuine Risk*, J. Vasquez
1981 *Pleasant Colony*, J. Velasquez
1982 *Gato del Sol*, E. Delahoussaye
1983 *Sunny's Halo*, E. Delahoussaye
1984 *Swale*, L. Pincay
1985 *Spend a Buck*, A. Cordero
1986 *Ferdinand*, W. Shoemaker

* *Dancer's Image* finished first but was disqualified after drug tests.

Largest Grandstand

The largest at a racecourse is at Belmont Park, Long Island, NY, which seats 30,000 and is 440 yd long.

Longest Race

The longest recorded horse race was one of 1,200 miles in Portugal, won by "Emir," a horse bred from Egyptian-bred Blunt Arab stock. The holder of the world record for long distance racing and speed is "Champion Crabbet," who covered 300 miles in 52 hours 33 min, carrying 245 lb, in 1920.

Most Horses in a Race

In the Grand National (England) on Mar 22, 1929, there were 66 horses.

Trainers

The greatest number of wins by a trainer is 496 in one year by Jack Van Berg in 1976, and 4,400 in his career to 1986. The greatest amount won in a year is $11,802,701 by D. Wayne Lucas (US) in 1985. The only trainer to saddle the first 5 finishers in a championship race is Michael Dickinson in the 1983 Cheltenham Gold Cup. On Dec 27, 1982, he won a record 12 races in one day.

Jockeys

The most successful jockey of all time is William Lee (Bill or Willie) Shoemaker (b at 2½ lb on Aug 19, 1931) now weighing 94 lb and standing 4 ft 11 in. (His wife is nearly 1 ft taller than he is.) From Mar 1949 through 1986, he rode 8,621 winners from 38,853 mounts, earning $110,622,090. Laffitt Pincay, Jr (b Dec 29, 1946, Panama City, Panama) has earned a record $116,146,205 in 6,519 wins on 29,504 mounts, 1966–86.

Chris McCarron (US), (b 1955), won a total of 546 races in 1974 out of 2,199 mounts, an average of 6 races a day. He earned $12,038,213 in 1984, the greatest amount ever won by any jockey in a year.

The most winners ridden on one card is 8 by Hubert S. Jones, 17, out of 13 mounts at Caliente, Calif, on June 11, 1944 (of which 5 were photo-finishes); by Oscar Barattuci at Rosario, Argentina, on Dec 15, 1957; by Dave Gall from 10 mounts at Cahokia Downs, East St Louis, Ill, on Oct 18, 1978; and by Chris Loseth, 29, out of 10 mounts at Exhibition Park in Vancouver, BC, Canada on Apr 9, 1984.

The youngest jockey was Australian-born Frank Wootton (1893–1940) (Eng champion 1909–12), who rode his first winner in Africa, aged 9 years 10 months. The oldest jockey is Bill Shoemaker (see above) who won the Kentucky Derby in 1986 at the age of 55.

The lightest jockey recorded was Kitchener (Eng) (d 1872), who won the Chester Cup on "Red Deer" in 1844 at 49 lb. He is said to have weighed only 35 lb in 1840.

HORSESHOE PITCHERS Dale Lipousky (left) and Phyllis Negaard, both from Minn, show the correct grip for lefties and righties. (Las Vegas News Bureau)

HORSESHOE PITCHING

Origins

This sport was derived from military blacksmiths and is of great antiquity. The first formal World Championships were staged at Bronson, Kansas, in 1909.

Most Titles

The record for men's titles is 10 by Ted Allen (Boulder, Colorado) in 1933–34–35–40–46–53–55–56–57–59. The women's record is also 10 by Vicki Chapelle Winston (LaMonte, Missouri) in 1956–58–59–61–63–66–67–69–75–81.

Highest Percentage

The record for consecutive ringers is 72 by Ted Allen in 1955 for men, and 42 by Ruth Hangen in 1974 for women. The highest percentage for a single game is 100 percent by two different players: Guy Zimmerman (Alamo, Calif) 44 ringers in 44 shoes in 1948, and Elmer Hohl (Wellesley, Ont, Canada) 30 in 30 in 1968.

Most Ringers

The most ringers in a single game is 175 by Glen Henton of Maquoketa, Iowa, in 1965.

Marathon

The longest continuous session of a 4-man contest, two teams pitching continuously and without substitutions, is 96 hours by Gary Alexander, Ralph Lewis, Mylin Sorber and Patricia Reynolds in Idaho Springs, Colorado, August 6–10, 1980.

SAND YACHT SPEED of 66.48 mph for a world record was attained by "Mobil" in a 75-mph wind on the beach at Le Touquet, France, in Mar 1981.

ICE and SAND YACHTING

Origins

The sport originated in The Netherlands and Belgium from the year 1600 (earliest patent granted) and along the Baltic coast. The earliest authentic record is Dutch, dating from 1768. Land or sand yachts of Dutch construction were first reported on beaches (now in Belgium) in 1595. The earliest international championship was staged in 1914.

Largest Yacht

The largest ice yacht was *Icicle,* built for Commodore John E. Roosevelt for racing on the Hudson River, NY, in 1869. It was 68 ft 11 in long and carried 1,070 sq ft of canvas.

Highest Ice Speeds

The highest speed officially recorded is 143 mph by John D. Buckstaff in a Class A stern-steerer on Lake Winnebago, Wis, in 1938. Such a speed is possible in a wind of 72 mph.

Highest Sand Speeds

The official world record for a sand yacht is 66.48 mph set by Christian-Yves Nau (b 1944) (France) in *Mobil* at Le Touquet, France on Mar 22, 1981, when the wind speed reached 75 mph. A speed of 88.4 mph was attained by Nord Embroden (US) in *Midnight at the Oasis* at Superior Dry Lake, Calif, on Apr 15, 1976.

ICE SKATING

Origins

The earliest skates were made of animal bones, such as those found in France and thought to be 20,000 years old. The first reference to skating is in early Norse literature *c.* 200 AD but the earliest report of skating as a sport or pastime is in a British chronicle by William Fitzstephen of 1180. The first club

ON THE WAY TO STARDOM: Dorothy Hamill (US) started by winning the Olympic figure skating gold in 1976 and the World title that year too. She went on to star in ice shows. (UPI)

was founded in Edinburgh in 1744, and the earliest artificial ice rink was opened in London in 1876.

Speed skating or racing must have taken place from the earliest times, although curved rinks, especially for racing, did not appear until the 1880s. Two Americans developed figure skating into an art. E. W. Bushnell invented steel blades in 1848 and thereby provided the precision skate needed for ever more intricate figures, and the first true innovator and teacher was Jackson Haines. He was a ballet master who transferred the artistry of the dance to the ice when he went to Vienna in 1864. Louis Rubinstein was a founder of the Amateur Skating Association of Canada in 1878, the first national governing body in the world. In 1892 the International Skating Union was set up at Scheveningen, Netherlands.

Longest Race

The longest race regularly held was the "Elfstedentocht" ("Tour of the Eleven Towns") in The Netherlands, covering 200 km (124 miles 483 yd). The fastest time was 6 hours 5 min 12 sec by Jan-Roelof Kruithof (Neth) on Feb 25, 1979 at Oulu, Finland. Kruithof won the race 8 times, 1974, 76–77, 79–83. The race was transferred to Finland in 1964 and subsequently to Canada, but it was returned to The Netherlands in 1985. An estimated 16,000 skaters took part in 1986.

MOVIE STAR Sonja Henie (Norway) (left) earned an estimated $47 million in ice shows and films after winning 3 Olympic golds in 1928-32-36 and 10 world titles. GOLD MEDALIST Scott Hamilton (right) was the only American ice skater to win a gold medal in the 1984 Olympics.

MOST DIFFICULT JUMP-LIFT: Marina Tcherkasova was only 12 years old when she and Sergei Shakrai first performed their unique quadruple twist lift in 1977. Shakrai was 18 years old at the time. (Popperfoto)

Largest Rink

The world's largest indoor artificial ice rink is in the Moscow Olympic arena which has an ice area of 86,800 sq ft. The largest outdoors is the Fujikyu Highland Promenade Rink complex in Japan with 285,243 sq ft.

Marathon

The longest recorded skating marathon is 109 hours 5 min by Austin McKinley of Christchurch, NZ, June 21–25, 1977.

FIGURE SKATING

Most Difficult Jumps

Many of the most difficult jumps in skating are named after their originators, such as the Axel (after Axel Paulsen of Norway) and the Salchow (after Ulrich Salchow of Sweden).

The first woman to attempt a jump in major com-

petition is said to have been Theresa Weld (US) who was reprimanded for her "unfeminine behavior" in the 1920 Olympic events. Cecilia Colledge (GB) was the first woman to achieve two turns in the air a few years later. In the 1962 World Championships Donald Jackson (Can) performed the first triple Lutz in a major competition and in the 1978 championships Vern Taylor, another Canadian, achieved the first triple Axel. Among women, the first triple Salchow was done by Sonja Morgenstern (E Ger) in 1972, and the first triple Lutz by Denise Beilmann (Switz) in the 1978 European championships. Incidentally, the latter has a spin named after her.

The first quadruple twist was performed by Marina Tcherkasova and Sergei Shakrai (USSR) in a pairs competition in Helsinki in 1977. They were able to achieve this because of the unusual difference in size between the tiny 12-year-old girl and her tall male partner.

A backward somersault jump was successfully negotiated by Terry Kubicka (US) in the 1976 world championships but it was immediately banned as being too dangerous.

Highest Marks

The highest score from a single set of marks in any world figure skating competition was gained by Jayne Torvill (b Oct 7, 1957) and Christopher Dean (b July 27, 1958) of Great Britain when awarded maximum sixes by all 9 judges for artistic presentation of their free dance "Barnum-on-ice" routine in the World Ice-Dance championships at Helsinki, Finland, Mar 12, 1983.

The highest number of maximum sixes awarded for one performance in an international championship was 13 to Torvill and Dean in the World Ice Dancing Competition in Ottawa, Canada, on Mar 24, 1984.

Donald Jackson (Canada) was awarded 7 "sixes" (the most by a soloist) in the world men's championship at Prague, Czechoslovakia, in 1962.

World Titles

The greatest number of individual world men's figure skating titles (instituted 1896) is 10 by Ulrich Salchow (1877–1949), of Sweden, in 1901–05, 07–11. The women's record (instituted 1906) is also 10 individual titles, by Sonja Henie (Apr 8, 1912–Oct 12, 1969), of Norway, between 1927 and 1936. Irina Rodnina (b Sept 12, 1949), of the USSR, has won 10 pairs titles (instituted 1908)—four with Aleksiy Ulanov (1969–72) and six with her husband Alek-

sandr Zaitsev (1973–78). The most ice dance titles
(instituted 1952) won is 6 by Aleksandr Gorshkov (b
Oct 8, 1946) and his wife, Ludmilla Pakhomova
(1946–86), both of the USSR, in 1970–74 and 76.

Olympic Titles in Figure Skating

The most Olympic gold medals won by a figure
skater is 3 by Gillis Grafström (1893–1938), of Sweden, in 1920, 24 and 28 (also silver medal in 1932); by
Sonja Henie (see *World Titles*) in 1928, 32 and 36;
and by Irina Rodnina (see *World Titles*) in the pairs
event in 1972, 76 and 80.

Distance

Robin Cousins (GB) (b Mar 17, 1957) achieved 19
ft 1 in in an Axel jump and 18 ft with a back flip at
Richmond Ice Rink, Surrey, Eng on Nov 16, 1983.

Barrel Jumping (on ice skates)

The official distance record is 29 ft 5 in over 18
barrels by Yvon Jolin at Terrebonne, Quebec, Canada, in 1981. The feminine record is 20 ft 4½ in over
11 barrels by Janet Hainstock in Mich on Mar 15,
1980.

SPEED SKATING

World Titles

The greatest number of world overall titles (instituted 1893) won by any skater is 5 by Oscar Mathisen
(Norway) (1888–1954) in 1908–09, 12–14, and Clas
Thunberg (1893–1973) of Finland, in 1923, 25, 28–29
and 31. The most titles won by a woman is 4 by Mrs
Inga Voronina, *née* Artomonova (1936–66) of Moscow, USSR, in 1957–58, 62 and 65, and Mrs Atje
Keulen-Deelstra of The Netherlands (b Dec 31,
1938) in 1970, 72–74.

The record score achieved in the world overall title
is 162.973 points by Eric Heiden (US) at Oslo, Norway, Feb 10–11, 1979. The record by a woman is
171.760 points by Andrea Schöne of E Germany at
Medeo, USSR Mar 23–24, 1984.

Olympic Titles

The most Olympic gold medals won in speed skating is 6 by Lidia Skoblikova (b March 8, 1939), of
Chelyabinsk, USSR, in 1960 (2) and 1964 (4). The
male record is held by Clas Thunberg (see above)
with 5 gold (including 1 tied gold) and also 1 silver
and 1 tied bronze in 1924–28; and by Eric Heiden

WORLD SPEED SKATING RECORDS
(Ratified by the I.S.U.)

Distance	min:sec	Name and Nationality	Place	Date
MEN				
500 m	36.49*	Igor Zhelezovsky (USSR)	Moscow, USSR	Dec 21, 1985
1000 m	1:12.58	Pavel Pegov (USSR)	Medeo, USSR	Mar 25, 1983
1500 m	1:53.00	Igor Zhelezovsky (USSR)	Medeo, USSR	Dec 15, 1985
3000 m	4:03.22	Viktor Shasherin (USSR)	Davos, Switzerland	Jan 19, 1986
5000 m	6:49.15	Viktor Shasherin (USSR)	Medeo, USSR	Mar 23, 1984
10,000 m	14:12.14	Geir Karlstad (Norway)	Inzell, W Ger	Feb 16, 1986
WOMEN				
500 m	39.52	Karin Kania (*née* Enke) (E Ger)	Medeo, USSR	Mar 21, 1986
1000 m	1:18.84	Karin Kania (E Ger)	Karulzawa, Japan	Feb 23, 1986
1500 m	1:59.30	Karin Kania (E Ger)	Medeo, USSR	Mar 22, 1986
3000 m	4:18.02	Karin Kania (E Ger)	Medeo, USSR	Mar 21, 1986
5000 m	7:20.99	Ehrig (*née* Schöne) (E Ger)	Medeo, USSR	Mar 22, 1986

* Represents an average speed of 30.65 mph. Note that Medeo, Alma-Ata, USSR is situated at an altitude of 1,691 m.

SPEED SKATING DOUBLE GOLD MEDALIST: At the 1985 Winter Olympics, Karin Kania (E Ger) won 2 golds and in 1986 regained 4 of her world records.

AMERICAN SPEEDSTER: His unprecedented 5-event sweep of the 1980 Olympic speed skating competition made Eric Heiden the first Olympic athlete to earn 5 individual (that is, not relay or team) gold medals at one Games.

(US) (b June 14, 1958) who won 5 gold medals, all at Lake Placid, NY, in 1980.

24 Hours

Ton Smits (Neth) skated 314.65 mi in 24 hours in Eindhoven, Neth, Dec 15–16, 1984.

OFF THE WALL: Jai-alai features the highest projectile speed of any ball game, the fastest measured speed being 188 mph. The exciting acrobatic game is most often played on a 3-walled court (front, back, and side), with the fourth side open for spectators.

JAI-ALAI (Pelota)

Origins

The game, which originated in Italy as *longue paume* and was introduced into France in the 13th century, is said to be the fastest of all ball games. The glove or *gant* was introduced *c.* 1840 and the *chistera* was invented by Jean "Gantchiki" Dithurbide of Ste Pée, France. The *grand chistera* was invented by Melchior Curuchague of Buenos Aires, Argentina in 1888.

The world's largest *frontón* (enclosed stadium) is the World Jaï Alaï at Miami, Fla, which had a record attendance of 15,052 on Dec 27, 1975.

World Championships

The Federacion Internacional de Pelota Vasca stages world championships every four years (first in 1952). The most successful pair has been Roberto Elias and Juan Labat (Argentina), who won the *Trinquete Share* four times, 1952, 1958, 1962 and 1966. Labat won a record 7 world titles in all. The most wins in the long court game *Cesta Punta* is 3 by Hamuy of Mexico, with two different partners, 1958, 1962 and 1966.

Highest Speed

An electronically measured ball velocity of 188 mph was recorded by José Ramon Arieto at the Newport Jai Alai, RI, on Aug 3, 1979.

Longest Domination

The longest domination as the world's No. 1 player was enjoyed by Chiquito de Cambo (*né* Joseph Apesteguy) (France), (1881–1955) from the beginning of the century until succeeded in 1938 by Jean Urruty (France) (b Oct 19, 1913).

Biggest Payout

The highest parimutuel payout in the US was for a group of bettors who won $988,326 (less $197,664 paid to the Internal Revenue) for a $2 ticket naming six consecutive winning Jai-Alai players at Palm Beach, Fla on Mar 1, 1983.

JUDO

Origins

Judo is a modern combat sport which developed out of an amalgam of several old Japanese fighting arts, the most popular of which was *ju-jitsu* (*jiu-jitsu*), which is thought to be of Chinese origin. Judo has developed greatly since 1882, when it was first devised by Dr. Jigoro Kano (1860–1938). World Championships were inaugurated in Tokyo on May 5, 1956. The International Judo Federation was founded in 1951, and it no longer considers judo one of the martial arts, only a sport.

Grades

The efficiency grades in Judo are divided into pupil (*kyu*) and master (*dan*) grades. A white belt signifies a beginning student. The next 3 grades upwards are a brown belt, and the highest grade or black belt *(dan)* is divided into 10 degrees, with the 6th, 7th and 8th entitled to wear a red and white belt, and the 9th and 10th degrees a solid red belt. The solid red has been given to only 13 men, and the 11th *dan* never awarded.

A 12th *dan,* entitling the wearer to a white belt twice as wide as an ordinary belt, and the title *Shihan* (Doctor) was awarded to the founder of the sport, Jigoro Kano.

The highest degree for a woman is 7th *dan* and only 2 Japanese have attained it, one being Ms Keiko Fukuda, living in San Francisco.

TWO OF THE GREATEST KARATEKAS: Masotashi Nakoyama (left) and Hirokazu Kanazawa (right) demonstrate their art.

FLIPPERS: Japan's Shinobu Sekine (above) beat Brian Jacks in this semi-final match enroute to the middleweight gold medal in the 1972 Olympics. Wilhelm (Wim) Ruska (right) celebrates his second gold medal in the same (1972) Games, this one in the Open division. Ruska won an additional 2 world titles.

Olympics

Included since 1964, with the exception of 1968. Only Wim Ruska (Neth) has won more than one title, with the over 93 kg and the Open classes in 1972. One of the biggest upsets to national pride in any sport occurred in 1964 when the giant 6 ft 6 in Dutchman, Anton Geesink, won the Open category in Tokyo before some 15,000 partisan Japanese spectators. Yasuhiro Yamashita (Japan) (b June 1, 1957) added to his 7-year unbeaten record by winning the Open category.

Open
1964 Anton Geesink (Neth)
1972 Wim Ruska (Neth)
1976 Haruki Uemura (Jap)
1980 Dietmar Lorenz (E Ger)
1984 Yasuhiro Yamashita (Jap)
Over 95 kg (formerly over 93 kg)
Isao Inokuma (Jap)
Wim Ruska (Neth)
Sergei Novikov (USSR)
Angelo Parisi (France)
Hitoshi Saito (Jap)
95 kg (formerly 93 kg)
1964 Not held
1972 Shota Chochoshvili (USSR)
1976 Kazuhiro Ninomiya (Jap)
1980 Robert van de Walle (Belgium)
1984 Ha Hyoung-Zoo (S Korea)
86 kg (formerly 80 kg)
Isao Okano (Jap)
Shinobu Sekine (Jap)
Isamu Sonoda (Jap)
Jürg Röthlisberger (Swi)
Peter Seisenbacher (Austria)
78 kg
1980 Shota Khabareli (USSR)
1984 Frank Wiencke (W Ger)
65 kg
Nikolai Soludkhin (USSR)
Yoshiyuki Matsucka (Japan)
70 kg (formerly 71 kg)
1964 Not held
1972 Kazutoyo Nomura (Jap)
1976 Vladimir Nevzorov (USSR)
1980 Ezio Gamba (Italy)
1984 Byeong Kuen Ahu (S Korea)
60 kg (formerly 63 kg)
Takehide Nakatani (Jap)
Takao Kawaguchi (Jap)
Hector Rodriguez (Cuba)
Thierry Ray (France)
Shinji Hosokawa (Jap)

World Champions

Judo World Championships were first held in Tokyo in 1956 and are now held biennially. New weight categories were applied to the 1979 competition and there are now 8 weight classes. Women's championships were first held in NYC in 1980.

Three men have won 4 world titles. Yasuhiro Ya-

mashita won heavyweight in 1979, 1981, 1983 and Open 1981, and retired undefeated after 203 successive wins, 1977–85. Wilhelm Ruska (b Aug 29, 1940) of The Netherlands won the 1967 and the 1971 heavyweight and the 1972 Olympic heavyweight and Open titles, and Shozo Fujii (Japan) (b May 12, 1950) won the middleweight title in 1971, 1973, 1975, and 1979. Ingrid Berghmans (Belgium) with 8 has won most medals by a woman, gold and bronze in 1980, gold and silver in 1982, 2 golds in 1984, and gold and silver in 1986.

Marathon

The longest recorded Judo marathon with continuous play by pairs is 245½ hours by 5 of 6 people at the Smithfield RSL Youth Club, NSW, Australia, Jan 3–13, 1984.

KARATE

Origins

Originally *karate* (empty hand) is known to have been developed by the unarmed populace as a method of attack on, and defense against, armed Japanese aggressors in Okinawa, Ryukyu Islands, based on techniques devised from the 6th century Chinese art of Shaolin boxing (Kempo). Transmitted to Japan in the 1920's by Funakoshi Gichin, this method of combat was refined and organized into a sport with competitive rules.

The five major schools of *karate* in Japan are *Shotokan, Wado-ryu, Goju-ryu, Shito-ryu,* and *Kyokushinkai,* each of which places different emphasis on speed, power, etc. Other styles include *Sankukai, Shotokai* and *Shukokai.* The military form of *Taekwan-do* with 9 *dans* is a Korean equivalent of *karate. Kung fu* is believed to have originated in Nepal or Tibet but was adopted within Chinese temples *via* India, and has in recent years been widely popularized through various martial arts films.

Wu shu is a comprehensive term embracing all Chinese martial arts.

Grades

The white belt in karate signifies beginner grade 9. As the student progresses he rises to grades 8 and 7 (yellow belt), 6 and 5 (green), 4 (purple), 3, 2, and 1 (brown) and finally black belt.

pre-Olympic tournament in 1984. Canada won in 1978, beating the US 17–16 in overtime. World Championships for women were instituted in 1969, and have been contested 4 times. Great Britain won the first title, the US won in 1974 and 1982, but were beaten 10–7 by Australia in the 1986 final.

Highest Score

The highest score in any international match was US over Canada, 28–4, at Stockport, Eng, on July 3, 1978. The highest total goal output in the World Games competition was seen in Australia's win over Canada, 24–18, in the 1982 World Games in Baltimore.

Collegiate

Johns Hopkins University has won or shared 39 national championships.

John Cheek (Washington College) netted 200 career goals, while Doug Fry (Maryland-Baltimore County) holds the collegiate record with 70 goals in one season.

Rick Gilbert (Hobart) holds the USILA record for single season assists (88) and points (122). He also holds career records with 287 assists and a remarkable 444 points.

Jeff Singer made a record 909 career saves as goaltender for MIT.

TEACHING KARATE TO ROYALTY: Mas Oyama (left), Japanese master, author of the book "Mas Oyama's Essential Karate," is instructing a prince of the Jordanian royal family in the fine points of the sport.

Most Titles

The only winner of 3 All-Japanese titles has been Takeshi Oishi, who won in 1969–70–71.

The leading exponents among karatekas are a number of 10th *dans* in Japan.

LACROSSE

Origin

The game is of American Indian origin, derived from the inter-tribal game *baggataway,* and was played by Iroquois Indians at lower Ontario, Canada, and upper NY State, before 1492. The French named it after their game of *Chouler à la crosse,* known in 1381. The game was included in the Olympic Games of 1904 and 1908, and featured as an exhibition sport in 1928 and 1948 Games.

World Championship

The US won 4 of the 5 Men's World Championships, in 1967, 1974, 1982, and 1986 and also won the

DOUBLE VICTORIES: Candy Finn (in white) achieved an unusual double when Penn State won the AIAW titles in both field hockey and lacrosse. Finn scored the winning goals in both championship games.

NATIVE SPORT: Lacrosse was derived from a game played by Iroquois Indians, whose contests would cover several miles and last several days. This illustration depicts a contest between Iroquois and early Canadian settlers.

Women's Championship

The Association for Intercollegiate Athletics for Women (founded 1971) and the US Women's Lacrosse Association (founded 1931) jointly sponsored collegiate championships from 1978 to 1980. In 1981, the tournament was run solely by the A.I.A.W. Since then it has been sponsored by the National Collegiate Athletic Association. The rules differ considerably from the men's game.

MARATHONS (Running)

The inaugural marathon races were staged in Greece in 1896. There were two trial races before the first Olympic marathon at Athens. The race commemorated the legendary run of an unknown Greek courier, possibly Pheidippides, who in 490 BC ran some 24 miles from the Plain of Marathon to Athens with the news of a Greek victory over the numeri-

CHAMPS: The Tar Heels of North Carolina rose to the top in 1981 and 1982 over defending champion Johns Hopkins in the NCAA championship game, but Johns Hopkins came back in 1984.

cally superior Persian army. Delivering his message—"Rejoice! We have won."—he collapsed and died. The Olympic races were run over varying distances until 1924 when the distance was standardized at 26 miles 385 yd, the distance first instituted in the 1908 Games in London.

There are no official records for the distance due to the variety of courses used and their varying severity, but the figures below are generally accepted to be the progressive best-known times on record.

The NYC Marathon in 1986 drew the largest number of competitors—20,595 started and 19,412 finished. In 1982, it drew the largest number of spectators—2,500,000 estimated to have lined the city streets along the route.

In the NYC Marathon in 1986, won by Gianni Poli of Italy and Grete Waitz of Norway, no new records were set.

Marathon Progressive Record

Men

2:55:18.4	Johnny Hayes (US)	1908
2:52:45.4	Robert Fowler (US)	1909
2:46:52.6	James Clark (US)	1909
2:46:04.6	Albert Raines (US)	1909
2:42:31.0	Fred Barrett (GB)	1909
2:40:34.2	Thore Johansson (Swed)	1909
2:38:16.2	Harry Green (GB)	1913
2:36:06.6	Alexis Ahlgren (Swed)	1913
2:32:35.8	Hannes Kolehmainen (Fin)	1920
2:29:01.8	Albert Michelsen (US)	1925
2:27:49.0	Fusashige Suzuki (Japan)	1925
2:26:44.0	Yasao Ikenaka (Japan)	1935
2:26:42.0	Kitei Son (Japan)	1935
2:25:39.0	Yun Bok Suh (S Korea)	1947
2:20:42.2	Jim Peters (GB)	1952
2:18:40.2	Jim Peters (GB)	1953
2:18:34.8	Jim Peters (GB)	1953
2:17:39.4	Jim Peters (GB)	1954
2:15:17.0	Sergey Popov (USSR)	1958
2:15:16.2	Abebe Bikila (Ethiopia)	1960
2:15:15.8	Toru Terasawa (Japan)	1963
2:14:28.0*	Buddy Edelen (US)	1963
2:13:55.0	Basil Heatley (GB)	1964
2:12:11.2	Abebe Bikila (Ethiopia)	1964
2:12:00.0	Morio Shigematsu (Japan)	1965
2:09:36.4	Derek Clayton (Australia)	1967
2:08:33.6	Derek Clayton (Australia)	1969
2:08:05.2†	Alberto Salazar (US)	1981
2:08:05.0	Stephen Jones (GB)	1984
2:07:11.06	Carlos Lopes (Port)	1985

* 36 yd (about 6 sec) under standard distance.
† NYC course later found to be 170 yd short.

Women

3:40:22.0	Violet Piercy (GB)	1926
3:27:45.0	Dale Greig (GB)	1966
3:19:33.0	Mildred Sampson (NZ)	1964
3:15:22.0	Maureen Wilton (Can)	1967
3:07:26.0	Anni Pede (W Ger)	1967
3:02:53.0	Caroline Walker (US)	1970
3:01:42.0	Elizabeth Bonner (US)	1971
2:46:30.0	Adrienne Beames (Australia)	1971
2:46:24.0	Chantal Langlace (France)	1974
2:43:54.5	Jackie Hansen (US)	1974
2:42:24.0	Liane Winter (W Ger)	1975
2:40:15.8	Christa Vahlensieck (W Ger)	1975
2:38:19.0	Jackie Hansen (US)	1975
2:35:15.4	Chantal Langlace (France)	1977
2:34:47.5	Christa Vahlensieck (W Ger)	1977
2:32:29.8†	Grete Waitz (Nor)	1978
2:27:32.6†	Grete Waitz (Nor)	1979
2:25:41.0†	Grete Waitz (Nor)	1980
2:25:28.8†	Allison Roe (NZ)	1981
2:25:28.7†	Grete Waitz (Nor)	1983
2:22:43.0	Joan Benoit (US)	1984
2:21:06.0	Ingrid Kristiansen (Nor)	1985

THE BOSTON MARATHON (above), the oldest US race of its kind, was won 7 times by Clarence DeMar. This was 1930. The NYC MARATHON (left) with 20,000 or more runners, gets its start on the Verrazano Bridge. BALANCING A BOTTLE on a tray is the way Roger Bourban (right) runs in every marathon.

RIDE, FENCE, SHOOT, SWIM AND RUN: András Balczó (left) of Hungary won a record 6 world titles and 3 Olympic gold medals (team) as well as the 1972 Olympic individual title, an extraordinary feat in this multifaceted event. Lars Hall (right) of Sweden has won 2 individual Olympic golds, 1952 and 1956.

MODERN PENTATHLON

Origins

In the ancient Olympics the Pentathlon was the most prestigious event of the Games. Traditionally inspired by the city of Sparta, it consisted of the discus and javelin throws, running, jumping and wrestling, and the competitors were eulogized by Aristotle. The concept of the five-event all-round sporting contest was held dear by the founder of the modern Games, Baron de Coubertin, but it was not until 1912 that it was first held.

The events of the Modern Pentathlon are riding (on an unfamiliar horse over an 800-meter course with 15 fences), fencing (with electrically wired épées against all others one at a time), shooting (with .22 caliber pistols at turning targets set at 25 meters), swimming (300 meter freestyle), and finally a 4000 meter cross-country run, each event held on a different day.

There is a story that the competitor is supposed to represent a King's messenger. First he rides like the wind to outdistance his pursuers; then when his horse is brought down, he fences his way out of trouble, following up with some good shooting to drive back

the enemy's reserves. Then he crosses the final obstacle, a river, and finally runs home to deliver his message. Certainly the qualities required of a Modern Pentathlete are not far removed from those of the messenger in the story.

Points are awarded for each activity with 1,000 being the standard for a good performance, excellence earning bonuses, and penalty points deducted for a sub-par performance. The winner is the one with the highest total after the five events. Initially only military personnel competed, but since the founding of the Union Internationale de Pentathlon Moderne et Biathlon (UIPMB) in 1948, non-military competitors have been allowed. Originally the same Union administered Biathlon 1957–58. Women's competitions for 14-year-olds and over were first held internationally in 1981.

Most World Championship Titles

World championships were first held in 1949 and annually since, except in Olympic years, when the Olympic and world titles are held simultaneously.

The record number of world titles won is 6 by András Balczó (Hungary) in 1963, 65–67 and 69, and the Olympic title in 1972. He also won 7 team titles (1960–70) with 5 world and 2 Olympic titles.

Highest Scores

	Points	Name and Nationality	Date and Place
Shooting			
200/200	—[1]	Charles Leonard (US) (b Feb 23, 1913)	Aug 3, 1936 W Berlin, Germ
200/200	1,132	Daniele Masala (Italy) (b Feb 12, 1955)	Aug 21, 1978 Jönkoping, Swed
200/200	1,132	Geo Horvath (Swed) (b Mar 14, 1960)	July 22, 1980 Moscow, USSR
Swimming			
3 min 08.22 sec	1,368	John Scott (US) (b Apr 14, 1962)	Aug 27, 1982 London, Eng

[1] Points not awarded in 1936 Olympic Games.

Point scores in riding, fencing, cross-country and hence overall scores have no comparative value between one competition and another. In shooting and swimming (300 m), where measurements are absolute, the point scores are of record significance.

Olympic Titles

The greatest number of Olympic gold medals won is 3 by Balczó, a member of Hungary's winning team in 1960 and 68, and the 1972 individual champion. Lars Hall (Sweden) (b Apr 30, 1927) uniquely has won 2 individual championships (1952 and 56). Pavel Lednev (USSR) (b Mar 25, 1943) has won a record 7 medals (2 gold, 2 silver, 3 bronze), 1968–80.

Probably the greatest margin of victory was by William Oscar Guernsey Grut (b Sept 17, 1914) (Sweden) in the 1948 Games in London, when he won three events and placed fifth and eighth in the other two events.

The gold medal winner in 1984 was Daniele Masala of Italy with 5,469 points. The Italian team won with 16,060 points, the highest number of points scored in any Games.

MOTORCYCLING

Earliest Motorcycle

On Nov 10, 1885, a single-track vehicle, powered by an internal-combustion engine designed by Gottlieb Daimler, was ridden a little over 7 mi from Canstatt to Unterturkheim, Germany. Daimler's vehicle, due to its engine location and basic design features which remain current today, is universally acknowledged as the world's first motorcycle, predating the first automobile—also by Daimler—by several months.

Earliest Races and Circuits

The first motorcycle race was held on an oval track of 1 mi at Sheen House, Richmond, Surrey, England, on Nov 29, 1897, won by Charles Jarrott (1877–1944) on a Fournier.

In the early days many races were for both motorcycles and cars, and often took the form of long-distance inter-city or inter-country events. These were heavily criticized following the aborted Paris to Madrid race of 1903 which resulted in a number of deaths of competitors and spectators. In 1904 the International Cup Race was held in France for motorcycles only, and on a closed road circuit. However, in 1905 the race was held again, and this is recognized as the first international motorcycling event. The venue was Dourdon near Paris, and it was organized by the newly formed Fédération Internationale des Clubs Motocyclistes (FICM), the predecessor of the Fédération Internationale Motocycliste (FIM). The race was a success and was won by an Austrian named Wondrick.

The Auto-Cycle Union Tourist Trophy (TT) series was first held on the 15.81-mile "Peel" ("St John's") course on the Isle of Man on May 28, 1907, and is still run on the island, on the "Mountain" circuit.

Longest Circuit

The 37.73-mile "Mountain" circuit on the Isle of Man, over which the two main TT races have been run since 1911, has 264 curves and corners and is the longest used for any motorcycle race.

Fastest Circuits

The highest average lap speed attained on any closed circuit is 160.288 mph by Yvon du Hamel (Canada) (b 1941) on a modified 903-cc four-cylinder Kawasaki Z1 on the 31-degree banked 2.5-mile Daytona International Speedway, Fla, in March 1973. His lap time was 56.149 sec.

The fastest road circuit has been the Francor-

QUICK AS A VINK: Henk Vink of The Netherlands set world records in 1977 for 1 kilometer and for 440 yds on his Kawasaki in 2-way runs from standing starts.

champs circuit near Spa, Belgium. It is 14.12 km (8 miles 1,340 yd) in length and was lapped in 3 min 50.3 sec (average speed of 137.150 mph) by Barry S. F. Sheene (b Holborn, London, England, Sept 11, 1950) on a 495-cc four-cylinder Suzuki during the Belgian Grand Prix on July 3, 1977.

The TT circuit (Isle of Man) speed record is 118.47 mph by Joey Dunlop on a Honda on June 4, 1984.

Fastest Race

The fastest track race in the world was held at Grenzlandring, W Germany, in 1939. It was won by Georg "Schorsh" Meier (b Germany Nov 9, 1910) at an average speed of 134 mph on a supercharged 495-cc flat-twin BMW.

The fastest road race is the 500-cc Belgian Grand Prix on the Francorchamps circuit (see above). The record time for this 10-lap 87.74-mile race is 38 min 58.5 sec (average speed of 135.068 mph) by Barry Sheene (UK) on a 495-cc four-cylinder Suzuki on July 3, 1977.

Longest Race

The longest race is the Liège 24 Hours, run on the Francorchamps circuit. The greatest distance ever covered is 2,761.9 miles (average speed 115.08 mph) by Jean-Claude Chemarin and Christian Leon of France on a 941-cc four-cylinder Honda on the Francorchamps circuit on Aug 14–15, 1976 (see above).

Most Successful Machines

Italian MV-Agusta motorcycles won 37 world championships between 1952 and 1973 and 276 world championship races between 1952 and 1976. Japanese Honda machines won 29 world championship races and 5 world championships in 1966. In the

DOUBLE WINNER: World champion Barry Sheene (UK) holds both the lap and race records for the Belgian Grand Prix, the road race held at Francorchamps.

SPEEDWAY CHAMPION: Racing on a dirt track (the event began in the US in 1902), Erik Gundersen of Denmark in 1985 became the first to hold 4 world titles simultaneously.
(All Sport)

7 years that Honda contested the championship (1961–67) its annual average was 20 race wins. In the sidecar class BMW machines won an unprecedented 19 consecutive championships between 1955 and 1973.

Speed Records

Official world speed records must be set with two runs over a measured distance within a time limit (one hour for FIM records, two hours for AMA records).

Donald Vesco (b Loma Linda, Calif, Apr 8, 1939) riding his 21-ft-long *Lightning Bolt* streamliner, powered by two 1,016-cc Kawasaki engines on Bonneville Salt Flats, Utah, on Aug 28, 1978, set AMA and FIM absolute records with an overall average of 318.598 mph and had a fastest run at an average of 318.66 mph.

The world record average speed for two runs over 1 km (1,093.6 yd) from a standing start is 16.68 sec by Henk Vink (b July 24, 1939) (Netherlands) on his supercharged 984-cc 4-cylinder Kawasaki, at Elvington Airfield, Yorkshire, England, on July 24, 1977. The faster run was made in 16.09 sec.

The world record for two runs over 440 yd from a standing start is 8.805 sec by Henk Vink on his supercharged 1,132-cc 4-cylinder Kawasaki, at Elvington Airfield, Yorkshire, England, on July 23, 1977. The faster run was made in 8.55 sec.

The fastest time for a single run over 440 yd from a standing start is 7.08 sec by Bo O'Brechta (US) riding a supercharged 1,200-cc Kawasaki-based machine at Ontario, Calif, in 1980. The highest terminal velocity recorded at the end of a 440-yd run from a standing start is 201.34 mph by Elmer Trett at Indianapolis, on Sept 5, 1983.

World Championships

Races are currently held for the following classes of motorcycles: 50 cc, 125 cc, 250 cc, 350 cc, 500 cc, and sidecars.

Most world championship titles (instituted by the *Fédération Internationale Motocycliste* in 1949) won are 15 by Giacomo Agostini (b Lovere, Italy, June 16, 1942) in the 350-cc class 1968–74 and in the 500-cc class 1966–72 and 75. Agostini is the only man to win two world championships in five consecutive years (350 and 500 cc titles 1968–72). Freddie Spencer (US) in 1985 became the first ever to win world titles at both 250 and 500 cc in the same year. Agostini won 122 races in the world championship series between Apr 24, 1965, and Aug 29, 1976, including a record 19 in 1970, also achieved by Stanley Michael "Mike" Hailwood, (b Oxford, England, 1940, d 1981) in 1966.

A record 3 world trials championships have been won by Yrjö Vesterinen (Finland) (1976–8) and by Eddie Lejeune (Belgium).

Klaus Enders (Germany) (b 1937) won 6 world sidecar titles, 1967, 69–70, 72–74.

CROSS-U S TREK: In this 260-lb 125-cc revised Suzuki, without refueling, Matt Guzzetta rode 2,443 mi from San Diego to Daytona Beach on 11.83 gallons in Mar 1984, for a record 214.37 mpg.

Alberto "Johnny" Cecotto (b Caracas, Venezuela, Jan 25, 1956) was the youngest person to win a world championship. He was aged 19 years 211 days when he won the 350-cc title on Aug 24, 1975. The oldest was Hermann-Peter Müller (1909–76) of W Germany, who won the 250-cc title in 1955, aged 46.

Cross-US Trek

Joseph Railton (b 1920) of Park City, Utah, rode a motorcycle from San Francisco to NYC in 64 hours June 1–4, 1985 for the fastest transcontinental trip, averaging 45.84 mph over the 2,934-mi distance.

Matthew P. Guzzetta, 31, of Don Vesco Products, Spring Valley, Calif claims to have ridden a 260-lb, 125-cc revised Suzuki motorcycle whose shell he designed and built, from San Diego, Calif, to Daytona Beach, Fla, without refueling, Mar 3–17, 1984. With a writer-friend, Gerald Foster, he covered the 2,443 mi on 11.83 gallons, for a record consumption of 214.37 mpg. In a snowstorm, they had to put the motorcycle in a van for 36 mi.

Moto-Cross (Scrambling)

This is a very specialized sport in which the competitors race over rough country including steep climbs and drops, sharp turns, sand, mud and water. The sport originated in England in 1924 when some riders competed in "a rare old scramble." Until the Second World War it remained mainly a British interest but the Moto-Cross des Nations was inau-

MOTO-CROSS RACE in progress. André Malherbe (Belgium) almost takes flight on his way to victory in the 500-cc contest in 1980.

FASTEST VELOCITY: Elmer Trett sped 201.34 mph at the end of a 440-yd run from a standing start to set the record for highest terminal velocity.

gurated in 1947, and became an annual event, with the current rules formulated in 1963. In 1961 the Trophée des Nations, for 250 cc machines, was introduced by the FIM. World championships had been instituted in 1957.

Joël Robert (b Chatelet, Belgium, Nov 11, 1943) has won six 250-cc moto-cross (also known as "scrambles") world championships (1964, 68–72). Between Apr 25, 1964, and June 18, 1972, he won a record fifty 250-cc Grands Prix. He became the youngest moto-cross world champion on July 12, 1964, when he won the 250-cc championship aged 20 years 244 days.

MOUNTAINEERING

Origins

Although Bronze-Age artifacts have been found on the summit (9,605 ft) of the Riffelhorn, Switzerland, mountaineering, as a sport, has a continuous history dating back only to 1854. Isolated instances of climbing for its own sake exist back to the 13th century. The Atacamenans built sacrificial platforms near the summit of Llullaillaco in South America (22,058 ft) in late pre-Columbian times, c. 1490.

Greatest Wall

The highest final stage in any wall climb is that on the south face of Annapurna I (26,545 ft). It was

PARTNERS IN CLIMB: Tenzing Norgay stood atop Mt Everest as Edmund Hillary took this historic photograph after the two men became the first to successfully climb the 29,028-ft mountain. Since then, so many climbers have made the attempt that the Nepalese Government is concerned about all the garbage left behind.

climbed by the British expedition led by Christian John Storey Bonington (UK) (b Aug 6, 1934) when

Progressive Mountaineering Altitude Records

ft	Mountain	Climbers	Date	
17,887	Popocatepetl, Mexico	Francisco Montano		1521
18,400	Mana Pass, Zaskar Range, Kashmir	A. de Andrade, M. Morques	July	1624
18,893	On Chimborazo, Ecuador	Dr. Alexander Von Humboldt, Aimé Bonpland, Carlos Montufar	June 23,	1802
19,411	On Leo Pargyal Range, Himalaya	Garrard and Lloyd		1818
22,260	On E. Abi Gamin, Garhwal Himalaya	A. & R. Schlagintweit	Aug	1855
22,606	Pioneer Peak on Baltoro Kangri, Kashmir	William M. Conway, Matthias Zurbiggen	Aug 23,	1892
22,834	Aconcagua, Andes	Matthias Zurbriggen	Jan 14,	1897
23,394	On Pyramis Peak, Karakoram, Tibet	William H. Workman, J. Petigax Snr & Jnr, C. Savoie	Aug 12,	1903
23,787	On Gurla Mandhata, Tibet	Thomas G. Longstaff, Alexis & Henri Brocherel	July 23,	1905
c.23,900	On Kabru, Sikkim-Nepal	Carl W. Rubenson and Monrad Aas	Oct 20,	1907
24,607	On Chogolisa, Karakoram, Tibet	Duke of the Abruzzi, J. Petigax, H. & E. Brocherel	July 18,	1909
c.24,900	Camp V, Everest, Tibet-Nepal	G. L. Mallory, E. F Norton, T. H. Somervell, H. T. Morshead	May 20,	1922
26,986	On Everest (North Face), Tibet	George L. Mallory, Edward F. Norton, T. Howard Somervell	May 21,	1922
c.27,300	On Everest (North Face), Tibet	George I. Finch, J. Granville Bruce	May 27,	1922
28,126	On Everest (North Face), Tibet	Edward Felix Norton	June 4,	1924
28,215	South Shoulder on Everest, Nepal	Raymond Lambert, Tenzing Norgay	May 28,	1952
28,721	South Shoulder on Everest, Nepal	Thomas D. Bourdillon, Robert C. Evans	May 26,	1953
29,028	Everest, Nepal-Tibet	Edmund P. Hillary, Tenzing Norgay	May 29,	1953

from Apr 2–May 27, 1970, Donald Whillans, 36, and Dougal Haston, 27, scaled to the summit. They used 18,000 ft of rope.

The longest wall climb is on the Rupal-Flank from the base camp at 11,680 ft to the South Point (26,384 ft) of Nanga Parbat—a vertical ascent of 14,704 ft. This was scaled by the Austro-Germano-Italian Expedition led by Dr Karl Maria Herrligkoffer in Apr 1970.

The most demanding free climbs are those rated at 5.13, the premier location for these being in the Yosemite Valley, Calif.

Mount Everest

Mount Everest (29,028 ft) was first climbed at 11:30 a.m. on May 29, 1953, when the summit was reached by Edmund Percival Hillary (b July 20,

LADY AT THE TOP: Junko Tabei was the first woman to reach the summit of Mt Everest on May 16, 1975. On the right is the south wall which she ascended. (Popperfoto)

1919), of New Zealand, and the Sherpa, Tenzing Norgay (b as Namgyal Wangdi, in Nepal in 1914, formerly called Tenzing Khumjung Bhutia). The successful expedition was led by Col (later Hon Brigadier) Henry Cecil John Hunt (b June 22, 1910).

The first climber to succeed three times was the Sherpa, Sundare (or Sungdare) on Oct 5, 1982. The first to succeed via three different routes was Yasuo Kato (Japan) (1949–82), who died shortly after his third ascent on Dec 27, 1982.

Franz Oppurg (1948–81) (Austria) was the first to make the final ascent solo, on May 14, 1978, while Reinhold Messner (Italy) was the first to make the entire climb solo on Aug 20, 1980. Messner and Peter Habeler (b July 22, 1942) (Austria) made the first entirely oxygen-less ascent on May 8, 1978.

Five women have reached the summit, the first being Junko Tabei (b Sept 22, 1939) (Japan) on May 16, 1975. The oldest person was Richard Daniel Bass (b Dec 21, 1929) aged 55 years 130 days on Apr 30, 1985.

Reinhold Messner, with his ascent of Kangchenjunga in 1982, became the first person to climb the world's three highest mountains, having earlier reached the summits of Everest and K2. He is the only person to have successfully scaled all of the world's 14 main summits of over 8,000 m (26,250 ft), all without oxygen.

Highest Bivouac

Two Japanese, Hironobu Kamuro (1951–83) and Hiroshi Yoshino (1950–83), bivouacked at 28,870 ft on Mt. Everest on the night of Oct 8/9, 1983. Yoshino died on Oct 9 while Kamuro died either during the bivouac night or next day.

LEGATOR: Baron Pierre de Coubertin was the main force behind reviving the Olympic Games after a 1,503-year hiatus. Now, not even 100 years after the first modern Olympics, politics, nationalism, drug abuse and uncertain standards of amateurism threaten to end the Baron's dream of competition open to athletes of all nations.

OLYMPIC GAMES

Note: These records include the un-numbered Games held at Athens in 1906. World Records set at the 1984 Olympiad in Los Angeles will be found under some of the sports.

Origins

The earliest celebration of the ancient Olympic Games of which there is a certain record is that of July 776 BC (when Coroibos, a cook from Elis, won a foot race), though their origin probably dates from perhaps as early as *c.* 1370 BC. The ancient Games were terminated by an order issued in Milan in 393 AD by Theodosius I, "the Great" (*c.* 346–95), Em-

OLYMPICS OF 1900-04-08 and 1920 had contests in archery, and one medal winner was Queenie Newell (GB) who managed to be dressed fashionably as well as functionally.

MOST MEDALS: It is unlikely that any Olympian will ever match the 10 gold medals won by Ray Ewry (US) in the standing jumps in four Games.

peror of Rome. At the instigation of Pierre de Fredi, Baron de Coubertin (1863–1937), the Olympic Games of the modern era were inaugurated in Athens on Apr 6, 1896.

Most Medals

In the ancient Olympic Games, victors were given a chaplet (head garland) of olive leaves. Leonidas of Rhodos won 12 running titles from 164 to 152 BC.

The most individual gold medals won by a male competitor in the modern Games is 10 by Raymond Clarence Ewry (US) (b Oct 14, 1874, at Lafayette, Ind; d Sept 29, 1937), a jumper (see *Track and Field*). The female record is 7 by Vera Caslavska-Odlozil (b May 3, 1942) of Czechoslovakia, a gymnast.

The only Olympian to win 4 consecutive individual titles in the same event has been Alfred A. Oerter (b Sept 19, 1936, NYC) who won the discus title in 1956, 60, 64 and 68.

The only man to win a gold medal in both the Summer and Winter Games is Edward F. Eagan (US) (1898–1967) who won the 1920 light-heavyweight boxing title and was a member of the winning four-man bob in 1932.

Gymnast Larissa Latynina (b Dec 27, 1934) (USSR) won a record 18 medals (see *Gymnastics*). The record at one celebration is 8 medals by gymnast Alexander Ditiatin (b Aug 7, 1957) (USSR) in 1980.

ATHENS STADIUM (Panathenean): Built for the 1896 Olympics, the first in modern times, this arena was used again for the 1906 Games. In 1987, Greeks are making a strong bid to have their homeland, where the Olympics originated, named as the permanent site for all Games from the anniversary year of 1996 onwards.

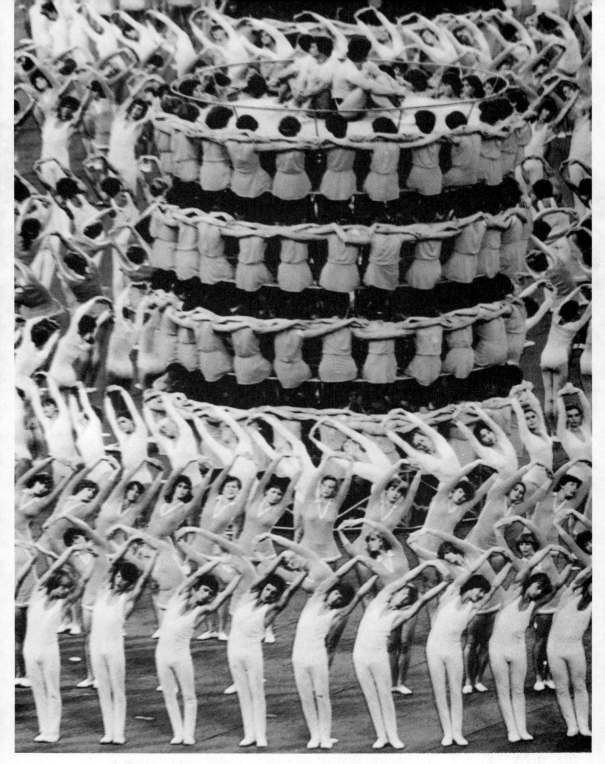

OLYMPIC CENTERPIECE: Americans never saw this Russian gymnastic display on TV as it happened in Moscow in 1980 when the Americans boycotted the Games.

LARGEST OLYMPIC SKI CROWD: This record-breaking audience witnessed the ski jump at Holmenkollen, outside Oslo, Norway, at the 1952 Winter Games.

KING MEETS DUKE: In the 1912 Olympics in Stockholm, King Gustavus V presented Duke Kahanamoku of Hawaii—his first name was Duke—with the gold medal he won in the 100-m freestyle swim. No Games in 1916 but in 1920 Duke won the gold again, and a silver in 1924 when Johnny Weissmuller outswam him.

IN DISCUS SUPREME: Al Oerter (US) won this event in 4 successive Olympics— 1956, 60, 64, 68—a unique achievement in field events. (E. D. Lacey)

Olympic Sports

There are 21 different sports currently on the Summer Games program and eight on the Winter Games schedule, as follows (with year of first inclusion):

Summer

Archery (1900)
Basketball (1936)
Boxing (1904)
Canoeing (1936)
Cycling (1896)
Equestrianism (1900)
Fencing (1896)
Field Hockey (1908)
Gymnastics (1896)
Handball (1972)
Judo (1964)
Modern Pentathlon (1912)
Rowing (1900)
Shooting (1896)
Soccer (1900)
Swimming (including Diving & Water
  Polo) (1896)
Track and Field (1896)
Volleyball (1964)
Weight Lifting (1896)
Wrestling (1896)
Yachting (1900)

Winter

Alpine Skiing (1936)
Bobsledding (1924)
Figure Skating (1908)
Ice Hockey (1920)
Luging (Tobogganing) (1964)
Nordic Skiing (1924), Ski-jumping (1964), Biathlon (1960)
Speed Skating (1924)

Youngest and Oldest Medalists

The youngest woman to win a gold medal is Marjorie Gestring (US) (b Nov 18, 1922) aged 13 years 9 months, in the 1936 women's springboard event.

The oldest person was Oscar Swahn (Swe) who won a silver medal for shooting in 1920, aged 72 years 280 days. Swahn had won a gold medal in 1912 at the record age of 64 years 258 days.

The youngest to win an Olympic gold medal was a French boy who coxed the winning Dutch rowing pairs crew in the 1900 Games. His name is not known as he was a last-minute substitute but he was no more than 10 years old and may even have been as young as seven.

RUSSIA in the Olympics: 40 years elapsed between 1912 (shown here) when Czarist Russia fielded a team, and 1952, when the first Soviet team participated.

MEDALS RESTORED:
Jim Thorpe in decathlon,
1912. (See below.)

Olympic Medals Restored

The star of the 1912 Olympic Games was an American Indian named Jim Thorpe. Held in Stockholm, the Games provided him with an opportunity to win two gold medals, one in the decathlon and one in the pentathlon. He also placed well in the high jump and long jump. He was greeted in New York with a ticker-tape parade, but in 1913 the International Olympic Committee demanded his medals back after it had come to light that prior to the Olympics he had played baseball for $25 a week and therefore was not strictly an amateur athlete. On Oct 13, 1982, 29 years after Thorpe's death, the I.O.C. presented his gold medals to his children and reinstated his name in the record books.

Longest Span

The longest competitive span of any Olympic competitor is 40 years by Dr Ivan Osiier (Denmark) (1888–1965), in fencing, 1908–32 and 48, and by Magnus Konow (Norway) (1887–1972) in yachting, 1908–20 and 36–48. The longest span for a woman is 24 years (1932–56) by the Austrian fencer Ellen Müller-Preiss. Raimondo d'Inzeo (b Feb 8, 1925) competed for Italy in equestrian events in a record 8

celebrations (1948–76), gaining one gold medal, 2 silver and 3 bronze medals. Janice Lee York Romary (b Aug 6, 1928), the US fencer, competed in all 6 Games from 1948 to 1968, and Lia Manoliu (Romania) (b Apr 25, 1932) competed 1952–72, winning the discus title in 1968.

Most Olympic Gold Medals at One Games

Mark Spitz (US), the swimmer, won a record 7 gold medals at one celebration (4 individual and 3 relay) at Munich in 1972.

The most gold medals won in individual events at one celebration is 5 by speed skater Eric Heiden (b June 14, 1958) (US) at Lake Placid, NY in 1980.

Most and Fewest Competitors

The greatest number of competitors in any Summer Olympic Games has been 7,147 at Munich in 1972. A record 122 countries competed in the 1972 Munich Games. The fewest was 311 competitors from 13 countries in 1896. In 1904 only 12 countries participated. The largest team was 880 men and 4 women from France at the 1900 Games in Paris.

OLYMPIC CROWD: It was at this arena, the Hoosier Dome in Indianapolis, that tryouts for the 1984 Games were held. On July 9, 1984, a crowd of 67,596 gathered.

TORCH LEADS WAY at 1956 Olympics in Melbourne. Australian long-distance runner Ron Clarke was chosen to carry it.

Largest Crowd

The largest crowd at any Olympic site was 150,000 at the 1952 ski-jumping at the Holmenkollen, outside Oslo, Norway. Estimates of the number of spectators of the marathon race through Tokyo on Oct 21, 1964, have ranged from 500,000 to 1,500,000.

Most Participations

Four countries have never failed to be represented at the 21 celebrations of the Summer Games: Australia, Greece, Great Britain and Switzerland. Of these, only Great Britain has been present at all Winter celebrations as well.

ORIENTEERING

Origins

Orienteering is basically a combination of cross-country running and map reading. Competitors in this unrenowned sport are given a map, marked with the locations of control points, and a compass. In some versions of the sport, the control points must be achieved in specified order, and the fastest time wins. In other versions, a time limit is declared and point values are assigned to finding the control points, so competitors must decide which control points they can get to to amass the highest score.

Orienteering as now known was invented by Major Ernst Killander in Sweden in 1918. It was based on military exercises of the 1890's. The term was first used for an event at Oslo, Norway, on October 7, 1900.

TOP WOMAN ORIENTEER: Sharon Crawford of Concord, Mass, who has been US Champion 9 times in the last 10 years, is reading her map, planning her routes, as she runs from the start. (Photo from Orienteering/North America)

Most Competitors

The most competitors at an event in one day is 22,510 on the first day of the Swedish O-Ringen at Smaalaand on July 18, 1983.

World Championships

	Men's Individual	Women's Individual
1966	Aage Hadler (Nor)	Ulla Lindqvist (Swe)
1968	Karl Johansson (Swe)	Ulla Lindqvist (Swe)
1970	Stig Berge (Nor)	Ingred Hadler (Nor)
1972	Aage Hadler (Nor)	Sarolta Monspart (Fin)
1974	Bernt Frilen (Swe)	Mona Norgaard (Den)
1976	Egil Johansen (Nor)	Liisa Veijalainen (Fin)
1978	Egil Johansen (Nor)	Anne Berit Eid (Nor)
1979	Ogvin Thon (Nor)	Outi Bergonstrom (Fin)
1981	Ogvin Thon (Nor)	Annichen Kringstad (Swe)
1983	Morton Berglia (Nor)	Annichen Svennson (Swe)
1985	Kari Sallinen (Fin)	Annichen Svennson (Swe)

Sweden has won the men's relay six times between 1966 and 1979 and the women's relay seven times, 1966, 1970, 1974, 1976, 1981, 1983, and 1985.

U.S. Champions

	Men
1973	Jerry Rice, Quantico
1974–75	Bob Turbyfill, Quantico
1975–76	Bob Turbyfill, Quantico
1976–77	Peter Gagarin, New Eng
1977	Peter Gagarin, New Eng
1978	Peter Gagarin, New Eng
1979	Peter Gagarin, New Eng
1980	Eric Weyman, Hudson Valley
1981	Eric Weyman, Hudson Valley
1982	Eric Weyman, Hudson Valley
1983	Peter Gagarin, New Eng
1984	Eric Weyman, Hudson Valley
1985	Dan Meenehan, St Louis
1986	Mikell Platt, Quantico

Women
1973   Heidi Green, Trojan OC, NC
1974–75 Cindy Prince (Fuller), Grazoo
1975–76 Joannie Pezdir (Gunther), Quantico
1976–77 Jenny Tuthill, New Eng
1977   Sharon Crawford, New Eng
1978   Sharon Crawford, New Eng
1979   Sharon Crawford, New Eng
1980   Sharon Crawford, New Eng
1981   Sharon Crawford, New Eng
1982   Sharon Crawford, New Eng
1983   Virginia Lehman, New Eng
1984   Sharon Crawford, New Eng
1985   Sharon Crawford, New Eng
1986   Sharon Crawford, New Eng

At each US meet, there may be as many as 6 courses varying in degree of difficulty by how far off the main path the orienteer must go.

World championships were inaugurated in 1967 and are held biennially under the auspices of the International Orienteering Federation (founded 1961), located in Sweden. The US Orienteering Federation was founded in 1971 to serve as the governing body for the sport in America and to choose teams for world championship competition.

PARACHUTING

Origins

Parachuting became a regulated sport with the institution of world championships in 1951. A team title was introduced in 1954, and women's events were included in 1956.

Most Titles

The USSR won the men's team titles in 1954, 58, 60, 66, 72, 76, 80, and the women's team titles in 1956, 58, 66, 68, 72, 76. Nikolai Ushamyev (USSR) has won the individual title twice, 1974 and 1980.

Most Jumps

The greatest number of consecutive jumps completed in 24 hours is 236 by Alan Jones (Capt America) of Bellevue, Wash, over Issaquah Parachute Center near Seattle, July 13–14, 1984.

A record 10,000 jumps have been made by Yuri Baranov (USSR) and Anatoli Ossipov (USSR) to the end of 1980. The women's record is 8,000 by Valentina Zakoretskaya (USSR) 1964–80.

For full table on Parachute Jumping Records, see next page.

LANDING ON A DIME: Staff Sergeant Dwight Reynolds of the Golden Knights at Fort Bragg, NC demonstrates accuracy landing. Reynolds holds the record of 105 daytime dead centers.

Formations

During the National Skydiving Championships at Davis Field, Muskogee, Okla, a team of 100 led by Guy Manos and Tom Piras of Deland, Fla, linked in a cluster formation for 7.67 sec on July 5, 1986. They jumped at 15,000 ft and took 61 sec to make the formation.

Greatest Accuracy

Jacqueline Smith (GB) (b March 29, 1951) scored ten consecutive dead center strikes (4-inch disk) in the World Championships at Zagreb, Yugoslavia, September 1, 1978. At Yuma, Arizona, in March, 1978, Dwight Reynolds scored a record 105 daytime dead centers, and Bill Wenger and Phil Munden tied with 43 nighttime DCs, competing as members of the US Army team, the Golden Knights. With electronic

First from Tower	Louis-Sébastian Lenormand (1757–1839)	quasi-parachute	Montpellier, France	1783
First from Balloon	André-Jacques Garnerin (1769–1823)	2,230 ft	Monçeau Park, Paris	Oct 22, 1797
First from Aircraft (man)	"Capt" Albert Berry	aerial exhibitionist	St Louis	Mar 1, 1912
(woman)	Mrs Georgina "Tiny" Broadwick		Griffith Park, Los Angeles	June 21, 1913
Longest Base Jump[3]	Carl Ronald Boenische; Jean K. Campbell Boenische	5,784 ft	Trollveggan Spire, Romsdal, Norway	July 4, 1984
Lowest Escape	Squad Leader T. Spencer, RAF	30–40 ft	Wismar Bay, Baltic Sea	Apr 19, 1945
Longest Duration Fall	Lt Col Wm. H. Rankin, USMC	40 min, due to thermals	North Carolina	July 26, 1956
Highest Escape	Flt Lt J. de Salis and Fg Off P. Lowe, RAF	56,000 ft	Monyash, Derby, Eng	Apr 9, 1958
Longest Delayed Drop (man)	Capt Joseph W. Kittinger[1]	84,700 ft (16.04 miles) from balloon at 102,800 ft	Tularosa, NM	Aug 16, 1960
(woman)	O. Kommissarova (USSR)	46,250 ft	over USSR	Sept 21, 1965
(civilian)	R. W. K. Beckett (GB) Harry Ferguson (GB)	30,000 ft from 32,000 ft	D. F. Malan Airport, Capetown, So Africa	Nov 23, 1969
Most Southerly	T/Sgt Richard J. Patton (d 1973)	Operation Deep Freeze	South Pole	Nov 25, 1956
Most Northerly	Dr Jack Wheeler (US)	Pilot, Capt Rocky Parsons (−25 °F)	in Lat 90° 00′ N	Apr 15, 1981
Career Total (man)	Yuri Baranov (USSR) and Anatolyi Osipov (USSR)	10,000	over USSR	to Sept 1980
(woman)	Valentina Zakoretskaya (USSR)	8,000	over USSR	1964–Sept 1980
Highest Landing	Ten USSR parachutists[2]	23,405 ft	Lenina Peak	May 1969
Heaviest Load	US Space Shuttle Columbia (external rocket retrieval)	80 ton capacity triple array each 120 ft dia	Atlantic, off Cape Canaveral, Fla	Apr 12, 1981
Highest from Bridge	Donald R. Boyles	1,053 ft	Royal Gorge, Colo	Sept 7, 1970
Highest Tower Jump	Herbert Leo Schmidtz (US)	KTUL-TV Mast 1,984 ft	Tulsa, Okla	Oct 4, 1970
Connected Free Fall (Biggest Star)	99-man team	Formation held 17 sec (US rules)	Freeport, Ill	Apr 3, 1985
(Canopy formation)	23 parachutists	Exited at 15,000 ft	Houston Gulf Airport	June 16, 1985
Highest Column	28-man US team	United Parachute Club	Gilbertsville, Pa	Dec 17, 1985
Lowest Indoor Jump	Andy Smith and Phil Smith	192 ft	Houston Astrodome, Tex	Jan 16–17, 1982
Most Traveled	Kevin Seaman from a Cessna Skylane (pilot, Charles Merritt)	12,186 miles	Jumps in all 50 US states	July 26–Oct 15, 1972
Oldest Man	Edwin C. Townsend	89 years	Vermillion Bay, La	Feb 6, 1986
Oldest Woman	Mrs Stella Davenport (GB)	75 years 8 mos	Humberside, Eng	June 27, 1981
24-Hour Total	David Huber (US)	250	Issaquah, Wash	July 3–4, 1985

[1] Maximum speed in rarefied air was 825.2 mph at 90,000 ft—marginally supersonic. [2] Four were killed. [3] "Base" is an acronym for jumping from fixed objects—Building, Antenna, Span and Earth. Carl Boenische was killed on July 7, 1984.

measuring the official FAI record is 50 DCs by Alexander Aasmiae (USSR) at Ferghana, USSR, in October, 1979.

The Men's Night Accuracy Landing Record on an electronic score pad is 27 consecutive dead centers by Cliff Jones (US) in 1981.

POLO

Origins

Polo is usually regarded as being of Persian origin, having been played as *Pulu c.* 525 BC. Other claims have come from Tibet and the Tang dynasty of China 250 AD.

The earliest club of modern times was the Kachar

ELEPHANT POLO: Polo was first played on elephant-back in Jaipur, India in 1976. The World Elephant Polo Association, formed in 1982, staged their first championships at Tiger Tops, Nepal in 1983, when the winners were the Tiger Tops Tuskers captained by Mark Payne. Other Polo Associations "take no cognisance" of elephant polo.

Club (founded in 1859) in Assam, India. The game was introduced into England from India in 1869 by the 10th Hussars at Aldershot, Hampshire, and the earliest match was one between the 9th Lancers and the 10th Hussars on Hounslow Heath, west of London, in July, 1871. The earliest international match between England and the US was in 1886.

Playing Field

The game is played (by two teams of four) on the largest field of any ball game in the world. The ground measures 300 yards long by 160 yards wide with side-boards or, as in India, 200 yards twice without boards.

Highest Handicap

The highest handicap based on eight 7½-minute "chukkas" is 10 goals, introduced in the US in 1891 and in the United Kingdom and in Argentina in 1910. The latest of the 42 players to have received 10-goal handicaps are Thomas Wayman (US) and Guillermo Gracida, Jr (Mex), and in 1984 the Argentinians, Gonzalo Perez, Alfonso Pierez, and Alfredo Harriott. A match of two 40-goal handicap teams was staged for the only time at Palermo, Buenos Aires, Argentina, in 1975.

Highest Score

The highest aggregate number of goals scored in an international match is 30, when Argentina beat the US 21–9 at Meadowbrook, Long Island, NY, in Sept, 1936.

Largest Crowd

Crowds of more than 50,000 have watched floodlit matches at the Sydney, Australia, Agricultural Shows.

Most Olympic Medals

Polo has been part of the Olympic program on five occasions: 1900, 1908, 1920, 1924 and 1936. Of the 21 gold medalists, a 1920 winner, John Wodehouse, the 3rd Earl of Kimberley uniquely also won a silver medal (1908).

Most Internationals

Thomas Hitchcock, Jr. (1900–44) played five times for the US vs. England (1921–24–27–30–39) and twice vs. Argentina (1928–36).

Polo on Elephant Back

A crowd of 40,000 watched a game played at Jaipur, India, in 1976, when elephants were used instead of ponies and longer than normal polo sticks were used.

POWERBOAT RACING

Origins

The first recorded race by powered boats was for steamboats at the Northern Yacht Club Regatta at Rothesay, Scotland in 1827. It was won by *Clarence,* a locally built vessel. Paddle steamers on the Mississippi were often pitted against each other in the 1840s for purely commercial reasons, such as getting to the markets first with their cargoes. In 1870 the *Robert E. Lee* had her famous race with the *Natchez* from New Orleans to St Louis, a distance of 1,027 miles, which the former won in 90 hours 30 min. This time was not beaten by any boat until 1929.

After 1903, racing developed mainly as a "circuit" or short, sheltered course type competition. Offshore or sea passage races also developed, initially for displacement (non-planing) cruisers. Offshore events for fast (planing) cruisers began in 1958 with a 170-mile passage race from Miami, Fla to Nassau, Bahamas. Outboard motor, *i.e.,* the combined motor/transmission detachable propulsion unit type racing began in the US in about 1920. Both inboard and outboard motor boat engines are mainly gasoline-fueled, but since 1950 diesel (compression ignition) engines have appeared and are widely used in offshore sport.

Highest Speeds

The "official" water speed record is 229 mph by Eddie Hill in a propeller-driven boat, *The Texan,* in Chowchilla, Calif, Sept 5, 1982. He also set a 440-yd elapsed time record of 5.16 sec in this boat at Firebird Lake, Ariz on Nov 13, 1983.

The official record for a woman is 116.279 mph by Fiona Brothers (UK) in a Seebold marathon hull at Holme Pierrepont, Nottingham, Eng, on Sept 1, 1981. However, the fastest attained on water by a woman driver is 190 mph by Mary Rife (US) in a drag boat.

The official American Drag Boat Association record is 223.88 mph by *Final Effort,* a blown-fuel hydro boat driven by Bob Burns at Creve Coeur Lake, St Louis, Mo, on July 15, 1985 over a ¼ mile course.

Records are recognized by the Union Internationale Motonautique. The fastest speed recognized by the UIM is now for Class (e)GP: 177.61 mph by P. R. Knight on Lake Ruataniwha, New Zealand, in a Chevrolet-engined Lauterbach hull powerboat.

The fastest speed recognized by the UIM for an offshore boat was set by *Innovation,* a 35-ft Maelstrom boat powered by 3 Johnson Evinrude outboard engines each of 214 cu in driven by Mike Drury at a mean speed for two runs of 131.088 mph at New Orleans, La, on March 31, 1984.

The fastest speed recorded for a diesel (compression ignition) boat is 135.62 mph by the hydroplane *Iveco World Leader,* powered by an Alfo-Fiat engine, driven by Carlo Bonomi at Venice, Italy in 1985.

Gold Cup

The Gold Cup (instituted 1903 by the American Power Boat Association) was won 8 times by Bill Muncey (1929–81) (US) (1956–57, 61–62, 72, 77–79). The highest lap speed reached in the competition is 128.338 mph by the hydroplane *Atlas Van Lines,* driven by Muncey in a qualifying round on the Columbia River, Wash in July 1977, and again in July 1978. Three boats have won on four occasions, *Slo-Mo-Shun IV* 1950–53, *Miss Budweiser* in 1969–70, 1973 and 1980, and *Atlas Van Lines* in 1972, 1977–79. The race speed record is 117.391 mph by *Miss Budweiser* driven by Dean Chenoweth in 1980.

Cowes International Offshore Powerboat Classic

Instituted in 1961, and originally held from Cowes to Torquay, Eng, in 1968 it was extended to include the return journey, a total distance of 246.13 miles. In 1982 the race became the Cowes International Powerboat Classic. The record for the race is 3 hours 4 min 35 sec by *Satisfaction* driven by Bill Elswick (US) averaging 79.64 mph in Aug 1980. The only 4-time winner is Renato Della Valle (Italy), 1982–85.

Longest Race

The longest offshore race has been the Port Richborough (London) to Monte Carlo Marathon Offshore International event. The race extended over 2,947 miles in 14 stages, June 10–25, 1972. It was won by *H.T.S.* (UK), driven by Mike Bellamy, Eddie Chater and Jim Brooks in 71 hours 35 min 56 sec (average speed 41.15 mph).

The longest circuit race has been the 24-hour race held annually since 1962 on the River Seine at Rouen, France. It was won by a Johnson outboard-engined Piranha boat driven by Francois Greens, Jan van Brockels and Roger Robin (Belgium) at 46.63 mph.

RIDING THE AIRWAVES: From a takeoff speed of 55 mph, Peter Horak jumped a powerboat 120 ft through the air for a television documentary. (Greg Meny)

ON THE MOVE: Chip Hanauer piloted "Atlas Van Lines U-00" to an unlimited hydroplane one-lap speed record at the time of 140.801 mph in Aug 1982. As a sponsor, Atlas Van Lines, Inc, one of the nation's larger household carriers, had 42 unlimited hydroplane victories to its credit by Oct 1982.

Longest Jump

The longest jump achieved by a jetboat has been 120 ft by Peter Horak (b May 7, 1943) (US) in a Glastron Carlson CVX 20 Jet Deluxe with a 460 Ford V8 engine (takeoff speed 55 mph) for a documentary TV film "The Man Who Fell from the Sky," at Salton Sea, Calif, on Apr 26, 1980.

The longest boat jump onto land is 172 ft by Norm Bagrie (NZ) from the Shotover River on July 1, 1982, in the 1½-ton jetboat *Valvolene*.

Fastest Transatlantic Crossing

A 65-ft powerboat, the *Virgin Atlantic Challenger II,* sailed by Richard Branson, a 35-year-old US businessman and his crew of 6, set a world record in June 1986 for all types of boats, by taking only 3 days 8 hours 31 min from NYC to Bishop's Rock off the coast of Eng. This beat the record held by the 51,988 gross ton transatlantic liner *United States* by 2 hours 11 min.

START OF A POWERBOAT RACE: This 1978 Cowes-Torquay contest in England was won by a woman for the first time at a then record average speed of 77.42 mph.

RACQUETBALL

Marathon

For 41 hours 22 min, Jean Gratton and Marc Ouellette (Canada) played racquetball Jan 18–19, 1986, at St. Antoine, Canada.

Playing against a series of opponents, Frank Araque (b Caracas, Venezuela 1957) of Edgewater Park, NJ, 5-ft-4-in tall, weighing 140 lb, played for 168 hours Apr 4-12, 1980. He won 225 of the 325 games he played.

Fastest Serve

In a club contest on Dec 2, 1979, Sol Abrevaya of Santa Monica, Calif, was officially clocked with a radar gun to have served before 100 witnesses at 179 mph, for the fastest serve in racket sports.

RODEO

Origins

While there is no known "first rodeo," as early as 1860 cowboys were competing at railheads and on trails for unofficial titles for bronc riding and other skills of their trade. After the great cattle drives were eliminated, due to the introduction of more and more railroads, large ranches began to "give a rodeo." As towns developed, they adopted the rodeo with Cheyenne, Wyo, claiming to have had the first in 1872.

A rodeo has been held each year in Prescott, Ariz, on the Fourth of July since 1888.

The sport was not organized until 1936 when a group of rodeo contestants founded the Cowboys Turtle Association (now the Professional Rodeo Cowboys Association) to standardize the sport. The official events now are saddle bronc riding, bareback riding, bull riding, calf roping, steer wrestling, and, in some states, team roping.

Largest Prize Money

The largest rodeo in the world is the U.S. National Finals Rodeo, held annually in Dec by the PRCA. The total prize money for the 1985 rodeo held in Las Vegas was $1,790,000.

The top 24 cowboys in the 1984 championship standings were invited to compete in the Winston Tour during which $1 million was awarded in prizes for calf roping, saddle bronc riding, bareback riding, steer wrestling, bull riding, barrel racing and team roping.

Most World Titles

The record number of all-round titles in the Professional Rodeo Cowboys Association world championships is 6 by Larry Mahan (US) (b Nov 21, 1943) in 1966–70 and 1973 and, consecutively, 1974–9 by Tom Ferguson (b Dec 20, 1950). Jim Shoulders (b 1928) of Henryetta, Okla, won a record 16 world championships between 1949 and 1959.

Champion Bull

The top bucking bull was probably "Tornado," who bucked out of the chute 220 times before Freckles Brown in 1967 became the first cowboy to ride him to the 8-sec bell. "Tornado" retired a year later after a 14-year career.

YOUNG BARREL-RACING CHAMP, Charmayne James, 16, is rounding a corner on her way to winning a record $151,969 in one year, 1986. (Springer)

SIXTEEN TITLES: Jim Shoulders won 5 all-around championships, 4 bareback titles, and 7 bull-riding titles in amassing his record 16 world rodeo titles. (Rodeo Information Commission)

KNOWS THE ROPES: Chris Lybbert parlayed his calf-roping and steer-wrestling skills into a then record $123,709 in the 1982 All-Around Championship on the Professional Rodeo Cowboys Association (PRCA) circuit. Since Lybbert joined the PRCA in 1976, total prize money has nearly doubled with over $13 million to be divided up nowadays.

Youngest Champion

The youngest winner of a world title is Metha Brorsen of Okla, who was only 11 years old when she won the International Rodeo Association Cowgirls barrel-racing event in 1975.

The youngest women's champion in the female division of the Professional Rodeo Cowboys Association competition is Jackie Jo Perrin of Antlers, Okla, who won the barrel-racing title in 1977 at age 13.

Time Records

Records for timed events, such as calf roping and steer wrestling, are not always comparable, because of the widely varying conditions due to the size of arenas and amount of start given the stock. The fastest time recently recorded for roping a calf is 5.7 sec by Lee Phillips in Assiniboia, Saskatchewan, Canada, in 1978, and the fastest time for overcoming a

steer is 2.4 sec by James Bynum at Marietta, Okla, in 1955; by Carl Deaton at Tulsa, Okla, in 1976; and by Gene Melton at Pecatonica, Ill, in 1976.

The standard required time to stay on in bareback, saddle bronc and bull riding events is 8 sec. In the now discontinued ride-to-a-finish events, rodeo riders have been recorded to have survived 15 min or more, until the mount had not a buck left in it.

The highest score in bull riding was 98 points out of a possible 100 by Denny Flynn on "Red Lightning" at Palestine, Ill, in 1979.

Highest Earnings

The record figure for prize money in a single season is $153,391 by Roy Cooper (b 1956) in 1983. The greatest earnings in a rodeo career is $978,809 by Tom Ferguson through 1985. The record for the

THREE IN ONE YEAR: Roy Cooper not only earned more than $150,000 in prizes in 1983, but his world championships were in steer roping, calf roping and all-round cowboy work.

most money won at one rodeo is $30,677 by Dee Pickett at the National Finals Rodeo in Oklahoma City in Dec 1984.

Charmayne James (b June 23, 1970), of Clayton, NM, won a record $151,969 in women's barrel (slalom) racing in 1986.

Champion Bronc

Traditionally a bronc called "Midnight" owned by Jim McNab of Alberta, Canada, was never ridden in 12 appearances at the Calgary Stampede.

ROLLER SKATING

Origins

The first roller skate was undoubtedly a pair of wooden spools, attached to a pair of ice skates minus the blades, sometime around 1700. The first recorded use of roller skates was in a play by Tom Hood, performed in 1743 at the Old Drury Lane Theatre, London, England. The first documented roller skate was invented by Jean Joseph Merlin of Huy, Belgium, in 1760, and demonstrated by him in London but with disastrous results. The forerunner of the modern four-wheel skate was invented by James L. Plimpton of Medfield, Mass, patented in 1863. The first indoor rink was opened in the Haymarket, London, in about 1824.

Largest Rink

The largest indoor rink ever to operate was located in the Grand Hall, Olympia, London, England. It had an actual skating area of 68,000 sq ft. It first opened in 1890 for one season, then again from 1909 to 1912.

The largest indoor rink now in operation is Gup-

STAYING POWER: Larry Mahan shares the record for most all-round world titles with 6.

ROLLER HOCKEY championships held annually draw teams from both coasts. Here, Cliff Molette of the Olympia (Wash) Tornadoes chases the ball that Harry Cage of the Cumberland (Md) Raiders has under control. (Skate magazine)

till's Arena, Latham, NY. The main rink measures 35,142 sq ft, and an addition increases the skating area by 6,400 sq ft.

Most Titles

Most world speed titles have been won by Alberta Vianello (Italy) with 16 between 1953 and 1965. The records for figure titles are 5 by Karl Heinz Losch in 1958–59, 61–62, 66, and 4 by Astrid Bader, both of W Germany, in 1965–68. Most world pairs titles have been taken by Dieter Fingerle (W Germany) with 4 in 1959, 65–67.

Most consecutive world pairs titles have been 4 won by John Arishita and Tammy Jerue (US) 1983–86.

DOUBLE WINNER: At the 1985 World Championships, Scott Myers captured the bronze medal in figure skating, and he and partner Anna Marie Danks won the silver in dance, making Myers the only American to win 2 medals in the tournament. (Skate magazine)

ROLLER SKATE RACING (left) is not the only competition on roller skates. The US Amateur Federation of Roller Skating of Lincoln, Neb, also holds dance contests (right).

Speed Records

The fastest speed (official world's record) is 25.78 mph by Giuseppe Cantarella (Italy) who recorded 34.9 sec for 440 yd on a road at Catania, Italy, on Sept 28, 1963. The mile record on a rink is 2 min 25.1 sec by Gianni Ferretti (Italy). The greatest distance skated in one hour on a rink by a woman is 23.051 mi by Annie Lambrechts (Belgium) at Louvain in July 1985. The men's record on a track is 23.133 mi by Alberto Civolani (Italy) at Inzell, W Germany, on Sept 28, 1968. He went on to skate 50 mi in 2 hours 20 min 33.1 sec.

Marathon

The longest recorded continuous roller skating marathon was one of 344 hours 18 min by Isamu Furugen at Naka Roller Skate Land, Okinawa, Japan, Dec 11–27, 1983.

Endurance

Theodore J. Coombs (b 1954) of Hermosa Beach, Calif, skated 5,193 miles from Los Angeles to NYC and back to Yates Center, Kan, from May 30 to Sept 14, 1979. His longest 24-hour distance was 120 mi, June 27–28.

ROWING

Oldest Race

The Sphinx stela of Amenhotep II (1450–1425 BC) records that he *stroked* a boat for some three miles. Warships were driven by human power in ancient times. The earliest literary reference to rowing is by the Roman poet Virgil in the *Aeneid,* published after his death in 19 BC. Rowing regattas were held in Venice *c* 1300 AD. The world's oldest annual race was inaugurated on Aug 1, 1716 by Thomas Doggett, an Irish-born actor. He presented "an Orange Colour Livery with a Badge" for the winner of a competition for London watermen over a 4½-mi course from London Bridge to Chelsea. The world governing body, FISA, was founded in 1892, and the first major international meeting, the European championships, was held a year later.

Olympic and World Championships

In a 1986 revision of rowing rules, lightweight events are now to be held at the World Champion-

TRIPLE GOLD MEDALIST: John Kelly (US), winner in single and double sculls in 1920, and again in double in 1924, later saw his son win a bronze medal in rowing and his movie star daughter, Grace, marry a prince.

ships, but are not scheduled for the 1988 Olympics. Lightweight is defined as an average of 154.32 lb with a maximum of 159.84 lb for men, and an average of 125.66 lb with a maximum of 130.07 lb for women. Also, the distance for women has been increased from 1,000m to 2,000m since 1985.

Six oarsmen have won 3 Olympic gold medals: John B. Kelly (US) (1889–1960), father of the late Princess Grace of Monaco, in the sculls (1920) and double sculls (1920 and 24); his cousin Paul V. Costello (US) (b Dec 27, 1899) in the double sculls (1920, 24 and 28); Jack Beresford, Jr (GB) (1899–1977) in the sculls (1924), coxless fours (1932) and double sculls (1936); Vyacheslav Ivanov (USSR) (b July 30, 1938) in the sculls (1956, 60 and 64); Siegfried Brietzke in the coxless pairs (1972) and the coxless fours (1976 and 80); and Pertti Karppinen (Finland) in the single sculls (1976, 1980, 1984), who also won 2 world championships.

Karppinen, three-time Olympic gold medalist, set a world best at the World Championship, Sept 1, 1985, in Willebroek, Belgium. His time was 6:48.08.

Olympic Championships were first held in 1900. Separate world championships were first held for men in 1962 and for women in 1974. The East German coxless pairs team of Bernd and Jorg Landvoigt have won their event 4 times in world championships and twice in Olympic competition, setting a record for any event. The female sculler Christine Scheiblich-Hann (E Ger) nearly matched this with one Olympic and four world titles.

The most world gold medals won is five by Ulrich Diessner (E Ger) (b Dec 27, 1954), four at coxed fours 1977–9 and 1982 and one at coxed pairs in 1983. He also won an Olympic gold medal at coxed fours in 1980. (Karppinen has also won five golds; *see*

SINGLE SCULLS RECORDHOLDER: Pertti Karppinen (Finland) set a world mark in Sept 1985 after having earned 3 Olympic golds (1976, 80, 84). (Sporting Pictures)

above. Five were also won by Peter-Michael Kolbe (W Ger) (b Aug 2, 1953) at single sculls, 1975, 78, 81, 83 and 86.) In the women's events Christine Hahn (née Schieblich) (E Ger) (b Dec 31, 1954), won 5, in 1974–5, 1977–8 (as well as the 1976 Olympic title).

Highest Speed

Speeds in tidal or flowing water are of no comparative value. The greatest speed attained on non-tidal water, over the standard men's rowing distance of 2000 m (2,187 yd), is 13.68 mph by the US eight on the Rootsee, Lucerne, Switzerland, in June 1984 when they clocked 5 min 27.14 sec. A team from the Penn AC (US) was timed in 5 min 18.8 sec (14.03 mph) in the FISA Championships on the Meuse River, Liège, Belgium, on Aug 17, 1930, but with the help of the river current.

The fastest by a female eight is also by a US crew, who clocked 2 min 54.05 sec for the standard women's distance of 1000 m (1,093.6 yd), achieving an average of 12.85 mph on the Rootsee, Lucerne in 1984. The fastest time over 2000 m by a single sculler, 6 min 49.68 sec by Nikolai Dovgan (USSR) in 1978,

BY A NOSE: The US won a close finish in the Eights race for a gold medal in the 1932 Olympics at Los Angeles.

WINNERS OF THE FIRST WOMEN'S OLYMPICS in rowing. The E German eight was victorious in the inaugural race in 1976 and again in 1980. In fact, in all but two inaugural rowing events in 1976, E Germans were winners, namely, single sculls, quadruple sculls, coxed fours and eights. Of course, in 1984, the E Germans did not compete. (Tony Duffy—All Sport)

"DRAGON BOAT" RACE in Hong Kong draws 2,400 rowers. Canton Chinese boat raises oars in victory sign as they beat US Rowing Association (Phila) crew in 1983 final.

represents an average speed of 10.92 mph. The best by a female sculler over 1000 m, 3 min 30.74 sec by Cornelia Linse (E Ger) in 1984, represents an average of 10.61 mph.

> John Kelly was thought to be a victim of class distinction when he was refused entry into the Diamond Sculls at Henley, Eng, in 1920, being unofficially informed that the muscles he had developed as a bricklayer gave him an unfair advantage over "gentlemen" competitors. Later, as a rich businessman, he saw his son John Kelly, Jr win the Diamond Sculls twice, in 1947 and 1949, and his film-star daughter become Princess Grace of Monaco. Benjamin Spock, later author of a best-selling baby and child care book, was a member of the Yale crew which represented the US and won the 1924 Olympic Eights.

3 OLYMPIC GOLDS were won by only 6 oarsmen. Jack Beresford, Jr (GB) (above) is one of them. He also won the Wingfield Sculls 7 times. (Below): Vyacheslav Ivanov (USSR) is one who also shares the record for 3 gold Olympic medals. Here (in shell at top) he has just won the singles in an international regatta. (CAP)

Heaviest Oarsman

The heaviest man ever to row in a British Boat Race has been Stephen G. H. Plunkett, the No 5 in the 1976 Oxford boat at 229 lb. The 1983 Oxford crew averaged a record 204.3 lb.

The lightest coxes weighed 72 lb: Francis Archer (Cambridge) in 1862, and Hart Parker Vincent Massey (Oxford) in 1939.

Longest Race

The longest rowing race is the annual Tour du Lac Léman, Geneva, Switzerland for coxed fours (the five-man team taking turns as cox) over 99 miles. The record winning time is 12 hours 52 min by LAGA, Delft, The Netherlands, Oct 3, 1983.

The longest distance rowed in 24 hours by a crew of 8 is 130 mi by members of the Renmark Rowing Club of S Australia Apr 1, 1984.

Sculling

The record number of wins in the Wingfield Sculls on the Thames in London (Putney to Mortlake) (instituted 1830) is 7 by Jack Beresford, Jr 1920–26. The fastest time has been 21 min 11 sec by Leslie Frank Southwood (b Jan 18, 1906) on Aug 12, 1933. The most world professional sculling titles (instituted 1831) won is 7 by William Beach (Australia) (1850–1935), 1884–87.

SHOOTING

Earliest Club

The Lucerne Shooting Guild (Switzerland) was formed *c.* 1466, and the first recorded shooting match was held at Zurich in 1472. Early contests had to be over very short range as it was not until rifling, to spin the bullet, was introduced to gun barrels in *c.* 1480 that accuracy over greater distances could be achieved.

Trap-shooting was introduced in the US in 1830, and skeet shooting in 1915, "skeet" being the old Norse word for "shoot."

Olympic Games

The record number of medals won is 11 by Carl Townsend Osburn (US) (1884–1966) in 1912, 1920 and 1924, consisting of 5 gold, 4 silver and 2 bronze. Six other marksmen have won 5 gold medals. The only marksman to win 3 individual gold medals has been Gudbrand Gudbrandsönn, Skatteboe (Norway) (1875–1965) in 1906. Separate events for women were first held in 1984.

> The first woman to win a medal at shooting was Margaret Murdock (US) in the small-bore rifle (3 positions) event in 1976. It was originally announced that she had won by a single point, but an error was discovered and she was tied with her teammate Lonny Bassham. Then an examination of the targets indicated that one of the latter's shots was 1/25th of an inch closer to the center than previously determined, and so the gold medal was given to Bassham, who gallantly invited Murdock to share first place position on the award rostrum.

Clay Pigeon Shooting

The record number of clay birds shot in an hour is 2,215 by Joseph Kreckman at the Paradise Shooting Center, Cresco, Pa, Aug 28, 1983. Graham Douglas Geater (b July 21, 1947) shot 2,264 targets in an hour on a trap-shooting range at the NILO Gun Club, Papamoa, NZ on Jan 17, 1981.

Most world titles have been won by Susan Nattrass (Canada) (b Nov 5, 1950) with 6, 1974–5, 77–9, 81.

A unique maximum 200/200 was achieved by Ricardo Ruiz Rumoroso at the Spanish clay pigeon championships at Zaragoza on June 12, 1983.

SHARP SHOOTER Annie Oakley (1860–1926) joined the Buffalo Bill Circus while still in her teens and soon became famous for her remarkable shooting skills. She could hit a dime in mid-air at 30 paces and score 100 out of 100 consistently when trapshooting. (Amateur Trapshooting Assoc. Hall of Fame)

Bench Rest Shooting

The smallest group on record at 1,000 yd is 5.093 in by Rick Taylor with a 300 Weatherby at Williamsport, Pa, on Aug 24, 1980.

Small-Bore Rifle Shooting

Richard Hansen shot 5,000 bull's-eyes in 24 hours at Fresno, Calif, on June 13, 1929.

Highest Score in 24 Hours

The Easingwold (England) Rifle & Pistol Club team of John Smith, Edward Kendall, Paul Duffield and Philip Kendall scored 120,242 points (averaging 95.66 per card) on Aug 6–7, 1983.

GAME SHOOTING

Record Heads

The world's finest head is the 23-point stag head in the Maritzburg collection, E Germany. The outside span is 75½ in, the length 47½ in and the weight 41½ lb. The greatest number of points is probably 33 (plus 29) on the stag shot in 1696 by Frederick III (1657–1713), the Elector of Brandenburg, later King Frederick I of Prussia.

Largest Shoulder Guns

The largest bore shoulder guns made were 2-bore. Less than a dozen of these were made by two English wildfowl gunmakers *c.* 1885. Normally the largest guns made are double-barreled 4-bore weighing up to 26 lb which can be handled only by men of exceptional physique. Larger smooth-bore guns have been made, but these are for use as punt-guns.

Biggest Bag

The largest animal ever shot by any big game hunter was a bull African elephant (*Loxodonta africana africana*) shot by E. M. Nielsen of Columbus, Neb, 25 miles north-northeast of Mucusso, Angola, on Nov 7, 1974. The animal, brought down by a Westley Richards 0.425, stood 13 ft 8 in tall at the shoulder.

In Nov 1965, Simon Fletcher, 28, a Kenyan farmer, claims to have killed two elephants with one 0.458 bullet.

The greatest recorded lifetime bag is 556,813 birds, including 241,234 pheasants, by the 2nd Marquess of Ripon (1852–1923) of England. He himself dropped dead on a grouse moor after shooting his 52nd bird on the morning of Sept 22, 1923.

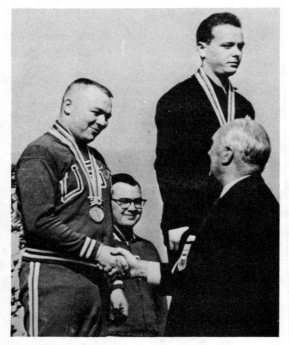

SILVER BULLETS: American Lones Wigger (left) is congratulated after receiving a silver medal in the 1964 Tokyo Olympics. He picked up a gold medal in the same competition.

GAME SHOOTING: Out after grouse is King Manoel of Portugal with the Marquess of Ripon (Radio Times Hulton)

INDIVIDUAL WORLD SHOOTING RECORDS
(as ratified by the International Shooting Union—UIT)

			Max-Score		
Free Rifle	300m	3 × 40 shots	1200–1160	Lones W. Wigger (US)	Seoul, 1978
			1160	Lones W. Wigger (US)	Rio de Janeiro, 1981
		60 shots prone	600–595	K. Leskinen (Finland)	Oslo, Norway, 1983
			595	T. Muller (Switz)	Oslo, Norway, 1983
Standard Rifle	300m	3 × 20 shots	600–580	Lones W. Wigger (US)	Rio de Janeiro, 1981
Small-Bore Rifle	50m	3 × 40 shots	1200–1180	Kiril Ivanov (USSR)	Lvov, USSR, Dec 1982
	50m	60 shots prone	600–600	Alistair Allan (GB)	Titograd, Yugo, 1981
			600	Ernest Van de Zande (US)	Rio de Janeiro, 1981
			600	(also by 5 others)	Suhl, E Ger, 1986
Free Pistol	50m	60 shots	600–581	Aleksandr Melentev (USSR)	Moscow, 1980
Rapid-Fire Pistol	25m	60 shots	600–599	Igor Puzyrev (USSR)	Titograd, Yugo, 1981
Center-Fire Pistol	25m	60 shots	600–597	Thomas D. Smith (US)	São Paulo, Brazil, 1963
Standard Pistol	25m	60 shots	600–584	Eric Buijong (US)	Caracas, Venez, 1983
Running Target	50m	60 shots "normal runs"	600–595	Igor Sokolov (USSR)	Miskulc, Hungary, 1981
Trap	—	200 birds	200–200	Danny Carlisle (US)	Caracas, Venez, 1983
Skeet	—	200 birds	200–200	Matthew Dryke (US)	São Paulo, Brazil, 1981
Air Rifle	10m	60 shots	600–590	Harald Stenvaag (Norway)	The Hague, Neth, 1982
Air Pistol	10m	60 shots	600–591	Vladas Tourla (USSR)	Caracas, Venez, 1983

TRIPLE WINNER IN 1984 OLYMPICS: Marja-Liisa Haemaelainen (Fin) dominated the women's cross-country skiing events, taking all three individual gold medals.

SKIING

Origins

The most ancient ski in existence was found well preserved in a peat bog at Höting, Sweden, dating from *c.* 2500 BC. However, in 1934 a Russian archaeologist discovered a rock carving of a skier at Bessovysledki, USSR, which dates from *c.* 6000 BC. These early skiers used the bones of animals whereas wooden skis appear to have been introduced to Europe from Asia. The first reference in literature is in a work by Procopius *c.* 550 AD who referred to "Gliding Finns." Additionally in the Scandinavian sagas there occur gods of skiing. By 1199, the Danish historian Saxo was reporting the military use of troops on skis by Sigurdsson Sverrir, the Norwegian King.

The modern sport did not develop until 1843 when the first known competition for civilians took place at Tromsó, Norway. The first ski club, named the Trysil Shooting and Skiing Club, was founded in Norway in 1861. Twenty years later ski bindings were invented by Sondre Nordheim, from Morgedal in the Telemark area, and the people of this region were the pioneers of the sport. The legendary "Snowshoe" Thompson, whose parents were Norwegian, was the earliest well-known skier in the US (1856) although skiing took place here in the 1840s. It was not until Olaf Kjeldsberg went to Switzerland in 1881 that the sport began to take hold in that country, and in 1889

one of the earliest of British exponents, Arthur Conan Doyle, began skiing at Davos, Switz. The first downhill race—as opposed to the Scandinavian races across country—was held at Kitzbuhel, Austria in 1908. The International Ski Federation (FIS) was founded on Feb 2, 1924. The Winter Olympics were inaugurated on Jan 25, 1924, and Alpine events have been included since 1936. The FIS recognizes both the Winter Olympics and the separate World Ski Championships as world championships.

Most Alpine World Titles

The World Alpine Championships were inaugurated at Mürren, Switzerland, in 1931. The greatest number of titles won has been 13 by Christel Cranz (b July 1, 1914), of Germany, with 7 individual—4 Slalom (1934, 37–39) and 3 Downhill (1935, 37, 39); and 5 Combined (1934–35, 37–39). She also won the gold medal for the Combined in the 1936 Olympics. The most titles won by a man is 7 by Anton "Toni" Sailer (b Nov 17, 1935), of Austria, who won all 4 in 1956 (Giant Slalom, Slalom, Downhill and the non-Olympic Alpine Combination) and the Downhill, Giant Slalom and Combined in 1958.

Most Olympic Victories

Marja-Liisa Haemaelainen (Fin), after having twice won the women's World Cup title in Nordic,

AMERICAN TWINS WON gold and silver in Giant Slalom in 1984 Olympics: Phil Mahre beat his twin brother Steve by 21/100ths of a second.

WORLD ALPINE CHAMPION: Christel Cranz of Germany in the 1930's won 13 times for a record number of titles.

1983–84, won all 3 individual gold medals in the 1984 Olympics.

The most Olympic gold medals won by a man for skiing is 4 by Sixten Jernberg (b Feb 6, 1929), of Sweden, in 1956–64 (including one for a relay). In addition, Jernberg has won 3 silver and 2 bronze medals for a record 9 Olympic medals. Four were also won by Nikolai Zimjatov (b June 28, 1955) (USSR) in 1980 (30 km, 50 km and on the team for 4 × 10-km relay) and in 1984 (30 km).

The only woman to win 4 Olympic gold medals is Galina Koulakova (b Apr 29, 1942) of USSR who won the 5 km and 10 km (1972) and was a member of the winning 3 × 5-km relay team in 1972 and the 4 × 5-km team in 1976. Koulakova also has won 2 silver and 2 bronze medals, 1968, 76, 80.

The most Olympic gold medals won in men's Alpine skiing is 3, by Anton "Toni" Sailer in 1956 and Jean-Claude Killy in 1968.

Most Nordic World Titles

The first world Nordic championships were those of the 1924 Winter Olympics at Chamonix, France. The greatest number of World titles won is 9 by Galina Koulakova (b Apr 29, 1942) (USSR), 1968–78. She also won 4 silver and 4 bronze medals for a record total of 17. The most won by a man is 8, in-

NORDIC SKIING: Sweden's Sixten Jernberg earned 4 Olympic golds, and dominated the sport (1956–64) with a total of 9 Olympic medals.

SNOWBIRD: In a sport that may be humankind's closest approach to unaided flight, Armin Kogler of Austria won the jumping World Cup twice, in 1981 and 1982. His longest jump was 590½ ft, a record at the time.

cluding relays, by Sixten Jernberg (b Feb 6, 1929) (Sweden), 1956–64. Johan Grottumsbraaten (1899–1942), of Norway, won 6 individual titles (2 at 18 km cross-country and 4 Nordic Combined) in 1926–32. The record for a jumper is 5 by Birger Ruud (b Aug 23, 1911), of Norway, in 1931–32 and 1935–37. Ruud is the only person to win Olympic titles in each of the dissimilar Alpine and Nordic disciplines. In 1936 he won the ski-jumping and the Alpine downhill (which was not then a separate event, but only a segment of the Combined event).

World Cup

The Alpine World Cup, instituted in 1967, and extended to include Nordic in 1981, has been won 4 times by Gustavo Thoeni (Italy) (b Feb 28, 1951) in 1971–73, and 75. The women's cup has been won 6

MOST TITLED NORDIC SKIER: Galina Koulakova (right) (USSR) pushes on to one of her record 4 Olympic gold medals. She won 9 world championships as well.

GOING DOWNHILL: Austria's Annemarie Proll Moser won the Alpine World Cup 6 times, winning 62 events in her career, including 11 straight downhill wins over a 13-month stretch. She was frustrated in her attempts to win an Olympic gold medal until she took the downhill title at Lake Placid in 1980. (AP)

times by the 5-ft-6-in 150-lb Annemarie Moser (*née* Proll) (Austria) in 1971–75 and 79. From Dec 1972 to Jan 1974 she completed a record sequence of 11 consecutive downhill victories. She holds the women's record of 62 individual event wins (1970–79). The most by a man is 83 by Ingemar Stenmark (b Mar 18, 1956) (Sweden), 1974–86, including a record 14 in one season in 1979. Franz Klammer (Austria) (b Dec 3, 1953) won a record 35 downhill races, 1974–85.

Alexander Zavialov (USSR) (b June 2, 1955) has two wins, 1981 and 1983, in the cross-country or Nordic World Cup (inst 1979). Also with two wins are Marja-Liisa Hamalainen (Finland) in 1983 and 1984, and Gunde Svan (Sweden) in 1984 and 1985. The jumping World Cup (inst 1980) has been twice won by Armin Kogler (Austria) (b Sept 4, 1959) 1981–2, and by Matti Nykanen (Finland) 1983 and 1985.

Duration

The record distance covered in 48 hours of Nordic skiing is 319 mi 205 yd by Bjorn Lokken (Norway) (b Nov 27, 1937) Mar 11–13, 1982.

In 24 hours Teuvo Rantanen covered 195 miles at Jyväskylä, Finland Mar 24–25, 1984. The women's record is 122.9 miles by Marlene Severs at East Burke, Vt, Mar 7–8, 1985.

The longest time spent in downhill skiing under regulated conditions is 83 hours by Dave Phillips and Gerry O'Neill at Grouse Mt, N Vancouver, Canada, Feb 20–23, 1986. No time was wasted waiting for the lift.

Luc Labrie at Daie Comeau, Quebec, Canada, skied alone for 138 hours, Feb 20–25, 1984.

Highest Speed—Cross Country

Bill Koch (US) (b Apr 13, 1943) on Mar 26, 1981 skied ten times around a 5-km (3.11-mi) loop on Marlborough Pond, near Putney, Vt. He completed the 50 km in 1 hour 59 min 47 sec, an average speed of 15.57 mph. A race includes uphill and downhill sections; the record time for a 50-km race is 2 hours 10 min 49.9 sec by Gunde Svan in the 1985 World Championships, an average speed of 14.25 mph. The record for a 15-km Olympic or World Championship

race is 38 min 52.5 sec by Oddvar Braa (Nor) (b Mar 16, 1951) at the 1982 World Championships, an average speed of 14.38 mph.

Closest Verdict

The narrowest winning margin in a championship ski race was one hundredth of a second by Thomas Wassberg (Sweden) (b March 23, 1956) over Juha Mieto (Finland) in the Olympic 15 km cross-country race at Lake Placid, NY on Feb 17, 1980. His winning time was 41 min 57.63 sec.

The narrowest margin of victory in an Olympic Alpine event was 2/100ths of a sec by Barbara Cochran (US) over Daniele De Bernard (France) in the 1972 slalom at Sapporo, Japan.

Highest Speed

The highest speed ever achieved by any skier is 129.827 mph by Franz Weber (b Austria 1957) on Apr 21, 1984 at Les Arcs, France. The fastest by a woman is 124.759 mph by Melissa Dimino (US) Apr 19, 1984 at Les Arcs, France.

The highest average race speed in the Olympic downhill was 64.95 mph by Bill Johnson (US) (b

WINTER WONDER: Jean-Claude Killy (France) thrilled his countrymen when he swept all 3 Olympic gold medals in the 1968 Winter Olympics in Grenoble, France. Killy also won the Alpine Combination world title that year and 2 other world titles in 1966.

AERODYNAMICALLY ATTIRED for speed, Franz Weber (Austria) holds the downhill skiing record at 129.827 mph set in 1984. (Danny McClure)

Mar 30, 1960) at Sarajevo, Yugoslavia, on Feb 16, 1984. The fastest in a World Cup downhill is 67.00 mph by Harti Weirather (Austria) (b Jan 25, 1958) at Kitzbuhl, Austria on Jan 15, 1982.

Highest Altitude

Jean Atanassieff and Nicolas Jaeger (both France) skied down from 26,900 ft to 20,340 ft on Mt Everest in 1978.

Longest Run

The longest all-downhill ski run in the world is the Weissfluhjoch-Küblis Parsenn course (7.6 miles long), near Davos, Switzerland. The run from the Aiguille du Midi top of the Chamonix lift (vertical lift 9,052 ft) across the Vallée Blanche is 13 miles.

Longest Jump

The longest ski jump ever recorded is one of 626 ft by Matti Nykänen (Fin) (b July 17, 1963) at Planica, Yugoslavia on Mar 15, 1985, and by Andreas Felder (Aust) at Bad Mitterndorf, Austria, on Mar 6, 1986.

The women's record is 110 m (361 ft) by Tiina Lehtola (Fin) (b Aug 3, 1962) at Ruka, Finland, on Mar 29, 1981.

The longest dry ski jump is 92 m (301 ft 10 in) by

Hubert Schwarz (W Germany) at Berchtesgaden, W Germany, on June 30, 1981.

Steepest Descent

Sylvain Saudan (b Lausanne, Switzerland, Sept 23, 1936) achieved a descent of Mt Blanc on the northeast side down the Couloir Gervasutti from 13,937 ft on Oct 17, 1967, skiing gradients of about 60 degrees.

Longest Races

The world's longest ski races are the Grenader, run just north of Oslo, Norway, and the König Ludwig Lauf in Oberammergau, W Germany. Both are 90 km (55.9 miles). The Canadian Ski Marathon at 160 km (99 miles) is longer, but is run in two parts on consecutive days.

The world's greatest Nordic ski race is the Vasaloppet, which commemorates an event in 1521 when Gustavus Vasa (1496–1560), later King of Sweden, fled 85.8 km (53.3 miles) from Mora to Sälen, Sweden. He was overtaken by loyal, speedy scouts on skis, who persuaded him to return eastwards to Mora to lead a rebellion and become the king of Sweden. The re-enactment of this return journey is now an annual event at 89 km (55.3 mi), contested by about

RECORDHOLDER: Gunde Svan (Sweden) won the 1984 Olympic gold for 15,000 m. In setting the 50-km Nordic uphill and downhill record, his average time was 14.25 mph. (All Sport)

12,000 skiers. The fastest time is 3 hours 48 min 55 sec by Bengt Hassis (Swe) on Mar 2, 1986.

The Vasaloppet is now the longest of 10 long distance races, constituting the world loppet, staged in 10 countries.

The longest downhill race is the *Inferno* in Switzerland, 8.7 miles from the top of the Schilthorn to Lauterbrunnen. In 1981 there was a record entry of 1,401, with Heinz Fringen (Switz) winning in a record 15 min 44.57 sec.

Longest Lift

The longest gondola ski lift is 3.88 mi long at Grindelwald-Männlichen, Switzerland (in two sections, but one gondola). The longest chair lift was the Alpine Way to Kosciusko Châlet lift above Thredbo, near the Snowy Mountains, NSW, Australia. It took from 45 to 75 min to ascend the 3.5 mi, according to the weather. It has now collapsed. The highest is at Chacaltaya, Bolivia, rising to 16,500 ft.

Ski Parachuting

The greatest recorded vertical descent in parachute ski-jumping is 3,300 ft by Rick Sylvester (b Apr 3, 1942) (US), who on July 28, 1976, skied off the 6,600-ft summit of Mt Asgard in Auyuittuq National Park, Baffin Island, Canada, landing on the Turner Glacier. The jump was made for a sequence in the James Bond film *The Spy Who Loved Me.*

4 CUPS, 4 TITLES AND A GOLD: Gustavo Thoeni (Italy) used his slalom expertise to win 4 Alpine World Cups, 4 world titles and an Olympic gold. (George Konig)

WINNER OF 35 DOWNHILL RACES: In World Cup competition Franz Klammer (above) (Austria) led all competition with victories, 1974–85.

MOST TITLES WON in Alpine World Championships was 7 earned by Anton "Toni" Sailer of Austria including 4 in 1956 alone. Here he is looking over the landscape at his home town of Kitzbuhel. (Photo by Bruno Engler)

BACKFLIP: The record for this popular stunt (sometimes called "hotdogging") has increased from 19 (as shown here) to 28 in just a few years. (Gary McMillin)

Backflip on Skis

The greatest number of skiers to perform a back layout flip while holding hands is 28 at Bromont, Quebec, Canada, on Feb 10, 1982.

Ski-Bob

The ski-bob was invented by J. C. Stevenson of Hartford, Conn in 1891, and patented (No. 47334) on Apr 19, 1892 as a "bicycle with ski-runners." The Fédération Internationale de Skibob was founded on Jan 14, 1961 in Innsbruck, Austria, and the first world championships were held at Bad Hofgastein, Austria in 1967. The highest speed attained is 103.4 mph by Erich Brenter (b 1940) (Austria) at Cervinia, Italy, 1964.

The only ski-bobbers to retain a world championship are: men—Alois Fischbauer (Austria) (b Oct 6, 1951), 1973 and 1975, Robert Mühlberger (W Germany), 1979, and 1981; women—Gerhilde Schiffkorn (Austria) (b Mar 22, 1950), 1967 and 1969, Gertrude Geberth (Austria) (b Oct 18, 1951), 1971 and 1973.

BIATHLON CHAMP: Frank Ullrich (E Ger), who has won 6 titles including Olympics, shows how he handles the gun while on a ski run.

BIATHLON

The biathlon, which combines cross-country ski-ing and rifle shooting, was first included in the Olympic Games in 1960, and world championships were first held in 1958.

The biathlon is now competed over 10 km, 20 km and a 4 × 7.5 km relay.

Most Olympic Titles

Magnar Solberg (Norway) (b Feb 4, 1937), in 1968 and 1972, is the only man to have won two Olympic individual titles. The USSR has won all five 4 × 7.5 km relay titles, 1968–84. Aleksandr Tikhonov (b Jan 2, 1947) who was a member of the first 4 teams also won a silver in the 1968 20 km.

Most World Championships

Frank Ullrich (E Ger) (b Jan 24, 1958) has won a record six individual world titles, at 10 km, 1978–81, including the 1980 Olympics, and at 20 km 1982–83. Aleksandr Tikhonov was in ten winning USSR relay teams, 1968–80 and won four individual titles. Ullrich has also won the world cup (inst 1979) three times, 1980–82.

SNOWMOBILING

The record speed for a snowmobile is 158.53 mph, set by Marv Jorgenson of Minneapolis at the St Paul Winter Carnival at Lake Phelan, Minn, on Feb 3, 1985.

SNOWSHOE RACING

Records set in competition, recognized by the US Snowshoe Association are:

Men		
100m	Walter Prow	16.81 sec
200m	Crispin McDonald	37.60 sec
400m	Michael Mieszczak	1 min 24.27 sec
Women		
100 m	Laura Kleinke	21.95 sec
200 m	Gwenne Church	49.87 sec
400 m	Nancy Mieszczak	1 min 59.02 sec

RECORD SNOWMOBILE RUN: Marv Jorgenson of Minneapolis went more than 158 mph on this machine on Lake Phelan in Feb 1985.

SNOWSHOE RACING is a grueling sport. Most participants use specially designed snowshoes in the five officially sanctioned events: sprint, relay, hurdle, slalom, and biathlon. (David Verner/AMPS)

SOCCER

Origins

Ball-kicking games were played very early in human history.

A game with some similarities termed *Tsu-chu* was played in China in the 3rd and 4th centuries BC. One of the earliest references to the game in England is a Royal Proclamation by Edward II in 1314 banning the game in the City of London. A soccer-type game called Calcio was played in Italy in 1410. The earliest clear representation of the game is in a print from Edinburgh, Scotland, dated 1672–73. The game became standardized with the formation of the Football Association in England on Oct 26, 1863. Eleven players on a side was standardized in 1870.

The sport is nationally governed by the US Soccer Federation with headquarters in NYC, which is affiliated with the *Fédération Internationale de Football Association*. The North American Soccer League is affiliated with the USSF.

Highest Team Scores

The highest score recorded in any first-class match is 36. This occurred in the Scottish Cup match between Arbroath and Bon Accord on Sept 12, 1885, when Arbroath won 36–0 on their home ground. But for the lack of nets and the consequent waste of re-

trieval time, the score might have been even higher. Seven goals were disallowed for offside.

The highest margin recorded in an international match is 17, when England beat Australia 17–0 at Sydney June 30, 1951. This match is not listed as a *full* international.

World Cup

The 1986 World Cup Competition, the 13th tournament, was held in Mexico May 31–Jun 29. The *Fédération Internationale de Football Association*

HIGH SCORER in World Cup: Gerd Muller (W Germany) scored 14 goals in two World Cup finals (1970 and 1974).

ATHLETE OF THE CENTURY: Pelé celebrates one of his 1,285 goals, this one with the NY Cosmos of the NASL. In a seemingly premature poll of 20 international newspapers, the tremendously popular Brazilian soccer star was named "Athlete of the Century" by the French sports magazine "L'Equipe." Jesse Owens was runner-up.

(FIFA), which was founded on May 21, 1904, instituted the first World Cup on July 13, 1930, in Montevideo, Uruguay. Thirteen nations took part then, playing for a trophy named after Jules Rimet, the late Honorary President of FIFA from 1921–1954. The first team to win the competition three times was to keep the trophy, a feat achieved by Brazil in 1970.

The only countries to win three times have been Brazil (1958, 62, 70) and Italy (1934, 38, 82). Brazil was also second in 1950, and third in 1938 and 1978.

Antonio Carbajal (b 1923) played for Mexico in goal in a record 5 competitions, in 1950, 54, 58, 62 and 66. Uwe Seeler (W Ger) (b Nov 5, 1936) shares the record for the most appearances in final tournaments, playing as a center forward in 21 games in the 1958–70 events, while Pelé is the only player to have been with 3 World Cup winning teams. The youngest

World Cup player ever was Norman Whiteside, who played for N Ireland vs Yugoslavia, aged 17 years 42 days on June 17, 1982.

The record goal scorer has been Just Fontaine (France) with 13 goals in 6 games in the final stages of the 1958 competition. Gerd Müller (W Ger) (b Nov 3, 1945) scored 10 goals in 1970 and 4 in 1974 for the highest aggregate of 14 goals. Fontaine and Jairzinho (Brazil) are the only two players to have scored in every game in a final series, as Jairzinho scored 7 in 6 games in 1970. The most goals scored in the final game is 3 by Geoffrey Hurst (b Dec 8, 1941) for England vs W Germany in 1966. Three players have scored in 2 finals: Vava (real name, Edwaldo Izito Neto) (Brazil) in 1958 and 62, Pelé in 1958 and 70, and Paul Breitner (W Ger) in 1974 and 82.

The highest score in a World Cup match is New Zealand's 13–0 defeat of Fiji in a qualifying match at Auckland on Aug 16, 1981. The highest score in the Finals Tournament is Hungary's 10–1 win over El Salvador at Elche, Spain, on June 15, 1982. The highest match aggregate in the Finals Tournament is 12 when Austria beat Switzerland in 1954.

The highest-scoring team in a Finals Tournament has been W Germany, which scored 25 in 6 games in

1954 for the highest average of 4.17 goals per game. England has the best defensive record, conceding only 3 goals in 6 games in 1966. Curiously, no team has ever failed to score in a World Cup Final.

The fastest goal scored in World Cup competition was one in 27 sec by Bryan Robson for England vs France in Bilbao, Spain, on June 16, 1982.

World Cup Winners

Winner	Locale
1930 Uruguay	Uruguay
1934 Italy	Italy
1938 Italy	France
1950 Uruguay	Brazil
1954 W Germany	Switzerland
1958 Brazil	Sweden
1962 Brazil	Chile
1966 England	England
1970 Brazil	Mexico
1974 W Germany	W Germany
1978 Argentina	Argentina
1982 Italy	Spain
1986 Argentina	Mexico

Marathons

The longest outdoor game played was 74½ hours by two teams trying to establish a record at Liswerry Leisure Centre, Gwent, Wales, June 23–26, 1983. The indoor soccer record is 104 hours 10 min set by two teams of students at Summerhill College, Sligo, Ireland, Mar 27–31, 1983.

Individual Scoring

The most goals scored by one player in a first-class match is 16 by Stephan Stanis (né Stanikowski, b Poland, July 15, 1913) for Racing Club de Lens vs Aubry-Asturies, in Lens, France, on Dec 13, 1942.

The record number of goals scored by one player in an international match is 10 by Sofus Nielsen (1888–1963) for Denmark vs France (17–1) in the 1908 Olympics and by Gottfried Fuchs for Germany, which beat Russia 16–0 in the 1912 Olympic tournament (consolation event) in Sweden.

The most goals scored in a specified period is 1,216 by Edson Arantes do Nascimento (b Baurú, Brazil, Oct 23, 1940), known as Pelé, the Brazilian inside left, in the period Sept 7, 1956 to Oct 2, 1974 (1,254 games). His best year was 1959 with 126 goals. His *milesimo* (1,000th) came in a penalty for his club, Santos, in the Maracaña Stadium, Rio de Janeiro, on Nov 19, 1969, when he was playing in his 909th first-class match. He came out of retirement in 1975 to add to his total with the New York Cosmos of the North American Soccer League. By his retirement on Oct 1, 1977 his total had reached 1,281 in 1,363 games. He added 4 more goals later in special appearances.

Franz ("Bimbo") Binder (b Dec 1, 1911) scored 1,006 goals in 756 games in Austria and Germany between 1930 and 1950.

Largest Tournament

In the Metropolitan Police 5-a-side Youth Competition in 1981 a record 7,008 teams entered.

Most Postponements

In the winter of 1978–79, the tie-breaking match for the Scottish Cup between Inverness Thistle and Falkirk had to be postponed 29 times due to weather conditions. Falkirk finally won 4–0.

Longest Matches

The world duration record for a first-class match is

NET WEIGHT: At 6 ft 3 in and 311 lb, Fatty Foulke was the most massive goalkeeper ever. One of his greatest exploits came off the field, however, when, appearing at the dinner table early one evening, Foulke ate the team's entire meal before any of his teammates arrived.

BALL JUGGLERS: The Brazilian youngster (left) in the street in Rio dreams of being a star soccer player like his fellow countryman Pelé. Mikael Palmquist (Sweden) has kept a soccer ball in midair for 14 hours 14 min non-stop.

3 hours 30 min (with interruptions), in the Copa Libertadores championship in Santos, Brazil, Aug 2–3, 1962, when Santos drew 3–3 with Penarol FC of Montevideo, Uruguay.

A match between St Ignatius College Preparatory of San Francisco and Bellarmine College Preparatory of San Jose lasted 4 hours 56 min (230 min playing time) at San Francisco on Feb 6, 1982.

Goalkeeping

The longest that any goalkeeper has succeeded in preventing any goals being scored past him in international matches is 1,142 min for Dino Zoff (Italy) from Sept 1972 to June 1974.

The biggest goalie on record was Willie J. ("Fatty") Foulke of England (1874–1916) who stood 6 ft 3 in and weighed 311 lb. By the time he died, he tipped the scales at 364 lb. He once stopped a game by snapping the cross bar.

Fastest Goals

The record for an international match is 3 goals in 3½ min by Willie Hall (Tottenham Hotspur) for England against Ireland on Nov 16, 1938, at Old Trafford, Manchester, England.

The fastest authenticated time for a goal from kickoff is 6 sec by Albert Mundy (1958), Barnie Jones (1962), Keith Smith (1964) and Tommy Langley (1980). Wind-aided goals in 3 sec after kickoff have been scored by a number of players.

In amateur soccer, Tony Bacon, of Schalmont HS, scored three goals vs Ichabod Crane HS in 63 sec at Schenectady, NY on Oct 8, 1975.

Most Olympic Wins

The only country to have won the Olympic soccer title three times is Hungary in 1952, 1964 and 1968. The UK won in 1908 and 1912 and also the unofficial tournament of 1900. The highest Olympic score is Denmark 17 vs France "A" 1 in 1908.

Winners:
1908 Great Britain
1912 Great Britain
1920 Belgium
1924 Uruguay
1928 Uruguay
1932 not held
1936 Italy
1948 Sweden
1952 Hungary
1956 USSR
1960 Yugoslavia
1964 Hungary
1968 Hungary
1972 Poland
1976 E Germany
1980 Czechoslovakia
1984 France

Ball Control

Mikael Palmquist (Sweden) juggled a regulation soccer ball for 14 hours 14 min non-stop with feet, legs and head without the ball ever touching the ground at Göteborg, Sweden, on Apr 6, 1986. He also headed a regulation soccer ball non-stop for 4½ hours at Göteborg, Sweden in 1984.

Radoslav Metdiev Nikolov juggled a ball with his feet for 2 hours 57 min 3 sec while covering a distance of 11.15 mi around a running track at Plovdiv, Bulgaria on Aug 18, 1984. He kicked the ball 18,110 times.

The greatest distance covered while juggling a soccer ball is 13.11 mi by Uno Lindstrom of Boden, Sweden, on May 10, 1985.

Penalties

All 11 players and 2 substitutes were "booked" before the start of a game played by Glencraig United (UK) because the referee took exception to the chant which greeted his arrival.

Crowds

The greatest recorded crowd at any soccer match was 205,000 (199,854 paid) for the Brazil vs Uruguay World Cup final in Rio de Janeiro, Brazil, on July 16, 1950.

The greatest crowd to see a soccer game in the US and Canada was the 77,691 spectators at Giants Stadium, NJ, who watched an NASL playoff game between the NY Cosmos and Ft Lauderdale Strikers on Aug 14, 1977.

The highest attendance at any amateur match is 120,000 at Senayan Stadium, Djakarta, Indonesia, on Feb 26, 1976, for the Pre-Olympic Group II Final between North Korea and Indonesia.

DOMINATING SOFT-BALL: Ty Stofflet (US) has struck out 33 in one game and 98 in a year with his underhand fast-pitch.

SOFTBALL

Origins

Softball, as an indoor derivative of baseball, was invented by George Hancock at the Farragut Boat Club of Chicago, in 1887. Rules were first codified in Minneapolis in 1895 as Kitten Ball. The name Softball was introduced by Walter Hakanson at a meeting of the National Recreation Congress in 1926. The name was adopted throughout the US in 1930. Rules were formalized in 1933 by the International Joint Rules Committee for Softball and adopted by the Amateur Softball Association of America. The International Softball Federation was formed in 1950 as governing body for both fast pitch and slow pitch, and reorganized in 1965.

Marathons

The longest fast pitch marathon is 61 hours 36 min 33 sec by two teams of 9 (no substitutes) belonging to

← **SOFTBALL QUEEN: Rosie Black heads a team of 4 that plays exhibitions against teams of 9. She claims to pitch a softball 100 mph, and has an assortment of pitches that enables her "court" to win almost all of their games.**

WORLD CHAMPIONSHIP FAST PITCH SOFTBALL
RECORDS

MEN
Batting

Highest batting average:	.583	Takayuki Ietke, Japan	1984
Most hits:	17	Basil McLean, New Zealand	1976
Most runs scored:	14	Takayuki Ietke, Japan	1984
Most runs batted in:	14	Chuck Teuscher US	1966
	14	Bob Burrows, Canada	1976
Most doubles:	5	Hector Serranto, Puerto Rico	1966
	5	Luis Delgado, Mexico	1966
	5	Frank Hurtt, US	1968
	5	Filomeno Codinera, Philippines	1968
Most triples:	3	Akira Nakagawa, Japan	1976
	3	Jesus Augon, Guam	1976
Most home runs:	4	Bob Burrows, Canada	1976

Pitching (in a year)

Most wins:	6	Owen Walford, New Zealand	1976
	6	Owen Walford, US	1980
Most strikeouts:	99	Kevin Herlihy, New Zealand	1972
	98	Ty Stofflet, US	1976
Most strikeouts in one game:	33	Ty Stofflet, US in 20 innings 1–0 win over New Zealand	1976
Most innings pitched:	59	Ty Stofflet, US	1976
	58⅔	Kevin Herlihy, New Zealand	1972
Lowest earned run average:			
(59 innings pitched)	0.00	Ty Stofflet, US	1976
(32⅓ innings pitched)	0.00	Chuck Richard, US	1966
(34⅔ innings pitched)	0.00	Owen Walford, US	1980
Most consecutive wins:	15	Owen Walford, US and New Zealand	1976, 80, 84
Perfect games:	7	tied	1968–84

WOMEN
Batting

Highest batting average:	.550	Tamara Bryce, Panama	1978
Most hits:	17	Miyoko Naruse, Japan	1974
Most runs scored:	13	Kathy Elliott, US	1974
Most runs batted in:	11	Miyoko Naruse, Japan	1974
	11	Keiko Uoul, Japan	1974
	11	Kathy Elliott, US	1974
Most doubles:	4	Vicki Murray, NZ	1983
	4	Suh-Chiung Ju, Taiwan	1983
Most triples:	6	Miyoko Naruse, Japan	1974
	6	Yug-Feng Yang, Taiwan	1982

Pitching

Most wins:	6	Lorraine Woolley, Australia	1965
	6	Nancy Welborn, US	1970
Most innings pitched:	50	Nancy Welborn, US	1970
Most strikeouts:	76	Joan Joyce, US	1974
Most no-hitters:	3	Joan Joyce, US	1974
	3	Kathy Arendsen, US	1978
Most perfect games:	2	Joan Joyce, US	1974

NOTE: Records are totals for all games in each particular championship.

the Marines of the 2nd Radio Battalion at Camp Lejeune, NC, May 3–5, 1984. The game went 266 innings and the score was 343-296.

The longest slow pitch softball game was an unratified 101 hours 32 min, played by 2 teams of 10 at Franke Park, Fort Wayne, Ind, Aug 7–11, 1986.

World Championships

The US has won the men's world championship (instituted in 1966) four times, 1966, 68, 76 (shared) and 80. The US has also won the women's title (instituted in 1965) 3 times, in 1974, 78 and 86.

In 1981, junior world championships for boys and girls were started, with Japan winning both divisions that year. In 1985, New Zealand won the boys' world championship and China the girls' division.

SQUASH

Earliest Champion

Although racquets with a soft ball (called "squashy") was played in 1817 at Harrow School (England), there was no recognized champion of any country until J. A. Miskey of Philadelphia won the American Amateur Singles Championship in 1907.

British Open Championship

The most wins in the Open Championship (amateur or professional), held annually in Britain, is 7 by Geoffrey Hunt (Australia) in 1969, 74, and 76–80. Hashim Khan (b 1915) (Pakistan) won 7 times and has also won the Vintage title 6 times, 1978–83.

The most wins in the Women's Squash Rackets Championship is 16 by Heather Pamela McKay (*née* Blundell) (b July 31, 1941) of Australia, 1961 to 1977. She also won the World Open title in 1976 and 79. In her career from 1959 to 1980 she lost only two games.

World Titles

Geoffrey B. Hunt (b Mar 11, 1947) (Australia) won a record four World Open (inst 1976) titles, 1976–7 and 1979–80, and three World Amateur (inst 1967) titles. Australia has won a record four amateur team titles, 1967, 1969, 1971 and 1973.

Jahangir Khan (Pakistan) has won 3 times (1981–82–83), and was the youngest champion in 1981 at age 17 years 354 days. He was beaten for the first time since 1981 when Ross Norman (NZ) beat him in 1986.

Heather McKay (see photo) won twice (1976 and 1979). No women's tournament was held in 1977 and 1978.

HOLDING COURT: The winner of 16 British and 2 World Open championships, Heather McKay has not lost a match since 1961. She won all but 2 of the games she played.

MOST SQUASH VICTORIES: Geoff Hunt (Aust) (nearer to camera) won 4 World Open tournaments and 3 World Amateur titles. Here he shows his 1969 form before becoming World champ. (AP)

Longest and Shortest Championship Matches

The longest recorded championship match was one of 2 hours 45 min when Jahangir Khan (b Dec 10, 1963) (Pakistan) beat Gamal Awad (Egypt) (b Sept 8, 1955) 9–10, 9–5, 9–7, 9–2, the first game lasting a record 1 hour 11 min, in the final of the Patrick International Festival at Chichester, W Sussex, England, Mar 30, 1983.

Suzanne Burgess beat Carolyn Mett in just 8 min, in the British Under-23 Open Championship at The Oasis Club, Marlow, Buckinghamshire, Eng, on Jan 20, 1986.

Marathon Record

The longest squash marathon is 122 hours 44 min by Amir Shailch and Phillip Marlowe at Wembley Squash Centre, Eng, Nov 8–13, 1985. (*This category is now confined to two players only.*)

SURFING

Origins

The traditional Polynesian sport of surfing in a canoe was first recorded by Captain James Cook (GB) (1728–79) on his first voyage at Tahiti in Dec 1771. Surfing on a board was first described "most perilous and extraordinary . . . altogether astonishing and is scarcely to be credited" by Lt (later Capt) James King (GB) in Mar 1779 at Kealakekua Bay, Hawaii Island. A surfer was first depicted by this voyage's official artist John Webber. The sport was revived at Waikiki by 1900. Hollow boards were introduced in 1929 and the light plastic foam type in 1956.

Most Titles

World Amateur Championships were inaugurated in May 1964 at Sydney, Australia; the only surfer to win two titles has been Joyce Hoffman (US) in 1965 and 1966. A World Professional circuit was started in 1975 and Mark Richards (Australia) has won the men's title four times, 1979–82. Tommy Curren (US) won the World Pro title in 1986.

Highest Waves Ridden

Makaha Beach, Hawaii provides the reputedly highest consistently tall waves, often reaching the ridable limit of 30–35 ft. The highest wave ever ridden was the *tsunami* of "perhaps 50 ft," which struck Minole, Hawaii on Apr 3, 1868. It was ridden by a Hawaiian named Holua to save his life.

Longest Ride

About four to six times each year ridable surfing waves break in Matanchen Bay near San Blas, Nayarit, Mexico which makes a ride of *c.* 5,700 ft possible.

The longest ride on a surfboard standing or lying down was 2.94 mi by Colin Kerr Wilson (b June 23, 1954) (UK) on May 23, 1982 on the bore of the Severn River, Eng.

SURFING was described in 1779 as "most perilous and extraordinary . . . altogether astonishing . . . scarcely to be credited," and the waves haven't changed much since then, but surfboards became lighter in 1956. (Debbie Beacham)

SWIMMING

Earliest References

Egyptian hieroglyphics, c. 3000 BC, indicate swimming figures, and a bronze of a diver dating from c. 510 BC was found near Perugia, Italy. Both Julius Caesar and Charlemagne were known to be good swimmers. Competitions took place in Japan in 36 BC, and that country was the first to take to the sport in a major way with an Imperial edict by the Emperor Go-Yozei decreeing its introduction in schools. In Britain, sea bathing was practiced as early as 1660 at Scarborough, but competitive swimming was not introduced until 1837, when competitions were held in London's artificial pools organized by the National Swimming Society, founded in that year. Australia was in the forefront of modern developments and an unofficial world 100-yd championship was held in Melbourne in 1858. With the foundation of the Amateur Swimming Association (though not known by this name till later) in Britain in 1869 came the distinction between amateurs and professionals.

The first recognizable stroke style seems to have been the breaststroke, although the "dog-paddle" technique may well have preceded it. From this developed the sidestroke, which is the breaststroke per-

FIRST CHANNEL SWIMMER: British navy captain Matthew Webb swam breaststroke the whole way in 1875. It took him 21¾ hours, compared to the current record of 7 hours 40 min. (Mary Evans)

formed sideways, a style which was last used by an Olympic champion in 1904, when Emil Rausch (Ger) won the 1-mi event. About the middle of the 19th century, some American Indians had swum in London exhibiting a style resembling the crawl. An Englishman, John Trudgen, noted a variation of this style while on a trip to South America in the 1870s. His forerunner to the modern crawl used the legs in basically a breaststroke way. However, from ancient carvings and wall paintings it would seem that the trudgen stroke was in use in early times.

Another "throwback" was the front or Australian crawl which is credited to a British emigrant to Australia, Frederick Cavill, and his sons, who noticed the unusual style of South Sea Island natives, and modified it to their own use. American swimmers developed this even further by variations of the kicking action of the legs. At the beginning of the 20th century some had shown their prowess by attempting the breaststroke on their backs, and later the crawl action was tried in the same position. Thus the backstroke was born. In the 1930s the idea of recovering the arms over the water in the breaststroke was developed, and led to a drastic revision of the record book, until the new style was recognized as a separate stroke, the butterfly, in 1952. Also in the 1930s

came the introduction, mainly in the US, of medley events in which swimmers use all four major strokes during one event, a real test of all-around ability.

World Titles

In the world swimming championships (instituted in 1973), the greatest number of medals won is 10 by Kornelia Ender of E Germany (8 gold, 2 silver) in 1973 and 75. The most by a man is 8 (5 gold, 3 silver) by Ambrose "Rowdy" Gaines (US, b Feb 17, 1959) in 1978 and 1982. The most gold medals is 6 by James Montgomery (b Jan 24, 1955) in 1973 and 1975.

The most medals in a single championship is 7 by Matt Biondi (US) in 1986 with 3 gold, 1 silver and 3 bronze. The women's second is 6, shared by Tracy Caulkins (US) (b Jan 11, 1963) in 1978 with 5 gold and a silver; by Kristin Otto (E Ger) with 4 gold and 2 silver in 1986; and by Mary Meagher (US) with 1 gold, 3 silver, and 2 bronze in 1986. She won a record 48 US titles before she retired in 1984.

The most successful country in the championships has been the US with a total of 57 swimming, 11 diving and 8 synchronized swimming titles. However, in

women's swimming events alone E Germany has a record total of 44 victories.

Other than relays, the only gold medalist in the same event at three championships is Phil Boggs (US) in springboard diving.

Most World Records

Men: 32, Arne Borg (Sweden) (b 1901), 1921–29. Women: 42, Ragnhild Hveger (Denmark) (b Dec 10, 1920), 1936–42. Under modern conditions (only metric distances in 50-meter pools) the most is 26 by Mark Spitz (US, b Feb 10, 1950), 1967–72, and 23 by Kornelia Ender (now Matthes) (E Germany, b Oct 25, 1958), 1973–76.

Hveger's record of 42 gained for her the name "Golden Torpedo." Her records came in 18 different events. She was a virtual certainty to win at the 1940 Olympic Games, but, of course, war intervened. Retiring in 1945, she made a comeback for the 1952 Games and placed fifth in the 400 m freestyle.

Most Individual Gold Medals

The record number of individual gold medals won is 4 shared by four swimmers: Charles M. Daniels (US) (1884–1973) (100 m freestyle 1906 and 1908, 220 yd freestyle 1904, 440 yd freestyle 1904); Roland Matthes (E Germany) (b Nov 17, 1950) with 100 m and 200 m backstroke 1968 and 1972; and Mark Spitz and Mrs Patricia McCormick (see next item).

Most Olympic Gold Medals

The greatest number of Olympic gold medals won is 9 by Mark Andrew Spitz (US) (b Feb 10, 1950), as follows:

100 m freestyle	1972
200 m freestyle	1972
100 m butterfly	1972
200 m butterfly	1972
4 × 100 m freestyle relay	1968 and 1972
4 × 200 m freestyle relay	1968 and 1972
4 × 100 m medley relay	1972

All but one of these performances (the 4 × 200 m relay of 1968) were also world records at the time. He also won a silver (100 m butterfly) and a bronze (100 m freestyle) in 1968 for a record 11 medals.

The record number of gold medals won by a woman is 4 shared by Mrs Patricia McCormick (née Keller) (US) (b May 12, 1930) with the high and springboard diving double in 1952 and 1956 (also the women's record for individual golds); by Dawn Fraser (Australia) (b Sept 4, 1937) with the 100 m freestyle (1956, 60, 64) and the 4 × 100 m freestyle relay (1956); and by Kornelia Ender (E Germany) with the 100 and 200 m freestyle (1976), the 100 m butterfly (1976) and the 4 × 100 m medley relay (1976). Dawn Fraser is the only swimmer to win the same event on three successive Olympic occasions.

Most Olympic Medals

The most medals won is 11 by Spitz, who in addition to his 9 golds (see above), won a silver (100 m

MOST RECORDS: A young Mark Spitz (17 years old in this photo) is congratulated after setting a world record early in his career. Spitz might be considered the most successful swimmer ever. Of his 9 Olympic gold medals (including the unequaled haul of 7 in 1972), 8 were won in world record time. In his 6-year career, Spitz set a total of 26 world records. (UPI)

butterfly) and a bronze (100 m freestyle), both in 1968.

The most medals won by a woman is 8 by Dawn Fraser, who in addition to her 4 golds (see above) won 4 silvers (400 m freestyle 1956, 4 × 100 m freestyle relay 1960 and 1964, 4 × 100 m medley relay 1960); by Shirley Babashoff (US) who won 2 golds (4 × 100 m freestyle relay 1972 and 1976) and 6 silvers (100 m freestyle 1972, 200 m freestyle 1972 and 1976, 400 m and 800 m freestyle 1976, and 400 m medley 1976); and by Kornelia Ender (E Germany) who, in addition to her 4 golds (see above), won 4 silvers (200 m individual medley 1972, 4 × 100 m medley 1972, 4 × 100 m freestyle 1972 and 1976).

Swimming into the Movies

The ability to move well in water has been the key to a movie career for a number of champion swimmers. The first star was Australian Annette Kellerman who made a number of silent films, and was the first woman to wear a one-piece bathing suit. However, it was the 1924 and 1928 Olympic gold medalist, Johnny Weissmuller (US), who became the first major box-office attraction from the swimming world, playing the role of Tarzan in a dozen films. His 1928 Olympic teammate, Clarence "Buster" Crabbe, who later won the 1932 400 m freestyle title, also went to Hollywood, where he was the hero in the long-running Buck Rogers and Flash Gordon serials.

Another 1932 Olympic champion, the glamorous Eleanor Holm (US) made several movies, although she did not go to Hollywood until she was dropped from the 1936 team for disciplinary reasons. Perhaps the best-known swimming star was Esther Williams, American 100 m champion in 1939 and favorite for the cancelled Olympics of 1940. Turning professional

SWIMMING WORLD RECORDS (MEN)

At distances recognized by the Fédération Internationale de Natation Amateur as of July 16, 1983. FINA no longer recognizes any records made for non-metric distances. Only performances in 50-m pools are recognized as World Records.

Distance	min:sec	Name and Nationality	Place	Date
		FREESTYLE		
50 m	22.33	Matthew Biondi (US)	Orlando, Fla	June 26, 1986
100 m	48.74	Matthew Biondi (US)	Orlando, Fla	June 24, 1986
200 m	1:47.44	Michael Gross (W Ger)	Los Angeles	July 29, 1984
400 m	3:47.80	Michael Gross (W Ger)	Remscheid, W Ger	June 27, 1985
800 m	7:50.64	Vladimir Salnikov (USSR)	Moscow, USSR	July 4, 1986
1,500 m	14:54.76	Vladimir Salnikov (USSR)	Moscow	Feb 22, 1983
4 × 100 m Relay	3:17.08	US National Team (Scott McCadam, Michael Heath, Paul Wallace, Matthew Biondi)	Tokyo	Aug 17, 1985
4 × 200 m Relay	7:15.69	US National Team (Michael Heath, David Larson, Jeff Float, Bruce Hayes)	Los Angeles	July 30, 1984
		BREASTSTROKE		
100 m	1:01.65	Steve Lundquist (US)	Los Angeles	July 29, 1984
200 m	2:13.34	Victor Davis (Canada)	Los Angeles	Aug 2, 1984
		BUTTERFLY STROKE		
100 m	52.84	Pedro Pablo Morales (US)	Orlando, Fla	June 23, 1986
200 m	1:56.24	Michael Gross (W Ger)	Hanover, W Ger	June 27, 1986
		BACKSTROKE		
100 m	55.19	Richard (Rick) Carey (US)	Caracas, Venezuela	Aug 21, 1983
200 m	1:58.14	Igor Polyansky (USSR)	Erfurt, E Ger	Mar 3, 1985
		INDIVIDUAL MEDLEY		
200 m	2:01.42	Alex Baumann (Canada)	Montreal, Canada	Mar 4, 1986
	2:01.42	Alex Baumann (Canada)	Los Angeles	Aug 4, 1984
400 m	4:17.41	Alex Baumann (Canada)	Los Angeles	July 30, 1984
		MEDLEY RELAY (Backstroke, Breaststroke, Butterfly Stroke, Freestyle)		
4 × 100 m	3:38.28	US National Team (Richard "Rick" Carey, John Moffett, Pablo Morales, Matthew Biondi)	Tokyo	Aug 18, 1985

she created a new vogue in the cinema, the swimming musical, in which she was supreme throughout the 1940s. One of her co-stars was Fernando Lamas, who had been a national swimming champion in his native Argentina, and whom she later married.

Closest Race

In the women's 100 m freestyle final in the 1984 Olympics, Carrie Steinseifer (US) and Nancy Hogshead (US) won in a tie at 55.92 sec, and were both awarded gold medals. It was not in record time, but it was the first dead heat in Olympic swimming history.

Fastest Swimmers

The fastest 50 m in a 50-m pool is 22.33 sec (5.01 mph) by Matthew Biondi (US) in Orlando, Fla, June 26, 1986.

The fastest by a woman is 25.28 sec (4.42 mph) by Tamara Costache (Rom) (b 1970) at Madrid, Spain, Aug 23, 1986.

Largest Pools

The largest swimming pool in the world is the saltwater Orthlieb Pool in Casablanca, Morocco. It is 480 m (1,574 ft) long, 75 m (246 ft) wide, and has an area of 8.9 acres.

The world's largest competition pool is at Osaka, Japan. It accommodates 13,614 spectators.

Synchronized Swimming

Started in 1904 by Annette Kellerman when she swam underwater and performed water ballets on the stage of the NYC Hippodrome, this did not become an Olympic event for women until 1984 at Los Angeles. The contestants are judged on presentation and showmanship as well as the athlete's skill and technique.

WORLD RECORDS SET IN OLYMPICS: Michael Gross (above) (W Ger) who set 200-m freestyle and 100-m butterfly records in the 1984 Games, went on to new records in the 400-m freestyle (1985) and 200-m butterfly (1986). Steve Lundquist (right) (US) set the 100-m breaststroke world mark in the 1984 Olympics that still prevails.

24-Hour Swim

David Goch (US) swam 55.682 mi in a 25-yd pool at Univ of Mich, May 17–18, 1986. In a 50-m pool, Bertrand Malegue swam 54.39 mi at St Etienne, France, May 31–June 1, 1980. The women's record is 42.05 mi in 25-m pool by Alyson Gibbons (UK) in Birmingham, Eng, Sept 7–8, 1985.

Greatest Lifetime Distance

Gustave Brickner (b Feb 10, 1912) of Charleroi, Pa, recorded 38,512 mi of swimming from 1926 to his retirement in 1986.

Underwater Swimming

Paul Cryne (UK) and Samir Sawan al Aw swam 49.04 mi underwater in a 24-hour period at Doha, Qatar on Feb 21–22, 1985 using sub-aqua equipment. They were swimming underwater for 95.5% of the time.

The first underwater cross-Channel swim was achieved by Fred Baldasare (US), aged 38, who completed a 42-mile swim from France to England with SCUBA in 18 hours 1 min, July 10–11, 1962.

Treading Water

The duration record for treading water (vertical posture in an 8-ft square without touching the pool

SWIMMING WORLD RECORDS (WOMEN)

Distance	min:sec	Name and Nationality	Place	Date
		FREESTYLE		
50 m	25.28	Tamara Costache (Romania)	Madrid, Spain	Aug 23, 1986
100 m	54.73	Kristin Otto (E Ger)	Madrid, Spain	Aug 19, 1986
200 m	1:57.55	Heike Friedrich (E Ger)	E Berlin	June 18, 1986
400 m	4:06.28	Tracey Wickham (Aust)	W Berlin	Aug 24, 1978
800 m	8:24.62	Tracey Wickham (Aust)	Edmonton, Canada	Aug 5, 1978
1,500 m	16:04.49	Kim Linehan (US)	Ft Lauderdale	Aug 19, 1979
4 × 100 m Relay	3:40.57	East Germany	Madrid, Spain	Aug 19, 1986
		(Kristin Otto, Manuella Stellmach, Sabina Schulze, Heike Friedrich)		
4 × 200 m Relay	7:59.33	E Germany	Madrid, Spain	Aug 17, 1986
		(Manuella Stellmach, Astrid Strauss, Nadja Bergknecht, Heike Friedrich)		
		BREASTSTROKE		
100 m	1:08.11	Sylvia Gerasch (E Ger)	Madrid, Spain	Aug 21, 1986
200 m	2:27.40	Silke Horner (E Ger)	Madrid, Spain	Aug 18, 1986
		BUTTERFLY STROKE		
100 m	57.93	Mary Meagher (US)	Milwaukee	Aug 16, 1981
200 m	2:05.96	Mary Meagher (US)	Milwaukee	Aug 13, 1981
		BACKSTROKE		
100 m	1:00.59	Ina Kleber (E Ger)	Moscow	Aug 24, 1984
200 m	2:08.60	Betsy Mitchell (US)	Orlando, Fla	June 27, 1986
		INDIVIDUAL MEDLEY		
200 m	2:11.73	Ute Geweniger (E Ger)	E Berlin	July 4, 1981
400 m	4:36.10	Petra Schneider (E Ger)	Guayaquil, Ecuador	Aug 1, 1982
		MEDLEY RELAY		
		(Backstroke, Breaststroke, Butterfly Stroke, Freestyle)		
4 × 100 m Relay	4:03.69	E German National Team	Moscow	Aug 24, 1984
		(Ina Kleber, Sylvia Gerasch, Ines Geissler, Birgit Meineke)		

BUTTERFLY CHAMPION: Mary Meagher (US) set 100 m and 200 m butterfly records in 1981 that still stand. She also set Olympic records in these events in 1984.

sides or bottom or lane markers) is 98½ hours set by Reginald (Moon) Huffstetler of Belmont, NC, at The Reef in Myrtle Beach, SC, May 20–24, 1986.

Albert Rizzo trod water in the sea at Gzira, Malta, for 108 hours 9 min Sept 7–12, 1983.

Diving Titles

Greg Louganis (US) (b Jan 29, 1960), won 5 world diving titles, one in 1978, and 2 in both 1982 and 1986, as well as 2 Olympic golds in 1984. At Guayaquil, Ecuador, he became the first to score over 700

DIVING CHAMPION: Greg Louganis (US), considered by many to be the best diver in the world in the 1980's, is one of two divers to earn perfect 10's from all 7 judges for one dive. He achieved the feat while winning his 2nd and 3rd world championships. In the 1984 Olympics he won 2 gold medals and set new world records for springboard and highboard.

OLYMPIC GOLD MEDALISTS: Mrs Pat McCormick (below) (US) and Dawn Fraser (right, below) (Aust) share the record, along with Kornelia Ender (E Ger) for the most gold medals won by a woman. McCormick uniquely won all 4 in individual events while Fraser is the only swimmer to win the same event at 3 consecutive Games.

MOST WORLD
RECORDS for a woman
(23): Kornelia Ender (E
Ger) holds the most
records in swimming in
metric-measured pools.
Here she is getting
started with her mouth
open. (Tony Duffy—All-
Sport)

points for the 11-dive springboard event with 752.67 on Aug 1, 1982. He went on to be awarded a score of 10.0 by all 7 judges for his highboard inward 1½ somersault in the pike position. In the 1984 Olympics, Louganis won two gold medals and set record totals of 754.41 for springboard and 710.91 for highboard.

Klaus Dibiasi (Italy, b Austria, Oct 6, 1947) won a total of 5 Olympic diving medals (3 gold, 2 silver) in 4 Games from 1964 to 1976. He is also the only diver to win the same event (highboard) at 3 successive Games (1968, 72 and 76). He also won 4 medals (2 gold, 2 silver) in world events in 1973 and 1975.

Irina Kalinina (USSR) (b Feb 8, 1959) has won 5 medals (3 gold, one silver, one bronze) in 1973, 1975 and 1978.

Perfect Dive

In the 1972 US Olympic Trials, held in Chicago, Michael Finneran (b Sept 21, 1948) was awarded a

BEST IN USA: Tracy Caulkins, here wearing her record 6 medals (5 gold, 1 silver) from the 1978 World Championships, eclipsed Johnny (Tarzan) Weissmuller's 54-year-old record as winner of the most US national titles. To these, she added more gold medals, including 1984 Olympic awards. (Tony Duffy, All-Sport)

STARTING YOUNG: Gertrude Ederle (US) (left), the first woman to swim the English Channel (1926), was also the youngest to break a non-mechanical world record. At the age of 12 years 298 days (1919) she set a new 880-yd freestyle mark. CHANNEL ENERGY (right) Jon Erikson, the first swimmer to make a triple crossing of the English Channel, relaxes here with his father, Ted. Both had held records for the fastest double crossing.

score of 10 by all seven judges for a backward 1½ somersault 2½ twist (free) from the 10-m platform, an achievement then without precedent. Greg Louganis matched this feat in 1982.

Long Distance Swimming

A unique achievement in long distance swimming was established in 1966 by Mihir Sen of Calcutta, India. He swam the Palk Strait from Sri Lanka to

LONGEST TOUGH SWIM: Using the exhausting butterfly stroke exclusively, the di Donato twins, James and Jonathan, swam 40.6 miles in 20 hours 6 min from Gun Cay, Bahamas, to near the Fla coast before foul weather stopped them. They also swam the 28+ miles around Manhattan Island in 9 hours 42 min using the butterfly stroke.

LONG-TIME CHAMPIONS: No one has been able to beat the record of Petra Schneider of E Germany (left) in the 400 m individual medley since 1982. Cindy Nicholas of Canada (right) was the first woman to make a double crossing of the English Channel in 1977, knocking 10 hours off the men's mark. She beat this by an hour in 1982.

India (in 25 hours 36 min, Apr 5–6); the Straits of Gibraltar (Europe to Africa in 8 hours 1 min on Aug 24); the Dardanelles (Gallipoli, Europe, to Sedulbahir, Asia Minor, in 13 hours 55 min on Sept 12); the Bosphorus (in 4 hours on Sept 21) and the entire length of the Panama Canal (in 34 hours 15 min, Oct 29–31). He had earlier swum the English Channel in 14 hours 45 min on Sept 27, 1958.

The longest ocean swim was one of 128.8 miles by Walter Poenisch (US) (b 1914), who started from Havana, Cuba, and arrived at Little Duck Key, Fla (in a shark cage and wearing flippers) 34 hours 15 min later, July 11–13, 1978.

The greatest recorded distance ever swum is 1,826 miles down the Mississippi from Ford Dam, near Minneapolis, to Carrollton Avenue, New Orleans, July 6 to Dec 29, 1930, by Fred P. Newton, then 27, of Clinton, Okla. He was in the water a total of 742 hours, and the water temperature fell as low as 47° F. He protected himself with petroleum jelly.

The longest swim using the highly exhausting butterfly stroke exclusively was 40.6 miles from Gun Cay, the Bahamas to near Florida by twins James and Jonathan di Donato (b Oct 24, 1953) (US) June 23, 1985. They were stopped by foul weather after 20 hours 6 min.

The fastest swim around Manhattan was made by a woman, Shelley Taylor of Australia (b 1961) who set a record of 6 hours 12 min 29 sec on Oct 15, 1985. The men's record was set by Drury J. Gallagher in 6 hours 41 min 35 sec on Sept 7, 1983. The longest swim around Manhattan was done over a period of 6 days in a row—Aug 15–20, 1985—28½ mi each day (except for the first day—20 mi) by Julie Ridge of NYC, who was an actress in the cast of a Broadway show.

The longest duration swim ever achieved was one of 168 continuous hours, ending on Feb 24, 1941, by the legless Charles Zibbelman, *alias* Zimmy (b 1894), of the US, in a pool in Honolulu, Hawaii.

The longest duration swim by a woman was 87 hours 27 min in a salt water pool at Raven Hall, Coney Island, NY by Mrs Myrtle Huddleston of NYC, in 1931.

The greatest distance covered in a continuous swim is 299 miles by Ricardo Hoffmann (b Oct 5, 1941) from Corrientes to Santa Elena, Argentina, in the River Paraná in 84 hours 37 min, Mar 3–6, 1981.

Earliest Channel Swimmers

The first to swim the English Channel (without a life jacket) was the merchant navy captain Matthew Webb (1848–83) (GB), who swam breaststroke from Dover, England, to Calais Sands, France, in 21 hours 45 min, Aug 24–25, 1875. Webb swam an estimated 38 miles to make the 21-mile crossing. Paul Boyton (US) had swum from Cap Gris Nez to the South Foreland in his patented lifesaving suit in 23 hours

MANHATTAN ROUND-TRIPPERS: Shelley Taylor (left) of Australia came to NY to set a record for swimming around the 28½-mi island in 6 hours 12 min 29 sec in Oct 1985. Here she is under the George Washington Bridge. Julie Ridge (right) a native of NY City, spent 6 days in a row in Aug 1985 in the treacherous waters swimming 20 mi the first day (when she was stopped by a tide turn), and the full 28½ mi circle the other 5 days. (Photos by Luca Del Borgo/Coplan & Assoc)

30 min, May 28–29, 1875. There is good evidence that Jean-Marie Saletti, a French soldier, escaped from a British prison hulk off Dover by swimming to Boulogne in July or Aug 1815. The first crossing from France to England was made by Enrico Tiraboschi, a wealthy Italian living in Argentina, who crossed in 16 hours 33 min on Aug 12, 1923, to win a $5,000 prize. By the end of 1981 the English Channel had been swum by 228 persons on 366 occasions.

The first woman to succeed was Gertrude Ederle (b Oct 23, 1906) (US) who swam from Cap Gris Nez, France, to Deal, England, on Aug 6, 1926, in the then record time of 14 hours 39 min. The first woman to swim from England to France was Florence Chadwick of California, in 16 hours 19 min on Sept 11, 1951.

Most Conquests of the English Channel

The greatest number of Channel conquests is 31 by Michael Read (GB), to Aug 19, 1984, including a record 6 in one year. Cindy Nicholas made her first crossing of the Channel on July 29, 1975, and her 19th (and fifth 2-way) on Sept 14, 1982.

SALT-WATER POOL 524 yd long and 82 yd wide in Casablanca, Morocco, is the world's largest.

Youngest and Oldest Channel Swimmers

The youngest conqueror is Marcus Hooper (b June 14, 1967) of Eltham, England, who swam from Dover to Sangatte, France, in 14 hours 37 min, when he was aged 12 years 53 days. The youngest woman was Samantha Claire Druce (b Apr 21, 1971) aged 12 years 119 days when she swam from England to France in 15 hours 27 min on Aug 18, 1983.

The oldest is Ashby Harper (b Oct 1, 1916) of Albuquerque, N Mex, at 65 years 332 days. He swam from Dover to Cap Blanc Nez in 13 hours 52 min on Aug 28, 1983. He also held the record as the oldest person to swim around Manhattan before that record was broken on Aug 26, 1984 by the 73-year-old Dr Adrian Kanaar of Poughkeepsie, NY.

The oldest woman to conquer the Channel is Stella Ada Rosina Taylor (b Bristol, Avon, England, Dec 20, 1929), aged 45 years 350 days when she swam it in 18 hours 15 min on Aug 26, 1975.

Double Crossings of the Channel

Antonio Abertondo (Argentina), aged 42, swam from England to France in 18 hours 50 min (8:35 a.m. on Sept 20 to 3:25 a.m. on Sept 21, 1961) and after about 4 minutes' rest returned to England in 24 hours 16 min, landing at St Margaret's Bay at 3:45 a.m. on Sept 22, 1961, to complete the first "double crossing" in 43 hours 10 min.

The fastest double crossing was by Philip Rush (NZ) (b Nov 6, 1963), who swam the fastest, 17 hours 56 min, beating the 18 hours 15 min set in 1983.

The fastest by a relay team is 15 hours 36 min 30 sec by the West One International Team on Sept 24, 1985.

Triple Crossing of the Channel

The first triple crossing of the English Channel was by Jon Erikson (b Sept 6, 1954) (US) in 38 hours 27 min, Aug 11–12, 1981.

Fastest Channel Crossings

The official Channel Swimming Association record is 7 hours 40 min by Penny Dean (b March 21, 1955) of California, who swam from Shakespeare Beach, Dover, England to Cap Gris Nez, France on July 29, 1978.

The fastest crossing by a relay team is 7 hours 17 min by 6 Dover (Eng) lifeguards from England to France on Aug 9, 1981.

Relay Records

The New Zealand national relay team of 20 swimmers swam a record 113.59 mi in Lower Hutt, NZ in 24 hours, passing 100 mi in 20 hours 47 min 13 sec on Dec 9–10, 1983.

The most participants in a one-day swim relay is 2,135, each swimming a length, organized by the Syracuse (NY) YMCA, Apr 11, 1986. A team of 4 from Capalaba State Primary School, Kim Wilson, Tanya Obstoj, Paul Giles, Daren Sheldrick, set an endurance record of 168 hours with one of the team in the water at any time, covering 336 mi on Dec 12–19, 1983 at Sheldon, Queensland, Australia.

The fastest time recorded for 100 miles in a pool by a team of 20 swimmers is 21 hours 41 min 4 sec by the Dropped Sports Swim Club of Indiana State University at Terre Haute, Ind, Mar 12–13, 1982. Four swimmers from the Darien YMCA, Conn, covered 300 miles in relay in 122 hours 59 min 40 sec, Nov 25–30, 1980.

Tony Boyle, Eddie McGettigan, Laurence Thermes and Gearoid Murphy swam a relay of 332.88 mi underwater in 168 hours using sub-aqua equipment at the Mosney Holiday Centre, Co. Meath, Ireland, June 22–29, 1985.

FASTEST MAN AROUND MANHATTAN: Drury Gallagher (left) swam around the island at 6:41.35. His time was surpassed by a woman (see page 196). Tom Hetzel (right) has swum around the island 8 times. (Gerard Malanga/Coplan & Assoc)

TABLE TENNIS

Earliest Reference

In 1879 some Cambridge University students indulged in a diversion in which they hit champagne corks to each other over a pile of books in the center of a table, using cigar boxes as crude bats. Rubber balls soon followed, but it was not until about 1900 that James Gibb, a former English world record-breaking runner, introduced a celluloid ball to the game.

At first the game was called "indoor tennis" and it marked the beginning of the game in the US. In 1902 the game was called Flim-Flam, *Gossima*, Klik-Klak, and Whiff-Whaff. The origin of the word Ping Pong is in doubt. Some claim it came from the use of banjo rackets which had two sides of vellum. The impact of the celluloid ball against this hollow racket made the sound "Ping" and the impact of the ball on the table, the sound "Pong." The game thrived for a period, and in 1902 the first Ping Pong Association was formed in Britain. But the monotony of play due to plain wooden bats soon led to a decline in interest until the 1920s.

The next stage in the history of the game was the use of wooden, cork and sandpaper rackets. In 1920, the studded rubber racket was invented, which allowed a spin to be imparted to the ball. Then, in 1952, sponge rackets were introduced by the Japanese at the world championships in Bombay, India.

The International Table Tennis Federation was founded in 1926 with 7 nations and now there are about 121 nations.

World Championships

Instituted in 1927, the world championships were held annually until 1957, when the competitions became biennial (rendering most of the following personal records virtually unbreakable).

The most world titles were 25 won by G. Victor Barna (1911–72) (Hungary and England), with 5 men's singles, 8 men's doubles, 2 mixed doubles, 3 Jubilee Cups and 7 men's team titles.

The women's records are 18 titles won by Maria Mednyanszky (1901–79) (Hungary) with 5 women's singles, 7 women's doubles and 6 mixed doubles; but Angelica Rozeanu (b Oct 15, 1921) (Romania) has more titles in women's singles (6) but fewer in total (17).

The most victories in the men's team championships (Swaythling Cup) is 12 by Hungary from 1927 through 1979. The women's team title (Marcel Corbillon Cup, instituted in 1934) has been won most often by Japan, with 8 victories from 1952–1971.

Over the years, Hungary has won 10 men's singles, 10 women's singles, 12 men's doubles, 7 women's doubles (plus 5 halves), 13 mixed doubles (plus 4 halves) and 6 men's consolations. Czechoslovakia won 4 women's consolations and Eng won 4 Jubilee Cups.

In 1937, the US was the first nation to win both Cups, a record that was not broken until 17 years later by Japan.

US National Titles

Three contestants have won 31 titles. In the women's division, Leah Thall (Ping) Neuberger (Columbus, O, and NYC) won a record 9 women's singles plus 12 women's doubles, 8 mixed doubles, one senior women's (for a total of 30 US Opens) and one US Closed. In the men's division, Sol Schiff (Bronx,

"PING" MEETS CHOU: The leading US women's table tennis player of her era, Leah "Ping" Neuberger was the first American to visit China (Apr 14, 1971).

NYC) has won 28 US Opens and 3 US Closed, while Eric Boggan (Merrick, NY) has won 15 US Opens and 16 US Closed. Richard Miles has 10 men's singles victories for a record.

Canadian International Open

Leah Thall (Ping) Neuberger won 48 titles, of which 11 were women's singles, 19 women's doubles, 11 mixed doubles and 7 on the women's team.

Longest Match

In the Swaythling Cup final match between Austria and Romania in Prague, Czechoslovakia, in 1936, the play lasted for 11 hours.

Longest Rally

In a Swaythling Cup match in Prague on March 14, 1936, between Alex Ehrlich (Poland) and Farcas Paneth (Romania), the first point was not scored until 2 hours 5 min after play began.

170 HITS IN ONE MINUTE is the record these table tennis internationals from Britain, Desmond Douglas (left) and Alan Cooke, set in Eng Feb 28, 1986.

Rick Bowling and Richard De Witt staged a rally lasting 10 hours 9 min at the YWCA in New Haven, Conn, on July 26, 1983.

Youngest International Contestant

The youngest international (in any sport) was Joy Foster, aged 8, when she represented Jamaica in the West Indies Championships at Port of Spain, Trinidad, in Aug 1958.

Fastest Rallying

The record number of hits in 60 sec is an unofficial 170 by Desmond Douglas (GB) and Alan Cooke (GB) (b Mar 23, 1966) at Scotswood Sports Centre, Newcastle-upon-Tyne, Eng, on Feb 28, 1986. The women's record is 163 by sisters Lisa and Jackie Bellinger at Luton, Eng on June 23, 1985.

With a paddle in each hand, Gary D. Fisher of Olympia, Wash, completed 5,000 consecutive volleys over the net in 44 min 28 sec on June 25, 1979.

Highest Speed

No conclusive measurements have been published, but in a lecture M. Sklorz (W Germany) stated that a smashed ball had been measured at speeds up to 105.6 mph.

Marathon

The longest recorded time for a marathon singles match by two players is 147 hours 47 min by S. Unterslak and J. Boccia at Dewaal Hotel, Cape Town, S Africa, Nov 12–18, 1983.

The longest doubles marathon by 4 players is 101 hours 1 min 11 sec by Lance, Phil and Mark Warren and Bill Weir at Sacramento, Calif, Apr 9–13, 1979.

TENNIS

Origins

The modern game of lawn tennis is generally agreed to have evolved as an outdoor form of the French Royal Tennis or *Jeu de Paume* from the 11th century. "Field Tennis" was mentioned in an English magazine (*Sporting Magazine*) on Sept 29, 1793. In 1858 Major Harry Gem laid out a "court" on the lawn of a friend in Birmingham, Eng, and in 1872 he founded the Leamington Club. In Feb 1874, Major Walter Clopton Wingfield of England (1833–1912) patented a form called "sphairistike," which was nicknamed "sticky," but the game soon became known as lawn tennis. The US Lawn Tennis Association (USLTA) was founded in 1881.

Amateurs were permitted to play with and against professionals in Open tournaments starting in 1968.

"Grand Slams"

The "grand slam" is to hold at the same time all four of the world's major championship titles: Wimbledon, the US Open, Australian and French championships. The first time this occurred was in 1935 when Frederick John Perry (GB) (b 1909) won the French title, having won Wimbledon (1934), the US title (1933–34) and the Australian title (1934).

The first player to hold all four titles simultaneously was J. Donald Budge (US) (b June 13, 1915), who won the championships of Wimbledon (1937), the US (1937), Australia (1938), and France (1938). He subsequently retained Wimbledon (1938) and the US (1938). Rodney George Laver (Australia) (b Aug 9, 1938) achieved this grand slam in 1962 as an ama-

PAST PERFORMERS: (Below, left) Charlotte "Lottie" Dod (GB) won the first of 5 Wimbledon titles in the late 1800's before she was 16, and also excelled at golf, archery, field hockey, skating and tobogganing. (Right) SUPERSTAR Suzanne Lenglen (France) was unbeaten in US singles 1916–26.

TENNIS IN ITS INFANCY: Leslie's magazine pictured women's entry into the sport in the late 19th century.

FIRST "GRAND SLAMMERS": (Left) Fred Perry (GB) won all major titles in 1934–35. Don Budge (US) (right) in 1937–38 held all 4 simultaneously. (Perry photos, AP)

teur and repeated as a professional in 1969 to become the first two-time grand slammer.

Three women players also have won all these four titles in the same tennis year. The first was Maureen Catherine Connolly (US). She won the US title in 1951, Wimbledon in 1952, retained the US title in 1952, won the Australian in 1953, the French in 1953, and Wimbledon again in 1953. She won her third US title in 1953, her second French title in 1954, and her third Wimbledon title in 1954. Miss Connolly (later Mrs Norman Brinker) was seriously injured in a riding accident shortly before the 1954 US championships; she died in June 1969, aged only 34.

The second woman to win the "grand slam" was Margaret Smith Court (Australia) (b July 16, 1942) in 1970. Martina Navratilova (US) (b Prague, Oct 18,

DOUBLES VISION: "Bunny" Ryan (US) is the all-time Wimbledon doubles champion with 19 titles (12 women's and 7 mixed). Her 19 victories were the overall record until Billie Jean King won the 1979 doubles title. Ryan, who had said she didn't want to live to see her record broken, died the night before Billie Jean's 20th victory.

1956) became the most recent "grand slam" winner on June 9, 1984 when she won the French title, beating Christine Evert Lloyd (US), after winning the other three titles in 1983. She won 6 successive "grand slam" singles titles 1983-Sept 1984, and with her partner Pamela Howard Shriver (US) (b July 4,

MOST "GRAND SLAMMERS": In 1962 as an amateur, Rod Laver (Aust) (left) won the Big 4 tournaments and again as a pro in 1969. Martina Navratilova (US) won all the "grand slam" events in 1983-84, and became the woman athlete with the highest earnings—more than $11 million by 1986. (USTA)

STILL MORE "GRAND SLAMMERS": The only women before Martina Navratilova to win the "grand slam" were Maureen Connolly (left) and Margaret Smith Court (right). Connolly (US) performed the feat in 1953; she might well have repeated had she not suffered a serious, career-ending injury in 1954. Court (Australia), who won the "grand slam" in 1970, is the all-time leading title winner. She won 22 titles in the Australian Open (including a record 10 in singles), 18 titles in the US Championships, and 13 titles in the French tournament (including 5 in singles)

1962) won 8 successive "grand slam" tournament women's doubles titles, and 109 successive doubles matches from Apr 24, 1983 through July 6, 1985.

The most singles championships in "grand slam" tournaments is 24 by Margaret Court (11 Australian, 5 French, 5 US, 3 Wimbledon), 1960–73. The men's record is 12 by Roy Emerson (Australia) (b Nov 3, 1936) (6 Australian, 2 each French, US, Wimbledon), 1961–67.

In doubles, the only men to win a "grand slam" are Frank Sedgman (Aust) and Ken McGregor (Aust) in 1951. Margaret Smith Court (Aust) and Ken Fletcher (Aust) won it in mixed doubles in 1961. Martina Navratilova (US) and Pam Shriver (US) managed a "grand slam" in doubles in 1983–84, the same year Martina got her "grand slam" in singles.

WIMBLEDON RECORDS

The first Championship was in 1877. Professionals first played in 1968. From 1971 the tie-break system

YOUNGEST WIMBLEDON WINNER: Boris Becker (W Ger) was not yet 18 when he beat the favorites and was victorious in 1985. A year later he won again. (Photo by David L. Boehm/Tamron)

was introduced, which effactually prevents sets proceeding beyond a 17th game, i.e., 9–8.

Most Wins

Six-time singles champion Billie Jean King (*née* Moffitt) has also won 10 women's doubles and 4 mixed doubles during the period 1961 to 1979, to total a record 20 titles.

The greatest number of singles wins was 8 by Helen N. Moody (*née* Wills) (b Oct 6, 1905) (US), who won in 1927–30, 32–33, 35 and 38.

The greatest number of singles wins by a man since the Challenge Round (wherein the defending champion was given a bye until the final round) was abolished in 1922 is 5 consecutively by Bjorn Borg (Sweden) in 1976–80. The all-time men's record was seven by William C. Renshaw, 1881–86 and 1889.

The greatest number of doubles wins by men was 8 by the brothers Doherty (GB)—Reginald Frank

BIGGEST WINNER in the 1920's: Bill Tilden (US) won only 4 times at Wimbledon (3 singles and one doubles) but 16 times in the US Open (including 7 singles) between 1920 and 1929.

Wimbledon Tournament Winners

Men's Singles

1919 Gerald Patterson (Aus)
1920 Bill Tilden (US)
1921 Bill Tilden (US)
1922 Gerald Patterson (Aus)
1923 William Johnston (US)
1924 Jean Borotra (Fra)
1925 René Lacoste (Fra)
1926 Jean Borotra (Fra)
1927 Henri Cochet (Fra)
1928 René Lacoste (Fra)
1929 Henri Cochet (Fra)
1930 Bill Tilden (US)
1931 Sidney Wood (US)
1932 Ellsworth Vines (US)
1933 Jack Crawford (Aus)
1934 Fred Perry (GB)
1935 Fred Perry (GB)
1936 Fred Perry (GB)
1937 Donald Budge (US)
1938 Donald Budge (US)
1939 Bobby Riggs (US)
1940–45 not held
1946 Yvon Petra (Fra)
1947 Jack Kramer (US)
1948 Bob Falkenburg (US)
1949 Ted Schroeder (US)
1950 Budge Patty (US)
1951 Dick Savitt (US)
1952 Frank Sedgman (Aus)
1953 Vic Seixas (US)
1954 Jaroslav Drobny (Cze)
1955 Tony Trabert (US)
1956 Lew Hoad (Aus)
1957 Lew Hoad (Aus)
1958 Ashley Cooper (Aus)
1959 Alex Olmedo (US)
1960 Neale Fraser (Aus)
1961 Rod Laver (Aus)
1962 Rod Laver (Aus)
1963 Chuck McKinley (US)
1964 Roy Emerson (Aus)
1965 Roy Emerson (Aus)
1966 Manuel Santana (Spa)
1967 John Newcombe (Aus)
1968 Rod Laver (Aus)
1969 Rod Laver (Aus)
1970 John Newcombe (Aus)
1971 John Newcombe (Aus)
1972 Stan Smith (US)
1973 Jan Kodes (Cze)
1974 Jimmy Connors (US)
1975 Arthur Ashe (US)
1976 Bjorn Borg (Swe)
1977 Bjorn Borg (Swe)
1978 Bjorn Borg (Swe)
1979 Bjorn Borg (Swe)
1980 Bjorn Borg (Swe)
1981 John McEnroe (US)
1982 Jimmy Connors (US)
1983 John McEnroe (US)
1984 John McEnroe (US)
1985 Boris Becker (W Ger)
1986 Boris Becker (W Ger)

Women's Singles

1919 Suzanne Lenglen (Fra)
1920 Suzanne Lenglen (Fra)
1921 Suzanne Lenglen (Fra)
1922 Suzanne Lenglen (Fra)
1923 Suzanne Lenglen (Fra)
1924 Kathleen McKane (GB)
1925 Suzanne Lenglen (Fra)
1926 Kathleen Godfree (GB)
1927 Helen Wills (US)
1928 Helen Wills (US)
1929 Helen Wills (US)
1930 Helen Wills Moody (US)
1931 Cilly Aussem (Ger)
1932 Helen Wills Moody (US)
1933 Helen Wills Moody (US)
1934 Dorothy Round (GB)
1935 Helen Wills Moody (US)
1936 Helen Jacobs (US)
1937 Dorothy Round (GB)
1938 Helen Wills Moody (US)
1939 Alice Marble (US)
1940–45 not held
1946 Pauline Betz (US)
1947 Margaret Osborne (US)
1948 Louise Brough (US)
1949 Louise Brough (US)
1950 Louise Brough (US)
1951 Doris Hart (US)
1952 Maureen Connolly (US)
1953 Maureen Connolly (US)
1954 Maureen Connolly (US)
1955 Louise Brough (US)
1956 Shirley Fry (US)
1957 Althea Gibson (US)
1958 Althea Gibson (US)
1959 Maria Bueno (Bra)
1960 Maria Bueno (Bra)
1961 Angela Mortimer (GB)
1962 Karen Susman (US)
1963 Margaret Smith (Aus)
1964 Maria Bueno (Bra)
1965 Margaret Smith (Aus)
1966 Billie Jean King (US)
1967 Billie Jean King (US)
1968 Billie Jean King (US)
1969 Ann Jones (GB)
1970 Margaret Smith Court (Aus)
1971 Evonne Goolagong (Aus)
1972 Billie Jean King (US)
1973 Billie Jean King (US)
1974 Christine Evert (US)
1975 Billie Jean King (US)
1976 Christine Evert (US)
1977 Virginia Wade (GB)
1978 Martina Navratilova (Cze)
1979 Martina Navratilova (Cze)
1980 Evonne Goolagong Cawley (Aus)
1981 Christine Evert Lloyd (US)
1982 Martina Navratilova (US)
1983 Martina Navratilova (US)
1984 Martina Navratilova (US)
1985 Martina Navratilova (US)
1986 Martina Navratilova (US)

Men's Doubles
First held 1884.

Most wins: 8 Laurence Doherty and Reginald Doherty (GB): 1897–1901, 1903–05

Winners since 1965:
1965 John Newcombe, Tony Roche (Aus)
1966 Ken Fletcher, John Newcombe (Aus)
1967 Bob Hewitt, Frew McMillan (S Af)
1968 John Newcombe, Tony Roche (Aus)
1969 John Newcombe, Tony Roche (Aus)
1970 John Newcombe, Tony Roche (Aus)
1971 Roy Emerson, Rod Laver (Aus)
1972 Bob Hewitt, Frew McMillan (S Af)
1973 Jimmy Connors (US), Ilie Nastase (Rom)
1974 John Newcombe, Tony Roche (Aus)
1975 Vitas Gerulaitis, Sandy Mayer (US)
1976 Brian Gottfried (US), Raul Ramirez (Mex)
1977 Ross Case, Geoff Masters (Aus)
1978 Bob Hewitt, Frew McMillan (S Af)
1979 Peter Fleming, John McEnroe (US)
1980 Peter McNamara, Paul McNamee (Aus)
1981 Peter Fleming, John McEnroe (US)
1982 Peter McNamara, Paul McNamee (Aus)
1983 Peter Fleming, John McEnroe (US)
1984 Peter Fleming, John McEnroe (US)
1985 Heinz Gunthardt (Switz) Bela Taroczi (Hungary)
1986 Mats Wilander (Swe) and Joakim Nystram (Swe)

Women's Doubles
First held 1899, but not a championship event until 1913.

Most wins: 12 Elizabeth (Bunny) Ryan (US): 1 with Agatha Morton 1914; 6 with Suzanne Lenglen 1919–23, 1925; 1 with Mary Browne 1926; 2 with Helen Wills Moody 1927, 1930; 2 with Simone Mathieu 1933–34

Winners since 1965:
1965 Maria Bueno (Bra), Billie Jean Moffitt (US)
1966 Maria Bueno (Bra), Nancy Richey (US)
1967 Rosemary Casals, Billie Jean King (*née* Moffitt) (US)
1968 Rosemary Casals, Billie Jean King (US)
1969 Margaret Court, Judy Tegart (Aus)
1970 Rosemary Casals, Billie Jean King (US)
1971 Rosemary Casals, Billie Jean King (US)
1972 Billie Jean King (US), Betty Stove (Hol)
1973 Rosemary Casals, Billie Jean King (US)
1974 Evonne Goolagong (Aus), Peggy Michel (US)
1975 Ann Kiyomura (US), Kazuko Sawamatsu (Japan)
1976 Christine Evert (US), Martina Navratilova (Cze)
1977 Helen Cawley (Aus), Joanne Russell (US)
1978 Kerr Reid, Wendy Turnbull (Aus)
1979 Billie Jean King (US), Martina Navratilova (Cze)
1980 Kathy Jordan, Anne Smith (US)
1981 Martina Navratilova (Cze), Pam Shriver (US)
1982 Martina Navratilova (US), Pam Shriver (US)
1983 Martina Navratilova (US), Pam Shriver (US)
1984 Martina Navratilova (US), Pam Shriver (US)
1985 Kathy Jordan (US), Liz Smylie (Aus)
1986 Martina Navratilova (US), Pam Shriver (US)

(1872–1910) and Hugh Lawrence (1875–1919). They won each year from 1897 to 1905 except for 1902. Hugh Doherty also won 5 singles titles (1902–06) and holds the record for most men's titles with 13.

The most wins in women's doubles was 12 by Elizabeth "Bunny" Ryan (US) (1894–1979). The greatest number of mixed doubles wins was 7 by Elizabeth Ryan, giving her a record total of 19 doubles wins 1914–34.

The men's mixed doubles record is 4 wins: by Elias Victor Seixas (b Aug 30, 1923) (US) in 1953–56; by Kenneth N. Fletcher (b June 15, 1940) (Australia) in 1963, 65–66 and 68; and by Owen Keir Davidson (Australia) (b Oct 4, 1943) in 1967, 71 and 73–74.

Youngest Champions

The youngest champion ever at Wimbledon was Charlotte (Lottie) Dod (1871–1960), who was 15 years 285 days old when she won in 1887.

The youngest male champion was Boris Becker (W Ger) (b Nov 22, 1967) who won the men's singles title in 1985 at 17 years 227 days.

The youngest-ever player at Wimbledon is reputedly Miss Mita Klima (Austria), who was 13 years old in the 1907 singles competition. The youngest player to win a match at Wimbledon is Kathy Rinaldi (b March 24, 1967) (US), who was 14 years 91 days old on June 23, 1981.

Oldest Champions

The oldest champion was Margaret Evelyn du Pont (*née* Osborne) (b Mar 4, 1918) (US) who was 44 years 125 days old when she won the mixed doubles in 1962 with Neale Fraser (Aust). The oldest singles champion was Arthur Gore (GB) at 41 years 182 days in 1909.

Greatest Attendance

The record crowd for one day at Wimbledon is 39,813 on June 26, 1986. The total attendance record was set at the 1986 Championships with 400,032.

Tennis Olympics

Tennis was part of the Olympic program up until 1924 and it was also a demonstration sport at Mexico City in 1968 and LA in 1984. It is likely to be reinstated to the Games proper in 1988.

The most gold and total medals won was by 1911 Wimbledon doubles champion Max Decugis (Fra)

with 4 gold, one silver and one bronze in 1900, 1906 and 1920. Kitty McKane Godfree (GB) set a women's record with one gold, 2 silver and 2 bronze in 1920 and 1924. In the latter year she won the first of her two Wimbledon singles championships. The 1908 Olympic tennis was played at the All-England Club, Wimbledon.

Most Appearances

Arthur W. Gore (1868–1928) (GB) made 36 appearances between 1888 and 1927.

In 1964 Jean Borotra (b Aug 13, 1898) of France made his 35th appearance since 1922. In 1977 he appeared in the Veterans' Doubles, aged 78. In Nov 1985, at the age of 87, Borotra played for the 100th time in the match between the International Clubs of France and GB at Wimbledon. Twice yearly he participated in every match since it was first staged in 1929.

U S CHAMPIONSHIPS

The USTA Championships were first held in 1881 and continued until 1969. The Tournament was superseded in 1970 by the US Open Championships which had first been held in 1968, and is now held at Flushing Meadow, New York.

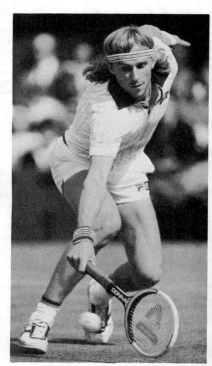

NEVER A WINNER IN US OPEN: Bjorn Borg (Sweden) won 5 Wimbledon titles and many others though.

THE WINNING MOMENT: Billie Jean King (US) jubilantly tosses her racket through the air because she knows, even if the scoreboard is a little slow, that she just won the championship point from Chris Evert (US) in the 1975 women's singles finals at Wimbledon. The victory was her 19th at Wimbledon (6th in singles), tying her with "Bunny" Ryan for the most wins in that tournament. King then won the 1979 doubles title, for her 20th victory, and became the winningest player in Wimbledon's history.

Most Wins

Margaret Evelyn du Pont (*née* Osborne) won a record 25 titles between 1936 and 1962. She won a record 13 women's doubles (12 with Althea Louise Brough), 8 mixed doubles and 3 singles. The men's record is 16 by William Tatem Tilden, including 7 men's singles, 1920–25, 1929—a record for singles shared with Richard Dudley Sears (1861–1943), 1881–87; William A Larned (1872–1926), 1901–02, 1907–11; and at women's singles by Molla Mallory (*née* Bjurstedt) (1892–1959), 1915–16, 1918, 1920–22, 1926 and Helen Moody (*née* Wills), 1923–25, 1927–29, 1931.

Youngest and Oldest

The youngest champion was Vincent Richards (1903–59) who was 15 years 139 days when he won the doubles with Bill Tilden in 1918. The youngest singles champion was Tracy Ann Austin (b Dec 12, 1962) who was 16 years 271 days when she won the women's singles in 1979.

The oldest champion was Margaret du Pont who won the mixed doubles at 42 years 166 days in 1960. The oldest singles champion was William Larned at 38 years 242 days in 1911.

U S Open Tournament Winners

Most wins:

Men's Singles: 7 Richard D. Sears 1881–87; 7 William A. Larned 1901–02, 1907–11; 7 William T. Tilden 1920–25, 1929

Women's Singles: 7 Helen Wills Moody 1923–25, 1927–29, 1931

Men's Singles	
1920 Bill Tilden	1923 Bill Tilden
1921 Bill Tilden	1924 Bill Tilden
1922 Bill Tilden	1925 Bill Tilden
	1926 René Lacoste

U S Open Winners (continued)

Men's Singles

1927 René Lacoste	1957 Malcolm Anderson
1928 Henri Cochet	1958 Ashley Cooper
1929 Bill Tilden	1959 Neale A. Fraser
1930 John Doeg	1960 Neale A. Fraser
1931 H. Ellsworth Vines	1961 Roy Emerson
1932 H. Ellsworth Vines	1962 Rod Laver
1933 Fred Perry	1963 Rafael Osuna
1934 Fred Perry	1964 Roy Emerson
1935 Wilmer Allison	1965 Manuel Santana
1936 Fred Perry	1966 Fred Stolle
1937 Don Budge	1967 John Newcombe
1938 Don Budge	1968 Arthur Ashe
1939 Robert Riggs	1969 Rod Laver
1940 Don McNeil	1970 Ken Rosewall
1941 Robert Riggs	1971 Stan Smith
1942 F. R. Schroeder Jr.	1972 Ilie Nastase
1943 Joseph Hunt	1973 John Newcombe
1944 Frank Parker	1974 Jimmy Connors
1945 Frank Parker	1975 Manuel Orantes
1946 Jack Kramer	1976 Jimmy Connors
1947 Jack Kramer	1977 Guillermo Vilas
1948 Pancho Gonzales	1978 Jimmy Connors
1949 Pancho Gonzales	1979 John McEnroe
1950 Arthur Larsen	1980 John McEnroe
1951 Frank Sedgman	1981 John McEnroe
1952 Frank Sedgman	1982 Jimmy Connors
1953 Tony Trabert	1983 Jimmy Connors
1954 E. Victor Seixas Jr	1984 John McEnroe
1955 Tony Trabert	1985 Ivan Lendl
1956 Ken Rosewall	1986 Ivan Lendl

U S OPEN CHAMPION and No. 1 in the world 1985–87: Ivan Lendl, the Czech who now lives in the US, has been winning almost all the major tournaments. (David L. Boehm/Tamron)

Women's Singles

1935 Helen Jacobs	1961 Darlene Hard
1936 Alice Marble	1962 Margaret Smith
1937 Anita Lizana	1963 Maria Bueno
1938 Alice Marble	1964 Maria Bueno
1939 Alice Marble	1965 Margaret Smith
1940 Alice Marble	1966 Maria Bueno
1941 Mrs. Sarah P. Cooke	1967 Billie Jean King
1942 Pauline Betz	1968 Virginia Wade
1943 Pauline Betz	1969 Margaret Smith Court
1944 Pauline Betz	1970 Margaret Smith Court
1945 Sarah P. Cooke	1971 Billie Jean King
1946 Pauline Betz	1972 Billie Jean King
1947 A. Louise Brough	1973 Margaret Smith Court
1948 Mrs. Margaret O. duPont	1974 Billie Jean King
1949 Mrs. Margaret O. duPont	1975 Chris Evert
1950 Mrs. Margaret O. duPont	1976 Chris Evert
1951 Maureen Connolly	1977 Chris Evert
1952 Maureen Connolly	1978 Chris Evert
1953 Maureen Connolly	1979 Tracy Austin
1954 Doris Hart	1980 Chris Evert Lloyd
1955 Doris Hart	1981 Tracy Austin
1956 Shirley J. Fry	1982 Chris Evert Lloyd
1957 Althea Gibson	1983 Martina Navratilova
1958 Althea Gibson	1984 Martina Navratilova
1959 Maria Bueno	1985 Hana Mandlikova
1960 Darlene Hard	1986 Martina Navratilova

RISING TENNIS STAR: (Right) Hana Mandlikova (Czech) won the US Open in 1985 and the Australian Open in 1987, beating her fellow countrywoman, Martina Navratilova, and is now seeded No. 2 woman player in the world.

U S Open Winners (continued)

Men's Doubles
1922 Bill Tilden—Vincent Richards
1923 Bill Tilden—Brian Norton
1924 Howard Kinsey—Robert Kinsey
1925 R. Norris Williams—Vincent Richards
1926 R. Norris Williams—Vincent Richards
1927 Bill Tilden—Francis Hunter
1928 George Lott—John Hennessey
1929 George Lott—John Doeg
1930 George Lott—John Doeg
1931 Wilmer Allison—John Van Ryn
1932 H. Ellsworth Vines—Keith Gledhill
1933 George Lott—Lester Stoefen
1934 George Lott—Lester Stoefen
1935 Wilmer Allison—John Van Ryn
1936 Don Budge—C. Gene Mako
1937 Baron G. von Cramm—Henner Henkel
1938 Don Budge—C. Gene Mako
1939 Adrian Quist—John Bromwich
1940 Jack Kramer—Frederick Schroeder Jr.
1941 Jack Kramer—Frederick Schroeder Jr.
1942 Gardner Mulloy—William Talbert
1943 Jack Kramer—Frank Parker
1944 Don McNeill—Robert Falkenburg
1945 Gardner Mulloy—William Talbert
1946 Gardner Mulloy—William Talbert
1947 Jack Kramer—Frederick Schroeder Jr.
1948 Gardner Mulloy—William Talbert
1949 John Bromwich—William Sidwell
1950 John Bromwich—Frank Sedgman
1951 Frank Sedgman—Kenneth McGregor
1952 Mervyn Rose—E. Victor Seixas Jr.
1953 Rex Hartwig—Mervyn Rose
1954 E. Victor Seixas Jr.—Tony Trabert
1955 Kosel Kamo—Atsushi Miyagi
1956 Lewis Hoad—Ken Rosewall
1957 Ashley Cooper—Neale Fraser
1958 Hamilton Richardson—Alejandro Olmedo
1959 Neale A. Fraser—Roy Emerson
1960 Neale A. Fraser—Roy Emerson
1961 Dennis Ralston—Chuck McKinley

COURT ARGUMENT: A young John McEnroe engages in a typical verbal battle with the umpire over a line call in an indoor finals match in 1981 against Jimmy Connors (below) at Wembley, England. (Connors photo by David L Boehm)

Men's Doubles
1962 Rafael Osuna—Antonio Palafox
1963 Dennis Ralston—Chuck McKinley
1964 Dennis Ralston—Chuck McKinley
1965 Roy Emerson—Fred Stolle
1966 Roy Emerson—Fred Stolle
1967 John Newcombe—Tony Roche
1968 Robert Lutz—Stan Smith
1969 Fred Stolle—Ken Rosewall
1970 Pierre Barthes—Nicki Pilic
1971 John Newcombe—Roger Taylor
1972 Cliff Drysdale—Roger Taylor
1973 John Newcombe—Owen Davidson
1974 Bob Lutz—Stan Smith
1975 Jimmy Connors—Ilie Nastase
1976 Marty Riessen—Tom Okker
1977 Bob Hewitt—Frew McMillan
1978 Stan Smith—Bob Lutz
1979 John McEnroe—Peter Fleming
1980 Stan Smith—Bob Lutz
1981 John McEnroe—Peter Fleming
1982 Kevin Curren—Steve Denton
1983 John McEnroe—Peter Fleming
1984 John Fitzgerald—Tomas Smid
1985 Ken Flach—Robert Seguso
1986 Andres Gomez-Slobodan Zivolinovic

Women's Doubles
1936 Mrs. M. G. Van Ryn—Carolin Babcock
1937 Mrs. Sarah P. Fabyan—Alice Marble
1938 Alice Marble—Mrs. Sarah P. Fabyan
1939 Alice Marble—Mrs. Sarah P. Fabyan
1940 Alice Marble—Mrs. Sarah P. Fabyan
1941 Mrs. S. P. Cooke—Margaret Osborne
1942 A. Louise Brough—Margaret Osborne
1943 A. Louise Brough—Margaret Osborne
1944 A. Louise Brough—Margaret Osborne
1945 A. Louise Brough—Margaret Osborne
1946 A. Louise Brough—Margaret Osborne
1947 A. Louise Brough—Margaret Osborne
1948 A. Louise Brough—Mrs. M. O. duPont
1949 A. Louise Brough—Mrs. M. O. duPont
1950 A. Louise Brough—Mrs. M. O. duPont
1951 Doris Hart—Shirley Fry
1952 Doris Hart—Shirley Fry
1953 Doris Hart—Shirley Fry
1954 Doris Hart—Shirley Fry
1955 A. Louise Brough—Mrs. M. O. duPont
1956 A. Louise Brough—Mrs. M. O. duPont
1957 A. Louise Brough—Mrs. M. O. duPont
1958 Darlene Hard—Jeanne Arth
1959 Darlene Hard—Jeanne Arth
1960 Darlene Hard—Maria Bueno
1961 Darlene Hard—Lesley Turner
1962 Maria Bueno—Darlene Hard
1963 Margaret Smith—Robyn Ebbern
1964 Billie Jean Moffitt—Karen Susman
1965 Carole C. Graebner—Nancy Richey
1966 Maria Bueno—Nancy Richey
1967 Rosemary Casals—Billie Jean King
1968 Maria Bueno—Margaret S. Court
1969 Françoise Durr—Darlene Hard
1970 M. S. Court—Judy Tegart Dalton
1971 Rosemary Casals—Judy Tegart Dalton
1972 Françoise Durr—Betty Stove
1973 Margaret S. Court—Virginia Wade
1974 Billie Jean King—Rosemary Casals
1975 Margaret Court—Virginia Wade
1976 Linky Boshoff—Ilana Kloss
1977 Betty Stove—Martina Navratilova
1978 Martina Navratilova—Billie Jean King
1979 Betty Stove—Wendy Turnbull
1980 Martina Navratilova—Billie Jean King
1981 Kathy Jordan—Anne Smith
1982 Rosemary Casals—Wendy Turnbull
1983 Martina Navratilova—Pam Shriver
1984 Martina Navratilova—Pam Shriver
1985 Claudia Kohde-Kilsch—Helena Sukova
1986 Martina Navratilova—Pam Shriver

Mixed Doubles
1946 Margaret Osborne—William Talbert
1947 A. Louise Brough—John Bromwich
1948 A. Louise Brough—Thomas Brown Jr.
1949 A. Louise Brough—Eric Sturgess
1950 Mrs. M. O. duPont—Kenneth MacGregor
1951 Doris Hart—Frank Sedgman
1952 Doris Hart—Frank Sedgman
1953 Doris Hart—E. Victor Seixas Jr.
1954 Doris Hart—E. Victor Seixas Jr.
1955 Doris Hart—E. Victor Seixas Jr.
1956 Mrs. M. O. duPont—Ken Rosewall
1957 Althea Gibson—Kurt Nielsen
1958 Mrs. M. O. duPont—Neale Fraser
1959 Mrs. M. O. duPont—Neale Fraser
1960 Mrs. M. O. duPont—Neale Fraser
1961 Margaret Smith—Robert Mark
1962 Margaret Smith—Fred Stolle
1963 Margaret Smith—Kenneth Fletcher
1964 Margaret Smith—John Newcombe
1965 Margaret Smith—Fred Stolle
1966 Donna Floyd Fales—Owen Davidson
1967 Billie Jean King—Owen Davidson
1968 Mary Ann Eisel—Peter Curtis
1969 Margaret S. Court—Marty Riessen
1970 Margaret S. Court—Marty Riessen
1971 Billie Jean King—Owen Davidson
1972 Margaret S. Court—Marty Riessen
1973 Billie Jean King—Owen Davidson
1974 Pam Teeguarden—Geoff Masters
1975 Rosemary Casals—Dick Stockton
1976 Billie Jean King—Phil Dent
1977 Betty Stove—Frew McMillan
1978 Betty Stove—Frew McMillan
1979 Greer Stevens—Bob Hewitt
1980 Wendy Turnbull—Marty Riessen
1981 Anne Smith—Kevin Curren
1982 Anne Smith—Kevin Curren
1983 Elizabeth Sayers—John Fitzgerald
1984 Manuela Maleeva—Tom Gullikson
1985 Martina Navratilova—Heinz Gunthardt
1986 Ken Flach—Kathy Jordan

Highest Earnings

(*Earnings from special restricted events and team tennis are not included.*)

The greatest reward for playing a single match is the $500,000 won by James Scott (Jimmy) Connors (US) (b Sept 2, 1952) when he beat John Newcombe (Australia) (b May 23, 1944) in a challenge match at Caesars Palace Hotel, Las Vegas, Nev, Apr 26, 1975. The highest total prize money is $3,450,800 for the 1986 US Championships.

The record for career earnings is held by Martina Navratilova, who won $11,488,658 by the end of 1986, having won $1,905,841 in that year.

The single season record for men is $2,028,850 by Ivan Lendl (Czechoslovakia) in 1982 (and including

FIVE-TIME DOUBLES WINNERS at Wimbledon: Rosemary Casals (jumping) and Billie Jean King (US) won in 5 of the 7 years 1967–73. (Leon Serchuk)

the Volvo Masters tournament held in January 1983). The women's record is $2,173,556 in 1984 (including a $1 million "Grand Slam" bonus) by Martina Navratilova in 1984.

Most Wins in One Day

When rain delayed play in the Italian Open on May 27, 1984, Manuela Maleeva, a 17-year-old Bulgarian, had to finish the last set of her quarter-final match the next day against Romania's Virginia Ruzici (winning), then faced Canada's Carling Basset in a semifinal match (winning). In the final on the same day, after a half-hour nap, Manuela met the top-seeded Chris Evert Lloyd, and vanquished her in straight sets, 6–3, 6–3, to win the $150,000 tournament. It was the first time anyone had won 3 escalating singles matches in the same day.

Longest Career

The championship career of C. Alphonso Smith (b March 18, 1909) of Charlottesville, Va, extended from winning the US National Boy's title at Chicago on Aug 14, 1924, to winning the National 70-and-over title at Santa Barbara, Calif, in Aug 1979. Smith has won 31 US National titles in all.

Dorothy May Bundy-Cheney (US) (b Sept 2,

1916) won 141 US titles at various age groups from 1941 to 1984.

Fastest Service

The fastest service ever *measured* was one of 163.6 mph by William Tatem Tilden (1893–1953) (US) in 1931.

A serve by Steve Denton (US) (b Sept 5, 1956) was timed at 138 mph at Beaver Creek, Colo on July 29, 1984, and is the record for fastest service timed with modern equipment.

Longest Game

The longest known singles game was one of 37 deuces (80 points) between Anthony Fawcett (Rhodesia) and Keith Glass (GB) in the first round of the Surrey championships at Surbiton, Surrey, England, on May 26, 1975. It lasted 31 min.

A junior game lasted 52 min (9 deuces) between Noelle Van Lottum and Sandra Begijn in the semi-finals of the under-13 Dutch National Indoor Championships in Ede, Gelderland, Holland on Feb 12, 1984.

The longest rally in tournament play is one of 643 times over the net between Vicky Nelson and Jean Hepner at Richmond, Va in October 1984. The 6 hour 22 min match was won by Nelson 6–4, 7–6. It concluded with a 1 hour 47 min tiebreaker, 13–11, for which one point took 29 min.

The longest tiebreaker was the 26–24 for the fourth and decisive set of a first round men's doubles at the Wimbledon Championship on July 1, 1985. Jan Gunnarsson (Sweden) and Michael Morterven (Denmark) defeated John Frawley (Australia) and Victor Pecci (Paraguay) 6–3, 6–4, 3–6, 7–6.

Tennis Marathons

The longest recorded tennis singles match is one of 117 hours by Mark and Jim Pinchoff at the Fitness Resort, Lafayette, La, May 14–19, 1985.

The duration record for doubles is 96 hours 25 minutes by Ann Wilkinson, Peter Allsopp, John Thorpe, and David Dicks at Mansfield Lawn Tennis Club, Nottingham, Eng, August 17–21, 1983.

Grand Prix Masters

The first WCT Masters Championships were staged in Tokyo, Japan in 1971 and have been held annually in NYC since 1977. Qualification to this annual event is by relative success in the preceding year's Grand Prix tournaments. John Patrick McEnroe (US) (b Feb 16, 1959) has won a record five titles, 1979, 1981, 1983–5. James Scott Connors (US) (b Sept 7, 1952) uniquely qualified for 14 consecutive years, 1972–85. He chose not to play in 1975, 1976 and 1985 and won in 1977.

Greatest Crowd

The greatest crowd at a tennis match was the 30,472 who came to the Houston Astrodome in Houston, Tex, on Sept 20, 1973, to watch Billie Jean King (US, b Nov 22, 1943) beat Robert Larimore (Bobby) Riggs (US, b Feb 25, 1918), over 25 years her senior, in straight sets in the so-called "Tennis Match of the Century."

The record for an orthodox match is 25,578 at Sydney, Australia, on Dec 27, 1954, in the Davis Cup Challenge Round vs the US (1st day).

Davis Cup

The most wins in the Davis Cup (instituted 1900), the men's international team championship, have been (inclusive of 1982) by the US with 28.

Roy Emerson (b Nov 3, 1936) (Australia) played on 8 Cup-winning teams, 1959–62, 1964–67.

TENNIS ON UNICYCLE: Manuel Vargas is the only man to have played 5 consecutive sets of respectable tennis without falling off the 24-inch unicycle. (UNIBALL ®)

Nicola Pietrangeli (Italy) (b Sept 11, 1933) played a record 163 rubbers, 1954 to 1972, winning 120. He played 109 singles (winning 78) and 54 doubles (winning 42). He took part in 66 ties.

Wightman Cup

The most wins in the Wightman Cup, contested annually by women's teams from the US and GB (instituted 1923) have been 48 by the US through 1986. Virginia Wade (b July 10, 1945) (GB) played in a record 21 ties and 56 rubbers between 1965 and 1985. Christine Evert Lloyd (b Dec 21, 1954) (US) won all 26 of her singles matches, 1971–85. Mrs Lloyd was selected by the Women's Sports Foundation in 1985 as the "greatest American Woman Athlete of the last 25 years."

Federation Cup

The most wins in the Federation Cup (instituted 1963), the women's international team champion-

WIMBLEDON WINNERS: Both Chris Evert Lloyd (left) and Evonne Goolagong Cawley (right) came back with victories after interrupting their successful careers to better enjoy their marriages. Evonne beat Chris in the 1980 Wimbledon finals, but in the following 2 years Chris won at Wimbledon. (Both photos by Leon Serchuk)

ship, is 12 (to 1986) by the US. Virginia Wade (GB) played each year from 1967 to 1983, in a record 55 ties, playing 100 rubbers, including 56 singles (winning 36) and 44 doubles (winning 30). Christine Evert Lloyd won 14 of 15 doubles, 1977–82, but her unbroken sequence of success in singles ended in 1986 after 29 victories.

TRACK AND FIELD

Earliest References

There is evidence that running was involved in early Egyptian rituals at Memphis *c.* 3800 BC, but usually track and field athletics date from the ancient Olympic Games. The earliest accurately known Olympiad dates from July 776 BC, at which celebration Coroibos won the foot race of 164–169 yd. The oldest surviving measurements are a long jump of 23 ft 1½ in by Chionis of Sparta *c.* 656 BC, and a discus throw of 100 cubits (*c.* 152 ft) by Protesilaus.

MILESTONE IN TRACK HISTORY: Breaking the 4-min mile was the outstanding achievement of 1954, and Roger Bannister (GB) was the man who set the record on May 6 of that year at 3:59.4 at Oxford.

"CHARIOTS OF FIRE," the popular movie, was the story of this athlete, Harold Abrahams (GB), who won the 100 m sprint in record time at the 1924 Olympics. Before that, in 1923 at Wembley (Eng), he won the long jump (seen here) for the combined Oxford/Cambridge team against the combined Harvard/Yale team. (BBC Hulton)

on May 6, 1954. John Walker (NZ) became the first man to run the mile in less than 4 min 100 times by Feb 17, 1985, in Auckland, NZ. His best time was 3:54.57.

Earliest Landmarks

The first time 10 sec ("even time") was bettered for 100 yd under championship conditions was when John Owen, then 30 years old, recorded 9 4/5 sec in the AAU Championships at Wash, DC, on Oct 11, 1890. The first recorded instance of 6 ft being cleared in the high jump was when Marshall Jones Brooks (1855–1944) jumped 6 ft 0⅛ in at Marston, near Oxford, England, on March 17, 1876. (He is reputed to have done much of his jumping while wearing a high hat.) The first man over 7 ft was Charlie Dumas (US) who jumped 7 ft 0½ in in June 1956. The breaking of the "4-minute barrier" in the one mile was first achieved by Dr Roger Gilbert Bannister (b Harrow, England, March 23, 1929), when he recorded 3 min 59.4 sec on the Iffley Road track, Oxford, at 6:10 p.m.

Most Records

The greatest number of official world records (in events on the current schedule) broken by one athlete is 14, by Paavo Nurmi (Fin) at various events between 1921 and 1931, and by Iolanda Balas (Rom) in the high jump from 1956 to 1961. Nurmi also set eight marks in events no longer recognized, giving him a grand total of 22.

The only athlete to have his name entered in the record book 6 times in one day (in fact, within one hour) was J. C. "Jesse" Owens (US) (1913–80) who at Ann Arbor, Mich, on May 25, 1935, equaled the 100-yd running record with 9.4 sec at 3:15 p.m.; long-jumped 26 ft 8¼ in at 3:25 p.m.; ran 220 yd (straight away) in 20.3 sec at 3:45 p.m.; and 220 yd over low hurdles in 22.6 sec at 4 p.m. The two 220-yd runs were also ratified as 200-m world records.

THE "FLYING FINN," Paavo Nurmi dominated distance running 1921–31, breaking 14 world records. (Right) Nurmi wins a special 3-mi race at LA Coliseum in 1925. (Wide World) (Left, below) Statue of the hero adorns the entrance to the Helsinki Stadium. (Finnish Tourist Assoc.) (Below, center) Nurmi crosses the finish line in England in a 4-mi invitational race with no competitors in sight. (Below, right) Nurmi has the honor of carrying the flame into the Helsinki Olympics in 1952. (AP wirephoto)

World Championships

The first-ever track and field world championships were staged at Helsinki, Finland, Aug 7–14, 1983. The most gold medals won was 3 by Carl Lewis (US) in the 100 m dash, long jump, and 4 × 100 m relay; and by Marita Koch (E Ger) in the 200 m dash, 4 × 100 m relay, and 4 × 400 m relay. With a silver medal in the 100 m dash, Koch was the top medal winner with 4.

Standing High Jump

The best high jump from a standing (as opposed to a running) position is 6 ft 2¾ in by Rune Almen (b Oct 20, 1952) (Sweden) at Karlstad, Sweden, on May 30, 1980. The best jump by a woman is 4 ft 11 in by Grete Bjørdalsbakke (b June 23, 1960) (Norway) at Orsta, Norway on Dec 12, 1979.

Fastest Speed

The fastest speed recorded in an individual world record is 22.69 mph, but this does not allow for the effects of the delay in reaching peak speed from a standing start. Maximum speeds exceeding 25 mph for men and 22.5 mph for women have been measured; for instance, for Carl Lewis and Evelyn Ashford, respectively, for their final 100 meters in the 1984 Olympic sprint relays.

MOST RECORDS IN ONE DAY: Jesse Owens, rated by many as the greatest athlete of the 20th century, and top vote-getter in the inaugural election for the US Olympic Hall of Fame, not only won 4 Olympic golds in one Games (1936), but set 6 world records in one hour at Ann Arbor, Mich (3 to 4 PM, May 25, 1935). Here he shows his hurdling and long jump style (left) and his running start (right). (Photos courtesy Atlantic Richfield Co—ARCO Jesse Owens Games and Mary Evans)

Standing Long Jump

Joe Darby (1861–1937), the famous Victorian professional jumper from Dudley, Worcestershire, England, jumped a measured 12 ft 1½ in *without* weights at Dudley Castle, on May 28, 1890. Arne Tverrvaag (Norway) jumped 12 ft 2¼ in in 1968. The best long jump by a woman is 9 ft 7 in by Annelin Mannes (Norway) at Flisa, Norway on March 7, 1981.

Oldest and Youngest Record Breakers

The greatest age at which anyone has broken a world track and field record is 41 years 196 days in the case of John J. Flanagan (1868–1938), who set a world record in the hammer throw on July 24, 1909. The female record is 36 years 139 days for Marina Stepanova (USSR) (née Makeyeva, b May 1, 1950)

4 GOLD MEDALS is the record that Carl Lewis (US) set in the 1984 Olympics, emulating Jesse Owens. Lewis is seen jumping 28 ft 0¼ in. (UPI)

LONG WINNING STREAK: Edwin Moses (US) has not been beaten in the 400 m hurdles since 1977. He had won 119 consecutive times including 104 finals to the end of 1986.

when she ran 400 m hurdles in 52.94 sec in Tashkent, USSR, Sept 17, 1986.

The youngest individual record breaker is Wang Yang (b Apr 9, 1971) (China) who set a women's 3,000 m walk record in 21 min 33.8 sec at Jian, China on Mar 9, 1986, when aged 14 years 334 days. The male record is 17 years 198 days by Thomas Ray (1862–1904) when he pole-vaulted 11 ft 2¼ in on Sept 19, 1879.

HISTORIC JUMP: Bob Beamon (US) is in midflight of his 29-foot-2½-inch long jump at the 1968 Olympics in Mexico City. The high altitude and a tail wind possibly helped Beamon shatter the record by 1 ft 9 in. The next best jump has been 28 feet 10¼ in by Carl Lewis in 1983.

WORLD TRACK AND FIELD RECORDS (MEN)

World Records for the 32 men's events (excluding the walking records) scheduled by the International Amateur Athletic Federation. Note: On July 27, 1976, IAAF eliminated all records for races measured in yards, except for the mile (for sentimental reasons). All distances up to (and including) 400 m must be electrically timed to be records. When a time is given to one-hundredth of a second, it represents the official electrically timed record.

RUNNING

Event	min:sec	Name and Nationality	Place	Date
100 m	9.93A	Calvin Smith (US)	Colorado Springs	July 3, 1983
200 m	19.72A	Pietro Mennea (Italy)	Mexico City	Sept 12, 1979
400 m	43.86A	Lee Edward Evans (US)	Mexico City	Oct 18, 1968
800 m	1:41.73	Sebastian Coe (GB)	Florence, Italy	June 10, 1981
1,000 m	2:12.18	Sebastian Coe (GB)	Oslo	July 11, 1981
1,500 m	3:29.45	Said Aouita (Morocco)	W Berlin	Aug 23, 1985
1 mile	3:46.32	Steve Cram (GB)	Oslo	July 27, 1985
2,000 m	4:51.39	Steve Cram (GB)	Budapest, Hungary	Aug 4, 1985
3,000 m	7:32.1	Henry Rono (Kenya)	Oslo	June 27, 1978
5,000 m	13:00.40	Said Aouita (Morocco)	Oslo	July 27, 1985
10,000 m	27:13.81	Fernando Mamede (Portugal)	Stockholm	July 2, 1984
20,000 m	57:24.2	Jos Hermens (Neth)	Papendal, Neth	May 1, 1976
25,000 m	1 hr. 13:55.8	Toshihiko Seko (Japan)	Christchurch, NZ	Mar 22, 1981
30,000 m	1 hr. 29:18.8	Toshihiko Seko (Japan)	Christchurch, NZ	Mar 22, 1981
1 hour	13 miles 24 yd 2 ft	Jos Hermens (Neth)	Papendal, Neth	May 1, 1976

FIELD EVENTS

Event	ft	in	Name and Nationality	Place	Date
High Jump	7	10¾	Igor Paklin (USSR)	Kobe, Japan	Sept 4, 1985
Pole Vault	19	8¾	Sergei Bubka (USSR)	Moscow	July 8, 1986
Long Jump	29	2½A	Robert Beamon (US)	Mexico City	Oct 18, 1968
Triple Jump	58	11½	Willie Banks (US)	Indianapolis, Ind	June 16, 1985
Shot Put	74	3½	Udo Beyer (E Ger)	E Berlin	Aug 20, 1986
Discus Throw	243	0	Jurgen Schult (E Ger)	Neubrandenburg, E Ger	June 6, 1986
Hammer Throw	284	7	Yuri Sedykh (USSR)	Stuttgart, W Ger	Aug 30, 1986
Javelin Throw*	343	10	Uwe Hohn (E Ger)	East Berlin	July 20, 1984

Note: One professional performance which was equal or superior to the IAAF marks, but where the same highly rigorous rules as to timing, measuring and weighing were not necessarily applied, was the Shot Put of 75 ft by Brian Ray Oldfield (US), at El Paso, Tex, on May 10, 1975. * Old javelin—new standards set in 1986—record under new rules is 281 ft 3 in by Klaus Tafelmeier (W Ger) at Como, Italy, Sept 21, 1986.

HURDLING

Event	min:sec	Name and Nationality	Place	Date
110 m (3'6")	12.93	Renaldo Nehemiah (US)	Zurich	Aug 19, 1981
400 m (3'0")	47.02	Edwin Corley Moses (US)	Coblenz, W Ger	Aug 31, 1983
3,000 m Steeplechase	8:05.4	Henry Rono (Kenya)	Seattle, Wash	May 13, 1978

RELAYS

Event		Name and Nationality	Place	Date
4 × 100 m	37.83	US Team (Sam Graddy, Ron Brown, Calvin Smith, Carl Lewis)	Los Angeles	Aug 11, 1984
4 × 200 m	1:20.26†	University of Southern California (US) (Joel Andrews, James Sanford, William Mullins, Clancy Edwards)	Tempe, Ariz	May 27, 1978
4 × 400 m	2:56.16A	US Olympic Team (Vincent Matthews, Ronald Freeman, G. Lawrence James, Lee Edward Evans)	Mexico City	Oct 20, 1968
4 × 800 m	7:03.89	Great Britain Team (Peter Elliott, Garry Cook, Steve Cram, Sebastian Coe)	London	Aug 30, 1982
4 × 1,500 m	14:38.8	W German Team (Thomas Wessinghage, Harald Hudak, Michael Lederer, Karl Fleschen)	Cologne, W Ger	Aug 17, 1977

† The time of 1:20.2 achieved by the Tobias Striders at Tempe, Ariz on May 27, 1978 was not ratified as the team was composed of varied nationalities.

DECATHLON

8,847 points (1985 scoring)	Francis Morgan "Daley" Thompson (GB)	Los Angeles	Aug 8–9 1984

(See next page)

GOLD MEDAL WINNERS IN 1984 OLYMPICS

Men

			min sec	
100 m	Carl Lewis (US)		9.99	
200 m	Carl Lewis (US)		19.80	OR
400 m	Alonzo Babers (US)		44.27	
800 m	Joachim Cruz (Brazil)		1: 43.00	OR
1500 m	Sebastian Coe (GB)		3: 32.53	OR
5000 m	Said Aouita (Morocco)		13: 05.59	OR
10000 m	Alberto Cova (Ita)		27: 47.54	
Marathon	Carlos Lopes (Portugal)		2 hr 9.21	OR
110 m hurdles	Roger Kingdom (US)		13.20	OR
400 m hurdles	Edwin Moses (US)		47.75	
3000 m steeplechase	Julius Korir (Ken)		8: 11.80	
4 × 100 m relay	US		37.83	WR
4 × 400 m relay	US		2: 57.91	
20 km road walk	Ernesto Canto (Mex)		1 hr 23.13	OR
50 km road walk	Raul Gonzalez (Mex)		3 hr 47.26	OR

		meters	
High jump	Dietmar Mögenburg (W Ger)	2.35	
Pole Vault	Pierre Quinon (Fra)	5.75	
Long Jump	Carl Lewis (US)	8.54	
Triple Jump	Al Joyner (US)	17.26	
Shot Put	Alessandro Andrei (Ita)	21.26	
Discus	Rolf Danneberg (W Ger)	66.60	
Hammer	Juha Tiainen (Fin)	78.08	
Javelin	Arto Härkönen (Fin)	86.76	
Decathlon	Daley Thompson (GB)	8797 points (1984 scoring)	OR

Women

			min sec	
100 m	Evelyn Ashford (US)		10.97	OR
200 m	Valerie Brisco-Hooks (US)		21.81	OR
400 m	Valerie Brisco-Hooks (US)		48.83	OR
800 m	Doina Melinte (Romania)		1: 57.60	OR
1500 m	Gabriella Dorio (Ita)		4: 03.25	
3000 m	Maricica Puica (Romania)		8: 35.96	*
Marathon	Joan Benoit (US)		2 hr 24.52	*
100 m hurdles	Benita Fitzgerald-Brown (US)		12.84	
400 m hurdles	Nawal El Moutawakel (Morocco)		54.61	*
4 × 100 m relay	US		41.65	
4 × 400 m relay	US		3: 18.29	OR

		meters	
High Jump	Ulrike Meyfarth (W Ger)	2.02	OR
Long Jump	Anisoara Stanciu (Romania)	6.96	
Shot Put	Claudia Losch (W Ger)	20.48	
Discus	Ria Stalman (Neth)	65.36	
Javelin	Tessa Sanderson (GB)	69.56	OR
Heptathlon	Glynis Nunn (Aust)	6,390 points	*

* not previously held
WR = World Record   OR = Olympic Record

24-Hour Record

The greatest distance run on a standard track in 24 hours is 170 miles 974 yd by Dave Dowdle (b Nov 7, 1954) (Gloucester AC) at Blackbridge, Gloucester, England, May 22–23, 1982. The best by a woman is 133 miles 939 yd by Lynn Fitzgerald (b Sept 9, 1947) (Highgate Harriers) in the same race.

Longest Winning Sequence

Iolanda Balas (Romania) (b Dec 12, 1936) won 140 successive high jump competitions from 1956 to 1967. The record for track races is 116 (including 101 finals) at 400-meter hurdles by Edwin Corley Moses (US) (b July 31, 1955) from 1977 to Aug 1986.

NOTE to opposite page: Records marked A were set at high altitude—Mexico City 7,349 ft, Colorado Springs 7,201 ft. Best marks at low altitude have been: Carl Lewis (US) (b July 1, 1961) 200 m—19.75 and long jump—28 ft 10¼ in, both at Indianapolis, June 19, 1983. Ben Johnson (Canada) 100 m—9.95, Moscow, July 9, 1986. Alberto Juantorena (Cuba) (b Nov 21, 1950) 400 m—44.26, Montreal, July 29, 1976, and the US 4 × 100 m relay team—2:58.65, Montreal, July 31, 1976.

GOLD MEDALISTS: Fanny Blankers-Koen (Neth) (left) and Betty Cuthbert (Aust) (far right) share, with Barbel Wöckel (below) (E Ger), the women's record for most Olympic gold medals with 4 apiece. Blankers-Koen was 30 years old with 2 children when she captured her 4 golds, all in the 1948 Games. Cuthbert won 3 golds in 1956 and picked up her fourth 8 years later.

WORLD TRACK AND FIELD RECORDS (WOMEN)

RUNNING

Event	min:sec	Name and Nationality	Place	Date
100 m	10.76	Evelyn Ashford (US)	Zurich	Aug 22, 1984
200 m	21.71	Marita Koch (E Ger)	Potsdam, E Ger	July 21, 1984
	21.71	Heike Dreschler (E Ger)	Stuttgart, W Ger	Aug 29, 1986
400 m	47.60	Marita Koch (E Ger)	Canberra, Australia	Oct 6, 1985
800 m	1:53.28	Jarmila Kratochvilova (Czech)	Munich	July 26, 1983
1,000 m	2:30.6	Tanyana Providokhina (USSR)	Podolsk, USSR	Aug 20, 1978
1,500 m	3:52.47	Tatyana Kazankina (USSR)	Zurich, Switz	Aug 13, 1980
1 mile	4:16.71	Mary Decker Slaney (US)	Zurich, Switz	Aug 21, 1985
2,000 m	5:28.69	Maricica Puica (Romania)	London, Eng	July 11, 1986
3,000 m	8:22.62	Tatyana Kazankina (USSR)	Leningrad	Aug 26, 1984
5,000 m	14:37.33	Ingrid Kristiansen (Norway)	Stockholm, Sweden	Aug 5, 1986
10,000 m	30:13.74	Ingrid Kristiansen (Norway)	Oslo, Norway	July 5, 1986

FIELD EVENTS

Event	ft	in	Name and Nationality	Place	Date
High Jump	6	9¾	Stefka Kosadinova (Bulgaria)	Sofia, Bulgaria	May 31, 1986
Long Jump	24	5½	Heike Drechsler (E Ger)	Dresden, E Ger	July 3, 1986
Shot Put	73	11	Natalya Lisovskaya (USSR)	Sochi, USSR	May 27, 1984
Discus Throw	244	7	Zdena Silhava (Czech)	Nitra, Czech	Aug 26, 1984
Javelin Throw	254	1	Fatima Whitbread (GB)	Stuttgart, W Ger	Aug 28, 1986

HURDLES

Event	min:sec	Name and Nationality	Place	Date
100 m (2′9″)	12.26	Yordanka Donkova (Bulgaria)	Ljubljana, Yugoslavia	Sept 7, 1986
400 m (2′6″)	52.94	Marina Stepanova (USSR)	Tashkent, USSR	Sept 17, 1986

RELAYS

4 × 100 m	41.37	E Germany (Silke Gladisch, Sabine Rieger, Ingrid Auerswold, Marlies Göhr)	Canberra, Australia	Oct 6, 1985
4 × 200 m	1:28.15	E Germany (Marlies Göhr, Romy Müller, Barbel Wöckel, Marita Koch)	Jena, E Ger	Aug 10, 1980
4 × 400 m	3:15.92	E Germany (Gesine Walther, Sabine Busch, Dagmar Ruebsam, Marita Koch)	Erfurt, E Ger	June 3, 1984
4 × 800 m	7:50.17	USSR (Nadezha Olizarenko, Lyubov Gunina, Lyudmila Borisova, Irina Padyalovskaya)	Moscow, USSR	Aug 7, 1984

HEPTATHLON

7,161 points		Jackie Joyner (US) (100-m hurdles 13.16 sec; high jump 6 ft 2 in; shot put 49 ft 10½ in, 200-m 22.85 sec; long jump 23 ft 0¼ in; javelin 164 ft 5 in; 800-m 2 min 9.69 sec)	Houston, Tex	Aug 1–2, 1986

RUSSIAN FOR THE GOLD: Star Soviet distance runner Tatyana Kazankina (#340) is first across the finish line in the Olympic 800 m in 1976. Kazankina, who also won the 1,500 m in both 1976 and 1980, holds world records for 1,500 and 3,000 m.

OLYMPIC INCIDENT at Los Angeles in 1984 caused Mary Decker (US) (left) to fall down. She later ran the world best mile. Marita Koch (E Ger) (above, #552) holds 200 and 400 m outdoor and 3 indoor world sprint records. Here, she is running with the great Polish sprinter Irena Szewinska, winner of 7 Olympic medals.

COLLAPSING WITH VICTORY IN HER GRASP: In the Commonwealth Games in Edinburgh, Scotland, a New Zealand schoolteacher, Sylvia Potts, came within 4 yd of winning the gold and setting a record in a 1500 m race, but her stamina gave out, limbs aching, lungs bursting and eyes burning. (London Daily Express)

Most Olympic Gold Medals in Field and Track

The most Olympic gold medals won in field events is 10 individual medals by Ray C. Ewry (US) (1874–1937) with:

Standing High Jump	1900, 1904, 1906, 1908
Standing Long Jump	1900, 1904, 1906, 1908
Standing Triple Jump	1900, 1904

The most gold medals won by a woman is 4, a record shared by Francina E. Blankers-Koen (Netherlands) (b Apr 26, 1918) with 100 m, 200 m, 80 m hurdles and 4 × 100 m relay (1948); Betty Cuthbert (Australia) (b Apr 20, 1938) with 100 m, 200 m, 4 × 100 m relay (1956) and 400 m (1964); and Barbel Wöckel (née Eckert) (b March 21, 1955) (E Germany) with 200 m and 4 × 100 m relay in 1976 and 1980.

The most gold medals at one Olympic celebration is 5 by Nurmi in 1924 and the most individual is 4 by Alvin C. Kraenzlein (US) (1876–1928) in 1900 with 60 m, 110 m hurdles, 200 m hurdles and long jump.

Oldest and Youngest Olympic Champions

The oldest athlete to win an Olympic gold was Irish-born Patrick J. "Babe" McDonald (US) (1878–1954) who was aged 42 years 26 days when he won the 56-lb weight throw at Antwerp, Belgium on Aug 21, 1920. The oldest female champion was Lia Manoliu (Romania) (b Apr 25, 1932) aged 36 years 176 days when she won the discus at Mexico City on Oct 18, 1968.

The oldest Olympic medalist was Tebbs Lloyd Johnson (1900–84), aged 48 years 115 days when he was third in the 1948 50,000 m walk. The oldest woman medalist was Dana Zatopkova aged 37 years 248 days when she was second in the javelin in 1960.

The youngest gold medalist was Barbara Pearl Jones (US) (b March 26, 1937) who was a member of the winning 4 × 100 m relay team, aged 15 years 123 days, at Helsinki, Finland, on July 27, 1952. The youngest male champion was Robert Bruce Mathias (US) (b Nov 17, 1930) aged 17 years 263 days when he won the decathlon at London, Aug 5–6, 1948.

Most US Gold Medals in Track and Field in One Olympiad

Carl Lewis won 4 gold medals—in the 100 and 200 m sprints, the long jump, and as the anchor runner of the world-record-setting 4 × 100 m relay team in 1984—matching the record Jesse Owens (US) set in the 1936 Olympics.

Most Olympic Medals in Track and Field

The most Olympic medals won in track is 12 (9 gold and 3 silver) by Paavo Johannes Nurmi (Finland) (1897–1973) with:

1920	Gold: 10,000 m; Cross-Country, Individual and Team; silver: 5,000 m
1924	Gold: 1,500 m; 5,000 m; 3,000 m Team; Cross-Country, Individual and Team.
1928	Gold: 10,000 m; silver: 5,000 m; 3,000 m steeplechase.

The most medals won by a woman athlete is 7 by Shirley de la Hunty (née Strickland) (b July 18, 1925) (Australia) with 3 gold, 1 silver and 3 bronze in the 1948, 1952 and 1956 Games. A recently discovered photo finish indicates that she finished third, not fourth, in the 1948 200 m event, thus unofficially increasing her total to 8. Irena Szewinska (née Kirszenstein) of Poland has also won 7 medals (3 gold, 2 silver, 2 bronze) in 1964, 1968, 1972 and 1976. She is the only woman ever to win Olympic medals in track and field in 4 successive Games.

OLDEST RACE RECORD: The 3-legged race record of 100 yards in 11 seconds was set 76 years ago by Harry Hillman (left) and Lawson Robertson (right), both Olympic medalists in 1904.

WORLD'S FASTEST HUMAN at 200 meters: Pietro Mennea (Italy) has held the record of 19.72 sec since 1979 when he won in the high-altitude air of Mexico City.

RUNNING BACKWARD: Donald Davis, winner of the 1-mile reverse race in 6 min 7.1 sec, shows how he does it.

Longest Race

The longest races ever staged were the 1928 (3,422 miles) and 1929 (3,665 miles) transcontinental races from NYC to Los Angeles. The Finnish-born Johnny Salo (1893–1931) was the winner in 1929 in 79 days, from March 31 to June 18. His elapsed time of 525 hours 57 min 20 sec gave a running average of 6.97 mph. His margin of victory was only 2 min 47 sec.

IN THIN AIR: Helped by the lower air resistance at the US Air Force Academy's high elevation in Colorado Springs, Calvin Smith (far right) broke the world record for the 100-meter dash that Jim Hines had set 15 years earlier under similar conditions in 1968 in the thin air of Mexico City. His mark remains unbeaten. (AP)

FOSBURY FLOPS: (Left) This high jump style was originated in 1968 by Dick Fosbury (US) who set the high jump record at 7 ft 4¼ in going over the bar backwards.

Progressive Pole Vault Records

Sergei Bubka (USSR) (right) set four world records in 1984, from 19 ft 1 in to 19½ ft. He improved to 19 ft 8¼ in in 1985, and 19 ft 8¾ in in 1986.

1963—a record ten outdoor world records, seven by John Pennel (US) and three by Brian Sternberg (US), were set in one year. In this year also Pentti Nikula (Fin), jumping indoors, registered the first 16-ft vault.

The first world record to be set with a fiber-glass pole was in 1961 when George Davies (US) cleared 15¾ ft.

Cornelius "Dutch" Warmerdam (US) set records from 15 ft to 15 ft 5 in (and 15 ft 6 in indoors). No other man cleared 15 ft until 1951.

The first 13-ft vault was 13 ft 0¾ in by Marcus Wright (US) in 1912.

POLE-VAULT RECORDHOLDER Sergei Bubka (USSR) keeps breaking his own record every time he leaps. By July 1986, he had reached 19 ft 8¾ in.

DECATHLON CHAMPION: (Left) In the shot put, Daley Thompson (GB) scored most points (4,550) in the first day and a world record total of 8,847 points in the 1984 Olympic Games in LA. YOUNGEST OLYMPIC MALE GOLD MEDALIST: (above) Bob Mathias (US) was only 17 years 263 days when he first won the decathlon in London, Aug 5–6, 1948.

TRIPLE JUMPING has never been as popular as today. A major reason is the ebullient enthusiasm and popularity of Willie Banks (left) (US), who holds the world record. LONG DISTANCE RUNNER Said Aouita (right) (Morocco) is the first person in 30 years to hold concurrent world records at 1,500 and 5,000 m. (All Sport)

Greatest Mileage

Jay F. Helgerson (b Feb 3, 1955) of Foster City, Calif, ran a certified marathon (26 miles 385 yd) or longer, each week for 52 weeks from Jan 28, 1979 to Jan 19, 1980, totalling 1,418 racing miles.

Sy Mah (1926–), an instructor at Toledo University (Ohio), has run 374 "marathons" of 26.2 mi or longer since 1966 for a total of 9,800 mi. He paces himself to take 3½ hours for each run.

Douglas Alistair Gordon Pirie (b Feb 10, 1931) (GB), who set 5 world records in the 1950s, estimated that he had run a total distance of 216,000 miles in 40 years to 1981.

The greatest distance run in one year is 15,472 miles by Tina Maria Stone (b Naples, Italy, Apr 5, 1934) of Irvine, Calif, in 1983.

> The longest-ever solo run is 10,608 miles by Robert J. Sweetgall (US) (b Dec 8, 1947) around the perimeter of the 48 states, starting and finishing in Wash, DC, Oct 9, 1982–July 15, 1983.

Ron Grant (Aust) (b Feb 15, 1943) ran around Australia, 8,316 miles in 217 days 3 hours 45 min, running every day Mar 28–Oct 31, 1983.

THREE WORLD RECORDS IN 20 DAYS: Steve Cram (GB) set a new record in running 1500 m on July 16, 1985 (3:29.67), in the mile run on July 27 (3:46.32), and 2000 m race on Aug 4 (4:51.39). On Aug 10 he came in with the world's second best time in 1000 m, against a head wind. Shown here, he exults over his victory in the mile. He set a better mark in the 1500 m in 1985. (IAAF Mobile Grand Prix)

Ernst Mensen (1799–1846) (Norway), a former seaman in the British Navy, is reputed to have run from Istanbul, Turkey, to Calcutta, in West Bengal, India, and back in 59 days in 1836, so averaging an improbable 92.4 miles per day.

Max Telford (b Hawick, Scotland, Feb 2, 1935) of New Zealand ran 5,110 miles from Anchorage, Alaska, to Halifax, Nova Scotia, in 106 days 18 hours 45 min from July 25 to Nov 9, 1977.

The greatest non-stop run recorded is 352.9 miles in 121 hours 54 min by Bertil Järlåker (Sweden) at Norrköping, Sweden, May 26–31, 1980. He was moving 95.04% of the time.

MILERS: Between them, Britishers Steve Ovett (left) and Sebastian Coe (right, #9) set 5 records for the mile run, including an amazing flurry of 3 records in 10 days during August, 1981. In their 1980 Olympic gold-medal runs, Ovett beat recordholder Coe at 800 meters before Coe beat recordholder Ovett at 1,500 meters. In 1984, Coe won the gold at 1,500 m and the silver at 800 m.

GREATEST DISTANCE run in one year is 15,472 mi by Tina Maria Stone (left) who was born in Italy, but is now running in Irvine, Calif. RUNNING ACROSS CANADA took Beryl Stott (right) 6½ months. She ran through all 10 provinces from Victoria to Nova Scotia, a total of 3,824 mi.

WON WITH HER FINAL THROW: Tiina Lillak (Fin) tossed the javelin 232 ft 4 in to win the 1983 World Championship.

ROAD RUNNER: (Right) Abebe Bikila (Ethiopia) won the 1961 Kosice Marathon in Czechoslovakia. Bikila is the only man to successfully defend the Olympic Marathon title, winning the gold medal in 1960 and 1964. DISTANCE WORLD RECORD HOLDER: (Below) Jos Hermens (Neth), No. 5, ran the fastest time for 20,000 m and the farthest distance for one hour in 1976, and the records still stand.

Fastest 100 Miles

The fastest recorded time for 100 miles is 11 hours 30 min 51 sec by Donald Ritchie (b July 6, 1944) at Crystal Palace, London, on Oct 15, 1977. The best by a woman is 15 hours 24 min 46 sec by Eleanor Adams (GB) (b Nov 20, 1947) at Honefoss, Norway, July 12–13, 1986.

Trans-America Run

The fastest time for the cross-US run is 46 days, 8 hours 36 min by Frank Giannino Jr (b 1952) (US) for the 3,100 miles from San Francisco to NYC, Sept 1–Oct 17, 1980.

When Johnny Salo won the 1929 Trans-America race from NYC to LA, his total elapsed time of 525 hours 57 min 20 sec gave him a margin of only 2 min 47 sec over second-place Peter Gavuzzi—after 3,665 miles.

Nicki Lewis, 50, of Santa Monica, Calif, is the first American woman to run across the continent, setting

100-METER UNBEATABLE: Evelyn Ashford (US) (far right) strains for the finish line on the day in 1983 when both she and Calvin Smith set world records for the 100-meter dash. In the 1984 Olympics she stood off all opposition to take the gold medal. (Tony Duffy/All-Sport; AP)

244-LB SHOT PUT CHAMP: Center of attention was Tamara Andreyevna (Fatty) Tyshkyevich (USSR), the gold medal winner in the 1956 Olympics.

ONE-LEGGED HIGH JUMPER: (Below) Arnie Boldt of Canada leaped 6 ft 8¼ in (2.04 m) high in Rome Apr 3, 1981, proving that he is not greatly handicapped.

a speed record of 3,224 miles in 75 days, Aug 16, 1983–Oct 30, 1983, running an average of 42.8 miles per day from Santa Monica to NYC. She was escorted by David Hermitage (Eng). She wore out one pair of shoes and had two other pairs sent by Nike to her, enroute.

In an attempt to beat the record, three women sponsored by The Greyhound Corporation set out from Boston, Mass in the summer of 1984 for San Francisco. Two of the women finished, Caroline Merrill, 42, and Annabel Marsh, 61, after 130 days and 3,261 miles. They wore out 12 pairs of shoes each.

Running unaccompanied, Sandy Goldstein, 38,

5,000-METER WORLD RECORDHOLDER, Zola Budd (GB), wearing number 007, heads the field in a cross-country race.

ran from Sacramento, Calif to Hyannis, Mass, her hometown, also in 1984 in 130 days, but covering 3,328 miles.

Trans-Canada Run

The only woman to have run across Canada from Victoria, BC, to Halifax, Nova Scotia, a distance of 3,824 mi in 6½ months, touching all 10 provinces, is Kanchan Beryl Stott of Ottawa, Ont. It was probably the longest run ever made by a woman.

One-Legged High Jump

Arnie Boldt (b 1958), of Saskatchewan, Canada, cleared a height of 6 ft 8¼ in in Rome, Italy, on Apr 3, 1981, in spite of the fact that he has only one leg.

Six-Day Race

The greatest distance covered by a man in six days (*i.e.* the 144 permissible hours between Sundays in Victorian times) was 635 miles 1,385 yards by Yiannis Kouros (Greece) (b Feb 13, 1956) at Colac,

Australia on Nov 26–Dec 1, 1984. On the same occasion Eleanor Adams (UK) (b Nov 20, 1947) set the women's record at 500 mi 1,452 yds.

Downhill Mile

Mike Boit (Kenya) ran what is believed to be the fastest mile ever when he won the Molenberg Mile in 3 min 28.36 sec over a carefully measured downhill course along Queen Street, Auckland, NZ, on Apr 16, 1983. The course had an overall vertical drop of nearly 208 yd.

Mass Relay Record

The record for 100 miles by 100 runners belonging to one club is 7 hours 53 min 52.1 sec by Baltimore Road Runners Club of Towson, Md, on May 17, 1981. The women's mark is 10 hours 47 min 9.3 sec by a team from the San Francisco Dolphins Southend Running Club, on Apr 3, 1977.

The best club time for a 100 × 400 m relay is 1 hour 29 min 11.8 sec (average 53.5 sec) by the Physical Training Institute, Leuven, Belgium, on Apr 19,

1978. The best women's club time for 100 × 100 meters relay is 23 min 28 sec by Amsterdanse dames athletiekvereniging, on Sept 26, 1981, in Amsterdam, Netherlands.

The longest relay ever run was 10,524 mi by 2,660 runners at Trondheim, Norway, Aug 26–Oct 20, 1985. Twenty members of the Melbourne Fire Brigade ran around Australia on Highway No. 1 in 43 days 23 hours 58 min, July 10–Aug 23, 1983. The most participants is 4,800 (192 teams of 25), in the Batavierenrace, 103.89 mi from Nijmegen to Enschede, The Netherlands, won in 9 hours 30 min 44 sec on Apr 23, 1983.

Running Backwards

The fastest time recorded for running 100 yd backwards is 12.8 sec by Ferdie Adoboe (Kenya, now US) in Amherst, Mass, on July 28, 1983.

Anthony "Scott" Weiland, 27, ran the Detroit marathon backwards in 4 hours 7 min 54 sec on Oct 3, 1982.

Donald Davis (b Feb 10, 1960) (US) ran 1 mi backwards in 6 min 7.1 sec at the University of Hawaii on Feb 21, 1983.

Arvind Pandya (India) ran LA-NY in 107 days, Aug 18–Dec 3, 1984.

Blind 100 Meters

The fastest time recorded for 100 m by a blind man is 11.4 sec by Graham Henry Salmon (b Sept 5, 1952) of Loughton, Essex, England, at Grangemouth, Scotland, on Sept 2, 1978.

DOUBLE WINNER: Valerie Briscoe-Hooks (US) won the 200 m and 400 m races in 1984, setting Olympic records in both events.

Fastest 100 Kilometers

Donald Ritchie ran 100 km in a record 6 hours 10 min 20 sec at Crystal Palace, London, on Oct 28, 1978. The women's best, run on the road, is 7 hours 27 min 22 sec by Chantal Langlace (b Jan 6, 1955) (France) at Amiens, France on Sept 6, 1980.

Three-Legged Race

The fastest recorded time for a 100-yd three-legged race is 11.0 sec by Olympic medalists Harry L. Hillman (1881–1945) and Lawson Robertson (1883–1951) in Brooklyn, NYC, on Apr 24, 1909.

Pancake Race Record

The annual "Housewives" Pancake Race at Olney, Buckinghamshire, England, was first mentioned in 1445. The record for the winding 415-yd course (three tosses mandatory) is 61.0 sec, set by Sally Ann Faulkner, 16, on Feb 26, 1974. The record for the counterpart race at Liberal, Kansas, is 58.5 sec by Sheila Turner (b July 9, 1953) in 1975.

Dale R. Lyons (b Feb 26, 1937) (GB) has run several marathons during which he tosses a 2-oz pancake repeatedly en route in a 1½ lb pan. His fastest time is 3 hours 6 min 48 sec in London, Apr 20, 1986.

TRAMPOLINING

Origins

The *sport* of trampolining (from the Spanish word *trampolin,* a springboard) dates from 1936, when the prototype "T" model trampoline was developed by George Nissen (US) in a garage in Cedar Rapids, Iowa. Trampolines were used in show business at least as early as "The Walloons" of the period, 1910–12.

Stunts

Septuple twisting back somersault to bed and quintuple twisting back somersault to shoulders was made by Marco Canestrelli to Belmonte Canestrelli at Madison Square Garden, NYC, on Jan 5 and Mar 28, 1979.

Richard Tisson performed a triple twisting triple back somersault for a Guinness TV program near Berchtesgaden, W Germany on June 30, 1981. The first person to perform this was Stuart Ransom of Memphis, Tenn, in 1977 in Lafayette, La.

Richard Cobbing of Gateshead, Eng performed 1,610 consecutive somersaults at Gateshead July 22, 1984. Damon Collins (GB) performed a record 68 somersaults in one minute in Gillingham, Kent, Eng, on Jan 23, 1986.

TWIST AND TURN: On the shores of the Konigsee, W Germany, Richard Tisson, a 2-time world champion, set a record by landing on his feet after performing a triple back somersault with 3 full twists. The Guinness TV cameras caught the action in 1981.

TRAMPOLINING LEAP: Marco Canestrelli (below) imitates Superman flying through the air over the backs of 4 elephants in the Ringling Bros and Barnum & Bailey Circus.

Marathon Record

The longest recorded trampoline bouncing marathon is one of 1,248 hours (52 days) set by a team of 6 in Phoenix, Ariz, from June 24 to Aug 15, 1974. The solo record is 266 hours 9 min by Jeff Schwartz, 19, at Glenview, Ill, Aug 14–25, 1981.

World Championships

Instituted in 1964 and since 1968 held biennially:

Men	Women
1964 Danny Millman (US)	Judy Wills (US)
1965 George Irwin (US)	Judy Wills (US)
1966 Wayne Miller (US)	Judy Wills (US)
1967 Dave Jacobs (US)	Judy Wills (US)
1968 Dave Jacobs (US)	Judy Wills (US)
1970 Wayne Miller (US)	Renee Ransom (US)
1972 Paul Luxon (GB)	Alexandra Nicholson (US)
1974 Richard Tisson (Fra)	Alexandra Nicholson (US)
1976 Richard Tisson (Fra) / Evgeni Janes (USSR)	Svetlana Levina (USSR)
1978 Evgeni Janes (USSR)	Tatyana Anisimova (USSR)
1980 Stewart Matthews (GB)	Ruth Keller (Switz)
1982 Carl Furrer (GB)	Ruth Keller (Switz)
1984 Lionel Pioline (Fra)	Sue Shotton (GB)
1986 Lionel Pioline (Fra)	Tatyana Luschina (USSR)

Coaching Record

Jeff Hennessey of Lafayette, La, has coached more world champions in trampoline, synchro trampoline, and double mini-trampoline.

TRIATHLON

A new type of competition, the Triathlon, began in Feb 1978 in Hawaii when two Navy men challenged each other to a particularly strenuous test of all the major muscles of the body in strength and endurance: a swim of 2.4 miles in the ocean, followed immediately by a 112-mile bike race, and then a full marathon run of 26 miles 385 yd, with no time-outs.

They were joined by 13 others in the first two Triathlons in Feb 1978 and Feb 1979. Then, in 1980 ABC on its "Wide World of Sports" began televising what began to be called the Ironman Triathlon and 108 competed. Now there are hundreds of triathlons—but not all are Ironman Triathlons. The "tinman" races cut the distances in half or less.

In the Bud Light Ironman Triathlon in Oct 1986, Dave Scott, 32, of Davis, Calif, shattered the previous course record in Kona, Hawaii, by winning his fifth championship in the record time of 8 hours 28 min 37 sec, some 22 min faster than the previous (1985) record for the 140.6-mi swim-bike-run event.

In the women's division in 1986, Paula Newby-Fraser, 24, of Zimbabwe broke the previous (1984) record by 36 min, finishing in 9 hours 49 min 13 sec.

The largest field in a triathlon of any kind has been 2,060 finishers in the US Triathlon (swim 1500 m, bike 40 km and run 10 km) in Chicago in July 1985.

VOLLEYBALL

Origins

The game was invented as Mintonette in 1895 by William G. Morgan at the YMCA gymnasium at Holyoke, Mass. The International Volleyball Association was formed in Paris in Apr 1947. The ball travels at a speed of up to 70 mph when smashed over the net, which stands 7 ft 11½ in high. In the women's game it is 7 ft 4¼ in high.

World Titles

World Championships were instituted in 1949 for men and 1952 for women. The USSR has won 6 men's titles (1949, 52, 60, 62, 78, and 82). The USSR won the women's championship in 1952, 56, 60 and 70. The record crowd is 90,000 for the 1983 world title matches in Brazil. The US won for the first time in 1986, following victory in the 1984 Olympics. China won the 1986 women's championship.

Most Olympic Medals

In the 1984 Olympics the US won the gold medal in the men's game, and China won in the women's.

The sport was introduced to the Olympic Games for both men and women in 1964. The only volleyball player to win four medals is Inna Ryskal (USSR) (b June 15, 1944), who won silver medals in 1964 and 76 and golds in 1968 and 72.

The record for medals for men is held jointly by Yuriy Poyarkov (USSR), who won gold medals in 1964 and 68, and a bronze in 1972, and Katsutoshi Nekoda (Japan) (b Feb 1, 1944) who won a gold in 1972, a silver in 1968, and a bronze in 1964.

TRIATHLON WINNERS: Dave Scott (left) finishing the 140-mi Ironman 1986 race in record time of 8 hours 28 min 37 sec. Paula Newby-Fraser (right) finished the same swim-bike-run race in record time in the women's division.

ONE-MAN VOLLEYBALL TEAM: (Below) Bob Schaffer of Newark, NJ (see inset) has won over 1,000 games with only 2 losses against 6-man teams.

IN 1976 OLYMPICS, the USSR (left) won the silver medal. Here they are beating Cuba, 3–0 in a semi-final. Poland (right), after beating Japan in the other semi-final, went on to win the gold medal. In 1984, the US won the men's gold medal.

Collegiate Championships

Since NCAA began sponsoring volleyball, only 4 teams have ever won a title. Pepperdine is the (1986) current champion, the other winners being UCLA, San Diego State and Southern Calif. Only twice have schools outside Calif vied for the championship: Ohio State in 1977 and Penn State in 1982. UCLA has won more matches than any other college with a record 32 wins and 3 defeats for a .914 percentage.

Marathon

The longest recorded volleyball marathon by two teams of six is 84 hours by players from Beta Theta Pi fraternity, Bethany College, Bethany, W Va, Sept 27–30, 1984.

WALKING

Longest Race

The Paris-Colmar event (until 1980 it was the Strasbourg-Paris event, instituted in 1926 in the reverse direction), now 322 miles, is the world's longest annual walk event. Gilbert Roger (France) has won 6 times (1949, 53–54, 56–58). The fastest performance

is by Robert Pietquin (b 1938) (Belgium) who walked 315 miles in the 1980 race in 60 hours 1 min 10 sec (deducting 4 hours of compulsory stops), averaging 5.25 mph. The first woman to complete the race was Annie van den Meer (Neth) (b Feb 24, 1947) who was 10th in 1983 in 82 hours 10 min.

Dumitru Dan (1890–1978) of Romania was the only man out of 200 entrants to succeed in walking 100,000 km (62,137 miles), in a contest organized by the Touring Club de France on Apr 1, 1910. By March 24, 1916, he had covered 96,000 km (59,651 miles), averaging 27.24 miles per day.

Longest in 24 Hours

The greatest distance walked in 24 hours is 140 mi, 1,229 yd by Paul Forthomme (Belgium), on a road course at Woluwé, Belgium Oct 13–14, 1984. The best by a woman is 125.7 miles by Annie van den Meer (Netherlands) at Rouen, France, Apr 30–May 1, 1984, over a 1.185-km-lap road course.

Most Olympic Medals

Walking races have been included in the Olympic schedule since 1906, but walking matches have been

WALKED FOR SIX YEARS at a rate of 27.24 mi per day: Dumitru Dan (Romania) (left) covered 100,000 kilometers in a contest 1910–16.

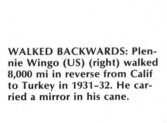

WALKED BACKWARDS: Plennie Wingo (US) (right) walked 8,000 mi in reverse from Calif to Turkey in 1931–32. He carried a mirror in his cane.

known since 1589. The only walker to win 3 gold medals has been Ugo Frigerio (Italy) (1901–68) with the 3,000 m and 10,000 m in 1920 and the 10,000 m in 1920 and 1924. He also holds the record of most medals with 4 (having additionally won the bronze medal in the 50,000 m in 1932), a total shared with

WALKING FOR 24 HOURS: Huw Neilson (GB) covered more than 133 miles in 1960, a record that still stands.

WALKING ACROSS AMERICA: John Lees (Eng) walked the 2,876 miles from LA to NYC in 53½ days in 1972. Lees' time was faster than the then-standing trans-America running record.

tional titles from 1958 to 1976, plus 4 Canadian championships.

Walking Around the World

The first person reported to have "walked around the world" is George M. Schilling (US), Aug 3, 1897–1904, but the first verified achievement was by David Kunst (b 1939), who started with his brother John from Waseca, Minn, on June 10, 1970. John

Vladimir Golubnichiy (USSR) (b June 2, 1936), who won gold medals for the 20,000 m in 1960 and 1968, the silver in 1972 and the bronze in 1964.

In the 1984 Olympics Ernesto Canto (Mex) won the 20,000 m in 1 hour 23 min 13 sec. Raul Gonzalez (Mex) won the 50,000 m walk in 3 hours 47 min 26 sec. Canto's world record at 20,000 m set May 5, 1984 in Fana, Norway, is 1 hour 18 min 39.9 sec. Gonzalez' world record at 50,000 m set May 25, 1979 at Fana, Norway, is 3 hours 41 min 38.4 sec.

Longest Non-Stop Walk

Tom Benson (GB) walked 414.74 miles in 6 days 12 hours 45 min at Moor Park, Preston, Eng, Apr 29–May 5, 1986. This was 233 laps of a 1.78-mi closed circuit. He was not permitted any stops for rest and was moving 98.78 percent of the time.

Most Titles

Four-time Olympian Ronald Owen Laird (b May 31, 1938) of the NYAC, won a total of 65 US Na-

OLYMPIC GOLD MEDALIST in the 20,000 m walk in Montreal was Daniel Bautista of Mexico. He also holds the world record of 1:20:06.8, three min better than the 1984 Olympic winner walked.

was killed in 1972 by Afghan bandits who thought they were carrying UNICEF funds they were soliciting. David was wounded, so another brother, Pete, joined him. David arrived home, after walking 14,500 miles, on Oct 5, 1974.

Tomas Carlos Pereira (b Argentina, Nov 16, 1942) spent 10 years, Apr 6, 1968, through Apr 8, 1978, walking 29,825 miles around all 5 continents.

John Lees, 27, of Brighton, England, Apr 11–June 3, 1972, walked 2,876 miles across the US from City Hall, Los Angeles, to City Hall, NYC, in 53 days 12 hours 15 min (53.746 miles per day).

Sean Eugene Maguire (b Sept 15, 1956) (US) walked 7,327 miles from the Yukon River, north of Livengood, Alaska, to Key West, Fla, in 307 days, from June 6, 1978 to Apr 9, 1979.

The record for the trans-Canada (Halifax to Vancouver) walk of 3,764 miles is 96 days by Clyde McRae, 23, from May 1 to Aug 4, 1973.

Walking Backwards

The greatest exponent of reverse pedestrianism has been Plennie L. Wingo (b Jan 24, 1895) then of Abilene, Tex, who started on his 8,000-mile transcontinental walk on Apr 15, 1931, from Santa Monica, Calif, to Istanbul, Turkey, and arrived on Oct 24, 1932. He celebrated the walk's 45th anniversary by covering the 452 miles from Santa Monica to San Francisco, Calif, backwards, in 85 days, aged 81 years.

The longest distance recorded for walking backwards in 24 hours is 84 mi by Anthony Thornton in Minneapolis, Dec 31, 1985–Jan 1, 1986.

WATER POLO

Origins

Water polo was developed in England as "Water Soccer" in 1869 and was first included in the Olympic Games in Paris in 1900. The US was introduced to the sport in 1898 but development was slow until after World War II. However, prior to that time the US won three Olympic medals. Since 1946 the popularity of water polo has grown rapidly, especially in California. Women's water polo has never been included in the Olympic program.

WALKING THE DOG: When Sean Maguire says he's taking his dog "Sweden" for a walk, he means it. They set out from the Yukon River, Alaska, and arrived at their destination (Key West, Fla) 10 months and 7,327 miles later.

Major water polo events include the FINA Cup held every other year; World University Games held every two years for collegians; Tungsram Cup in Budapest, Hungary, biannually; US Olympic Festival, annually except for the Olympic year; Pan American Games, the Olympics and World Championships every fourth year.

Most Goals

The greatest number of goals scored by an individual in an international tournament is 13 by Debbie Handley for Australia (16) vs Canada (10) at the World Championships in Guayaquil, Ecuador, in 1982.

Olympic Victories

Hungary has won the Olympic tournament most often with 6 wins, in 1932, 36, 52, 56, 64 and 76. Five

SLAM DUNK: Hungary's Gyorgy Karpati (#7) is one of the 5 players who have won 3 Olympic gold medals in water polo.

players share the record of 3 gold medals: George Wilkinson (1879–1946) in 1900, 08 and 12; Paulo (Paul) Radmilovic (1886–1968) and Charles Sidney Smith (1879–1951) in 1908, 12 and 20—all GB; and the Hungarians Deszö Gyarmati (b Oct 23, 1927) and György Kárpáti (b June 23, 1935) in 1952, 56 and 64. Gyarmati's wife (Eva Szekely) and daughter (Andrea) won gold and silver medals respectively in swimming. Radmilovic also won a gold medal for the 4 × 200 m freestyle relay in 1908. Yugoslavia won the gold medal in 1984.

Marathon

Two teams of seven from Eton College and Hammersmith Swimming Club, Eng played for 25 hours, July 5–6, 1986.

WATER SKIING

Origins

The sport originated with people walking on water with planks attached to their feet, possibly as early as the 14th century. A 19th century treatise on sorcerers refers to Eliseo of Tarentum who, in the 14th century, "walks and dances" on the water. The first report of aquaplaning on large boards behind a motorboat was from the Pacific coast of the US in the early 1900's. A photograph exists of a "plank-riding" contest in a regatta won by a Mr H. Storry at Scarborough, Yorkshire, England, on July 15, 1914. Competitors were towed on a *single* plank by a motor launch.

The present-day sport of water skiing was pioneered by Ralph W. Samuelson on Lake Pepin, Minn, on two curved pine boards in the summer of 1922, though claims have been made for the birth of the sport on Lake Annecy (Haute-Savoie), France, in 1920. The first world organization, the United Internationale de Ski Nautique, was formed in Geneva, Switz on July 27, 1946.

One of the earliest British aquaplaners was the Duke of York, later King George VI, who was intro-

SLALOM TWISTSTER: Deena Brush (US) rounding 4 buoys at 11.25-m line set a women's world record in Oct 1983 in Florida.

duced to the fad at Cowes, Isle of Wight, Eng, in 1921 by Lord Louis Mountbatten, himself one of the early band of true water skiers. Other early *aficionados* of the new sport in the 1930s were film stars David Niven and Errol Flynn. The first national governing body was the American Water Ski Association founded in 1939, and they organized the first national championships in that year. The first World Water Ski Organization was formed in Geneva, Switzerland, on July 27, 1946.

Slalom

The world record for slalom is 5 buoys on a 10.75-m line by Bob LaPoint (US) at Shreveport, Fla, 1984. Andy Mapple (GB) tied this record in Sept 1985.

The women's record is 4 buoys, on a 11.25-m line, on Oct 2, 1983, by Deena Brush (US) at Okeechellee Record Classic, W Palm Beach, Fla. This was tied in Aug 1985 by Jennifer Leachman.

Highest Speed

The fastest water skiing speed recorded is 143.08 mph by Christopher Michael Massey (Australia) on the Hawkesbury River, NSW, Australia, Mar 6, 1983. His drag-boat driver was Stanley Charles Sainty. Donna Patterson Brice (US) (b 1953) set a feminine record of 111.11 mph at Long Beach, Calif, on Aug 21, 1977.

Most Titles

World overall championships (instituted 1949) have been won three times by Sammy Duvall (US) in 1981, 1983 and 1985. The women's title has been won three times by Mrs Willa McGuire (*née* Worthington) of the US, in 1949–50 and 55, and Elizabeth Allan-Shetter (US) in 1965, 69, and 75. Allan-Shetter has also won a record 8 individual championship events and is the only person to win all 4 titles (slalom, jumping, tricks and overall) in one year, at Copenhagen, Denmark, in 1969. The US has won the team championship on 15 successive occasions, 1957–85.

ROUNDING A BUOY in the record slalom run is Kris LaPoint (US) at the International Cup event in Florida in Apr 1984. (American Water Ski Association)

SKI JUMP: Nine members of the US Water Ski Show Team leap 5½ ft in the air over a ramp on the Hudson River at Albany, NY. (Photo by Mike Nicholas)

Jumps

The first recorded jump on water skis was 50 ft by Ralph W. Samuelson, off a greased ramp at Lake Pepin, Wis, in 1925, and this was not exceeded officially until 1947.

The longest jump recorded is one of 203 ft by Michael Hazelwood (GB) at Birmingham, Ala, on June 28, 1986. The women's record is 150 ft 2 in by Sue Lipplegoes (Australia) at Reading, Eng, on July 31, 1983.

A high jump record of 5½ ft by 9 men simultaneously over a 14-ft-wide ramp was set by the US Water Ski Show Team on July 20, 1986, on the Hudson River at Albany, NY, as part of the city's Tri-Centennial.

Tricks

The tricks or freestyle event involves various maneuvers for which points are awarded according to the degree of difficulty and the speed at which they are performed.

BAREFOOT AUSTRALIAN Brett Wing set a record 61-ft 4-in jump in 1984.

The tricks record is 10,550 points by Patrice Martin (France) on Lake Cadevil near Royan, France, on Sept 28, 1986.

The women's record is 8,350 points by Ana Maria Carrasco (Venezuela) at McCormick, Fla, on Sept 13, 1984.

VENEZUELAN RECORDHOLDER: Ana Maria Carrasco scored 8,350 points in water ski tricks in 1984, and her world record still stands.

"TRICKS" SPECIALIST Patrice Martin outpointed Cory Pickos to win the World Championship in 1985. Pickos then set the world record score, but Martin has now come back with a new record of 10,550 points in Sept 1986.

Barefoot

The first person to water ski barefoot is reported to be Dick Pope, Jr, at Lake Eloise, Fla, on March 6, 1947. The barefoot duration record is 2 hours 42 min 39 sec by Billy Nichols (US) (b 1964) on Lake Weir, Fla, on Nov 19, 1978. The backwards barefoot record is 39 min by Paul McManus (Australia). The barefoot jump record is 65 ft 11¼ in by Mike Siepel in 1984. The official barefoot speed record (two runs) is 110.02 mph by Lee Kirk (US) at Firebird Lake, Phoenix, Ariz, on June 11, 1977. His fastest run was 113.67 mph. The fastest by a woman is 73.67 mph by Karen Toms (Australia) on Mar 31, 1984 in New South Wales, Australia. The fastest official speed backward and barefoot is 62 mph by Robert Wing (Australia) on Apr 3, 1982.

Longest Run

The greatest distance traveled is 1,304.6 miles by Will Coughey on Feb 18–19, 1984 on Lake Tikitapu, New Zealand.

MOST WORLD RECORDS: Vasili Alexeev (USSR) has 8 world titles, including Olympics, and has set 80 official world records in the heavyweight class, more than any other athlete.

WEIGHT LIFTING and POWER LIFTING

Origins

Competitions for lifting weights of stone were held in the ancient Olympic Games. The first "world" championship was staged at the Café Monico, Piccadilly, London, on March 28, 1891, and the first official championships were held in Vienna, Austria, July 19–20, 1898, subsequently recognized by the International Weightlifting Federation. Prior to that time, weight lifting consisted of professional exhibitions in which some of the advertised poundages were open to doubt.

The International Weightlifting Federation (IWF) was established in 1920, and their first official championships were held in Tallinn, Estonia on Apr 29–30, 1922.

The first to raise 400 lb was Karl Swoboda (1882–1933) (Austria) in Vienna, with 401¼ lb in 1910, using the continental and jerk style.

In weight lifting, an Olympic sport, there are two types of lifts. One is the "snatch," in which the lifter grips the bar with both hands, palms downward, and with one movement raises the weight to arms' length over his head. In the other lift, called "the clean and jerk," the lifter first brings the weight to his shoulders, pauses, then raises it to arm's length over his head.

Power lifting is a modern offshoot of weight lifting, popularized by body builders, in which sheer strength and less technique are required. Its three lifts are: (1) the "squat," in which the lifter stands with the bar on his shoulders, squats, and returns to the standing position; (2) the "bench press," in which the competitor, on his back, begins with the weight in outstretched arms, lowers it to his chest, and after a pause, presses it back to arms' length; (3) the "dead lift," in which the lifter removes the weight from the floor and stands erect with the weight hanging at arms' length.

Greatest Lift

The greatest weight ever raised by a human being is 6,270 lb in a back lift (weight raised off trestles) by the 364-lb Paul Anderson (US) (b Oct 17, 1932), the 1956 Olympic heavyweight champion, at Toccoa, Ga, on June 12, 1957. The greatest by a woman is 3,564 lb with a hip and harness lift by Josephine Blatt (*née* Schauer) (US) (1869–1923) at the Bijou Theatre, Hoboken, NJ, on Apr 15, 1895.

The greatest overhead lift ever made by a woman is 303 lb by 180-lb Karyn Tarter (b 1956) in a clean

GREATEST LIFT BY A WOMAN: Karyn Tarter of NYC made an overhead lift of 303 lb in a clean-and-jerk on Apr 20, 1985, beating the 286-lb official record set in 1911 by Katie Sandwina. Here Karyn is lifting two gymmates just to show she can lift live weights, too. (Carolyn Vesper)

LIFTING HER BROTHER OVERHEAD (below) was only one feat that Katie Sandwina was known for. She once shouldered a 1,200-lb cannon.

(b Jan 21, 1884, d as Mrs Max Heymann in NYC, in 1952) stood 5 ft 11 in tall, weighed 210 lb, and is reputed to have unofficially lifted 312½ lb and to have once shouldered a 1,200-lb cannon taken from the tailboard of a Barnum & Bailey circus wagon.

Most World Titles

The most world title wins, including Olympic Games, is 8 by John Davis (US) (1921–84) in 1938, 46–52; by Tommy Kono (US) (b June 27, 1930) in 1952–9; and by Vasili Alexeev (USSR) (b Jan 7, 1942) 1970–7.

Most Olympic Medals

Winner of most Olympic medals is Norbert Schemansky (US) with 4: gold, middle-heavyweight 1952; silver, heavyweight 1948; bronze, heavyweight 1960 and 1964.

and jerk in NYC Apr 20, 1985. She has been US national champion five times in three separate weight classes. Katie Sandwina, *née* Brummbach (Germany)

WORLD WEIGHT LIFTING RECORDS

Bodyweight Class	Lift	kg	lb	Name and Country	Place	Date
52 kg 114½ lb	Snatch	116	255¾	He Zhuggiang (China)	Donaueschingen, W Ger	May 26, 1986
	Jerk	152.5	336	Neno Terziyski (Bulgaria)	Vittoria, Spain	Apr 27, 1984
	Total	262.5	578½	Neno Terziyski (Bulgaria)	Vittoria, Spain	Apr 27, 1984
56 kg 123 lb	Snatch	133	293	Oksen Mirzoyan (USSR)	Varna, Bulgaria	Sept 12, 1984
	Jerk	170.5	375¾	Naum Shalamanov (Bulgaria)	Belgrade, Yugoslavia	Sept 12, 1984
	Total	300	661¼	Naum Shalamanov (Bulgaria)	Varna, Bulgaria	May 11, 1984
60 kg 132 lb	Snatch	147	324	Naum Shalamanov (Bulgaria)	Sofia, Bulgaria	Nov 9, 1986
	Jerk	188	414¼	Naum Shalamanov (Bulgaria)	Sofia, Bulgaria	Nov 9, 1986
	Total	335	738½	Naum Shalamanov (Bulgaria)	Sofia, Bulgaria	Nov 9, 1986
67.5 kg 148 lb	Snatch	155.5	342¾	Vladimir Grachev (USSR)	Minsk, USSR	Mar 15, 1984
	Jerk	200	440¾	Aleksandr Varbanov (Bulgaria)	Varna, Bulgaria	Sept 13, 1984
	Total	352.5	777	Andreas Behm (E Ger)	Schwedt, E Germany	July 20, 1984
75 kg 165 lb	Snatch	167.5	369¼	Vladimir Kuznyetsov (USSR)	Moscow, USSR	Oct 26, 1983
	Jerk	215	474	Aleksandr Varbanov (Bulgaria)	Sofia, Bulgaria	Nov 9, 1986
	Total	377.5	832	Zdravko Stoichkov (Bulgaria)	Varna, Bulgaria	Sept 14, 1984
82.5 kg 181 lb	Snatch	182.5	402¼	Yuri Vardanyan (USSR)	Varna, Bulgaria	Sept 14, 1984
	Jerk	224	493¾	Yuri Vardanyan (USSR)	Varna, Bulgaria	Sept 14, 1984
	Total	405	892¼	Yuri Vardanyan (USSR)	Varna, Bulgaria	Sept 14, 1984
90 kg 198 lb	Snatch	195.5	431	Blagoi Blagoyev (Bulgaria)	Varna, Bulgaria	May 1, 1983
	Jerk	233	513½	Viktor Solodov (USSR)	Varna, Bulgaria	Sept 15, 1984
	Total	422.5	931¼	Viktor Solodov (USSR)	Varna, Bulgaria	Sept 15, 1984
100 kg 220½ lb	Snatch	200	440¼	Yuri Zakharevich (USSR)	Odessa, USSR	Mar 4, 1983
	Jerk	241.5	532¼	Pavel Kuznyetsov (USSR)	Varna, Bulgaria	Sept 15, 1984
	Total	440	970	Yuri Zakharevich (USSR)	Moscow, USSR	Oct 30, 1983
110 kg 242½ lb	Snatch	200.5	442	Yuri Zakharevich (USSR)	Varna, Bulgaria	Sept 16, 1984
	Jerk	247.5	545½	Vyacheslav Klokov (USSR)	Moscow, USSR	Oct 30, 1983
	Total	442.5	975½	Leonid Taranenko (USSR)	Varna, Bulgaria	Sept 16, 1984
Over 110 kg 242½ lb	Snatch	211	465	Aleksandr Gunyashev (USSR)	Rheims, France	June 1, 1984
	Jerk	265	584	Anatoliy Pisarenko (USSR)	Varna, Bulgaria	Sept 16, 1984
	Total	465	1,025	Aleksandr Gunyashev (USSR)	Rheims, France	June 1, 1984

WORLD POWER LIFTING RECORDS Figures in kilograms

Class	Squat		Bench Press		Deadlift		Total	
MEN								
52 kg	242.5	Joe Cunha (US) 1981	146.5	Joe Cunha 1982	232.5	Haruji Watanabe (Jap) 1984	567.5	Hideaki Inaba (Jap) 1980
56 kg	237.5	Hideaki Inaba (Jap) 1982	151.5	Hiroyaki Isagawa (Jap) 1985	289.5	Lamar Gant (US) 1982	625	Lamar Grant 1982
60 kg	295	Joe Bradley (US) 1980	180	Joe Bradley 1980	296.5	Lamar Gant 1983	707.5	Joe Bradley 1982
67.5 kg	297	Robert Wahl (US) 1982	194	Kristoffer Hulecki (Swe) 1982	312.5	Raimo Välineva (Fin) 1981	732.5	Joe Bradley 1981
75 kg	327.5	Mike Bridges (US) 1980	217.5	James Rouse 1980	325.5	Eric Coppin (Bel) 1985	850	Rick Gaugler (US) 1982
82.5 kg	379.5	Mike Bridges 1982	240	Mike Bridges 1981	357.5	Veli Kumpuniemi (Fin) 1980	952.5	Mike Bridges 1982
90 kg	375	Fred Hatfield (US) 1980	255	Mike MacDonald (US) 1980	372.5	Walter Thomas (US) 1982	937.5	Mike Bridges 1980
100 kg	400	Fred Hatfield 1982	261.5	Mike MacDonald 1977	377.5	James Cash (US) 1982	952.5	James Cash 1982
110 kg	393.5	Dan Wohleber (US) 1981	270	Jeffrey Magruder (US) 1982	395	John Kuc 1980	1,000	John Kuc 1980
125 kg	412.5	David Waddington (US) 1982	278.5	Tom Hardman (US) 1982	385	Terry McCormick (US) 1982	1,005	Ernie Hackett (US) 1981
125+ kg	445	Dwayne Fely (US) 1982	320	Theodore Arcidi (US) 1985	402	Bill Kazmaier 1981	1,100	Bill Kazmaier 1981
WOMEN								
44 kg	140	Anna Liisa Prinkkala (Fin) 1983	75	Teri Hoyt (US) 1982	153	M. Vassart (Bel) 1984	350	Cheryl Jones (US) 1985
48 kg	147	Majik Jones (US) 1984	82.5	Michelle Evris (US) 1981	182.5	Majik Jones (US) 1984	390	Majik Jones 1984
52 kg	177.5	Sisi Dolman (Hol) 1983	95	Mary Ryan (US) 1984	172	Sisi Dolman 1984	405	Sisi Dolman 1985
56 kg	184	Vicki Steenrod (US) 1984	112	Vicki Steenrod 1984	190	Vicki Steenrod 1984	475	Vicki Steenrod 1984
60 kg	200.5	Ruthi Shafer (US) 1983	97.5	Eileen Todaro (US) 1981	213	Ruthi Shafer 1983	500	Ruthi Shafer 1983
67.5 kg	230	Ruthi Shafer (US) 1984	105.5	C. Gerard (Fra) 1981	244	Ruthi Shafer 1984	565	Ruthi Shafer 1984
75 kg	212.5	Beverley Francis (Aus) 1981	140	Beverley Francis 1981	212.5	L. Miller (Aus) 1981	550	Beverley Francis 1983
82.5 kg	218	Beverley Francis 1983	150	Beverley Francis 1981	227.5	Vicky Gagne (US) 1981	577.5	Beverley Francis 1983
90 kg	213	Gael Martin (Aus) 1983	120.5	Gael Martin 1983	210	Rebecca Waibler (W. Ger) 1982	525	Gael Martin 1982
90+ kg	247.5	Jan Todd (US) 1981	130	Gael Martin 1982	230	Wanda Sander (US) 1981	567.5	Gael Martin 1982

Body-Weight Feats

Lamar Gant (US) was the first man to deadlift five times his own body weight, lifting 661 lb when 132 lb in 1985. Stefan Topurov (Bulgaria) cleaned and jerked 396¾ lb, three times his body weight, at Moscow, USSR on Oct 24, 1983.

POWER LIFTER Jan Todd can carry her heavyweight husband, Terry, on her back. She raised 545½ pounds in a squat lift in 1981. Jan has since lost 82 lb, but is still setting records.

Youngest World Record Holder

Naum Shalamanov (Bulgaria) (b Nov 23, 1967) set 56 kg world records for clean and jerk (160 kg) and total (285 kg) at 15 years 123 days at Allentown, Pa, Mar 26, 1983. He became the youngest world champion at 15 years 334 days.

POWER LIFTING

Paul Anderson as a professional has bench-pressed 6,270 lb, achieved 1,200 lb in a squat, and deadlifted 820 lb.

Hermann Görner (Germany) performed a one-

GREATEST LIFT: Paul Anderson once raised 6,270 lb in a back lift from trestles. A gold medalist in the 1956 Olympics, he later turned professional, switching from weight lifting to power lifting, where he succeeded with a squat lift of 1,200 lb.

handed deadlift of 734½ lb in Dresden on July 20, 1920. He once raised 24 men weighing 4,123 lb on a plank with the soles of his feet, in London on Oct 12, 1927, and also carried on his back a 1,444-lb piano for a distance of 52½ ft on June 3, 1921.

Precious McKenzie (b June 6, 1936) was the first man to total 11 times his body weight (121 lb) with 1,339 lb at Honolulu, Hawaii on May 5, 1979. Lamar Grant (US) deadlifted five times his body weight (123¼ lb) with 617 lb at Dayton, Ohio on Nov 2, 1979. Mike MacDonald (US) was the first man to hold world records (bench press) in four different classes simultaneously. Dave Waddington (US) was the first power lifter to squat over 1,000 lb on June 13, 1981. Dan Wholeber (US) was the first to deadlift over 900 lb in official competition on Dec 12, 1982.

The newly instituted two-man deadlift record was raised to 1,448 lb by Clay and Doug Patterson in Arlington, Tex, on Dec 15, 1979.

Peter B. Cortese (US) achieved a one-arm deadlift of 370 lb—22 lb over triple his body weight—at York, Pa, on Sept 4, 1954.

A recently-formed organization called the American Drug Free Powerlifting Association is holding contests for men, women, teen-agers and collegians regularly. Contestants must be examined by 3 referees, an official weigher, and a drug tester, who also witness the event. Applications for the meets can be obtained from Jan Todd at the University of Tex, Austin.

The heaviest bench press by a woman is 332.5 lb by Debra Poston, Tampa, Fla in April, 1985.

The greatest power lift by a woman is a squat of 545½ lb by Jan Suffolk Todd (b May 22, 1952) (US) (weighing 195 lb) at Columbus, Ga, in Jan 1981. Cammie Lynn Lusko (b Apr 5, 1958) (US) became the first woman to lift more than her body weight with one arm, with 131 lbs at a body weight of 128.5 lb, at Milwaukee, Wis, on May 21, 1983.

John Decker lifted 25 tons by bench presses (1,000 lifts of 56 lb) within an hour at Congleton, Cheshire, Eng, on Aug 16, 1984.

The greatest lift by a woman is a deadlift of 551 lb by Terry Byland-Rohal (US) on Jan 27, 1985, in Boston, Mass. She also made the highest total of all time in all three lifts for women, regardless of body-weight classification, with 1,355 lb.

A deadlifting record of 5,244,169 lb in 24 hours was set by a team of ten from ASC Unterwössen at Kreuzheben, W. Ger, on Jan 27–28, 1984.

WINDSURFING

See Boardsailing

WRESTLING

Origins

The earliest depictions of wrestling holds and falls on wall plaques and a statue indicate that organized wrestling dates from *c.* 2750–2600 BC. It was the most popular sport in the ancient Olympic Games and victors were recorded from 708 BC. The Greco-Roman style is of French origin and arose about 1860. The International Amateur Wrestling Federation (FILA) was founded in 1912.

Best Records

In international competition, Osamu Watanabe (b Oct 21, 1940) (Japan), the 1964 Olympic freestyle 63 kg champion, was unbeaten and unscored-upon in 187 consecutive matches.

Wade Schalles (US) won 821 bouts from 1964 to 1984, with 530 of these victories by pin.

Most World Championships

The greatest number of world championships won by a wrestler is 10 by the freestyler Aleksandr Medved (USSR) (b Sept 16, 1937), with the 97 kg titles in 1962, 63, 64 (Olympic) and 66, the 97 kg in 1967 and 68 (Olympic), and the 100 kg title 1969, 70, 71 and 72 (Olympic). The only wrestler to win the same title in 7 successive years has been Valeriy Rezantsev (b Feb 2, 1947) (USSR) in the Greco-Roman 90 kg class, 1970–76, including the Olympic Games of 1972 and 1976.

Three wrestlers have won three Olympic gold medals. They are: Carl Westergren (1895–1958) (Sweden) in 1920, 24 and 32; Ivar Johansson (1903–79) (Sweden) in 1932 (two) and 36; and Aleksandr Medved (b Sept 16, 1937) (USSR) in 1964, 68 and 72.

Two wrestlers who won more medals are Imre Polyak (b Apr 16, 1932) (Hungary) who won the silver medal for the Greco-Roman 62 kg in 1952, 56 and 60, and the 63 kg gold in 1964, and Eino Leino (Finland) who won the gold in 1920, silver in 1924, and bronze in 1928 and 1932 as a freestyle at 75, 72, 66, and 72 kg.

HEAVIES: Hawaiian-born Jesse Kuhaulua (left), known as Takamiyama, takes on 2 US Marines in a charity exhibition. Kuhaulua, the first non-Japanese ever to win an official tournament, weighed as much as 450 lbs. Chris Taylor (US) (right) was the heaviest wrestler in Olympic history. At 6 ft 5 in tall, Taylor weighed over 420 lbs when he won the 1972 super-heavyweight bronze medal.

MOST TITLES: Ten-time world champion Aleksandr Medved drives India's Maruti Mane to the mat. Three of Medved's record 10 titles came in Olympic competition, as he moved up in class from light-heavyweight to super-heavyweight.

HEAVIEST SUMO WRESTLER: (Left) Samoan-born Honolulu resident Salevaa Atisnoe, 491 lb, 21 years old in this photo, dressed here in his ceremonial apron, was the second American to reach the rank of Grand Sumo. (Right) MOST SUCCESSFUL WRESTLER: "Strangler" Lewis (US) won all but 33 out of 6,200 bouts.

Sumo Wrestling

The sport's origins in Japan date from *c.* 23 BC. The heaviest ever *sumotori* is Samoan-American Salevaa Atisnoe Fuali of Hawaii, also known as Konishiki, who attained a height of 6 ft 1½ in and weight of 512 lb in 1986. Weight is amassed by overeating a high protein stew called *chankonabe*.

The most successful wrestlers have been Koki Naya (b 1940), *alias* Taiho ("Great Bird"), who won 32 Emperor's Cups until his retirement in 1971; Sadaji Akiyoshi (b 1912), *alias* Futabayama, who won 69 consecutive bouts in the 1930's; and the *ozeki* Torokichi, *alias* Raiden, who in 21 years (1789–1810) won 240 bouts and lost only 10 for the highest ever winning percentage of .962. Taiho and Futabayama share the record of 8 perfect tournaments without a single loss.

The youngest of the 59 men to attain the rank of *Yokozuna* (Grand Champion) was Toshimitsu Obata, *alias* Kitanoumi, in July 1974, aged 21 years 2 months. He set a record in 1978 winning 82 of the 90 bouts that top *rikishi* fight annually and has a career

record 951 wins. Hawaiian-born Jesse Kuhaulua (b June 16, 1944), now a Japanese citizen named Daigoro Watanabe, *alias* Takamiyama, was the first non-Japanese to win an official tournament in July 1972 and in 1981 set a record of 1,231 consecutive top division bouts. He weighed at least 450 lb before retiring in 1984.

Longest Bout

The longest recorded bout was one of 11 hours 40 min between Martin Klein (Estonia, representing Russia) and Alfred Asikáinen (Finland) in the Greco-Roman 75 kg "A" event for the silver medal in the 1912 Olympic Games in Stockholm, Sweden. Klein won.

Fastest Pin

William R. Kerslake (b Dec 27, 1929) reputedly recorded the fastest fall in national tournament competition when he threw Ralph Bartleman in 4 sec during the 1956 National Amateur Athletic Union

(NAAU) Greco-Roman Championships at Tulsa, Okla. Kerslake won 8 consecutive NAAU freestyle championships and 7 consecutive NAAU Greco-Roman championships, 1953–1960, a string of 76 consecutive victories.

Heaviest Heavyweight

The heaviest wrestler in Olympic history is Chris Taylor (1950–79), bronze medalist in 1972, who stood 6 ft 5 in tall and weighed over 440 lb. FILA introduced a top weight limit of 286 lb for international competition in 1985.

YACHTING

Origins

Yachting in England dates from the £100 stake race between King Charles II of England and his brother, James, Duke of York, on the Thames River, on Oct 1, 1661, over 23 miles, from Greenwich to Gravesend. The King won. The earliest club is the Royal Cork Yacht Club (formerly the Cork Harbour Water Club), established in Ireland in 1720, when the first recorded regatta was held.

The word "yacht" is from the Dutch, meaning to hunt or chase. The word "regatta"—meaning a gathering of boats—is Italian and was applied to the proceedings at Ranelagh on the Thames in June 1775. The sport did not really prosper until the seas became safer with the end of the Napoleonic Wars in 1815. That year The Yacht Club (later to become The Royal Yacht Squadron) was formed and organized races at Cowes, Isle of Wight, Eng, which was the beginning of modern yacht racing. In 1844 the New York YC was founded and held its first regatta the following year. The International Yacht Racing Union (IYRU) was established in 1907.

Highest Speed

The official world sailing speed record is 36.04 knots (41.50 mph) achieved by the 73½-ft *Crossbow II* over a 500-m (547-yd) course off Portland Harbor, Dorset, England, on Nov 17, 1980. The vessel, which had a sail area of 1,400 sq ft, was designed by Rod McAlpine-Downie and owned and steered by Timothy Colman. In an unsuccessful attempt on the record in Oct 1978, *Crossbow II* is reported to have momentarily attained a speed of 45 knots (51 mph).

Transatlantic Recordsetter Loses Race and Record

The man who finished first in record time in a race across the Atlantic Ocean lost the race to a countryman who had stopped to help a troubled sailor.

Philippe Poupon of France thought he had broken a world sailing record by more than one day when he arrived in Newport, RI on June 18, 1985 in 16 days, 11 hours, 56 min in the "Observer Singlehanded Trans-Atlantic Race." Some Marine experts believe that the record breaker should have been Yvon Fauconnier, who finished nearly 11 hours later. Fauconnier, at the helm of the 53-ft-trimaran *Unupro Jardin,* was given a 16-hour handicap for stopping to help Philippe Jeantot, whose boat, *Credit Agricole II,* capsized the week previous.

CONSISTENT OLYMPIC WINNER: Paul Elvstrom (Denmark) was the first Olympian to win individual gold medals in 4 successive Games, 1948–60.

The fastest 24-hour single-handed run by a sailing yacht was recorded by Nick Keig (b June 13, 1936), of the Isle of Man, who covered 340 nautical miles in a 37½-ft trimaran, *Three Legs of Mann I,* during the Falmouth to Punta, Azores, race, June 9–10, 1975, averaging 14.16 knots (16.30 mph). The fastest bursts of speed reached were about 25 knots (28.78 mph).

Olympic Victories

The first person ever to win individual gold medals in four successive Olympic Games was Paul B. Elvström (b Feb 24, 1928) (Denmark) in the Firefly class in 1948 and the Finn class in 1952, 56 and 60. He has also won 8 other world titles in a total of 6 classes.

The lowest number of penalty points by the winner of any class in an Olympic regatta is 3 points (5 wins [1 disqualified] and 1 second in 7 starts) by *Superdocious* of the Flying Dutchman class sailed by Lt Rodney Stuart Pattison (b Aug 5, 1943), British Royal Navy, and Ian Somerled Macdonald-Smith (b July 3, 1945), in Acapulco Bay, Mexico, in Oct 1968.

Greatest Distance

The greatest distance covered in a day's run under sail was set by the 80-foot catamaran *Formula Tag* (skipper: Michael Birch). During the 1984 Transat TAG Race between Quebec and St Malo, France, she covered 512.55 nautical mi in 23.70 hours for an average of 21.63 knots. She must have achieved at least 518 naut mi in the full 24 hours. For one period of 24.6 min she averaged 31.68 knots.

Longest Race

The longest regular sailing race is the quadrennial Whitbread Round the World race (instituted Aug 1973) organized by the Royal Naval Sailing Association. The distance is 26,180 nautical miles from Portsmouth, England, and return with stops and re-starts at Cape Town, Auckland and Mar del Plata. The record (sailing) time is 120 days 6 hours 35 min by *Flyer* crewed by Cornelius van Rietschoten (Netherlands), finishing on Mar 29, 1982.

Admiral's Cup

The ocean racing series to have attracted the largest number of participating nations (three boats allowed to each nation) is the Admiral's Cup held by the Royal Ocean Racing Club in the English Channel in alternate years. Up to 1981, Britain had a record 8 wins. A record 19 nations competed in the 1975, 77 and 79 competitions.

Largest Marina

The largest marina in the world is that of Marina Del Rey, Los Angeles, Calif, which has 7,500 berths.

Most Competitors

The most competitors ever to start in a single race was 1,947 (of which 1,767 finished) sailing boats in the Round Zeeland (Denmark) race, June 17–20, 1983, over a course of 233 miles.

Most Successful

The most successful racing yacht in history was the British Royal Yacht *Britannia* (1893–1935), owned by King Edward VII while Prince of Wales, and subsequently by King George V, which won 231 races in 625 starts.

America's Cup

The America's Cup was originally won as an outright prize by the schooner *America* on Aug 22, 1851, at Cowes, England, but was later offered by the NY Yacht Club as a challenge trophy. On Aug 8, 1870, J. Ashbury's *Cambria* (GB) failed to capture the trophy from the *Magic,* owned by F. Osgood (US). Since then the Cup was challenged by GB in 16 contests, by Canada in 2 contests, and by Australia 7 times, but the US holders never were defeated, winning 77 races in 132 years and only losing 8, until the 4–3 defeat in Sept 1983 of *Liberty* by *Australia II,* skippered by John Bertrand and owned by a syndicate headed by Alan Bond at Newport, RI. The closest race ever was in the trials held on Nov 4, 1986 when *White Crusader* (UK) beat *Canada II* by the margin of 1 sec. The fastest time ever recorded by a 12-m boat for the triangular course of 24.3 miles is 2 hours 27 min 42 sec by *Freedom* on Sept 25, 1980.

The America's Cup was returned to the US in Feb 1987 when *Stars and Stripes,* the yacht belonging to the San Diego Yacht Club, skippered by Dennis Conner, beat the Australian entry, *Kookaburra III,* in 4 of 4 races. Conner had been the skipper of the yacht *Liberty* which had lost to *Australia II* in Sept 1983, the first time the Cup had left the US in 132 years.

INDEX